A·N·N·U·A·L E·D·I·T·I·O·N·S

INTERNATIONAL BUSINESS 99/00

99/00

Eighth Edition

Dr. Fred Maidment
Park College

Dr. Fred Maidment is associate professor and department chair of the Department of Business Education at Park College. He received his bachelor's degree from New York University and his master's degree from Bernard M. Baruch College of the City University of New York. In 1983 he received his doctorate from the University of South Carolina. His research interests include training and development in industry. He resides in Kansas City, Missouri, with his wife and children.

Dushkin/McGraw-Hill
Sluice Dock, Guilford, Connecticut 06437

Visit us on the Internet
http://www.dushkin.com/annualeditions/

nsin

Credits

1. The Nature of International Business
Facing overview—© 1998 by PhotoDisc, Inc.
2. The International Environment: Organizations and Monetary Systems
Facing overview—photo courtesy New York Stock Exchange
3. Foreign Environment
Facing overview—UN Photo/Derek Lovejoy
4. How Management Deals with Environmental Forces
Facing overview—UN Photo/Kay Muldoon Ibrahim. 197—AP/Wide World photo by Robert Horn. 198—*Business Week* map by Ray Vella.

Copyright

Cataloging in Publication Data
Main entry under title: Annual Editions: International Business. 1999/2000.
    1. International business enterprises—Periodicals. 2. Business—
Periodicals. I. Maidment, Fred, *comp.* II. Title: International business.
ISBN 0–07–040337–6   338.88′05   ISSN 1091–1731

© 1999 by Dushkin/McGraw-Hill, Guilford, CT 06437, A Division of The McGraw-Hill Companies.

Eighth Edition

Cover image © 1999 PhotoDisc, Inc.

Printed in the United States of America   1234567890BAHBAH54321098   Printed on Recycled Paper

iii

To the Reader

In publishing ANNUAL EDITIONS we recognize the enormous role played by the magazines, newspapers, and journals of the public press in providing current, first-rate educational information in a broad spectrum of interest areas. Many of these articles are appropriate for students, researchers, and professionals seeking accurate, current material to help bridge the gap between principles and theories and the real world. These articles, however, become more useful for study when those of lasting value are carefully collected, organized, indexed, and reproduced in a low-cost format, which provides easy and permanent access when the material is needed. That is the role played by ANNUAL EDITIONS.

New to ANNUAL EDITIONS is the inclusion of related World Wide Web sites. These sites have been selected by our editorial staff to represent some of the best resources found on the World Wide Web today. Through our carefully developed topic guide, we have linked these Web resources to the articles covered in this ANNUAL EDITIONS reader. We think that you will find this volume useful, and we hope that you will take a moment to visit us on the Web at *http://www.dushkin.com/* to tell us what you think.

When the first edition of *Annual Editions: International Business* was being compiled a few years ago, the world was extremely unstable. Power in the Soviet Union was very much in question. Hardliners had conducted a coup against the reform government. On August 19, 1991, Russian president Boris Yeltsin jumped on a tank outside the Russian parliament building and denounced the coup leaders, galvanizing the people to take back their government. On that same day, I was writing the introductory essay for the section of this book that included articles on the Soviet Union. In fact, I was typing the essay at the very moment when the news bulletin reporting Yeltsin's act came over the radio. Needless to say, I had to rewrite the essay.

With the subsequent dissolution of the Soviet Union and the turn to capitalism by its newly independent states, many new opportunities for international business have opened. In the future, virtually all countries and all organizations will be engaged in doing business with other organizations outside of their home countries. Students of business administration and, indeed, all people involved in business need to be aware of the new international environment. They need to recognize the opportunities and the problems associated with doing business outside of their home markets. They need to understand that the same types of opportunities await all who engage in business.

Business must respond to this change in the environment by keeping an open mind about the opportunities available to it on a global basis. The articles that have been chosen for *Annual Editions: International Business 99/00* comprise a cross section of the current literature on the subject. The collection addresses the various aspects of international business, with emphasis on the foundations and environment of international trade and on how corporations respond to and deal with this environment. To this editor, the general tone of the articles seems to be growing more optimistic than it was a few years ago. This trend has been borne out in this latest edition. No one claims that all the news is good (because it is not) or that all the problems have been solved (because they never will be), but there has been a change. Most of the literature seems to be more hopeful and less bleak and foreboding than it was at the start of the last decade of the twentieth century. There is more talk about opportunity and success and less talk about problems and failure. A new era seems to be dawning.

This edition of *Annual Editions: International Business 99/00* contains a number of features designed to make it useful for people interested in international business. These features include a *topic guide* for locating articles on specific subjects and a *table of contents* with abstracts that summarize each article and draw attention to key words in bold italics. This edition also has *World Wide Web* sites, which are cross-referenced by number to the topic guide, for further exploration of the topics. The volume is organized into four units dealing with specific interrelated topics in international business. Each unit begins with an overview that provides the necessary background information to allow the reader to place a selection in the context of the book. Important topics are emphasized, and challenge questions address major themes.

We would like to know what you think about our book. Please take a few minutes to complete and return the postage-paid *article rating form* in the back of the volume. We need your advice and assistance to help improve future editions of *Annual Editions: International Business*.

Fred Maidment

Fred Maidment
Editor

Contents

UNIT 1

The Nature of International Business

Seven selections describe the
dynamics of today's international
business community.

The concepts in bold italics are developed in the article. For further expansion please refer to the Topic Guide and the Index.

UNIT 2

The International Environment: Organizations and Monetary Systems

Four articles examine international organizations, the international monetary system, and the finance of international businesses.

UNIT 3

Foreign Environment

Fifteen selections discuss how international markets are influenced by the common pressures of financing, the economy, sociocultural dynamics, politics, the legal system, labor relations, and other forces.

The concepts in bold italics are developed in the article. For further expansion please refer to the Topic Guide and the Index.

The concepts in bold italics are developed in the article. For further expansion please refer to the Topic Guide and the Index.   **vii**

UNIT 4

How Management Deals with Environmental Forces

Twenty articles discuss challenging aspects of managing in the international business community.

The concepts in bold italics are developed in the article. For further expansion please refer to the Topic Guide and the Index.

The concepts in bold italics are developed in the article. For further expansion please refer to the Topic Guide and the Index.

The concepts in bold italics are developed in the article. For further expansion please refer to the Topic Guide and the Index.

The concepts in bold italics are developed in the article. For further expansion please refer to the Topic Guide and the Index.

This topic guide suggests how the selections and World Wide Web sites found in the next section of this book relate to topics of traditional concern to international business students and professionals. It is useful for locating interrelated articles and Web sites for reading and research. The guide is arranged alphabetically according to topic.

The relevant Web sites, which are numbered and annotated on pages 4 and 5, are easily identified by the Web icon (☺) under the topic articles. By linking the articles and the Web sites by topic, this ANNUAL EDITIONS reader becomes a powerful learning and research tool.

TOPIC AREA	TREATED IN	TOPIC AREA	TREATED IN
Communication	1. Growth through Global Sustainability	**Economic Trends**	1. Growth through Global Sustainability
	3. International Business		2. American and the Global Economy
	4. Building Effective R&D		4. Building Effective R&D
	8. Riding the Dragon		6. World Education League
	9. Multinational Corporations		8. Riding the Dragon
	15. Global Transfer		10. Great Escape
	17. Can Multinational Businesses Agree on How to Act Ethically?		11. Reining in the IMF
	18. Us and Them		12. International Monetary Arrangements
	24. Global Economy, Local Mayhem?		13. Asia Sets a New Challenge
	27. How to Succeed in the Global Marketplace		14. Africa's New Dawn
	28. World of Advertising		15. Global Transfer
	29. Asia's Next Tiger?		16. Scaling the Great Wall
	30. Troubles Ahead in Emerging Markets		21. Antitrust Regulation
	35. Building Successful Partnerships		24. Global Economy, Local Mayhem?
	37. World as a Single Machine		25. Global Deregulation
	38. Erasing Boundaries		26. Controlling Economic Competition in the Pacific Rim
	43. Global Culture		30. Troubles Ahead in Emerging Markets
	44. Don't Get Burned		32. Myth of the China Market
	45. Why HR Managers Need to Think Globally		34. Heat Is On
	46. Globe Trotting		36. Strengthening the Architecture
	☺ *2, 7, 9, 18, 25, 30*		37. World as a Single Machine
			38. Erasing Boundaries
Developing Countries	1. Growth through Global Sustainability		41. Company without a Country?
	2. American and the Global Economy		42. Opportunity Knocks
	3. International Business		45. Why HR Managers Need to Think Globally
	8. Riding the Dragon		46. Globe Trotting
	9. Multinational Corporations		☺ *1, 2, 3, 4, 5, 7, 8, 9, 11, 12, 13, 17, 19, 20, 21, 23, 24, 25, 27, 29, 30*
	10. Great Escape		
	11. Reining in the IMF	**European Union**	3. International Business
	12. International Monetary Arrangements		6. World Education League
	13. Asia Sets a New Challenge		17. Can Multinational Businesses Agree on How to Act Ethically?
	14. Africa's New Dawn		19. Government and National Parliaments
	15. Global Transfer		20. Trade Free or Die
	16. Scaling the Great Wall		21. Antitrust Regulations across National Borders
	17. Can Multinational Businesses Agree on How to Act Ethically?		25. Global Deregulation
	22. Rule by Law		36. Strengthening the Architecture
	23. Wanted: Muscle		37. World as a Single Machine
	24. Global Economy, Local Mayhem?		38. Erasing Boundaries
	26. Controlling Economic Competition in the Pacific Rim		46. Globe Trotting
	29. Asia's Next Tiger?		☺ *1, 5, 7, 10, 23, 29*
	30. Troubles Ahead in Emerging Markets		
	32. Myth of the China Market	**Finance**	1. Growth through Global Sustainability
	33. "Compromise Increases the Risk of War"		2. America and the Global Economy
	34. The Heat Is On		3. International Business
	35. Building Successful Partnerships		5. Back to the Land
	37. World as a Single Machine		7. Balancing Act
	38. Erasing Boundaries		10. Great Escape
	41. Company without a Country?		11. Reining in the IMF
	42. Opportunity Knocks		12. International Monetary Arrangements
	44. Don't Get Burned		13. Asia Sets a New Challenge
	☺ *1, 8, 14, 16, 21, 24*		

● AE: International Business

The following World Wide Web sites have been carefully researched and selected to support the articles found in this reader. If you are interested in learning more about specific topics found in this book, these Web sites are a good place to start. The sites are cross-referenced by number and appear in the topic guide on the previous two pages. Also, you can link to these Web sites through our DUSHKIN ONLINE support site at *http://www.dushkin.com/online/*.

The following sites were available at the time of publication. Visit our Web site—we update DUSHKIN ONLINE regularly to reflect any changes.

General Sources

1. Internet Resources for International Economics & Business
http://dylee.keel.econ.ship.edu/intntl/int_home.htm
Dr. Daniel Y. Lee of the College of Business at Shippensburg University maintains this site, which lists Internet resources related to economics and business in general, references, and specific international business topics such as international development.

2. NewsPage
http://pnp1.individual.com/
This site from Individual, Inc. provides daily business briefings and more in-depth stories related to such fields as computing and media, banking and finance, health care, insurance, and transportation and distribution.

3. STAT-USA
http://www.stat-usa.gov/stat-usa.html
This essential site, a service of the U.S. Department of Commerce, presents daily economic news; a myriad of links to databases, statistical releases, and selected publications; and general information on export and international trade as well as business leads and procurement opportunities.

The Nature of International Business

4. Business Policy and Strategy
http://www.aom.pace.edu/bps/bps.html
This site, the home page of the Business Policy and Strategy Division of the U.S. Academy of Management, is packed with information about the theory and practice of international business. The division is interested in "the roles and problems of general managers."

5. Harvard Business School
http://www.hbs.edu/
This Web site of the Harvard Business School provides useful links to library and research resources, to the Harvard Business Review, and to information regarding executive education as well as other topics.

6. Information Institute: Law about . . . Pages
http://www.law.cornell.edu/topical.html
Explore this site's extensive searchable index to learn about a myriad of international legal subjects. Organized by topic, it provides useful summaries with links to key primary source material and off-Net references.

7. International Business Resources on the WWW
http://ciber.bus.msu.edu/busres.htm
Michigan State University's Center for International Business Education and Research provides this invaluable site, which allows a keyword search and points you to a great deal of trade information and leads, government resources, and related periodicals. It also provides general and specific country and regional information.

8. OECD/FDI Statistics
http://www.oecd.org/daf/cmis/fdi/statist.htm
Explore foreign direct investment trends and statistics on this site from the Organization for Economic Cooperation and Development. It provides links to many related topics and addresses the issues on a country-by-country basis.

9. Sales & Marketing Executives International
http://www.smei.org/
Visit this home page of Sales & Marketing Executives (SME), a worldwide association of sales and marketing management. Through this "Digital Resource Mall," you can access research and useful articles on sales and management. You can even listen in as marketing leaders discuss their latest strategies and ideas.

10. World Trade Centers Association
http://www.wtca.org/
WTCA On-Line presents this site as a news and information service. Members can access the *Dun & Bradstreet Exporters' Encyclopaedia* and other valuable sources, but guests to the site can also gain entry to interesting trade-related information.

The International Environment: Organizations and Monetary Systems

11. Center for International Business Education and Research
http://www.cob.ohio-state.edu/ciberweb/
Surf this site for information about international business/ trade organizations and emerging markets, and for news links to related topics.

12. Finance (and Banking) Related Links
http://ananse.irv.uit.no/trade_law/nav/i-finance.html
Surf this site for information on international banking and finance. It provides links to popular sites for finance, stock research, and electronic banking.

13. Institute of International Bankers
http://www.iib.org/
Examine this site for information on the Institute of International Bankers, IBB events, and publications in order to become familiar with trends in international banking. The site also features regulatory compliance issues relating to the Year 2000 date change.

14. International Labour Organization
http://www.ilo.org/
ILO's home page leads to links that describe the goals of the organization and summarizes international labor standards and human rights. Its official UN Web site locator can point you to many other useful resources.

15. International Trade Law Monitor
http://ananse.irv.uit.no/trade_law/
Use this valuable site to access a wealth of resources related to international trade, including data on the European Union and the International Monetary Fund. Among its many links, it addresses such topics as Principles of International Commercial Contracts and UN Arbitration Laws.

16. RefLaw

http://lawlib.wuacc.edu/washlaw/reflaw/refgatt.html

This site from the Washburn University School of Law Library Reference Desk can direct you to primary documents related to GATT and other information about the Agreement. It also reproduces world constitutions and the text of NAFTA and other major treaties.

17. Resources for Economists on the Internet

http://coba.shsu.edu/EconFAQ/EconFAQ.html

This site and its links are essential reading for those interested in learning about the Organization for Economic Cooperation and Development, the World Bank, the International Monetary Fund, and other important international organizations.

Foreign Environment

18. Chambers of Commerce World Network

http://worldchambers.net/

This site of the World Network of Chambers of Commerce and Industry describes itself as "The world's first, oldest, and largest business network." Access a global index of Chambers of Commerce & Industry and Chambers for International Business, as well as information on "Strategic Alliance Partners" such as G-7.

19. Charts and Tables Related to Foreign Direct Investment in Japan

http://www.jef.or.jp/news/jp/index.html

This site from the Japan Economic Foundation presents charts illustrating trends of foreign direct investment in Japan.

20. CIBERWeb

http://ciber.centers.purdue.edu/

The Centers for International Business Education and Research work to increase and promote Americans' capacity for international understanding and economic enterprise. This site is useful for exploring issues of doing business in a global market.

21. Facilities and Incentives for Foreign Investment in India

http://india-times.com/frinvest/fr_inv.html

India Times summarizes salient features of the foreign-investment climate in India, one of the largest markets in the world. It discusses technology transfer, industrial licensing, capital market investment, and other topics.

22. International Economic Law Web Site

http://www.tufts.edu/fletcher/inter_econ_law/index.htm

This site of the International Economic Law Group of the American Society of International Law contains valuable research tools and links to Web resources regarding international law.

23. United States Trade Representative

http://www.ustr.gov/

This home page of the U.S. Trade Representative provides links to many other U.S. government resources of value to those interested in international business. It notes important trade-related speeches and agreements and describes the mission of the USTR.

24. WWW Virtual Library Demography & Population Studies

http://coombs.anu.edu.au/ResFacilities/ DemographyPage.html

Through this Internet guide to demography and population studies, learn about leading information facilities of value and/or significance to researchers in the field of demography. The site is provided by Australian National University.

How Management Deals with Environmental Forces

25. International Marketing Review

http://www.mcb.co.uk/cgi-bin/journal1/imr/

Visit this home page of the journal *International Marketing Review* to gather leads to a number of resources and articles. It also provides for interactive discussion and an "International Meeting Place."

26. IR-Net

http://www.ir-net.co.za/

Examine this site of South Africa's Industrial-Relations Network as a sample of how different countries address labor issues. It provides information on mediation and conciliation, discusses the International Labour Organization, and notes many library and resource links.

27. Kitchener Business Self-Help Office: Seven Steps to Exporting

http://www.city.kitchener.on.ca/kitchener_import_ export.html

This site describes seven steps to exporting, from selecting an export market to actually beginning to export. It addresses such critical topics as distribution, pricing, and subsidiaries.

28. MELNET

http://www.bradford.ac.uk/acad/mancen/melnet/ index.html

MELNET, self-described as a "World Class Business Network," is a virtual cooperative for people looking to improve the way they do business. Through this interactive site, you can learn about such important topics as branding.

29. Research and Reference (Library of Congress)

http://lcweb.loc.gov/rr/

This research and reference site of the Library of Congress will lead you to invaluable information on different countries. It provides links to numerous publications, bibliographies, and guides in area studies that can be of great help to the international businessperson.

30. Telecommuting as an Investment: The Big Picture—John Wolf

http://www.svi.org/telework/forums/messages5/48.html

This page deals with the many issues related to telecommuting, including its potential role in reducing environmental pollution. The site discusses such topics as dealing with unions, employment-law concerns, and the impact of telecommuting on businesses and employees.

We highly recommend that you review our Web site for expanded information and our other product lines. We are continually updating and adding links to our Web site in order to offer you the most usable and useful information that will support and expand the value of your Annual Editions. You can reach us at: *http://www.dushkin. com/annualeditions/*.

www.dushkin.com/online/

Unit 1

Key Points to Consider

❖ The world is growing smaller. How have improvements in transportation and communication affected international trade?

❖ Economies are growing all over the world, but the most rapid growth is in the emerging countries of the Pacific Rim. How is this important to businesspeople in the strategic planning of their businesses?

❖ How has the mobility of production factors changed their importance when considering theories of international trade?

 **Links**

www.dushkin.com/online/

These sites are annotated on pages 4 and 5.

The world is growing smaller each day. Communication and transportation have made planet Earth more closely knit for the people who live on it.

Global growth is accelerating, especially in the developing countries of the Pacific Rim (who, while they have had a temporary setback, will continue to grow), and it is starting to increase in Latin America. In the first unit article, "Growth through Global Sustainability," Robert Shapiro, the CEO of Monsanto, discusses how his company plans to deal with global growth. Industrialized countries, such as the United States, Japan, and Germany, will continue to grow, but at a much slower rate than the emerging "tigers" of the Pacific Rim. Not everyone will benefit from international trade, and there will be those who will be on the losing end. The consequences of this will certainly be felt in the political arena as well as in the economic sphere.

While international trade continues to grow, it is also becoming more and more complex. It is a simple equation: The more countries, the more trading blocs, and the more people involved, the more complicated trade becomes. Rules can be set, such as those associated with the General Agreement on Tariffs and Trade (GATT) and the World Trade Organization (WTO). But the more rules there are, the greater is the potential for gray areas between them. Not only is international trade becoming more complicated, but it is also becoming more competitive. The developing countries of the world are challenging the established countries in a variety of areas. Software is being developed in India; electronics manufacture is leaving Japan and going to other countries in Asia; and textiles, the traditional first step on the road to industrialization, have become a major industry in many emerging countries. The United States, faced with such complexity and competition, must not revert to isolationism and abandon world trade.

Theories of trade are also changing, and the resources necessary to engage in international trade are reflecting this change. In the past, utilitarians talked about the four factors of production—land, the entrepreneur, labor, and capital—and about how each country had certain advantages over other countries in these areas. Today, that old analysis does not necessarily work. Transportation and communication have made the relative advantages in the four factors of production less important. The factor of land, or raw material, has been made less imposing by the transportation system. Japan, for example, has virtually no natural resources, yet few would argue with the success of the Japanese economy. Education is likely to be the fifth factor of production, and how various countries stack up is addressed in the "World Education League, Who's Top?"

The entrepreneurial factor can be seen everywhere. It is not just North Americans who start new ventures, but Chinese, South Americans, and Europeans. The former Soviet bloc more than demonstrates the ability of former communists to become entrepreneurs, as do developments in mainland China over the past 10 years. Even in Bangladesh, local financing is being used to help small entrepreneurs. True, these new beehives of entrepreneurial activity may have their problems learning to negotiate the world of business, just as infants have difficulty learning to walk. But eventually, like small children, they will be on their feet and running everywhere.

Even labor, perhaps the most sedentary of all the factors of production, has shown signs of movement. Labor has always been willing to move, but historians have tended to view these movements as migrations of peoples, not as the movement of a mundane factor of production. Emigrations from Europe to Australia, South Africa, and North and South America have been made by people seeking a better life for themselves and their families. This same kind of movement goes on today. Australia is still gaining population through immigration; Europe is experiencing waves of new workers from former colonies, whether they are Algerians in France or Indians and Pakistanis in Great Britain; and the United States continues to receive immigrants, both legal and illegal, from all over the world, especially from Latin America. Whatever the reason for immigrating, these people represent potential labor, and they are all seeking better lives.

Finally, capital, or the means of production, has shown an ability to go global. Ever since the start of the industrial revolution, there have been countries that were "developed" (with the means of production) and countries that were "less" or "least" developed (generally without the means of production). But that is starting to change. Because of global transportation and communications systems, the location of production facilities is not as important as it once was. In addition, real and potential growth is now to be found in these developing countries. Any organization that is looking to grow will find it much easier to do so in an economy that is rapidly expanding than in one that is saturated and growing only as fast as the population. Capital and the division of production are global at last and will be even more so in the future.

GROWTH THROUGH GLOBAL SUSTAINABILITY

An Interview with Monsanto's
CEO, Robert B. Shapiro

by Joan Magretta

Robert B. Shapiro, chairman and CEO of Monsanto Company, based in St. Louis, Missouri, sees the conundrum facing his company this way. On the one hand, if a business doesn't grow it will die. And the world economy must grow to keep pace with the needs of population growth. On the other hand, how does a company face the prospect that growing and being profitable could require intolerable abuse of the natural world? In Shapiro's words, "It's the kind of question that people who choose to spend their lives working in business can't shrug off or avoid easily. And it has important implications for business strategy."

Sustainable development is the term for the dual imperative—economic growth and environmental sustainability—that has been gaining ground among business leaders since the 1992 United Nations Earth Summit in Rio de Janeiro. As Shapiro puts it, "We can't expect the rest of the world to abandon their economic aspirations just so we can continue to enjoy clean air and water. That is neither ethically correct nor likely to be permitted by the billions of people in the developing world who expect the quality of their lives to improve."

If companies genetically code a plant to repel pests, farmers don't have to spray with pesticides. That's what's meant by "replacing stuff with information."

Monsanto—with its history in the chemicals industry—may seem an unlikely company to lead the way on an emerging environmental issue. But a number of resource- and energy-intensive companies criticized as environmental offenders in the 1980s have been the first to grasp the strategic implications of sustainability.

Monsanto, in fact, is seeking growth through sustainability, betting on a strategic discontinuity from which few businesses will be immune. To borrow Stuart L. Hart's phrase, Monsanto is moving "beyond greening." (See "Beyond Greening: Strategies for a Sustainable World" in HBR. January-February 1997). In the following interview with HBR editor-at-large Joan Magretta, the 58-year-old Shapiro discusses how Monsanto has moved from a decade of progress in pollution prevention and clean-up to spotting opportunities for revenue growth in environmentally sustainable new products and technologies.

HBR: *Why is sustainability becoming an important component of your strategic thinking?*

Robert B. Shapiro: Today there are about 5.8 billion people in the world. About 1.5 billion of them live in conditions of abject poverty—a subsistence life that simply can't be romanticized as some form of simpler, preindustrial lifestyle. These people spend their days trying to get food and firewood so that they can make it to the next day. As many as 800 million people are so severely malnourished that they can neither work nor participate in family life. That's where we are today. And, as far as I know, no demographer questions that the world population will just about double by sometime around 2030.

Without radical change, the kind of world implied by those numbers is unthinkable. It's a world of mass migrations and environmental degradation on an unimaginable scale. At best, it means the preservation of a few islands of privilege and prosperity in a sea of misery and violence.

Our nation's economic system evolved in an era of cheap energy and careless waste disposal, when limits seemed irrelevant. None of us today, whether we're managing a house or running a business, is living in a sustainable way. It's not a question of good guys and bad guys. There is no point in saying, If only those bad guys would go out of business, then the world would be fine. The whole system has to change; there's a huge opportunity for reinvention.

We're entering a time of perhaps unprecedented discontinuity. Businesses grounded in the old model will become obsolete and die. At Monsanto, we're trying to invent some new businesses around the concept of environmental sustainability. We may not yet know exactly what those businesses will look like, but we're willing to place some bets because the world cannot avoid needing sustainability in the long run.

Can you explain how what you're describing is a discontinuity?

Years ago, we would approach strategic planning by considering "the environment"—that is, the economic, technological, and competitive context of the business—and we'd forecast how it would change over the planning horizon. Forecasting usually meant extrapolating recent trends. So we almost never predicted the critical discontinuities in which the real money was made and lost—the changes that really determined the future of the business. Niels Bohr was right when he said it is difficult to make predictions—especially about the future. But every consumer marketer knows that you can rely on demographics. Many market discontinuities were predictable—and future ones can still be predicted—based on observable, incontrovertible facts such as baby booms and busts, life expectancies, and immigration patterns. Sustainable development is one of those discontinuities. Far from being a soft issue grounded in emotion or ethics, sustainable development involves cold, rational business logic.

This discontinuity is occurring because we are encountering physical limits. You can see it coming arithmetically. Sustainability involves the laws of nature—physics, chemistry and biology—and the recognition that the world is a closed system. What we thought was boundless has limits, and we're beginning to hit them. That's going to change a lot of today's fundamental economics, it's going to change prices, and it's going to change what's socially acceptable.

Is sustainability an immediate issue today in any of Monsanto's businesses?

In some businesses, it's probably less apparent why sustainability is so critical. But in our agricultural business, we can't avoid it. In the twentieth century, we have been able to feed people by bringing more acreage into production and by increasing productivity through fertilizers, pesticides, and irrigation. But current agricultural practice isn't sustainable: we've lost something on the order of 15% of our topsoil over the last 20 years or so, irrigation is increasing the salinity of soil, and the petrochemicals we rely on aren't renewable.

Most arable land is already under cultivation. Attempts to open new farmland are causing severe ecological damage. So in the best case, we have the same amount of land to work with and twice as many people to feed. It comes down to resource productivity. You have to get twice the yield from every acre of land just to maintain current levels of poverty and malnutrition.

Now, even if you wanted to do it in an unsustainable way, no technology today would let you double productivity. With current best practices applied to all the acreage in the world, you'd get about a third of the way toward feeding the whole population. The conclusion is that new technology is the only alternative to one of two disasters: not feeding people—letting the Malthusian process work its magic on the population—or ecological catastrophe.

What new technology are you talking about?

We don't have 100 years to figure that out; at best, we have decades. In that time frame, I know of only two viable candidates: biotechnology and information technology. I'm treating them as though they're separate, but biotechnology is really a subset of information technology because it is about DNA-encoded information.

DRAWING BY GARISON WEILAND

Monsanto's Smarter Products

Scientists at Monsanto are designing products that use information at the genetic or molecular level to increase productivity. Here are three that are on the market today.

The NewLeaf Potato. The NewLeaf potato, bioengineered to defend itself against the destructive Colorado potato beetle, is already in use on farms. Monsanto also is working on the New Leaf Plus potato with inherent resistance to leaf virus—another common scourge. Widespread adoption of the product could eliminate the manufacture, transportation, distribution, and aerial application of millions of pounds of chemicals and residues yearly.

B.t. Cotton. In ordinary soil microbes known as B.t. microbes occur naturally and produce a special protein that, although toxic to certain pests, are harmless to other insects, wildlife and

people. If the destructive cotton budworm, for example eats B.t. bacteria, it will die.

Some cotton farmers control budworms by applying to their cotton plants a powder containing B.t. But the powder often blows or washes away, and reapplying it is expensive. The alternative is for farmers to spray the field with a chemical insecticide as many as 10 or 12 times per season.

But Monsanto's scientists had an idea. They identified the gene that tells the B.t. bacteria to make the special protein. Then they inserted the gene in the cotton plant to enable it to produce the protein on its own while remaining unchanged in other respects. Now when budworms attack, they are either repelled or killed by the B.t.

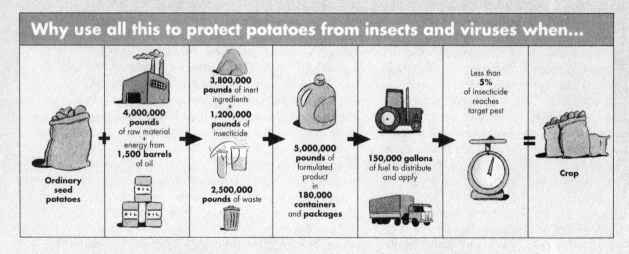

Why use all this to protect potatoes from insects and viruses when...

Ordinary seed potatoes + 4,000,000 pounds of raw material + energy from 1,500 barrels of oil | 3,800,000 pounds of inert ingredients + 1,200,000 pounds of insecticide | 2,500,000 pounds of waste → 5,000,000 pounds of formulated product in 180,000 containers and packages → 150,000 gallons of fuel to distribute and apply → Less than 5% of insecticide reaches target pest = Crop

Using information is one of the ways to increase productivity without abusing nature. A closed system like the earth's can't withstand a systematic increase of material things, but it can support exponential increases of information and knowledge. If economic development means using more stuff, then those who argue that growth and environmental sustainability are incompatible are right. And if we grow by using more stuff, I'm afraid we'd better start looking for a new planet.

But sustainability and development might be compatible if you could create value and satisfy people's needs by increasing the information component of what's produced and diminishing the amount of stuff.

How does biotechnology replace stuff with information in agriculture?

We can genetically code a plant, for example, to repel or destroy harmful insects. That means we don't have to spray the plant with pesticides— with stuff. Up to 90% of what's sprayed on crops today is wasted. Most of it ends up on the soil. If we put the right information in the plant, we waste less stuff and increase productivity. With biotechnology, we can accomplish that. It's not that chemicals are inherently bad. But they are less efficient than biology because you have to manufacture and distribute and apply them.

I offer a prediction: the early twenty-first century is going to see a struggle between information technology and biotechnology on the one hand and environmental degradation on the other. Information technology is going to be our most powerful tool. It will let us miniaturize things, avoid waste, and produce more value without producing and processing more stuff. The substitution of information for stuff is essential to sustainability. (See the insert "Monsanto's Smarter Products.") Substituting services for products is another.

Explain what you mean by substituting services for products.

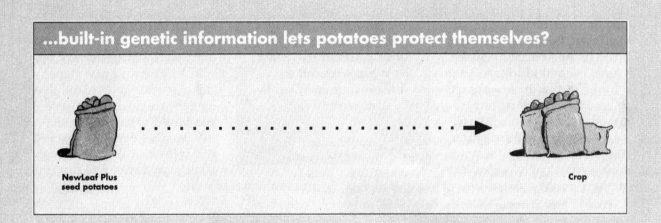

...built-in genetic information lets potatoes protect themselves?

NewLeaf Plus
seed potatoes

Crop

With products like B.t. cotton, farmers avoid having to buy and apply insecticides. And the environment is spared chemicals that are persistent in the soil or that run off into the groundwater.

Roundup Herbicide and No-Till Farming. Sustainability has become an important design criterion in Monsanto's chemically based products as well as in its bioengineered products. Building the right information into molecules, for example, can render them more durable or enhance their recyclability.

Roundup herbicide is a molecule designed to address a major problem for farmers: topsoil erosion. Topsoil is necessary for root systems because of its organic matter, friability in structure, and water-holding capabilities. The subsoil underneath is incapable of supporting root systems. Historically, farmers have tilled their soil primarily for weed control and only to a minor extent for seed preparation. But plowing loosens soil structure and exposes soil to erosion.

By replacing plowing with application of herbicides like Roundup—a practice called *conservation tillage*—farmers end up with better soil quality and less topsoil erosion. When sprayed onto a field before crop planting, Roundup kills the weeds, eliminating the need for plowing. And because the Roundup molecule has been designed to kill only what is growing at the time of its initial application, the farmer can come back a few days after spraying and begin planting; the herbicide will have no effect on the emerging seeds.

The Roundup molecule has other smart features that contribute to sustainability. It is degraded by soil microbes into natural products such as nitrogen, carbon dioxide, and water. It is nontoxic to animals because its mode of action is specific to plants. Once sprayed, it sticks to soil particles; it doesn't move into the ground-water. Like a smart tool, it seeks out its work.

Substituting services for products is one solution. Selling a carpet service instead of a carpet could be more sustainable.

Bill McDonough, dean of the University of Virginia's School of Architecture in Charlottesville, made this come clear for me. He points out that we often buy things not because we want the things themselves but because we want what they can do. Television sets are an obvious example. No one says, "Gee, I'd love to put a cathode-ray tube and a lot of printed circuit boards in my living room." People *might* say, "I'd like to watch the ball game" or "Let's turn on the soaps." Another example: Monsanto makes nylon fiber, much of which goes into carpeting. Each year, nearly 2 million tons of old carpeting go into landfills, where they constitute about 1 % of the entire U.S. municipal solid-waste load. Nobody really wants to own carpet; they just want to walk on it. What would happen if Monsanto or the carpet manufacturer owned that carpet and promised to come in and remove it when it required replacing? What would the economics of that look like? One of our customers is exploring that possibility today. It might be that if we got the carpet back, we could afford to put more cost into it in the first place in ways that would make it easier for us to recycle. Maybe then it wouldn't end up in a landfill.

We're starting to look at all our products and ask, What is it people really need to buy? Do they need the stuff or just its function? What would be the economic impact of our selling a carpet service instead of a carpet?

Can you cite other examples of how we can replace stuff with information?

Sure. Information technology, whether it's telecommunications or virtual reality—whatever that turns out to be—can eliminate the need to move people and things around. In the past, if you wanted to send a document from one place to another, it involved a lot of trains and planes and trucks. Sending a fax eliminates all that motion. Sending E-mail also eliminates the paper.

I have to add that any powerful new technology is going to create ethical problems—problems of privacy, fairness, ethics, power, or control. With any major change in the technological substrate, society has to solve those inherent issues.

You referred earlier to using information to miniaturize things. How does that work?

Miniaturization is another piece of sustainability because it reduces the amount of stuff we use. There are enormous potential savings in moving from very crude, massive designs to smaller and more elegant ones. Microelectronics is one example: the computing power you have in your PC would have required an enormous installation not many years ago.

We've designed things bigger than they need to be because it's easier and because we thought we had unlimited space and material. Now that we know we don't, there's going to be a premium on smaller, smarter design. I think of miniaturization as a way to buy time. Ultimately, we'd love to figure out how to replace chemical processing plants with fields of growing plants—literally, green plants capable of producing chemicals. We have some leads: we can already produce polymers in soybeans, for example. But I think a big commercial breakthrough is a long way off.

Today, by developing more efficient catalysts, for example, we can at least make chemical plants smaller. There will be a number of feasible alternatives if we can really learn to think differently and set design criteria other than reducing immediate capital costs. One way is to design chemical plants differently. If you looked at life-cycle costs such as energy consumption, for instance, you would design a plant so that processes needing heat were placed next to processes generating heat; you wouldn't install as many heaters and coolers that waste energy. We think that if you really dig into your costs, you can accomplish a lot by simplifying and shrinking.

Some people are talking about breakthroughs in mechanical devices comparable to what's being done with electronic devices. Maybe the next wave will come through nanotechnology, but probably in 10 or 20 years, not tomorrow.

The key to sustainability, then, lies in technology?

I am not one of those techno-utopians who just assume that technology is going to take care of everyone. But I don't see an alternative to giving it our best shot.

Business leaders tend to trust technology and markets and to be optimistic about the natural unfolding of events. But at a visceral level, people know we are headed for trouble and would love to find a way to do something about it. The market is going to want sustainable systems, and if Monsanto provides them, we will do quite well for ourselves and our shareowners. Sustainable development is going to be one of the organizing principles around which Monsanto and a lot of other institutions will probably define themselves in the years to come.

Describe how you go about infusing this way of thinking into the company?

It's not hard. You talk for three minutes, and people light up and say, "Where do we start?" And I say, "I don't know. And good luck."

Monsanto's Seven Sustainabililty Teams

Three of Monsanto's sustainability teams are working on tools and methodologies to assess, measure, and provide direction for internal management.

The Eco-efficiency Team. Because you can't manage what you don't measure, this team is mapping and measuring the ecological efficiency of Monsanto's processes. Team members must ask, In relation to the value produced, what inputs are consumed, and what outputs are generated? Managers have historically optimized raw material inputs, for example, but they have tended to take energy and water for granted because there is little financial incentive today to do otherwise. And although companies such as Monsanto have focused on toxic waste in the past, true eco-efficiency will require better measures of all waste. Carbon dioxide, for instance, may not be toxic, but it can produce negative environmental effects. Ultimately, Monsanto's goal is to pursue eco-efficiency in all its interactions with suppliers and customers.

The Full-Cost Accounting Team. This team is developing a methodology to account for the total cost of making and using a product during the product's life cycle, including the true environmental costs associated with producing, using, recycling, and disposing of it. The goal is to keep score in a way that doesn't eliminate from consideration all the environmental costs of what the company does. With better data, it will be possible to make smarter decisions today and as the underlying economics change in the future.

The Index Team. This team is developing criteria by which business units can measure whether or not they're moving toward sustainability. They are working on a set of metrics that balance economic, social, and environmental factors. Units will be able to track the sus-

People come to us and say, "I want to be involved, and this is the team I want to be involved in."

tainability of individual products and of whole businesses. These sustainability metrics will, in turn, be integrated into Monsanto's balanced scorecard approach to the management of its businesses. The scorecard links and sets objectives for financial targets, customer satisfaction, internal processes, and organizational learning.

Three teams are looking externally to identify sustainability needs that Monsanto might address.

The New Business/New Products Team. This team is examining what will be valued in a marketplace that increasingly selects products and services that support sustainability. It is looking at areas of stress in natural systems and imagining how Monsanto's technological skills could meet human needs with new products that don't aggravate—that perhaps even repair—ecological damage.

The Water Team. The water team is looking at global water needs—a huge and growing problem. Many people don't have access to clean drinking water, and there is a worsening shortage of water for irrigation as well.

The Global Hunger Team. This team is studying how Monsanto might develop and deliver technologies to alleviate world hunger. That goal has been a core focus for the company for a number of years. For example, Monsanto had been studying how it might use its agricultural skills to meet people's nutritional needs in developing countries.

The final team develops materials and training programs.

The Communication and Education Team. This team's contribution is to develop the training to give Monsanto's 29,000 employees a common perspective. It offers a framework for understanding what sustainability means, how employees can play a role, and how they can take their knowledge to key audiences outside the company.

DRAWINGS BY GARISON WEILAND

Maybe some context would help. We've been grappling with sustainability issues here long before we had a term for the concept. Part of our history as a chemical company is that environmental issues have been in our face to a greater extent than they've been in many other industries.

My predecessor, Dick Mahoney, understood that the way we were doing things had to change. Dick grew up, as I did not, in the chemical industry, so he tended to look at what was coming out of the plants. The publication of our first toxic-release inventory in 1988 galvanized attention around the magnitude of plant emissions.

Dick got way out ahead of the traditional culture in Monsanto and in the rest of the chemical industry. He set incredibly aggressive quantitative targets and deadlines. The first reaction to them was, My God, he must be out of his mind. But it was an effective technique. In six years, we reduced our toxic air emissions by 90%.

Not having "grown up in the chemical industry," as you put it, do you think differently about environmental issues?

Somewhat. Dick put us on the right path. We have to reduce—and ultimately eliminate—the negative impacts we have on the world. There is no argument on that subject. But even if Monsanto reached its goal of zero impact next Tuesday that wouldn't solve the world's problem. Several years ago, I sensed that there was something more required of us than doing no harm, but I couldn't articulate what that was.

So I did what you always do. I got some smart people together—a group of about 25 critical thinkers, some of the company's up-and-coming leaders—and sent them off to think about it. We selected a good cross-section—some business-unit leaders, a couple from the management board, and people from planning, manufacturing, policy, and safety and health. And we brought in some nontraditional outsiders to challenge our underlying assumptions about the world. My request to this group was, "Go off, think about what's happening to the world, and come back with some recommendations about what it means for Monsanto. Do we have a role to play? If so, what is it?"

That off-site meeting in 1994 led to an emerging insight that we couldn't ignore the changing global environmental conditions. The focus around sustainable development became obvious. I should have been able to come up with that in about 15 minutes. But it took a group of very good people quite a while to think it through, to determine what was real and what was just puff,

to understand the data, and to convince themselves that this wasn't a fluffy issue—and that we ought to be engaged in it.

People came away from that meeting emotionally fired up. It wasn't just a matter of Okay you threw me an interesting business problem, I have done the analysis, here is the answer, and now can I go back to work. People came away saying, "Damn it, we've got to get going on this. This is important." When some of your best people care intensely their excitement is contagious.

So now we have a bunch of folks engaged, recognizing that we have no idea where we're going to end up. No one—not the most sophisticated thinker in the world—can describe a sustainable world with 10 billion to 12 billion people, living in conditions that aren't disgusting and morally impermissible. But we can't sit around waiting for the finished blueprint. We have to start moving in directions that make us less unsustainable.

How are you doing that?

There's a quote of Peter Drucker's—which I will mangle here—to the effect that at some point strategy has to degenerate into work. At Monsanto, there was a flurry of E-mail around the world, and in a matter of four months a group of about 80 coalesced. Some were chosen; many others just heard about the project and volunteered. They met for the first time in October 1995 and decided to organize into seven teams: three focused on developing tools to help us make better decisions, three focused externally on meeting world needs, and one focused on education and communication. (See the insert "Monsanto's Seven Sustainability Teams.")

We realized that many of the things we were already doing were part of a sustainability strategy even if we didn't call it that. We'd been working on pollution prevention and investing in biotechnology for years before we thought about the concept of sustainability. As we made more progress in pollution prevention, it became easier for everyone to grasp how pollution—or waste—actually represents a resource that's lost. When you translate that understanding into how you run a business, it leads to cost reduction. You can ask, did we do it because it reduces our costs or because of sustainability? That would be hard to answer because optimizing resources has become part of the way we think. But having the sustainability framework has made a difference, especially in how we weigh new business opportunities.

One of the seven sustainability teams is discussing how to gain a deeper understanding of global water needs and whether we at Monsanto might meet some of those needs with our existing capabilities. That is an example of a conversation that might not have occurred—or might have occurred much later—if we weren't focused on sustainability. Agricultural water is becoming scarcer, and the salination of soils is an increasing problem. In California, for example, they do a lot of irrigation, and when the water evaporates or flushes through the soil, it leaves small amounts of minerals and salts. Over time, the build-up is going to affect the soil's productivity.

Should we address the water side of the problem? Or can we approach the issue from the plant side? Can we develop plants that will thrive in salty soil? Or can we create less thirsty plants suited to a drier environment? If we had plants that could adapt, maybe semidesert areas could become productive.

Another problem is drinking water. Roughly 40% of the people on earth don't have an adequate supply of fresh water. In the United States, we have a big infrastructure for cleaning water. But in developing countries that lack the infrastructure, there might be a business opportunity for in-home water-purification systems.

I realize this is still early in the process, but how do you know that you're moving forward?

One interesting measure is that we keep drawing in more people. We started off with 80; now we have almost 140. And a lot of this response is just one person after another saying, "I want to be involved, and this is the team I want to be involved in." It's infectious. That's the way most good business processes work. To give people a script and tell them, "Your part is on page 17; just memorize it" is an archaic way to run institutions that have to regenerate and re-create themselves. It's a dead end.

Today, in most fields I know, the struggle is about creativity and innovation. There is no script. You have some ideas, some activities, some exhortations, and some invitations, and you try to align what people believe and what people care about with what they're free to do. And you hope that you can coordinate them in ways that aren't too wasteful—or, better still, that they can self-coordinate. If an institution wants to be adaptive, it has to let go of some control and trust that people will work on the right things in the right ways. That has some obvious implications for the ways you select people, train them, and support them.

Would it be accurate to say that all of your sustainability teams have been self-created and self-coordinated?

Someone asked me recently whether this was a top-down exercise or a bottom-up exercise. Those don't sound like very helpful concepts to me. This is about *us*. What do *we* want to do? Companies aren't machines anymore. We have thousands of independent agents trying to self-coordinate because it is in their interest to do so.

There is no top or bottom. That's just a metaphor and not a helpful one. People say, Here is what I think. What do you think? Does that make sense to you? Would you like to try it? I believe we must see what ideas really win people's hearts and trust that those ideas will turn out to be the most productive.

People in large numbers won't give their all for protracted periods of time—with a cost in their overall lives—for an abstraction called a corporation or an idea called profit. People can give only to people. They can give to their coworkers if they believe that they're engaged together in an enterprise of some importance. They can give to society, which is just another way of saying they can give to their children. They can give if they believe that their work is in some way integrated into a whole life.

Historically, there has been a bifurcation between who we are and the work we do, as if who we are is outside our work. That's unhealthy, and most people yearn to integrate their two sides. Because of Monsanto's history as a chemical company, we have a lot of employees—good people—with a recurrent experience like this: their kids or their neighbors' kids or somebody at a cocktail party asks them what kind of work they do and then reacts in a disapproving way because of what they *think* we are at Monsanto. And that hurts. People don't want to be made to feel ashamed of what they do.

I don't mean to disparage economic motives—they're obviously important. But working on sustainability offers a huge hope for healing the rift between our economic activity and our total human activity. Instead of seeing the two in Marxist opposition, we see them as the same thing. Economics is part of human activity.

What are the organizational implications of that?

Part of the design and structure of any successful institution is going to be giving people permission to select tasks and goals that they care about. Those tasks have to pass some kind of economic screen; but much of what people care about will pass because economic gain comes from meeting people's needs. That's what economies are based on.

"If emerging economies have to relive the entire industrial revolution . . . I think it's all over."

The people who have been working on sustainability here have done an incredible job, not because there has been one presiding genius who has organized it all and told them what to do but because they want to get it done. They care intensely about it and they organize themselves to do it.

I don't mean to romanticize it, but, by and large, self-regulating systems are probably going to be more productive than those based primarily on control loops. There are some institutions that for a short period can succeed as a reflection of the will and ego of a single person. But they're unlikely to survive unless other people resonate with what that person represents.

We're going to have to figure out how to organize people in ways that enable them to coordinate their activities without wasteful and intrusive systems of control and without too much predefinition of what a job is. My own view is that as long as you have a concept called a job, you're asking people to behave inauthentically; you're asking people to perform to a set of expectations that someone else created. People give more if they can figure out how to control themselves, how to regulate themselves, how to contribute what they can contribute out of their own authentic abilities and beliefs, not out of somebody else's predetermination of what they're going to do all day.

How will you measure your progress toward sustainability? Do you have milestones?

For something at this early level of exploration, you probably want to rely for at least a year on a subjective sense of momentum. People usually know when they're going someplace, when they're making progress. There's a pace to it that says, yes, we're on the right track. After that, I would like to see some quantitative goals with dates and very macro budgets. As the teams begin to come to some conclusions, we will be able to ignite the next phase by setting some specific targets.

This is so big and complicated that I don't think we're going to end up with a neat and tidy document. I don't think environmental sustainability lends itself to that.

As your activities globalize, does the issue of sustainability lead you to think differently about your business strategy in different countries or regions of the world?

The developing economies can grow by brute force, by putting steel in the ground and depleting natural resources and burning a lot of hydrocarbons. But a far better way to go would be for companies like Monsanto to transfer their knowledge and help those countries avoid the mistakes of the past. If emerging economies have to relive the entire industrial revolution with all its waste, its energy use, and its pollution, I think it's all over.

Can we help the Chinese, for example, leapfrog from preindustrial to postindustrial systems without having to pass through that destructive middle? At the moment, the signs aren't encouraging. One that is, however, is China's adoption of cellular phones instead of tons of stuff: telephone poles and copper wire.

The fact that India is one of the largest software writing countries in the world is encouraging. You'd like to see tens of millions of people in India employed in information technology rather than in making more stuff. But there's an important hurdle for companies like Monsanto to overcome. To make money through the transfer of information, we depend on intellectual property rights, which let us reconcile environmental and economic goals. As the headlines tell you, that's a little problematic in Asia. And yet it's critically important to our being able to figure out how to be helpful while making money. Knowledge transfer will happen a lot faster if people get paid for it.

Will individual companies put themselves at risk if they follow sustainable practices and their competitors don't?

I can see that somebody could get short-term advantage by cutting corners. At a matter of fact, the world economy *has* seized such an advantage—short-term in the sense of 500 years—by cutting corners on some basic laws of physics and thermodynamics. But it's like asking if you can gain an advantage by violating laws. Yes, I suppose you can—until they catch you. I don't think it is a good idea to build a business or an economy around the "until-they-catch-you principle." It can't be the right way to build something that is going to endure.

The multinational corporation is an impressive invention for dealing with the tension between the application of broadly interesting ideas on the one hand and economic and cultural differences on the other. Companies like ours have gotten pretty good at figuring out how to operate in places where we can make a living while remaining true to some fundamental rules. As more countries enter the world economy, they are accepting—with greater or lesser enthusiasm—that they are going to have to play by some rules that are new for them. My guess is that, over time, sustainability is going to be one of those rules.

Doesn't all this seem far away for managers? Far enough in the future for them to think, "It won't happen on my watch"?

The tension between the short term and the long term is one of the fundamental issues of business—and of life—and it isn't going to go away. Many chief executives have gotten where they are in part because they have a time horizon longer than next month. You don't stop caring about next month, but you also have to think further ahead. What's going to happen next in my world? If your world is soft drinks, for example, you have to ask where your clean water will come from.

How do you react to the prospect of the world population doubling over the next few decades? First you may say, Great, 5 billion more customers. That is what economic development is all about. That's part of it. Now, keep going. Think about all the physical implications of serving that many new customers. And ask yourself the hard question, How exactly are we going to do that and still live here? That's what sustainability is about.

I'm fascinated with the concept of distinctions that transform people. Once you learn certain things—once you learn to ride a bike, say—your life has changed forever. You can't unlearn it. For me, sustainability is one of those distinctions. Once you get it, it changes how you think. A lot of our people have been infected by this way of seeing the world. It's becoming automatic. It's just part of who you are.

America And The Global Economy

INTERNATIONAL TRADE AND INVESTMENT

Address by SHERROD BROWN, *United States Congressman from the State of Ohio*
Delivered to The City Club of Cleveland, Cleveland, Ohio, January 9, 1998

Thank you very much for the opportunity to be with you here today at the City Club. It's a great honor to address this distinguished forum. The First Amendment comes alive every day at the City Club, and that is a public service of immeasurable value.

And that's certainly the case today, because I want to use this opportunity to call attention to an issue that garners a great deal of attention but very little informed analysis.

It's almost impossible these days to pick up the paper or turn on the radio or TV without hearing somebody mention "the global economy." But what exactly does that mean?

In a narrow sense the global economy has existed since Marco Polo and the Dutch traders fanned out to sell their wares in foreign lands.

The global economy has certainly been a reality since the end of World War II, when the United States had the wherewithal and the desire to help create new markets for its industrial machine by establishing the Bretton Woods system and rebuilding Western Europe and Japan after the ravages of global warfare.

But when people talk about the "global economy" today they are usually referring to the increasing interdependence of national economies, facilitated by air travel, telecommunications, and computers.

The "global village" that Marshall McLuhan first envisioned in the Sixties is now clearly in focus, thanks to the Internet and other technological marvels.

When people talk about a global economy they are talking about a world in which informed citizens and successful business people stay abreast of events not only in their own community, their own state, or their own nation, but also worldwide.

The effects of currency crises on the other side of the planet are no longer contained in a single country.

The interdependence of the world's major economies sometimes means that when Thailand catches a cold, South Korea gets pneumonia.

Indeed, the Asian currency crisis has proved highly communicable, thus, the term "Asian flu." And the deep concern now stems from a fear that this contagion might spread throughout the region, to Japan, and possibly even infect our own economy.

This increased interdependence, revolutionary in and of itself, as pretty much taken for granted among policy elites.

Jerry Mander, senior fellow at the Public Media Center, has observed:

"Economic globalization involves arguably the most fundamental redesign of the planet's political and economic arrangements since at least the Industrial Revolution. Yet the profound implications of these fundamental changes have barely been exposed to serious public scrutiny or debate. Despite the scale of the global reordering, neither our elected officials nor our educational institutions nor the mass media have made a credible effort to describe what is being formulated or to explain its root philosophies."

Elites in American society for decades have dominated the debate over international trade policy.

For many years, at least going back to World War II, international trade and commerce were hardly front-burner issues with the American public. The United States ruled the roost. We knew it. The world knew it. Everybody else in the world was playing catch up.

So strong was the U.S. economy in the post-war period that we were able to muster our resources to embark upon the Marshall Plan to rebuild Europe and also to design a peacetime economy for Japan.

And, meanwhile, in Washington, a handful of well-connected law firms and lobbying firms dominated the arcane area of international trade policy.

From *Vital Speeches of the Day*, March 1, 1998, pp. 293-296. © 1998 by City News Publishing Company, Inc. Reprinted by permission.

A doctrinaire version of so-called "free trade" brooked no dissent.

For most of our post-war history, trade policy was merely an adjunct of larger foreign policy goals, specifically, winning the Cold War.

Down in Athens, Ohio University Professor Alan Eckes, former chairman of the International Trade Commission under Ronald Reagan and now an Ohio Eminent Scholar in contemporary history, has done pioneering research on the history of American trade policy, particularly in his book, "Opening America's Market."

As Professor Eckes has noted, "During the Cold War Years, the United States treated trade policy as an instrument of foreign policy for fulfilling hegemonic responsibilities, not as an end in itself."

Those foreign policy objectives, such as rebuilding the economies of Western Europe and Japan, and defeating Communism, were laudable goals. And the United States may have succeeded, in the process of winning the Cold War over the Soviet Union, in helping to open up the world economy.

But, as Professor Eckes concludes, the U.S. also "lost critical commercial battles . . .unilaterally (opening) the American market without gaining commensurate advantages in foreign markets for the products of American workers and American factories."

When the first waves of Japanese exports started to hit the U.S. shores in the Seventies and Eighties, the public consensus over so-called "free trade" started to crumble.

The historic debate over the North American Free Trade Agreement in 1993 marked another watershed in the formation of American trade policy. For the first time in American history, at least since the great tariff battles of the 19th Century, an international trade issue took center stage in the political theater.

That debate in Congress in 1993 didn't turn out the way I would have liked, but it nevertheless changed forever the rules of engagement. No longer would a handful of high-powered law firms dictate U.S. trade policy.

The public had been engaged and had gotten the message that America's economic future was tied in part to the world economy. And in that respect, the NAFTA debate busted the monopoly that the elites in this country had held over the formation of international trade policy.

That debate came into full flower again last year in Congress when the House of Representatives derailed the Clinton-Gingrich "fast track" bill. Many commentators bought the line that the labor unions had coerced members of Congress into opposing "fast track."

That is a shockingly superficial analysis and wrong.

First of all, business interests contribute 11 times the campaign money that labor does.

More important, though, to attribute the defeat of "fast track" to campaign contributions by labor misses the key point: Congress is going to be actively involved in formulating trade policy and will no longer give President Clinton, or any other president, a blank check.

And this is only right, because the United States Constitution specifically grants to the legislative branch the power to regulate international trade.

To hear some of the Washington pundits tell it, the defeat of "fast track" legislation was nothing short of apocalyptic. One of the so-called experts and one of the so-called think tanks predicted a stock market crash if the House rejected the Clinton-Gingrich "fast track" bill. Indeed, there was no shortage of so-called mainstream economists and business commentators who now look foolish because of their predictions of imminent catastrophe.

In fact, the U.S. equity and bond markets have performed quite nicely by any measure, the Dow, the S&P 500, almost all the various indexes, since "fast track" was defeated.

The sky has not fallen.

Confidence in the American economy has not faltered.

The U.S. has completed a financial services agreement under the rubric of the World Trade Organization. (Incidentally, this is one of approximately 200 trade agreements that the Administration has successfully negotiated without fast track authority. Keep in mind, also, that fast track authority has existed since Richard Nixon came up with the idea in the early 1970s and it has been used only four times.)

Meanwhile, the U.S. economy continues to hum along in the most sustained peacetime expansion in our history.

And, most significant, not one single nation has turned its back on the U.S. consumer market, the greatest prize in all of world commercial history. Everybody is still desperately competing for access to the American market.

The defeat of "fast track" legislation will prove to be a blessing for the American economy, for workers and businesses alike, because it represents a rejection of the failed American trade policy of the past 25 years.

Through 1970, the U.S. international merchandise trade balance was almost always positive (we exported more than we imported).

In 1984, the U.S. merchandise trade deficit doubled from the previous year, for the first time exceeding $100 billion.

Now the deficit is hemorrhaging.

This year's merchandise trade deficit is en route to approximately $200 billion, and some commentators have said the deficit is likely to hit $300 billion next year.

The Asian currency crisis that we've been hearing so much about has already led to serious devaluations in the currencies of Thailand, Malaysia, Korea and Indonesia. As a result, products that are made in those countries will be significantly cheaper on the world market, leading to massive exports to the buyer of last resort, the United States.

Almost inevitably our trade deficit inevitably will soar.

Even mainstream economists who are schooled in the neoliberal trade theories acknowledge that America's massive and rising trade deficit threatens economic growth in this country.

The Merrill Lynch Chartbook predicts that economic growth in the United States will drop by more than a complete percentage point.

And of course there is a huge difference between 3 percent growth and 2 percent growth in an economy the size of America's.

Still, the defeat of fast track brings some much-needed glasnost to the trade debate in the United States.

The rejection of the "fast track" version of deregulated international commerce is an opportunity to retool American trade policy.

First we need to start with the language, because to many of the ideologues in this debate, the words "global economy" or "free trade" actually cloak a political agenda.

As economist Dr. Hennan Daly said in his landmark article in Scientific American published before the NAFTA and GATT debates, a more accurate name than the persuasive label free trade (because who can be opposed to freedom?) is deregulated international commerce. "(And) deregulation is not always good policy: Recall the . . . experience of the U.S. deregulation of the savings and loan institutions."

No wonder Newt Gingrich and Dick Armey and Bill Archer and the Republican leadership in the House of Representatives would be so enthusiastic about a fast track bill with no provisions for labor and the environment. For them, "fast track" was merely an opportunity to enact, through the back door of an international trade and investment agreement, the same extremist domestic agenda that failed with the collapse of their Contract with America.

But the defeat of fast track presents an opportunity finally to confront the hard questions that are raised by the global economy.

It is an opportunity to address fundamental economic policy issues that will determine America's economic future in the next millenium.

The issue is not whether the global economy exists. It does.

The issue is not whether the United States is going to participate. It is going to.

And the issue is not whether the United States will adopt a policy of free trade or protectionism. Protectionism is dead.

Indeed, the issue is much more complex than most elites have deigned to admit.

The issue is not whether we trade, but what shape our trade policy will take.

Not whether we participate in the global economy, but what rules we will put in place.

Will the global economy help promote rising standards of living and eliminate poverty, both here and abroad, or will it merely be a global race to the bottom?

Complete deregulation is unacceptable to all but the think tank elites and the editorial writers.

As William Greider says in his remarkably prescient book, One World, Ready or Not, published to great acclaim last year, "The utopian vision of the marketplace offers, after all, an enthralling religion, a self-satisfied belief system that attracts fervent and influential adherents . . . Many intelligent people have come to worship these market principles, like a spiritual code that will resolve all the larger questions for us, social and moral and otherwise, so long as no one interferes with its authority. In this modern secular age, many who think of themselves as rational and urbane have put their faith in this idea of the self-regulating market as piously as others put their trust in God."

Those who approach trade with an ideological agenda—usually, laissez-faire, blind faith in the unregulated marketplace—ignore the danger of allowing capital and investment to flow freely without regard to national borders, but not labor.

They would protect intellectual property from the dangers of an unregulated global economy, but deny it to people who work for a living. Somehow, they justify protecting a Madonna CD, but not the men and women who work with their hands.

Nonetheless, it's the trendy model for trade and investment agreement that the elites are pushing. It's the NAFTA model. It's the GATT model. It's the Clinton-Gingrich "fast track" model.

Why should agreements such as NAFTA and "fast track" specifically protect investors from the dangers of expropriation but prohibit protection for the environment? I believe in a progressive, positive trade policy for the future.

I believe that America needs to take the lead in the global economy by negotiating trade agreements that help lift people up, not investment agreements that protect only wealthy investors.

I believe America needs to take the lead in negotiating trade agreements that help create open world markets for American products while protecting the social consensus that we have built in this country over the past 50 years—clean air, clean water, safe food, and rights for working people.

I believe that America should take the lead in the global economy by negotiating trade agreements that help create new markets for American products, and thereby create jobs for American workers.

How do we do that? We need to remember the lesson of Henry Ford, who was ridiculed by his counterparts when he proposed paying his workers the outrageous sum of $5 a day so that they could save enough money to buy the products they were making.

America needs to take the lead in the global economy by negotiating trade agreements that help the poor in Mexico and other nations join the consumer class, not investment agreements that privatize the gains for multinational corporations and socialize their losses.

America needs to take the lead in the global economy by negotiating trade agreements that help the poor in Mexico and other nations join the consumer class, not investment agreements that privatize the gains for multinational corporations and socialize their losses.

America needs to take the lead in the global economy by negotiating trade agreements that incorporate labor and environmental rights—not investment agreements that make trickle-down economics the preferred policy of the global economy.

America needs to take the lead by negotiating trade agreements that put people first, not money-center banks and the bond market.

We need a trade policy that looks to the future, not to the past.

But earlier this year, I saw a future I didn't like.

Last fall, as Congress was gearing up for the fight over the president's "fast track" bill, I spent three days in Texas and the maquiladora zone on the Mexican side of the border.

NAFTA's epicenter.

I saw the global economy, NAFTA style.

It doesn't work. It cannot work.

In Reynosa, Mexico, just across the border, I met a typical working family: husband, wife, and two kids. Both parents were working in a factory run by General Motors, the largest private employer in Mexico. Each day they came home to a plywood shack with dirt floors and no running water and no electricity.

They told me their dreams of moving into a little nicer house and providing an education for their children, but they weren't making much headway because they were earning only 90 cents an hour—about $40 a week. It was barely enough to put food on the table and keep their kids in clothes.

They had a propane tank to fuel their cooking stove and they had hooked up a cheap little television to a car battery. Their roof leaked and they said they "suffered" in the winter because their house was so poorly constructed. As we talked, their children, happy as most children are when they have loving parents, ran barefoot on the dirt floors. The father was a proud man, but he worried aloud about his ability to provide. Chicken cost 30 pesos a kilogram, almost 10 percent of his weekly salary.

NAFTA had failed this family. Badly. For them, the global economy was a dead end.

It works pretty well for the elites, for the handful of super-rich families in Mexico, where the richest citizen's wealth is more than the combined annual income of the poorest 17 million people combined.

But the people I met were pawns in a global chess game in which big capital and multinational corporations can move across borders with ease, seeking the best deal, but workers are considerably less mobile.

The global economy had failed these people because the Mexican government refused to enforce its labor laws and they had nowhere else to go. They had migrated from the south of Mexico to the border region because there were jobs in the maquiladora factories, but now they were trapped.

"They're taking advantage of us for their own interests. We know the company doesn't want any bad publicity, so why is there such injustice? Don't the shareholders know about our situation? I am not afraid. I am going forward for myself and my family, for my children. We will not quit."

A neighbor also earned less than a dollar an hour. She had nine dollars taken out of her $40 paycheck every week to pay for a small stove—one you might find in a college dorm room in this country, in her tiny home. One quarter of her paycheck, for the next 52 weeks, would be deducted for an appliance that probably would sell for less than $200 in the United States.

Her brother-in-law has suffered some type of nerve damage to his face. His doctor told him it's from working around massive doses of lead at an American company which, of course, does not use lead in its U.S. operations.

Clearly NAFTA has failed to keep its promises to these people.

And they are merely three families among millions who are congregated along the U.S.-Mexico border. The American Medical Association has called that region "access pool of infectious disease."

I call it a ticking time bomb on our southern border.

And NAFTA is not a development strategy, it's an investment agreement to protect the interests of the elite. It's a step backward. It's more like the trickle-down economics of the Reagan Administration than the Kennedyesque idealism of the Alliance for Progress.

The momentum is building in this country for a humane trade policy.

A policy that not only protects American interests, American businesses, workers, and consumers, but also promotes sustainable economic development among our trading partners.

A trade policy tailored to the needs of the next century, not a past that no longer exists.

A trade policy that meets the challenges of the global economy head on and establishes American leadership around American values well into the next century.

NAFTA and "fast track" failed because they represented the policies of the past. Now we have to begin the hard work of fashioning a trade policy that will meet the challenges of the global economy and the next century.

International Business: The New Bottom Line

by Bruce Kogut

Multinational corporations are the primary players today in the world's most dynamic industries and the driving force behind the global economy. Privatization is reaching deep into the farthest corners of Latin America. Russian firms seek international capital by listing themselves on the New York Stock Exchange. Africa, rich in resources but desperately poor in other respects, sees in foreign investment the only hope for an otherwise dismal future. Indeed, the business of the world today is business. Prime ministers become famous by announcing their distaste for the global market, but their actions belie a different set of beliefs. While nation-states worry about guarding their sovereignty, their citizens pursue profit, higher living standards, and good old-fashioned durable goods, regardless of whether the products they buy come from next door or halfway around the world.

These are not the times for narrow balance-of-power considerations. As even an unchallenged superpower like the United States has seen, efforts to block the flow of trade and investment to nations such as Iran and Cuba are not just increasingly ineffective but costly. Multinational corporations—once made vulnerable to the expropriation of property or

BRUCE KOGUT *is professor of management and codirector of the Reginald H. Jones Center at the Wharton School, University of Pennsylvania.*

blockage of funds, and forbidden to trade with hostile countries and to buy and sell freely the latest high technology and scarce commodities—are now more likely to guide foreign policy than follow it. Individual donors such as George Soros and Ted Turner surpass the world's impoverished ministries of foreign affairs with their gifts to countries and world agencies. Every year, the financial flows of international organizations such as the World Bank and the International Monetary Fund (IMF) diminish in importance relative to the hefty direct and portfolio investments that private investors pour into emerging markets. Many forces, from technology to political ideas, are keeping the global bullet train of consumerism and privatization running.

The field of international business concerns the study of the international activities of firms, including their interactions with foreign governments, competitors, and employees. It seeks to address not only the question of why firms go overseas but also how they do it. The globalization of markets, and rapid changes in economic and political systems, have forced scholars to rethink the meaning of international business concepts such as location, competitive advantage, and transmission of knowledge among countries. Because multinational corporations dominate trade and world production, international business focuses on the ability of managers to coordinate and organize people—despite large variations in their national origins and culture—within the boundaries of a single firm that spans borders.

WHY INVEST IN ANOTHER COUNTRY?

Multinational corporations have long been the principal players in particular industries such as consumer products (from toothpaste to electronics), transportation, and chemicals. Consider competing firms such as Procter & Gamble, Hertel, Kao, Colgate, or Unilever that produce, for example, washing-machine detergent, and look at the various places they have set up shop: France, Japan, Mexico, Poland, and Saudi Arabia. Theirs is a long-standing oligopoly, an industry composed of a few firms who compete and produce in a recognized world market and whose business strategies are dictated as much by what their rivals do as by what their customers need. Yet, while all multinationals tend to be part of an oligopoly, not all oligopolistic firms become multinationals or even invest abroad.

Companies that operate in the soap or computer markets tend to be multinationals. Those that manufacture airplanes do not. Why?

Because rates of return on investment in industries such as aviation are higher at home, right? No. The empirical evidence shows that companies expand their operations elsewhere even when the returns are negligible. Moreover, this pattern is widespread enough that it cannot be written off as the result of mistakes made by overeager managers who insist on playing with shareholders' money.

In fact the rise of multinational corporations (companies that own and exert centralized control over firms in several other countries) was this puzzle that the first generation of international business scholars sought to solve. Prior to the publication in 1960 of Stephen Hymer's doctoral dissertation at MIT, most economists and policymakers thought that differences in the rates of return to capital among countries explained why money moves across borders. Hundreds of years have passed since British and Dutch firms began contracting production to local businesses in Asia and elsewhere. Alfred Chandler and Mira Wilkins have written stunning histories of American firms such as Singer and Westinghouse that built large factories in England prior to the early 1900s. Nor was this only an American experience. British firms dominated real investment across bor-

ders until the 1950s. German companies would have been far more important in overseas markets if not for losing their assets abroad after both world wars. Despite so much history and experience, the prevailing belief was that direct and portfolio investments were the same thing: both sought higher rates of return on invested capital.

Hymer simply asked why any firm would invest physical capital (exposed as it is to commercial and political risk) in one country when it could spread small amounts of financial capital across many companies and countries? If a firm wants to invest and own physical capital in a foreign country, it must believe that there is some additional advantage that outweighs the added costs of operating at a distance in an unknown business environment. Moreover, it must also believe that this advantage can only be exploited through the ownership and control of foreign operations. Otherwise a company could rely on exports to tap foreign markets without incurring the troubles, and added costs, of investing abroad. Hymer eliminated the country as an important factor in understanding direct investment. Now the focus would be on industries and firms themselves.

Since Hymer, there has been fairly universal agreement that the distinctive characteristic of direct investment is the intent to control. As a consequence, governments define foreign direct investment (FDI) as the controlling ownership of assets by foreign private individuals or firms. Thus, FDI is quite distinct from foreign portfolio investment, which usually implies the ownership of noncontrolling equities in companies whose shares are traded in a foreign stock market.

The forces that affect the two types of investments are quite different. In the case of portfolio investments, changes in investment conditions in a specific country or even across the globe, or a downturn in expectations, can spur a quick divestment from one particular company or potentially from the entire country or continent. With direct ownership and management of a corporation, investors are both less likely and less able to flee at the first sign of trouble. The effects on the receiving economy of these two kinds of foreign private investments are also quite different. Portfolio investments can have huge financial impacts and, as Ricardo Hausmann illustrated in the Fall 1997 issue of FOREIGN POLICY, are a driving force behind the macroeconomic roller coaster that often destabilizes many vulnerable emerging markets. FDIs tend to have more links to other sectors of the economy, mobilizing local resources that might otherwise be idle or less productive and contributing to the dissemination of productive skills and technology.

WHAT IT TAKES TO BE A MULTINATIONAL

Recognizing that multinational corporations tend to populate industries in which only a few firms dominate sales (i.e., oligopolistic markets), Hymer basically set out a necessary condition for direct investment and multinational corporations—namely, these firms should own some hard-to-replicate proprietary advantage (e.g. brand label, technology, efficiency due to size) that enables them to become dominant in domestic markets and, later, foreign markets. Ironically, this tendency to dominate markets that Hymer first identified as a result of the multinational corporation's advantage is also the target of popular political and economic attack, one that Hymer quickly came to join.

Even though these basic ideas were subsequently more fully developed by Charles Kindleberger of MIT and Richard Caves of Harvard, they still failed to capture the differences among firms and industries. Why is Boeing, which enjoys important competitive advantages and an oligopoly, still largely a domestic producer that operates internationally through exports? In contrast, why did companies that manufacture tires or sewing machines feel the need so early in their histories to establish similar operations in other countries?

In the decades after Hymer's contribution, there emerged an integrated view that John Dunning, a professor at the University of Reading in England, dubbed the eclectic theory of FDI. Dunning employed the acronym "OLI" to summarize the theory's three elements: *ownership*, *location*, and *internalization*. The first, ownership, is simply Hymer's idea that a firm has to own some unique advantage to offset the added costs of competing overseas. The second, location, seems obvious enough—a firm will locate its activities either to gain access to cheap labor, capital, materials, and other inputs, or to sell close to its customers and avoid transportation and tariff costs. In the parlance of economics, the sourcing decision is an act of "vertical" investment—as when a steel company buys a mine in Brazil to supply iron ore. The sales decision

Volkswagen of America, Inc.
How do you say "Love Bug" in Spanish?

represents a "horizontal" investment: Compaq computer, for example, opens an assembly plant to expand production of computers already made at home.

A tremendous amount of intellectual labor has been invested in the third element, internalization. Scholars such as Peter Buckley, Mark Casson, and Jean-François Hennart sought to explain why a firm would choose to exploit its advantage internationally through direct ownership of another company overseas instead of entering into a joint venture, offering a license, granting a franchise, or simply signing an export sales agreement with a company abroad. In practice, these different modes of entry into overseas markets are not mutually exclusive. A firm, for example, may decide to enter into a joint venture (i.e. share the equity ownership in a foreign operation with another partner) and allow others to "rent" its technology by granting them a license to use it. This license sells the right to use the technology in return for various kinds of payments, usually fees and royalties.

The United States has a healthy balance of payments on these transactions and for many years was the principal source of licensing technology in the world economy. Many critics understood these licenses as "giving away" U.S. technology. Japanese industrial policy in the 1950s and 1960s is often the example used as a warning of the consequences of selling technology to firms that later return as formidable competitors. However, a multinational corporation will frequently sell licenses to its own subsidiaries abroad or to joint ventures, thereby establishing property rights that can prevent the diffusion of technology to competitors or former partners.

Concerns about property rights and political vulnerability are examples of the reasons why a firm would opt to enter a country by one mode rather than another, or not enter at all. Historically, IBM has often refused requests by countries to license its technology, out of the belief that certain key technologies should be kept under proprietary control. This policy has generally worked to the company's benefit. If, for example, IBM had licensed its technology to Indian firms during the 1970s, it could conceivably be in a worse position today to establish brand label recognition in India. In contrast, Texas Instruments ultimately came out the loser in tough negotiations in Japan that led it to license its semiconductor-manufacturing technology to Japanese firms that later became dominant competitors. But these examples tend to exaggerate the dangers. It is improbable that IBM's licensing could have created Indian competitors (it could have set a dangerous example for other governments or permitted leakage of computer technology to military programs). Technical change occurs so frequently these days that transferring current technology—without including the capability to improve it—is not a threat in the future. Countries seeking to expand may offer their partners licenses for technology that will become quickly outdated, but only if these partners cannot innovate faster than they can.

RECOGNIZING COMPETITIVE ADVANTAGE

While for most of the 1970s and 1980s the eclectic theory (or OLI) provided a useful perspective, the growing globalization of markets is increasingly undermining its conceptual value. The earlier theories of direct investment sought to explain it as if a firm were investing in a foreign country for the first time. But by the 1980s, hundreds of corporations already had extensive networks of wholly owned subsidiaries in place around the globe. Increasingly, managers of such multinational corporations understood that the global nature of their operations provided an important advantage. They pursued global strategies that sometimes conflicted with the objectives of governments and that other times acted as powerful mechanisms for economic progress.

In the mid-1980's, I argued that FDI theory should redirect its focus away from the first investment made by a firm to the sequential advantages—those advantages gained by coordinating a multinational network of operations. One of the most important, and controversial, sequential sources of advantage for a multinational corporation is its ability to arbitrage internationally, which means profiting from the differences in costs and prices across borders. Such activities trouble both governments and workers. A multinational corporation often buys and sells across borders within its own network. Ford produces parts in many places in the world and then ships these parts for final assembly. For some countries such as the United States, Sweden, and the United Kingdom, as well as many developing nations, it is estimated that this "intrafirm" trade is responsible for 30 to 50 percent of their international trade in manufactured products.

Given such internal trade, it makes sense not just to produce in countries where the costs are reduced but to realize profits where the tax rates are also lower. Here is where arbitrage becomes important. But other kinds of arbitrage that defy effective government intervention are also possible and provide huge profit opportunities to multinational corporations. For example, the extent to which exchange rates move is astounding. A few years ago, the dollar was worth 70 yen or 1.4 deutsch Marks (DM). Recently, the dollar has been at more than 130 yen and 1.8 DM, appreciations of almost 90 and 40 percents over a course of two years. This appreciation of the dollar means that if productivity growth and inflation are about the same in these countries, it is now almost twice as expensive to produce in the United States as in Japan, and 40 percent more in the United States than in Germany. For exporters from the United States, these are tougher times. And the recent sharp drops in the exchange rates of Asian currencies only add further pressure. But American multinationals also own facilities in Asia and Europe (and of course in other countries too). Some of the production done in the United States can be moved to these locations. This shifting is arbitrage in response to exchange rates. Though these responses when measured in percentage are minimal, the value of switching production, as Subramanian Rangan has shown, is large. No wonder the president of a large European multinational corporation once whimsically wished to have his factories on his ships, moving from country to country depending on the day's exchange rates.

Of course, shifting production about is not like moving money in and out of the country using modern computer and communications technologies. That is why financial markets are much more subject to arbitrage. In their attempt to participate more fully in the international economy, many countries have sought to open their financial markets or at least to allow for the easy convertibility of their currencies. Multinational corporations and foreign investors in general do not like to invest in countries where they cannot take their money out easily. They also prefer to have stable currencies, so that an ....ment to build a large petrochemical plant as an export platform to other countries is not suddenly eradicated because costs (based on the home currency) suddenly go up. Countries also borrow abroad to help finance their own domestic companies or public projects to improve infrastructure and social programs. However, such borrowing (especially when loans must be refinanced every year and are denominated in foreign currency) can make a country vulnerable to investors who might refuse to relend (or "roll over") financing, as happened in Mexico in late 1994 and East Asia in 1997–98.

In contrast, investments by multinational corporations are less fungible. A multinational manufacturer hesitates before closing a factory and moving production elsewhere. After all, currency rates, and other costs, might become favorable again. Arbitrage remains attractive, of course, and large firms will adjust overtime shifts on an international basis to operate at full capacity those plants located in today's low-cost site. Multinational corporations help countries readjust. For example, Asia's financial disaster has caused currency there to depreciate, making exports cheaper and more internationally competitive. As a result, these countries are all the more attractive to multinational corporations looking for export bases for their products.

The contemporary multinational corporation is best viewed as a global network of subsidiaries. Thanks to advances in communications, transportation, and managerial science, managers enjoy an unprecedented degree of flexibility in moving production around, transferring knowledge, and reacting to threats and opportunities. The multinational corporation has become, in the words of Christopher Bartlett and Sumantra Ghoshal, transnational. A firm such as Philips may have scores of subsidiaries throughout the world, but it increasingly coordinates their management on a global basis.

Multinational corporations do not compete so much on scale, but on their ability to coordinate international activity.

Multinational corporations do not compete so much on scale, though they are large, but on their ability to coordinate international activities. Such coordination also includes transferring knowledge on how to organize for manufacturing, research, and sales from one country to the next. The terms ownership, internalization, and even location do not adequately capture this global role of the multinational corporation. Recent efforts to look at the multinational corporation start with a redefinition of what is meant by ownership. In this new scholarship, which builds on the ideas of Richard Nelson and Sidney Winter, a multinational corporation does not simply own an advantage. Rather, a firm is viewed as a repository of valuable knowledge that can be exploited either through new products or through the dissemination of existing products to new locations. This knowledge consists not just of what an individual employee knows but of collective information on how people, machines, and technology are best organized and directed. Toyota's investments in the United States surely consisted of real estate and capital equipment; but as John Paul MacDuffie of the Wharton School and his associates at the Sloan School of Management's program on autos have shown, Toyota's organizational knowledge (in this case, re-organizing workers and suppliers in a new system for fabricating cars) cannot be overlooked in any analysis of its operations.

This approach redefines FDI, encompassing within it the spread of a firm's organizational knowledge across national borders. Direct investment often consists of technology transfer, but this technology includes organizational and management skills. Consider McDonald's. When McDonald's set up operations in Russia, it had to train its Russian suppliers to bake the right kind of bread and to deliver it on time, every time. This training was costly and brought the best of Western-quality management to these suppliers. They were then able to use these same techniques to sell bread to Russian customers. Of course, McDonald's chose to own its Russian operations. This choice was based not on the dangers of franchising (i.e., the internalization argument fashionable in the 1980s) but on the recognition that company knowledge could be more safely, easily, and effectively transferred to Russia through channels managed inside the firm—a crucial consideration if McDonald's has the intention, as it does, to clone this knowledge for use in establishing operations throughout Russia.

TECHNOLOGY AND ITS LIFE CYCLE

So far, we have described the activities of the multinational corporation just in terms of transferring knowledge into one country. This transfer implies that knowledge is also being transferred from some other country. Raymond Vernon made this observation in the 1960s when he proposed that direct investment follows a "life cycle." The cycle starts with an innovation in the home market and ends with the firm investing in a foreign country to reproduce that innovation. John Cantwell made the important observation that if some countries innovate more than others in particular industries, then foreign firms should also be drawn to high-technology regions. Suddenly, FDI is no longer seen as the flow from advanced to lower-cost countries, but as the result of where firms decide to locate their activities to be able to learn and innovate most effectively.

In today's world, innovations move much faster across borders. Sun Microsystems had 25 percent of the workstation market in Japan only a few years after its founding in Silicon Valley; hence, its international life cycle is very short. Why should Japanese firms wait for Sun Microsystems to come to Japan? If the knowledge of new innovations is in Silicon Valley, then why not invest directly there? In other words, countries differ in what they innovate and how fast they do so. And for reasons that scholars are now exploring, this knowledge of how to innovate is geographically sticky; that is, firms may have to go to particular regions to acquire it. Somehow, simply buying the license or analyzing the components is not enough.

The older notion of sourcing cheap labor and raw materials is too restrictive. Firms also invest in source technologies, high-quality people, and ideas. Look at Japanese investment in Europe up until a few years ago. Nissan, Toyota, and Hitachi invested in lower-cost England and Spain but also in expensive Germany. Though German wages were steep, the high productivity of workers at that time made setting up shop there efficient. Investing in Germany also meant Japanese firms could sell directly to German manufacturers, procure from German suppliers and, in the process, learn new ideas and technologies from some of the most sophisticated companies in the world. This learning would in turn be disseminated within the corporations themselves and could then be profitably exploited in other countries by subsidiaries—another example of the arbitrage of ideas and techniques available to corporations that operate in many countries.

The work on these issues is still early, but we know already from the studies done by Paul Almeida that foreign subsidiaries do not just passively learn in regions such as Silicon Valley, but that they also contribute to the regions. And yet, corporations have a difficult time transferring this knowledge back to the parent office or other foreign sites. The static distinction between location and ownership advantages is irrelevant to understanding why knowledge is created in certain places. Just being there is what matters as far as the firm's ability to innovate.

THE GLOBAL DIVISION OF MENTAL LABOR

Adam Smith did not forecast the world of today, but he understood its principles. The division of labor operates, not at the level of industries still taught in textbooks on international economics, but at the level of activities. A car is no longer a mechanical machine with a combustion engine; it is also a computer, a mini-telecommunications center replete with advanced optical fiber. Auto firms do not look at Detroit, Baden-Württemberg, or Toyota

City as the only possible locations for their activities. They consider which places would offer them the best opportunity to develop design ideas (Newport Beach, California?), machine tools for quality production (Italy?), or high-grade steel (Germany or Korea?). Specialization and comparative advantage operate across countries, but within firms.

In today's integrated, knowledge-based, world economy, there is an international division of mental labor. Highly trained workers and engineers (of many nationalities) work in laboratories and factories throughout Europe, Japan, and the United States, but they are also found increasingly in hotbeds of technology such as India, Israel, Russia, and Taiwan. Often their activities are conducted in small firms or laboratories, and frequently these smaller entities have commercial relationships with one another. If these complex interlocking ties could be seen from space, they would show a dense pattern of activities in many regions in the world—Bangalore, Moscow, Palo Alto, Stuttgart, and Taichung—that are themselves linked together by countless strands spun by a few hundred multinational corporations.

The implications of these changes for research are exciting; for policymakers, they are critical. If the countries of the European Union wish to pump a billion euro into technology, they will likely have to think about these policies in terms of the competence not only of individual firms but also of regions. Policymakers in Europe, Japan, and the United States tend to recognize that technology policy requires cooperation among small and large firms situated close to one another. The participation of multinational corporations in these programs is a double-edged sword. Not only do such corporations have the requisite financial and technical capabilities to partner with governments, they form the communication highway that speeds the flow of technical knowledge among regions. For regions to renew their economies, they must be a node in the global network. There is, however, a policy quandary. What technology can governments fund with the expectation that the innovative knowledge will stay within their borders—not because of legal restraints but because, for some reason, it is sticky to that location?

The understanding of location is, of course, also linked to the overall challenge of discerning the implications of the global marketplace for individual countries. Much as multinational corporations seem to threaten national technology policies, the globalization of production and services through multinational FDI upsets the social welfare policies of European countries and the economic aspirations of industrializing countries. Global capitalism and national and regional policies appear to be historical contradictions. But the evidence that Geoffrey Garrett has shown for social welfare states is inconclusive: Integration in global markets does not mean that we must abandon the historical, corporatist agreements struck between labor, government, and the private sector. This issue of global markets, and the degrees of freedom for national policy, form the most important research agenda for international business studies.

WANT TO KNOW MORE?

For a comprehensive overview of economic theories of the multinational enterprise, read Richard Caves' *Multinational Enterprise and Economic Analysis,* second edition (Cambridge: Cambridge University Press, 1996). John Dunning's textbook *Multinational Enterprises and the Global Economy* (Reading, MA: Addison-Wesley, 1993) covers the economics of the multinational corporation from economics to cross-cultural studies. A useful collection of economic studies on FDI is given in *Foreign Direct Investment* (Chicago, IL: University of Chicago Press, 1995), edited by Kenneth Froot of the National Bureau of Economic Research.

Stephen Hymer's book *The International Operations of National Firms* (Cambridge, MA: MIT Press, 1976), based on his 1960 Ph.D thesis, remains an easy and interesting read. A seminal book on internalization theory, even if drier, is Peter Buckley & Mark Casson's *The Future of the Multinational Corporation* (London: Blackwell, 1976). *A Theory of Multinational Enterprise* by Jean-François Hennart (Ann Arbor, MI: University of Michigan, 1982) is a superbly written book, filled with clear logic and historical examples, which sets out the argument for internalization theory as a problem of information and incentives.

Bruce Kogut's chapter, "Foreign Direct Investment as a Sequential Process," in Charles Kindleberger & David Audretsch, eds., *The Multinational Corporation in the 1980s* (Cambridge, MA: MIT Press, 1986) is one of the first articles to argue for understanding FDI flows as influenced by the real option advantages of a global network. The most recent treatment of this topic is Subramanian Rangan's *"Do Multinationals Operate Flexibly? Theory and Evidence"* (Journal of International Business Studies, forthcoming).

John Cantwell's book *Technological Innovation and Multinational Corporations* (Oxford: Blackwell, 1989) is the first full-length study of the pull of innovation centers on FDI flows. Michael Porter's *The Competitive*

Advantage of Nations (New York, NY: Free Press, 1990) is an innovative work that combines history and corporate strategy with analysis of the national sources of competitive strength for global firms. The compiled essays in Mark Mason & Dennis Encarnation's *Does Ownership Matter? Japanese Multinationals in Europe* (Oxford: Oxford University Press, 1994) present a variety of arguments regarding the meaning of borders and global firms. There are many important statistical studies on productivity spillovers among multinational firms and domestic firms, but an easy introduction into the transfer of practices can be gleaned by reading the MIT study *The Machine that Changed the World* by James Womack, Daniel Jones, and Daniel Roos (New York, NY: Rawson Associates, 1990).

A fine read of the strategies and structure of multinational corporations is *Managing Across Borders* by Christopher Bartlett and Sumantra Ghoshal (Cambridge, MA: Harvard Business School Press, 1989). Geert Hofstede's *Culture's Consequences: International Differences in Work-Related Values* is a classic study of cultural differences (London: Sage Publications, 1984).

The literature on the political economy of direct investment is a fascinating topic, especially in light of globalization. Raymond Vernon's *Sovereignty at Bay: The Multinational Spread of United States Enterprises* (New York, NY: Basic Books, 1971) is a model statement on how innovation drives global firms and challenges national policy. Two books in the Brookings Institution's useful series on globalization that readers may find of particular interest are Richard Herring & Robert Litan's *Financial Regulation in a Global Economy* (1995) and Stephan Haggard's *Developing Nations and the Politics of Global Integration* (1995). Geoffrey Garrett presents the counterargument to the thesis that globalization signifies that national governments can no longer pursue social welfare policies in his *Partisan Politics in the Global Economy* (Cambridge: Cambridge University Press, 1998).

Finally, there are many excellent corporate and general histories of multinational corporations. Alfred Chandler's *Scale and Hope: The Dynamics of Industrial Capitalism* (Cambridge, MA: Harvard University Press, 1998) deserves to be singled out, as do Mira Wilkins' many books on the subject. Charles Kindleberger's *American Business Abroad* (New Haven, CT: Yale University Press, 1969) remains an interesting blend of history and theory and documents the rise of American corporations.

All foreign R&D sites fall into one of two categories,
and each type has different needs.

Building Effective R&D Capabilities Abroad

by Walter Kuemmerle

An increasing number of companies in technologically
intensive industries such as pharmaceuticals and electronics have abandoned the traditional approach to managing
research and development and are establishing global
R&D networks in a noteworthy new way. For example,
Canon is now carrying out R&D activities in 8 dedicated
facilities in 5 countries, Motorola in 14 facilities in 7 countries, and Bristol-Myers Squibb in 12 facilities in 6 countries. In the past, most companies—even those with a
considerable international presence in terms of sales and
manufacturing—carried out the majority of their R&D activity in their home countries. Conventional wisdom held
that strategy development and R&D had to be kept in
close geographical proximity. Because strategic decisions
were made primarily at corporate headquarters, the thinking went, R&D facilities should be close to home.

But such a centralized approach to R&D will no longer
suffice—for two reasons. First, as more and more sources
of potentially relevant knowledge emerge across the globe,
companies must establish a presence at an increasing
number of locations to access new knowledge and to absorb new research results from foreign universities and
competitors into their own organizations. Second, companies competing around the world must move new products from development to market at an ever more rapid
pace. Consequently, companies must build R&D networks

that excel at tapping new centers of knowledge and at
commercializing products in foreign markets with the
speed required to remain competitive. And more and
more, superior manufacturers are doing just that. (See the
exhibit "Laboratory Sites Abroad in 1995.")

In an ongoing study on corporate strategy and the geographical dispersion of R&D sites, I have been examining
the creation of global research networks by 32 U.S., Japanese, and European multinational companies.[1] The most
successful companies in my study brought each new site's
research productivity up to full speed within a few years
and quickly transformed knowledge created there into innovative products. I found that establishing networks of
such sites poses a number of new, complex managerial
challenges. According to my research, managers of the
most successful R&D networks understand the new dynamics of global R&D, link corporate strategy to R&D

*Walter Kuemmerle is an assistant professor at the Harvard
Business School in Boston, Massachusetts, where he
teaches technology and operations management, as well
as entrepreneurial finance. His research focuses on the
technology strategies of multinational companies, patterns
of strategic interaction between small and large companies,
and foreign direct investment.*

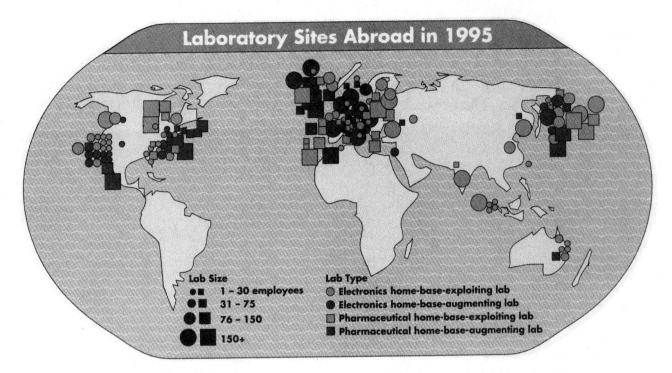

Laboratory Sites Abroad in 1995

Lab Size
● ■ 1 – 30 employees
● ■ 31 – 75
● ■ 76 – 150
● ■ 150+

Lab Type
○ Electronics home-base-exploiting lab
● Electronics home-base-augmenting lab
□ Pharmaceutical home-base-exploiting lab
■ Pharmaceutical home-base-augmenting lab

strategy, pick the appropriate sites, staff them with the right people, supervise the sites during start-up, and integrate the activities of the different foreign sites so that the entire network is a coordinated whole.

Adopting a Global Approach to R&D

Adopting a global approach to R&D requires linking R&D strategy to a company's overall business strategy. And that requires the involvement of managers at the highest levels of a company.

Creating a Technology Steering Committee. The first step in creating a global R&D network is to build a team that will lead the initiative. To establish a global R&D network, the CEOs and top-level managers of a number of successful companies that I studied assembled a small team of senior managers who had both technical expertise and in-depth organizational knowledge. The technology steering committees reported directly to the CEOs of their respective companies. They were generally small—five to eight members—and included managers with outstanding managerial and scientific records and a range of educational backgrounds and managerial responsibilities. The committees I studied included as members a former bench scientist who had transferred into manufacturing and had eventually become the head of manufacturing for the company's most important category of therapeutic drugs; a head of marketing for memory chips who had worked before in product development in the same electronics company; and an engineer who had started out in product development, had moved to research, and eventually had become the vice president of R&D. Members of these committees were sufficiently senior to be able to mobi-

lize resources at short notice; and they were actively involved in the management and supervision of R&D programs. In many cases, members included the heads of major existing R&D sites.

Categorizing New R&D Sites. In selecting new sites, companies find it helpful first to articulate each site's primary objective. (See the exhibit "Establishing New R&D Sites.") R&D sites have one of two missions. The first type of site—what I call a *home-base-augmenting site*—is established in order to tap knowledge from competitors and universities around the globe; in that type of site, information flows *from* the foreign laboratory *to* the central lab at home. The second type of site—what I call a *home-base-exploiting site*—is established to support manufacturing facilities in foreign countries or to adapt standard products to the demand there; in that type of site, information flows *to* the foreign laboratory *from* the central lab at home. (See the exhibit "How Information Flows Between Home-Base and Foreign R&D Sites.")

The overwhelming majority of the 238 foreign R&D sites I studied fell clearly into one of the two categories. Approximately 45% of all laboratory sites were home-base-augmenting sites, and 55% were home-base-exploiting sites. The two types of sites were of the same average size: about 100 employees. But they differed distinctly in their strategic purpose and leadership style.[2] (See the insert "Home-Base-Augmenting and Home-Base-Exploiting Sites: Xerox and Eli Lilly.")

Choosing a Location for the Site. Home-base-augmenting sites should be located in regional clusters of scientific excellence in order to tap new sources of knowledge. Central to the success of corporate R&D strategy is the ability of senior researchers to recognize and combine scientific advancements from different areas of science and technology. Absorbing the new knowledge can happen in a number of ways: through participation in formal or informal meeting circles that exist within a geographic area containing useful knowledge (a knowledge cluster), through hiring employees from competitors, or through sourcing laboratory equipment and research services from the same suppliers that competitors use.

For example, the Silicon Valley knowledge cluster boasts a large number of informal gatherings of experts as well as more formal ways for high-tech companies to exchange information with adjacent universities, such as industrial liaison programs with Stanford University and the University of California at Berkeley. In the field of communication technology, Siemens, NEC, Matsushita, and Toshiba all operate laboratory sites near Princeton University and Bell Labs (now a part of Lucent Technologies) to take advantage of the expertise located there. For similar reasons, a number of companies in the same industry have established sites in the Kanto area surrounding Tokyo. Texas Instruments operates a facility in Tsukuba Science City, and Hewlett-Packard operates one in Tokyo.

After a company has picked and established its major R&D sites, it might want to branch out. It might selectively set up secondary sites when a leading competitor or a university succeeds in building a critical mass of research expertise in a more narrowly defined area of science and technology outside the primary cluster. In order to benefit from the resulting miniclusters of expertise, companies sometimes establish additional facilities. For that reason, NEC operates a small telecommunications-oriented R&D facility close to a university laboratory in London, and

Canon operates an R&D facility in Rennes, France, close to one of France Telecom's major sites.

Home-base-exploiting sites, in contrast, should be located close to large markets and manufacturing facilities in order to commercialize new products rapidly in foreign markets. In the past, companies from industrialized countries located manufacturing facilities abroad primarily to benefit from lower wages or to overcome trade barriers. Over time, however, many of those plants have taken on increasingly complex manufacturing tasks that require having an R&D facility nearby in order to ensure the speedy transfer of technology from research to manufacturing. A silicon-wafer plant, for example, has to interact closely with product development engineers during trial runs of a new generation of microchips. The same is true for the manufacture of disk drives and other complex hardware. For that reason, Hewlett-Packard and Texas Instruments both operate laboratories in Singapore, close to manufacturing facilities.

The more complex and varied a manufacturing process is, the more often manufacturing engineers will have to interact with product development engineers. For example, in the case of one of Toshiba's laptop-computer-manufacturing plants, a new model is introduced to the manufacturing line every two weeks. The introduction has to happen seamlessly, without disturbing the production of existing models on the same line. In order to predict and remedy bugs during initial production runs, development engineers and manufacturing engineers meet several times a week. The proximity of Toshiba's laptop-development laboratory to its manufacturing plant greatly facilitates the interaction.

Establishing New R&D Sites

Types of R&D Sites	Phase 1 Location Decision	Phase 2 Ramp-Up Period	Phase 3 Maximizing Lab Impact
Home-Base-Augmenting Laboratory Site Objective of establishment: absorbing knowledge from the local scientific community, creating new knowledge, and transferring it to the company's central R&D site	–Select a location for its scientific excellence –Promote cooperation between the company's senior scientists and managers	–Choose as first laboratory leader a renowned local scientist with international experience—one who understands the dynamics of R&D at the new location –Ensure enough critical mass	–Ensure the laboratory's active participation in the local scientific community –Exchange researchers with local univesity laboratories and with the home-base lab
Home-Base-Exploiting Laboratory Site Objective of establishment: commercializing knowledge by ransferring it *from* the company's home base to the laboratory site abroad and from there to local manufacturing and marketing	–Select a location for its proximity to the company's existing manufacturing and marketing locations –Involve middle managers from other functional areas in start-up decisions	–Choose as first laboratory leader an experienced product-develement engineer with a strong companywide reputation, international experience, and knowledge of marketing and manufacturing	–Emphasize smooth relations with the home-base lab –Encourage employees to seek interaction with other corporate units beyond the manufacturing and marketing units that originally sponsored the lab

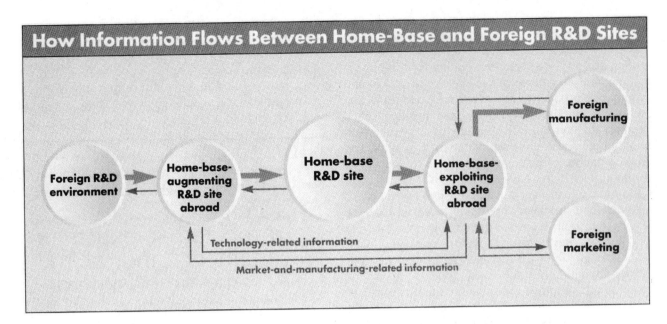

How Information Flows Between Home-Base and Foreign R&D Sites

Establishing a New R&D Facility

Whether establishing a home-base-augmenting or a home-base-exploiting facility, companies must use the same three-stage process: selecting the best laboratory leader, determining the optimal size for the new laboratory site, and keeping close watch over the lab during its start-up period in order to ensure that it is merged into the company's existing global R&D network and contributes sufficiently to the company's product portfolio and its economic performance.

Selecting the Best Site Leader. Identifying the best leader for a new R&D site is one of the most important decisions a company faces in its quest to establish a successful global R&D network. My research shows that the initial leader of an R&D site has a powerful impact not only on the culture of the site but also on its long-term research agenda and performance. The two types of sites require different types of leaders, and each type of leader confronts a particular set of challenges.

The initial leaders of home-base-augmenting sites should be prominent local scientists so that they will be able to fulfill their primary responsibility: to nurture ties between the new site and the local scientific community. If the site does not succeed in becoming part of the local scientific community quickly, it will not be able to generate new knowledge for the company. In addition to hiring a local scientist, there are a variety of other ways to establish local ties. For example, Toshiba used its memory-chip joint venture with Siemens to develop local ties at its new R&D site in Regensburg, Germany. The venture allowed Toshiba to tap into Siemens's dense network of associations with local universities. In addition, it helped Toshiba develop a better understanding of the compensation packages required to hire first-class German engineering graduates. Finally, it let the company gain useful insights into how to establish effective contract-research relationships with government-funded research institutions in Germany.

In contrast, the initial leaders of home-base-exploiting sites should be highly regarded managers from within the company—managers who are intimately familiar with the company's culture and systems. Such leaders will be able to fulfill their primary responsibility: to forge close ties between the new lab's engineers and the foreign community's manufacturing and marketing facilities. Then the transfer of knowledge from the company's home base to the R&D site will have the maximum impact on manufacturing and marketing located near that site. When one U.S. pharmaceutical company established a home-base-exploiting site in Great Britain, executives appointed as the initial site leader a manager who had been with the company for several years. He had started his career as a bench scientist first in exploratory research, then in the development of one of the company's blockbuster drugs. He had worked closely with marketing, and he had spent two years as supervisor of manufacturing quality at one of the company's U.S. manufacturing sites. With such a background, he was able to lead the new site effectively.

However, the best candidates for both home-base-augmenting and home-base-exploiting sites share four qualities: they are at once respected scientists or engineers and skilled managers; they are able to integrate the new site into the company's existing R&D network; they have a comprehensive understanding of technology trends; and they are able to overcome formal barriers when they seek access to new ideas in local universities and scientific communities.

Appointing an outstanding scientist or engineer who has no management experience can be disastrous. In one case, a leading U.S. electronics company decided to establish a home-base-augmenting site in the United Kingdom. The engineer who was appointed as the first site leader was an outstanding researcher but had little management experience outside the company's central laboratory environment. The leader had difficulties marshaling the necessary resources to expand the laboratory beyond its starting size of 14 researchers. Furthermore, he had a tough time mediating between the research laboratory and the company's product development area. Eleven of the 14 researchers had been hired locally and therefore lacked deep ties to the company. They needed a savvy corporate advocate who could understand company politics and could promote their research results within the company. One reason they didn't have such an advocate was that two of the three managers at the company's home base—people who had promoted the establishment of the new R&D lab—had quit about six months after the lab had opened because they disagreed about the company's overall R&D strategy. The third manager had moved to a different department.

In an effort to improve the situation, the company appointed a U.S. engineer as liaison to the U.K. site. He realized that few ideas were flowing from the site to the home base; but he attributed the problem to an inherently slow scientific-discovery process rather than to organizational barriers within the company. After about two years, senior management finally replaced the initial laboratory leader and the U.S. liaison engineer with two managers-one from the United Kingdom and one from the United States. The managers had experience overseeing one of the company's U.S. joint ventures in technology, and they also had good track records as researchers. Finally, under their leadership, the site dramatically increased its impact on the company's product portfolio. In conjunction with the increase in scientific output, the site grew to its projected size of 225 employees and is now highly productive.

> The best managers of foreign R&D sites are respected scientists or engineers and, at the same time, skilled managers.

In the case of both types of sites, the ideal leader has in-depth knowledge of both the home-base culture and the foreign culture. Consider Sharp's experience. In Japan, fewer corporate scientists have Ph.D.'s than their counterparts in the United Kingdom; instead they have picked up

Home-Base-Augmenting and Home-Base-Exploiting Sites: Xerox and Eli Lilly

The particular type of foreign R&D site determines the specific challenges managers will face. Setting up a *home-base-augmenting site*—one designed to gather new knowledge for a company—involves certain skills. And launching a *home-base-exploiting site*—one established to help a company efficiently commercialize its R&D in foreign markets—involves others. The cases of Xerox and Eli Lilly present an instructive contrast.

Xerox established a home-base-augmenting laboratory in Grenoble, France. Its objective: to tap new knowledge from the local scientific community and to transfer it back to its home base. Having already established, in 1986, a home-base-augmenting site in Cambridge, England, Xerox realized in 1992 that the research culture in continental Western Europe was sufficiently different and complementary to Great Britain's to justify another site. Moreover, understanding the most advanced research in France or Germany was very difficult from a base in Great Britain because of language and cultural barriers. One senior R&D manager in the United States notes, "We wanted to learn firsthand what was going on in centers of scientific excellence in Europe. Being present

at a center of scientific excellence is like reading poetry in the original language."

It was essential that managers from the highest levels of the company be involved in the decision-making process from the start. Senior scientists met with high-level managers and entered into a long series of discussions. Their first decision: to locate the new laboratory at a center of scientific excellence. Xerox also realized that it had to hire a renowned local scientist as the initial laboratory leader. The leader needed to be able to understand the local scientific community, attract junior scientists with high potential, and target the right university institutes and scholars for joint research projects. Finally, Xerox knew that the laboratory would have an impact on the company's economic performance only if it had the critical mass to become an accepted member of the local scientific community. At the same time, it could not become isolated from the larger Xerox culture.

Xerox considered a number of locations and carefully evaluated such aspects as their scientific excellence and relevance, university liaison programs, licensing programs, and university recruiting programs. The company came up with their knowledge and skills on the job. That difference presented a management challenge for Sharp when it established a home-base-augmenting facility in the United Kingdom. In order to cope with that challenge, the company hired a British laboratory leader who had previously worked as a science attaché at the British embassy in Japan. In that position, he had developed a good understanding of the Japanese higher-education system. He was well aware that British and Japanese engineers with different academic degrees might have similar levels of expertise, and, as a result, he could manage them better.

The pioneer who heads a newly established home-base-augmenting or home-base-exploiting site also must have a broad perspective and a deep understanding of technology trends. R&D sites abroad are often particularly good at combining knowledge from different scientific fields into new ideas and products. Because those sites start with a clean slate far from the company's powerful central laboratory, they are less plagued by the "not-invented-here" syndrome. For example, Canon's home-base-augmenting laboratory in the United Kingdom developed an innovative loudspeaker that is now being manufactured in Europe for a worldwide market. Senior researchers at Canon in Japan acknowledge that it would have been much more difficult for a new research team located in Japan to come up with the product. As one Canon manager puts it, "Although the new loudspeaker was partially based on knowledge that existed within Canon already,

Canon's research management in Japan was too focused on existing product lines and would probably not have tolerated the pioneering loudspeaker project."

Finally, leaders of new R&D sites need to be aware of the considerable formal barriers they might confront when they seek access to local universities and scientific communities. These barriers are often created by lawmakers who want to protect a nation's intellectual capital. Although foreign companies do indeed absorb local knowledge and transfer it to their home bases—particularly in the case of home-base-augmenting sites—they also create important positive economic effects for the host nation. The laboratory leader of a new R&D site needs to communicate that fact locally in order to reduce existing barriers and prevent the formation of new ones.

Determining the Optimal Size of the New R&D Site. My research indicates that the optimal size for a new foreign R&D facility during the start-up phase is usually 30 to 40 employees, and the best size for a site after the ramp-up period is about 235 employees, including support staff. The optimal size of a site depends mainly on a company's track record in international management. Companies that already operate several sites abroad tend to be more successful at establishing larger new sites.

Companies can run into problems if their foreign sites are either too small or too large. If the site is too small, the resulting lack of critical mass produces an environment in which there is little cross-fertilization of ideas among

four potential locations: Paris, Grenoble, Barcelona, and Munich. At that point, Xerox also identified potential laboratory leaders. The company chose Grenoble on the basis of its demonstrated scientific excellence and hired as the initial laboratory leader a highly regarded French scientist with good connections to local universities. Xerox designed a facility for 40 researchers and made plans for further expansion. In order to integrate the new laboratory's scientists into the Xerox community, senior R&D management in Palo Alto, California, allocated a considerable part of the initial laboratory budget to travel to other Xerox sites and started a program for the temporary transfer of newly hired researchers from Grenoble to other R&D sites. At the same time, the Grenoble site set out to integrate itself within the local research community.

In 1989, Eli Lilly considered establishing a home-base-exploiting laboratory in East Asia. The company's objective was to commercialize its R&D more effectively in foreign markets. Until then, Eli Lilly had operated one home-base-augmenting laboratory site abroad and some small sites in industrialized countries for clinical testing and drug approval procedures. But in order to exploit Lilly's R&D capabilities and product portfolio, the company needed a dedicated laboratory site in East Asia. The new site would support efforts to manufacture and market pharmaceuticals by adapting products to local needs. To that end, the management team decided that the new laboratory would have to be located close to relevant markets and existing corporate facilities. It also determined that the initial laboratory leader would have to be an experienced manager from Lilly's home base—a manager with a deep understanding of both the company's local operations and its overall R&D network.

The team considered Singapore as a potential location because of its proximity to a planned Lilly manufacturing site in Malaysia. But ultimately it decided that the new home-base-exploiting laboratory would have the strongest impact on Lilly's sales if it was located in Kobe, Japan. By establishing a site in the Kobe-Osaka region—the second-largest regional market in Japan and one that offered educational institutions with high-quality scientists—Lilly would send a signal to the medical community there that the company was committed to the needs of the Japanese market. Kobe had another advantage: Lilly's corporate headquarters for Japan were located there, and the company was already running some of its drug approval operations for the Japanese market out of Kobe. The city therefore was the logical choice.

The team assigned an experienced Lilly researcher and manager to be the initial leader of the new site. Because he knew the company inside and out—from central research and development to international marketing—the team reasoned that he would be able to bring the new laboratory up to speed quickly by drawing on resources from various divisions within Lilly. In order to integrate the new site into the overall company, some researchers from other Lilly R&D sites received temporary transfers of up to two years to Kobe, and some locally hired researchers were temporarily transferred to other Lilly sites. It took about 30 months to activate fully the Kobe operation—a relatively short period. Today the site is very productive in transferring knowledge from Lilly's home base to Kobe and in commercializing that knowledge throughout Japan and Asia.

researchers. And a small R&D site generally does not command a sufficient level of respect in the scientific community surrounding the laboratory. As a result, its researchers have a harder time gaining access to informal networks and to scientific meetings that provide opportunities for an exchange of knowledge. In contrast, if the laboratory site is too large, its culture quickly becomes anonymous, researchers become isolated, and the benefits of spreading fixed costs over a larger number of researchers are out-weighed by the lack of cross-fertilization of ideas. According to one manager at such a lab, "Once people stopped getting to know one another on an informal basis in the lunchroom of our site, they became afraid of deliberately walking into one another's laboratory rooms to talk about research and to ask questions. Researchers who do not know each other on an informal basis are often hesitant to ask their colleagues for advice: they are afraid to reveal any of their own knowledge gaps. We realized that we had crossed a critical threshold in size. We subsequently scaled back somewhat and made an increased effort to reduce the isolation of individual researchers within the site through communication tools and through rotating researchers among different lab units at the site."

> Managers must integrate a site's research agenda into the company's overall goals.

Supervising the Start-Up Period. During the initial growth period of an R&D site, which typically lasts anywhere from one to three years, the culture is formed and the groundwork for the site's future productivity is laid. During that period, senior management in the home country has to be in particularly close contact with the new site. Although it is important that the new laboratory develop its own identity and stake out its fields of expertise, it also has to be closely connected to the company's existing R&D structure. Newly hired scientists must be aware of the resources that exist within the company as a whole, and scientists at home and at other locations must be aware of the opportunities the new site creates for the company as a whole. Particularly during the start-up period, senior R&D managers at the corporate level have to walk a fine line and decide whether to devote the most resources to connecting the new site to the company or to supporting ties between the new site and its local environment.

To integrate a new site into the company as a whole, managers must pay close attention to the site's research agenda and create mechanisms to integrate it into the company's overall strategic goals. Because of the high de-

gree of uncertainty of R&D outcomes, continuous adjustments to research agendas are the rule. What matters most is speed, both in terms of terminating research projects that go nowhere and in terms of pushing projects that bring unexpectedly good results.

> Managing an R&D network is both delicate and complex. It requires constant tinkering—evaluation and reevaluation.

The rapid exchange of information is essential to integrating a site into the overall company during the start-up phase. Companies use a number of mechanisms to create a cohesive research community in spite of geographic distance. Hewlett-Packard regularly organizes an in-house science fair at which teams of researchers can present projects and prototypes to one another. Canon has a program that lets researchers from home-base-augmenting sites request a temporary transfer to home-base-exploiting sites. At Xerox, most sites are linked by a sophisticated information system that allows senior R&D managers to determine within minutes the current state of research projects and the number of researchers working on those projects. But nothing can replace face-to-face contact between active researchers. Maintaining a global R&D network requires personal meetings, and therefore many researchers and R&D managers have to spend time visiting not only other R&D sites but also specialized suppliers and local universities affiliated with those sites.

Failing to establish sufficient ties with the company's existing R&D structure during the start-up phase can hamper the success of a new foreign R&D site. For example, in 1986, a large foreign pharmaceutical company established a biotechnology research site in Boston, Massachusetts. In order to recruit outstanding scientists and maintain a high level of creative output, the company's R&D management decided to give the new laboratory considerable leeway in its research agenda and in determining what to do with the results—although the company did reserve the right of first refusal for the commercialization of the lab's inventions. The new site was staffed exclusively with scientists handpicked by a newly hired laboratory leader. A renowned local biochemist, he had been employed for many years by a major U.S. university, where he had carried out contract research for the company. During the start-up phase, few of the company's veteran scientists were involved in joint research projects with the site's scientists—an arrangement that hindered the transfer of ideas between the new lab and the company's other R&D sites. Although the academic community now recognizes the lab as an important contributor to the field, few of its inventions have been patented by the company, fewer have been targeted for commercialization, and none have reached the commercial stage yet. One senior scientist working in the lab commented that ten years after its creation, the lab had become so much of an "independent animal" that it would take a lot of carefully balanced guidance from the company to instill a stronger sense of commercial orientation without a risk of losing the most creative scientists.

There is no magic formula that senior managers can follow to ensure the success of a foreign R&D site during its start-up phase. Managing an R&D network, particularly in its early stages, is delicate and complex. It requires constant tinkering—evaluation and reevaluation. Senior R&D managers have to decide how much of the research should be initiated by the company and how much by the scientist, determine the appropriate incentive structures and employment contracts, establish policies for the temporary transfer of researchers to the company's other R&D or manufacturing sites, and choose universities from which to hire scientists and engineers.

Flexibility and experimentation during a site's start-up phase can ensure its future productivity. For example, Fujitsu established a software research laboratory site in San Jose, California, in 1992. The company was seriously thinking of establishing a second site in Boston but eventually re-considered. Fujitsu realized that the effort that had gone into establishing the San Jose site had been greater than expected. Once the site was up and running, however, its productive output also had been higher than expected. Furthermore, Fujitsu found that its R&D managers had gained an excellent understanding of the R&D community that created advanced software-development tools. Although initially leaning toward establishing a second site, the managers were flexible. They decided to enlarge the existing site because of its better-than-expected performance as well as the limited potential benefits of a second site. The San Jose site has had a major impact on Fujitsu's software development and sales—particularly in Japan but in the United States, too. Similarly, at Alcatel's first foreign R&D site in Germany, senior managers were flexible. After several months, they realized that the travel-and-communications budget would have to be increased substantially beyond initial projections in order to improve the flow of knowledge from the French home base. For instance, in the case of a telephone switchboard project, the actual number of business trips between the two sites was nearly twice as high as originally projected.

Integrating the Global R&D Network

As the number of companies' R&D sites at home and abroad grows, R&D managers will increasingly face the challenging task of coordinating the network. That will require a fundamental shift in the role of senior managers at the central lab. Managers of R&D networks must be global coordinators, not local administrators. More than being managers of people and processes, they must be managers of knowledge. And not all managers that a company has in place will be up to the task.

Consider Matsushita's R&D management. A number of technically competent managers became obsolete at the company once it launched a global approach to R&D. Today managers at Matsushita's central R&D site in Hirakata, Japan, continue to play an important role in the research and development of core processes for manufacturing. But the responsibility of an increasing number of senior managers at the central site is overseeing Matsushita's network of 15 dedicated R&D sites. That responsibility includes setting research agendas, monitoring results, and creating direct ties between sites.

How does the new breed of R&D manager coordinate global knowledge? Look again to Matsushita's central R&D site. First, high-level corporate managers in close cooperation with senior R&D managers develop an overall research agenda and assign different parts of it to individual sites. The process is quite tricky. It requires that the managers in charge have a good understanding of not only the technological capabilities that Matsushita will need to develop in the future but also the stock of technological capabilities already available to it.

Matsushita's central lab organizes two or three yearly off-site meetings devoted to informing R&D scientists and engineers about the entire company's current state of technical knowledge and capabilities. At the same meetings, engineers who have moved from R&D to take over manufacturing and marketing responsibilities inform R&D members about trends in Matsushita's current and potential future markets. Under the guidance of senior project managers, members from R&D, manufacturing, and marketing determine timelines and resource requirements for specific home-base-augmenting and home-base-exploiting projects. One R&D manager notes, "We discuss not only why a specific scientific insight might be interesting for Matsushita but also how we can turn this insight into a product quickly. We usually seek to develop a prototype early. Prototypes are a good basis for a discussion with marketing and manufacturing. Most of our efforts are targeted at delivering the prototype of a slightly better mousetrap early rather than delivering the blueprint of a much better mousetrap late."

To stimulate the exchange of information, R&D managers at Matsushita's central lab create direct links among researchers across different sites. They promote the use of videoconferencing and frequent face-to-face contact to forge those ties. Reducing the instances in which the central lab must act as mediator means that existing knowledge travels more quickly through the company and new ideas percolate more easily. For example, a researcher at a home-base-exploiting site in Singapore can communicate with another researcher at a home-base-exploiting site in Franklin Park, Illinois, about potential new research projects much more readily now that central R&D fosters informal and formal direct links.

Finally, managers at Matsushita's central lab constantly monitor new regional pockets of knowledge as well as the company's expanding network of manufacturing sites to determine whether the company will need additional R&D locations. With 15 major sites around the world, Matsushita has decided that the number of sites is sufficient at this point. But the company is ever vigilant about surveying the landscape and knows that as the landscape changes, its decision could, too.

As more pockets of knowledge emerge worldwide and competition in foreign markets mounts, the imperative to crate global R&D networks will grow all the more pressing. Only those companies that embrace a global approach to R&D will meet the competitive challenges of the new dynamic. And only those managers who embrace their fundamentally new role as global coordinators and managers of knowledge will be able to tap the full potential of their R&D networks.

1. In a systematic effort to analyze the relationship of global strategy and R&D investments in technologically intensive industries, I have been collecting detailed data on all dedicated laboratory sites operated by 32 leading multinational companies. The sample consists of 10 U.S., 12 Japanese, and 10 European companies. Thirteen of the companies are in the pharmaceutical industry, and 19 are in the electronics industry. Data collection includes archival research, a detailed questionnaire, and in-depth interviews with several senior R&D managers in each company. Overall, these companies operate 238 dedicated R&D sites, 156 of them abroad. About 60% of the laboratory sites abroad were established after 1984. I have used this sample, which is the most complete of its kind, as a basis for a number of quantitative and qualitative investigations into global strategy, competitive interaction, and R&D management.

2. My research on global R&D strategies builds on earlier research on the competitiveness of nations and on research on foreign direct investment, including Michael E. Porter, The Competitive Advantage of Nations (New York: The Free Press, 1990), and Thomas J. Wesson, "An Alternative Motivation for Foreign Direct Investment" (Ph.D. dissertation, Harvard University, 1993). My research also builds on an existing body of knowledge about the management of multinational companies. See, for example, Christopher A. Bartlett and Sumantra Ghoshal, Managing Across Borders (New York: The Free Press, 1989).

INVESTING

Back to the Land

Asian investors move in on Tokyo's property bargains but plenty of obstacles await them.

By Peter Landers in Tokyo

To Hong Kong's Richard Li it's all very simple. Punching a few figures into his calculator, he declares that when he paid 86.9 billion ($710 million) for a sliver of choice Tokyo property, it was just good business.

He's not alone. Major property players in Hong Kong, Singapore and Taiwan agree that quality Japanese real estate—whose value has plunged by up to 85% since 1991—has finally reached rock bottom and is an attractive overseas play. A joint venture between Singapore's government and Hong Kong firm HKR International headed by Payson Cha, for example, recently won an auction for part of a large plot near Tokyo's prestigious Ginza shopping area, as part of a group bid with Japanese companies totalling 138.2 billion.

To a nation starved for news of a real-estate recovery, it looks like the bandwagon is rolling. Japan's corporate chieftains certainly hope so: if overseas money jacks up local land prices, banks can at last shed their bad-loan problems and free Japan's economy of its biggest burden.

But for foreign investors, Japan often doesn't play by the rules to which they are accustomed elsewhere—and that applies to real estate as much as any other industry. On paper, the nation's store of property looks like a supermarket packed with bargains, yet many Asian shoppers may never get to the checkout line.

To see why, imagine a wealthy investor with a few hundred million dollars to put into property. He calls up a real-estate agent in Tokyo and asks for data on a few properties in that price range. Yasuo Kawakami, managing director at real-estate agent Richard Ellis in Tokyo, has been on the other end of such calls, and he always has to explain that Japanese sellers will only divulge information when they feel the potential buyer is serious. The seller wants to be sure of the buyer's liquidity, reputation and discretion, and often asks for a formal letter of interest. Foreign companies, other than a few multinationals, are just not known to the local players. The investors may well ask for brochures, says Kawakami, "but that's not how business is done here. They'll never get those."

Another reason Asian investors have run up against a wall, says Kawakami, is the "sense of shame and guilt" Japanese feel about selling property. In the most prestigious business district, the Marunouchi-Otemachi next to Tokyo Station, property almost never goes on the market. Yet Asian investors often aren't interested in buying lesser-quality real estate. They feel that top-notch property values will outpace the rest whether the market recovers or not.

Simply put, buying is heavily weighted against outsiders. "The whole machinery is catered to self-sufficiency without the need for foreign participation," concurs Li, the 30-year-old son of Hong Kong tycoon Li Ka-shing. The current business troubles of Japanese companies, he adds, are "the only reason there's a window for foreigners to play, and there may not be a window five to six years from now."

Li was looking for a year at Tokyo property before he found an opportunity that interested him: auctions of land by the company settling the debts of the former national railway. After two unsuccessful bids, he landed a 5,000-square-metre site right next to Tokyo Station, the central terminal for Japan's major rail lines. His Pacific Century company will put up a 28-storey building on the former railway offices site. Only a handful of other Asians, however, have had similar success. As Li's Tokyo representative, Andrew Reilly, puts it: "You could put all the Asians who have bought real estate in Japan into a taxi, and still have room to sit in the front seat."

If real-estate investors are finding Japan less than hospitable, they are only reaching the same conclusion that foreign companies in other sectors came to long ago. Direct foreign investment in Japan amounted to just $3.8 billion in the year ending March 1996, most of it by American and European companies. Compare that to the $50.7 billion in Japanese investment abroad, most of which was in industry and real estate. Much of it goes to Asia, which accounted for 24% of Japan's total foreign direct investment in fiscal 1995.

Now, Japanese officials insist, Asian interest in Japan is growing, and there are some indications to support that. South Korea's Samsung conglomerate has bought half of an office building in Tokyo and stepped up marketing investment to sell its TV sets in Japan. And an investment arm of Malaysia's government last year bought a stake in Nichiei Seiki, a medium-sized tool-and-die manufacturer, although the purchase was such a novelty it drew widespread media attention.

Officially Japan would like to see a lot more foreign investment, but many Japanese admit popular sentiment is not as welcoming. Minoru Mori, the president and CEO of major developer Mori Building Co., says there's a "feeling of resistance against investment from abroad," even though it would help Japan's economy recover more quickly.

"Money from abroad is the best reinforcement we could have. We ought to welcome it with open arms," says Mori. "But Japanese have a kind of fear that the small land area [of Japan] will be taken over by foreigners." Japanese know well the resentment that can be generated by foreign investment, having themselves been subject to opposition in the United States in the 1980s and early 1990s.

Mori estimates that commercial property in Tokyo now goes for about one-sixth of the peak in the late 1980s, a collapse that led to piles of bad loans at Japanese banks and a five-year economic slowdown. But for all its concern about an economic recovery the Japanese government has done little to invigorate the market. Anyone buying real estate, for instance, has to pay both na-

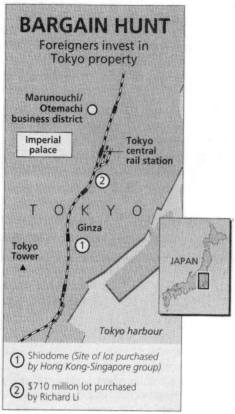

BARGAIN HUNT
Foreigners invest in Tokyo property

Marunouchi/Otemachi business district

Imperial palace

Tokyo central rail station

②

T O K Y O

Ginza

Tokyo Tower ▲

①

JAPAN

Tokyo harbour

① Shiodome (Site of lot purchased by Hong Kong-Singapore group)

② $710 million lot purchased by Richard Li

REVIEW GRAPHIC/DICKY TANG

tional and regional purchase taxes, plus a registration tax and a fee for the revenue stamp that must be affixed to the contract.

The government also doesn't look kindly on real-estate investors taking quick profits when prices go up, something that comes naturally to those used to Hong Kong's fast-and-loose property market. A confiscatory tax of up to 76% is levied on any capital gains within two years of a property purchase. Japanese developers know the tax system but foreigners often overlook its complexities and added costs, say property professionals.

And it is not just the tax system that can leave foreigners puzzled—not being clued-in about underhand business practices can leave outsiders exposed. Cosy relations between construction companies, for example, mean that they routinely confer and fix bids for developing sites to keep costs artificially high.

Li says he had to be wary when discussing his bidding plans with Japanese because he was afraid they might leak details to his competitors. "You never know who is friend or foe," he says. "There are no secrets in this town."

The fact that foreign investors are still interested in Japan despite all those difficulties illustrates just how attractive prices are. Li anticipates a 5%–6% return on his investment, well above the 2.2% yield on Japanese government bonds. While 5%–6% may not sound much for more hot-blooded bulls, the figure is regarded as a minimum return. If the market takes off, much more is expected. Property analysts also point out that conservative investors like the Singapore government are not buying Tokyo property for speculation, but for good, secure returns.

"If you compare on a global basis, Japan is a very good opportunity," says Kohei Ogawa, managing director for a Hong Kong property company, the Far East Consortium. "We can buy very cheaply." Far East took a 24.8% stake on April 1 in Mori Denki, a publicly traded manufacturer of industrial illumination equipment, hoping that real-estate investment would be easier through a listed vehicle.

Ogawa admits Japan is "to a certain extent a closed society," but he adds: "Japan is changing. I think we'll see many more deals in the next couple of years."

WORLD EDUCATION LEAGUE

Who's top?

Some countries seem to educate their children much better than others. Why? No comprehensive answer has emerged yet but plenty of lessons are being learnt from the tests which reveal the educational discrepancies

A CLASS has 28 students and the ratio of girls to boys is 4:3. How many girls are there? Which of the following is made using bacteria: yogurt, cream, soap or cooking oil? Simple enough questions in any language (the answers, by the way, are 16 and yogurt). But when half a million pupils from around the world were set questions like these, some countries, just like some pupils, did very well and some very badly.

The tests were set for the largest-ever piece of international education research, the Third International Maths and Science Study (TIMSS). Of the 41 nations participating in this first phase, Singapore was teacher's pet: the average scores of its pupils were almost twice those of South Africa, bottom of the class (see table 1).

East Asian countries have overtaken nations such as America and Britain which have had universal schooling for much longer. America came 17th in science and 28th in mathematics. England came 25th in maths and Scotland (whose pupils were tested separately) came 29th. The four richest East Asian economies took the first four places in maths.

Some former communist countries, notably the Czech Republic, Slovakia, Slovenia and Bulgaria, also did significantly better than their richer western neighbours, even though they spend much less on education. Six of the top 15 places in both maths and science went to East Europeans. It seems that how much a country can afford to spend has less than you might think to do with how well educated its children are. American children have three times as much money spent on their schooling as young South Koreans, who nevertheless beat them hands down in tests.

International educational comparisons like the TIMSS study have been subjects of growing academic enthusi-

2+2=?			**1**
13-year-olds' average score in TIMSS* (Int average =500)			
Maths		**Science**	
1 Singapore	643	Singapore	607
2 South Korea	607	Czech Republic	574
3 Japan	605	Japan	571
4 Hong Kong	588	South Korea	565
5 Belgium (F†)	565	Bulgaria	565
6 Czech Republic	564	Netherlands	560
7 Slovakia	547	Slovenia	560
8 Switzerland	545	Austria	558
9 Netherlands	541	Hungary	554
10 Slovenia	541	England	552
11 Bulgaria	540	Belgium (F†)	550
12 Austria	539	Australia	545
13 France	538	Slovakia	544
14 Hungary	537	Russia	538
15 Russia	535	Ireland	538
16 Australia	530	Sweden	535
17 Ireland	527	United States	534
18 Canada	527	Canada	531
19 Belgium (W‡)	526	Germany	531
20 Thailand	522	Norway	527
21 Israel	522	Thailand	525
22 Sweden	519	New Zealand	525
23 Germany	509	Israel	524
24 New Zealand	508	Hong Kong	522
25 England	506	Switzerland	522
26 Norway	503	Scotland	517
27 Denmark	502	Spain	517
28 United States	500	France	498
29 Scotland	498	Greece	497
30 Latvia	493	Iceland	494
31 Spain	487	Romania	486
32 Iceland	487	Latvia	485
33 Greece	484	Portugal	480
34 Romania	482	Denmark	478
35 Lithuania	477	Lithuania	476
36 Cyprus	474	Belgium (W‡)	471
37 Portugal	454	Iran	470
38 Iran	428	Cyprus	463
39 Kuwait	392	Kuwait	430
40 Colombia	385	Colombia	411
41 South Africa	354	South Africa	326

*Third International Maths and Science Study †Flanders ‡Wallonia
Source: TIMSS

asm and criticism since the 1960s (for the controversies, *see box,* "Answering the critics".) Teachers, though, have been almost entirely hostile and most governments have held themselves aloof from the arguments, fearing embarrassment. A poor showing in the league table would give political opponents ammunition, while the studies might be used to accuse ministers of starving their education system (or, possibly, of wasting taxpayers' money on a grand scale).

Now, attitudes are changing, at least among politicians. Over the past ten years or so, governments' desire to know more about how their schools compare with others, and what lessons can be learned from the comparison, have begun to outweigh fear of embarrassment. More countries took part in TIMSS than in its predecessors, and the attention paid to its findings by the world's politicians, educators and the news media was much greater than for previous studies.

Politicians do their homework

President Clinton described the test in his state-of-the-union message in February, as one "that reflects the world-class standards our children must meet for the new era." America's poor overall showing has sparked calls for the adoption of a national curriculum and national standards for school tests—including from Mr. Clinton himself. These calls are based on the observation that the countries which did best in the study tended to have national frameworks of this kind.

In a television interview in December, the French president, Jacques Chirac, described as "shameful" a decision by his education ministry to pull out of an international study of adult literacy which was showing that the French were doing badly. And in Britain last year, Michael Heseltine, the deputy prime minister, brushed aside objections from officials in the Department of Education and Employment, and published the unflattering results of a study he had commissioned comparing British workers with those in France, America, Singapore and Germany—chosen as key economic competitors.

The Germans, in turn, were shocked by their pupils' mediocre performance in the TIMSS tests. Their pupils did only slightly better than the English at maths, coming 23rd out of 41 countries. In science, the English surged ahead (though not the Scots) while the Germans were beaten by, among others, the Dutch, the Russians—and even the Americans. A television network ran a special report called "Education Emergency in Germany"; industrialists accused politicians of ignoring repeated warnings about declining standards in schools.

There are more studies to come. In December the Organisation for Economic Cooperation and Development (OECD), a club of 29 of the world's richest countries, launched its own series of annual reports. The OECD already collects data on how the governments spend their combined $1 trillion annual education budgets, and what proportion of each nation's population reaches a given level of education. The

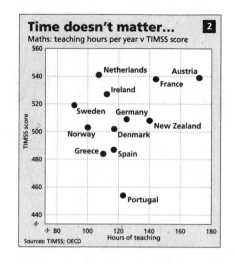

Time doesn't matter... `2`
Maths: teaching hours per year v TIMSS score
Sources: TIMSS; OECD

new studies will go much further, comparing how schools, colleges and universities are run in each country and analysing the implications for policymakers.

In some countries, international comparisons are already being used as a catalyst for education reform. The poor performance of Swedish children in maths, in one study in the mid 1980s, led to the setting up of a new programme of in-service training for teachers. The initial results from TIMSS suggest that Sweden has since pulled itself up to slightly above the international average.

Although Japanese children have repeatedly gained high overall marks in maths tests, some studies have suggested that they are not as advanced in other things, such as analysing data, as they are in basic arithmetic. The Japanese government has started using such findings to reform its national curriculum. Hungary, discovering in early studies that its children were among the world's best in maths and science but among the least literate, ordered its teachers to spend more time on reading.

Knowledge workers

Leaving aside the results of the tests, two main factors lie behind governments' increasing willingness to take part in international education studies to begin with. The first is the growing consensus that education is the key to getting rich—for countries as well as for individuals. It is widely believed that one of the main reasons why tiger economies like Singapore and South Korea have grown so quickly is that their governments have made determined and successful efforts to raise educational standards.

The other factor is value for money. Governments everywhere have woken up to the full economic significance of education just as they are making des-

Answering the critics

CROSS-COUNTRY comparisons have long been controversial. Among the doubts: Do tests put an unwarranted premium on certain qualities—speed of recall, mental arithmetic—while ignoring hard-to-measure ones like creative thinking? Were pupils from different countries really comparable? (For instance, in countries where children are made to repeat a year of their education if they fail to reach a certain standard, tests for, say, 13-year-olds may exclude those who have been sent to join a class of 12-year-olds.) Were pupils in some countries told that the tests were extremely important, while others were not? Did the tests give an unfair advantage to countries whose curriculum for 13-year-olds happens to include more of the topics included in them?

Wendy Keys of Britain's National Foundation for Educational Research, one of the bodies that organised the TIMSS project, says that a number of measures were taken to answer such

criticisms. The score for each country was adjusted to take account of any pupils who were held back a year. Teachers everywhere were given precise instructions on how to explain the tests to pupils, and independent monitors were sent to schools chosen at random. After the results were in, experts in each country looked at how their pupils had done on those questions which most closely matched the curriculum for children of their age.

The results? Broadly, the new study confirmed the relative positions of countries which had taken part in earlier studies. That consistency suggested the original criticisms may have been exaggerated. However, the refinements made in the recent study may overturn one of the theories that has been used to explain why America and Britain, in spite of having had universal education for longer than most nations, do so poorly. This is that they contain

an unusually large proportion of pupils who perform very badly. The comforting implication would be that ordinary pupils do reasonably well but that average scores are dragged down by a so-called "long tail of low achievers".

This explanation was given a colour of plausibility by earlier tests. In those, mediocre scores in Britain and America could be explained away by the failure of the tests to take account of countries where pupils are held back a year. The new version of the test puts that problem right—and the two countries are still doing poorly. Though the mass of results from TIMSS is still being analysed, Dr Keys says there is no sign so far of the "long tail". The implication would be that the average scores of American and British pupils are mediocre because average performance is mediocre, and not because of some peculiarity at the very bottom of the class.

perate attempts to rein in public spending. OECD countries already spend about 6% of national income on education; given the pressure to trim budgets there is no prospect that governments will chuck money at schools without checking to see whether standards are improving. Hence the enthusiasm for comparisons. If governments could discover what it is about their education system that helps growth, then perhaps, they hope, they could do better without spending more.

So do the tests help? They do not provide a sure-fire formula of exactly how much should be spent on schools, how schools should be managed and precisely how each subject should be taught.

All the same, the tests are already proving useful, especially for exposing myths. A popularly-held view has it that "opportunity to learn" is the key to educational success—ie, the more time children spend on a subject, the better they do at it. Alas, the evidence so far is not encouraging for the proponents of this theory. Taking the twelve countries which both took part in TIMSS and also had their average teaching hours measured in the OECD's recent study of school management, there seems little correlation between time spent on a subject and performance of pupils in tests (see chart 2). Young Austrians spend exceptionally long hours on maths and science lessons; for them, it pays off in higher test scores. But so do New Zealand's teenagers—and they do not do any better than, say, Norwegians, who spend an unusually short time on lessons in both subjects.

Next—and of particular interest to cash-strapped governments—there appears to be little evidence to support the argument, often heard from teachers' unions, that the main cause of educational under-achievement is under-funding. Low-spending countries such as South Korea and the Czech Republic are at the top of the TIMSS league table. High-spenders such as America and Denmark do much worse (see chart 3). Obviously, there are dozens of reasons other than spending why one country does well, another badly, but the success of the low-spending Czechs and Koreans does show that spending more on schools is not a prerequisite for improving standards.

Another article of faith among the teaching profession—that children are bound to do better in small classes—is also being undermined by educational

...nor does money 3
State spending per pupil*, $'000 PPP 1993
0 1 2 3 4 5 6 7

Country		Maths	Science
Switzerland		8	25
United States		28	17
Germany		23	18
Denmark		27	34
France		13	28
England	†	25	10
Japan		3	3
South Korea		2	2
Czech Rep.		6	2
Hungary		14	9

TIMSS ranking — Maths / Science

Sources: TIMSS; OECD   *Secondary   †Average for whole of Britain

research. As with other studies, TIMSS found that France, America and Britain, where children are usually taught in classes of twenty-odd, do significantly worse than East Asian countries where almost twice as many pupils are crammed into each class. Again, there may be social reasons why some countries can cope better with large classes than others. All the same, the comparison refutes the argument that larger is necessarily worse.

Further, the tests even cast some doubt over the cultural explanation for the greater success of East Asia: that there is some hard-to-define Asian culture, connected with parental authority and a strong social value on education, which makes children more eager to learn and easier to teach. Those who make this argument say it would of course be impossible to replicate such oriental magic in the West.

Yet the results of TIMSS suggest that this is, to put it mildly, exaggerated. If "culture" makes English children so poor at maths, then why have they done so well at science (not far behind the Japanese and South Koreans)? And why do English pupils do well at science and badly at maths, while in France it is the other way around? A less mystical, more mundane explanation suggests itself: English schools teach science well and maths badly; French schools teach maths better than science; East Asian schools teach both subjects well.

Apart from casting doubt on some widely-held beliefs, do international comparisons have anything constructive to say? So far, the conclusions are tentative, but some answers are emerging.

Teaching the teachers

As well as getting pupils to sit tests, the TIMSS researchers monitored the way lessons were taught in each country. Eventually this should point to which teaching method tends to be most successful, though the data are still being worked on. Meanwhile, other researchers have been searching for common factors among those countries whose schools seem to turn out well-educated pupils.

Julia Whitburn of Britain's National Institute of Economic and Social Research has studied the way maths is taught in Japan and Switzerland, two countries which are different in many ways but whose pupils seem to do consistently well at in the subject. She noted a number of common factors:
• Much more time is spent on the basics of arithmetic than on more general mathematical topics such as handling data;
• Pupils learn to do sums in their heads before they are taught to do them on paper; calculators are usually banned;
• Standardised teaching manuals, which are tested extensively in schools before being published, are used widely;
• A method known as "whole-class interactive teaching" is used widely. The teacher addresses the whole class at once, posing questions to pupils in turn, to ensure they are following the lesson. American and British schools have been criticised for letting pupils spend much of their time working in small groups, with the teacher rushing from one group to the next to see how they are doing. Ms. Whitburn notes that in Japan and Switzerland this method is only used in teaching arts and crafts;
• Finally, great efforts are made to ensure that pupils do not fall behind. Those that do are given extra coaching.

Learning, though, is not a one-way street. Just as western countries are busy seeking to emulate Japanese schools, schools and universities in Japan are coming under pressure from employers to turn out workers with the sort of creativity and individuality that the Japanese associate with western education. And just as American and British politicians are demanding that schools copy their more successful oriental counterparts and set their pupils more homework, the South Korean government is telling schools to give pupils regular homework-free days, so they can spend more time with their families—just like western children. Perhaps in education there is such a thing as a happy medium.

Balancing act

How might the worldwide boom in foreign direct investment affect international trade

TRADE figures are among the most politically sensitive statistics around. In the late 1980s and early 1990s Japan's colossal trade surpluses were regularly paraded as evidence of Japanese economic ascendancy. America's unbroken 21-year string of trade deficits is routinely presented as evidence of the country's economic weakness.

Many critics expected the worldwide growth in foreign direct investment to aggravate these "problems". Total flows of direct investment doubled, to $315 billion, between 1991 and 1995. In the United States, opponents of the North American Free-Trade Agreement, signed in 1994, feared a "giant sucking sound" as domestic manufacturers served American customers from new plants in low-wage Mexico. Politicians in many developed countries worried that the sharp rise in investment in China would trigger a flood of imported consumer goods.

So far, the critics have been wrong. As foreign direct investment has soared, trade has become more balanced, not less so (see chart). Although America's trade deficit is much the same in dollar terms as it was in the late 1980s, it is only 2.5% of GDP, compared with 3.4% in 1987. But Japan's trade surplus, which peaked at 4.7% of GDP in 1986, is now less than 2%. Why is trade seemingly moving closer to balance? One important reason, according to an article in the OECD's *Economic Outlook,* published last month, is a change in the ways in which companies make investments in foreign countries.

ECONOMICS FOCUS

The OECD's economists studied the behaviour of American and Japanese companies that invest in factory equipment and property or take large stakes in existing businesses outside their

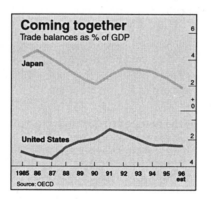

Coming together
Trade balances as % of GDP
Source: OECD

home countries. They found basic differences in the way those different nations' companies have planned their strategies. Those differences, it turns out, account for much of the recent change in the flow of trade.

American companies invest abroad mainly to serve foreign markets, rather than to produce finished or partly finished goods to ship back home. In 1992, about two-thirds of the sales of American companies' foreign subsidiaries took place in the regions in which they were based. In Europe, this share has been pretty static since the early 1980s. American companies' affiliates in Asia increasingly serve that region's markets. Asia accounted for 62% of those affiliates' sales in 1992, up from 41% in 1982.

Only in Canada and Mexico is there much evidence that American companies are investing to serve the American market. American-owned factories in these countries made 26% of their sales in the United States in 1992, up from 18% in 1982. That ratio may have increased further since the North American free-trade deal took effect in 1995.

Japanese companies, by contrast, are increasingly looking homeward as they expand overseas. About 10% of Japanese owned companies' total output took place outside Japan in 1995, compared with only 4% in 1986. Almost everything that Japanese companies make in America is sold there. But the Asian subsidiaries of Japanese companies have been exporting a growing proportion of their wares to Japan. Japanese sales accounted for 16% of the total turnover of Asian affiliates in 1992, compared with only 11% a decade before.

The OECD's economists argue that this shift in the nature of Japanese foreign investment will have durable effects on the country's trade patterns. Imports from foreign subsidiaries now account for 14% of all Japanese imports; in 1992, they were worth only 4%. As a proportion of GDP, imports of goods and services have risen from 9% in mid-1992 to 12% in mid-1996. Imports of consumer goods from Japanese-owned factories in Asia account for much of the increase.

How does all this translate into trade statistics? In principle, foreign investment can affect exports and imports in a number of ways, depending on the precise circumstances. Suppose, for instance, that a firm builds a factory abroad from which it will serve local markets. Sales from that factory could supplant exports from the home country, cutting the trade surplus or increasing the deficit. Or the sales could be entirely new, and therefore have no direct effect on the trade balance.

Trade's tricky arithmetic

There are other complications. Firms often rely on home-country partners to build their overseas factories, so construction of the foreign factory might raise exports of construction materials or machinery. And once the factory is up and running, some components or half-finished goods may be exported from home for assembly abroad. Or investment might not be in a factory, but in a distribution system. If the system is a successful one, exports to the foreign market will increase.

But foreign investment can also be a base for production for the home market. It may simply be cheaper to produce overseas than at home: wages may be lower, after taking differences in productivity into account; or foreign governments may levy lower taxes or provide investment incentives. Such investment is far more likely to increase the home country's imports and reduce its exports, because foreign production is a substitute for producing at home. The migration of Japanese factories to South-East Asia, whence goods are sent to Japan as well as the rest of the world, is an example of exactly this.

The OECD's economists reckon that this change in the nature of Japanese foreign investment appears to have made Japanese imports more responsive to changes in import prices. Thus smaller increases in the value of the yen should be needed to bring about a given increase in imports. This means that large Japanese trade surpluses may be less persistent than they have been in the past.

Whether the changes in the pattern of Japanese foreign direct investment are permanent, of course, remains to be seen. A weaker yen, for instance, might eventually shift some Japanese production from South-East Asia back to Japan—just as a strong yen made foreign production attractive in the first place. But even if changing investment patterns do rein in trade imbalances, they are unlikely to calm politicians' nerves about trade disputes for good.

Unit 2

Key Points to Consider

❖ Describe the role of international trade organizations. Do you think they help or hinder world trade? Why?

❖ Describe some efforts to stabilize world monetary markets.

❖ What do you think will happen in the future concerning international money systems? The IMF? The World Bank?

 **Links**   # www.dushkin.com/online/

These sites are annotated on pages 4 and 5.

One of the most obvious features of international trade has been the development of international trade organizations. Some of these organizations have existed for several decades while others are very new. They all have several things in common. The first is that, while there have been some global agreements such as the General Agreement on Tariffs and Trade (GATT) and the World Trade Organization (WTO), most of the trade organizations tend to be regional. The European Union (EU), which was known as the European Economic Community or Common Market until 1994, the North American Free Trade Agreement (NAFTA), and the Asia Pacific Economic Cooperation forum (APEC) are three of the more obvious examples.

The second common bond is that trade organizations involve nations in a sort of customs union, which tends to lower and/or remove trade barriers among its members while maintaining, at a somewhat higher level, trade restrictions for products and services from outside the association.

A few trade organizations, such as the EU, also have political ambitions of uniting the member countries into a political union. The EU headquarters is located in Brussels, Belgium. One of the problems that the EU has had over the years has been the struggle over sovereignty between the countries making up the union and its centralized government in Brussels.

One recently developed trade organization is the North American Free Trade Agreement (NAFTA), a trading agreement among the United States, Canada, and Mexico that took effect in January 1994. NAFTA was built on an agreement that was in force for several years between the United States and Canada. That agreement essentially removed the vast majority of trade barriers between these two countries. NAFTA added Mexico to the deal. This was not accomplished without great struggle in the U.S. Congress or without second thoughts, especially when the Mexican economy crashed shortly after U.S. ratification of the agreement in late 1993.

NAFTA does broaden opportunities for all businesses involved. However, one major problem is going to be the integration of Mexico, a country that for decades has seemed to be on the verge of joining the developed world, into a union with Canada and the United States. Integrating the Canadian and U.S. economies is a relatively simple task: The legal systems are based on the same philosophy of law; the most-used language is the same; the political systems are very similar; many U.S. and Canadian firms are already doing substantial business in each other's countries; and the standard of living, while not exactly the same, is certainly comparable. Mexico, however, is a very different story: The legal system is based on a whole different philosophy of law; the language is different; it has one-party rule; the standard of living is very different; and much of the business activity in Mexico is aimed at export to the United States. Still, economically, geographically, or politically, it does not make sense to exclude Mexico from economic integration with the rest of North America. The difficulty arises in how to do it.

Another recent development in world trade has been the creation of the World Trade Organization (WTO). The WTO was created as a result of the Uruguay Round (1986–1993) of the GATT talks and in many ways supersedes GATT. Many challenges face the WTO. One of the first is the trading conflict between the United States and Japan over automobiles. This conflict has been going on for over 25 years, and it is part of a larger balance of trade problem between the two countries. Much of the conflict is not to be found in official government policy, but in the way individual firms do business, something that has always been difficult to control and will surely prove a thorny problem for the WTO.

Financial markets have always been a major cause of concern for organizations engaged in world trade. Financial markets, along with the International Monetary Fund (IMF) and the World Bank, were the major focus of the Bretton Woods Agreement at the end of World War II. But the financial markets aspect of the agreement failed, and while the IMF and the World Bank have continued in their missions, the value of currencies has been unhitched and allowed to float. This has led banks and other international financial institutions to seek greater cooperation and stability in the world monetary markets. It also led to the recognition that world trade conditions were fluid and subject to change and that a mechanism was needed to help deal with the inherent risks associated with that change. Such a mechanism was found in the international market for currencies and the associated markets, such as derivatives, that have developed over the years. It is difficult to say what will happen in the future concerning the international monetary systems. Some problems and their possible solutions are outlined in the articles "The Great Escape" and "Reining in the IMF."

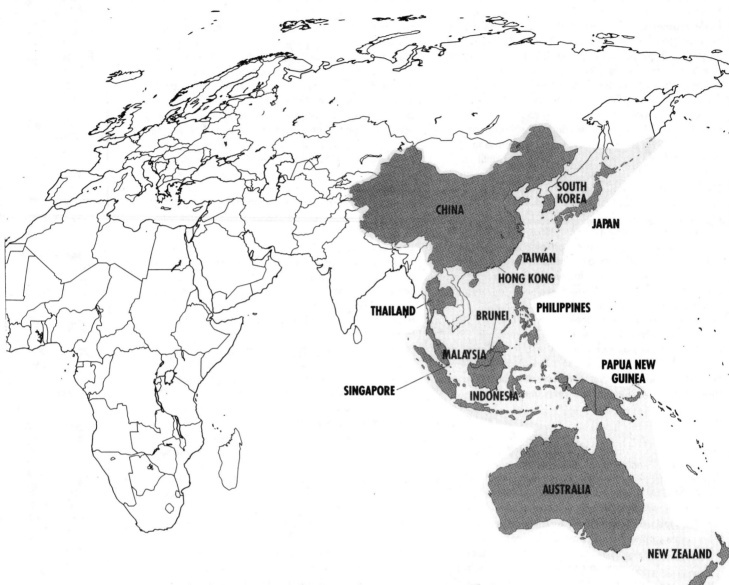

Riding the Dragon

Around the Pacific Rim, a new kind of power is emerging. APEC, the region's biggest trade network, can now influence more than half the world's economic production. The question is—will APEC make that production sustainable?

by Molly O'Meara

From *World Watch*, March/April 1997, pp. 8-18. © 1997 by the Worldwatch Institute. Reprinted by permission.

APEC MEMBER ECONOMIES

Australia	Mexico
Brunei	New Zealand
Canada	Papua New Guinea
Chile	Philippines
China	Singapore
Hong Kong	South Korea
Indonesia	Taiwan
Japan	Thailand
Malaysia	United States

"APEC Means Business!" Every few feet, it seemed, that slogan jumped from banners that lined the streets of Manila. The Philippines was hosting the 1996 meeting of the Asia Pacific Economic Cooperation forum, a loose conclave of 18 Pacific rim states—among them such economic giants as the United States, Japan, and China. To APEC's boosters, that slogan was a way of commending these annual meetings as a new paradigm in international negotiations—one that harnesses the private sector to achieve practical results. But in the mouths of critics, the slogan meant something very different. Many environmentalists, human rights advocates, and other ac-

tivists see APEC as a dangerous new variation on an old theme: a collusion of big business and government that shuts social and environmental concerns out of the loop. In the debate surrounding the Manila meeting, from November 20 to 25, perhaps the only point of agreement was that APEC could be changing the nature of the trading game.

The Philippine government intended the APEC meeting as a national "coming out" party. While many of its Southeast Asian neighbors had prospered during the 1980s, the Philippines had been mired in stagnant growth and burdened by runaway inflation. Frequent brown-outs plagued business and private life. But four years of economic reform under President Fidel Ramos had revived the economy, which grew by 7 percent in 1996. Foreign direct investment rose by 40 percent in the first half of that year; inflation had slowed to under 5 percent; and the lights were back on.

But the festivity in the streets was mingled with frustration. On Roxas Boulevard, the main route to the ministerial conference site, half the lanes had been reserved for the conference. On one side of the median, local traffic inched along in congestion even worse than usual; on the other side, in the nearly deserted "friendship lanes," a few shiny vehicles sped APEC visitors to their destinations. The highway between Manila and Subic Bay, where the heads of state were meeting, was lit by garlands of holiday

On the road to the summit, Ramos and Clinton burned in effigy.

lights—and by protestors who were burning Ramos and U.S. President Bill Clinton in effigy. The protestors' ire is not hard to understand: according to the government's own estimates, over a third of the population lives in poverty. Yet the country had just spent $15 million on cosmetic alterations for foreign visitors—a make-over that included the bulldozing of squatter settlements near the conference sites.

My own excursions in and around Manila showed me a reality that seemed almost entirely divorced from APEC's rhetoric. An estimated 1 million vehicles already clog Manila's streets and that number is expected to double by 2002. The current level of congestion is already costing at least $51 million a year in wasted fuel. Manila's trademark "jeepneys" (converted U.S. army jeeps used now for public transport) are powered by inefficient, second-hand diesel engines that belch exhaust with health-threatening levels of pollutants. My taxis often crossed over the fetid Pasig River, which snakes through Manila, carrying much of the city's sewage and industrial waste into Manila Bay. Fishery yields in the bay have declined by 39 percent from 1975 to 1988; some 30,000 tons of dead fish washed ashore there about a month before the conference began. Thousands of squatter families who lack access to safe water make their homes on the banks of the Pasig. The population of metropolitan Manila has ballooned from 1.5 million in 1950 to 8.9 million in 1990, an increase fed in part by the continual influx of migrants from the country's impoverished and environmentally degraded outer provinces.

It was against this backdrop that government officials, business leaders, and activists alike were all trying to articulate the long-term significance of APEC. How could the forum best foster trade and economic development in the Asia-Pacific region? And what will it mean for the region's already advanced state of environmental decay?

Avoiding "Euro-Sclerosis"

Every year, now, it seems that the APEC forum produces group photos of beaming presidents and prime ministers in local costume. But that simple, outward token of success belies the complexity within. APEC is a difficult creature to understand. Its structure grows more unwieldy every year and its acronym-rich language seems impenetrable—the Philippine government tried to decode it last year in an 83-page dictionary.

The reason for this complexity lies in APEC's unique history. APEC grew out of a set of less glamorous meetings convened by groups like the Pacific Basin Economic Council (PBEC), which was formed in the late 1960s and which continues to be important for business networking in the region. A more direct precursor is perhaps the Pacific Economic Cooperation Council (PECC), a forum set up in 1980 by academic economists and government officials to discuss trade and investment. In 1989, Bob Hawke, then Prime Minister of Australia, organized APEC to give these conversations a kind of official status. Hawke's original group consisted of Australia, New Zealand, Japan, South Korea, the United States, Canada, and the members of ASEAN. (ASEAN, the Association of Southeast Asian Nations, then included Brunei, Indonesia, Malaysia, the Philippines, Singapore, and Thailand. Vietnam has since joined.)

From its inception, then, APEC encompassed a huge range in level of development and wealth. The per capita GNP of Indonesia, for instance, is just $880, while Japan's is about $35,000. This disparity is largely responsible for APEC's amorphous structure, since ASEAN members initially feared that APEC would become a tool for strong-arming them in trade negotiations with the heavyweights. To coax them on board, Australian and Japanese diplomats had to assure them that APEC would be a purely consultative body, and that it would operate according to the model of consensus pioneered by ASEAN itself. This distaste for binding rules, along with the links to business and academia, became hallmarks of the forum. In his book on APEC, *Asia Pacific Fusion*, Japanese journalist Yoichi Funabashi calls this approach the "APEC way."

The "APEC way" grew even broader in 1991, when South Korea scored a diplomatic coup with an agreement in which China, Taiwan, and Hong Kong joined APEC simultaneously. China tries to bar Taiwan's entry into all clubs of nations in which China is itself a member, but was placated by the notion that APEC members would be

Guide to APEC's "Ad-Hocracy"

APEC's fluid structure makes it difficult for NGOs to get a firm grip on forum activities. But all of the bodies on this chart are potential recipients of NGO input. For contact possibilities and conference schedules, check the Web sites in the Resources box.

AD-HOC INFORMAL LEADERS' MEETING

Ad-hoc Eminent Persons Group (advisory panel of independent economists, 1993–'95)

Official Ministerial (Foreign and Trade Ministers)*

*PECC, the Pacific Economic Cooperation Council, is the only NGO granted official observer status. It can attend meetings at the ministerial level or at any of the levels below.

Ad-hoc Special Ministerials (includes Energy, Finance, Environment, Sustainable Development)

Senior Officials' Meeting

Ad-hoc Expert Groups

3 Official Committees:

Budget & Administrative
Trade & Investment
Economic

APEC Business Advisory Council

Ad-hoc Task Forces

10 Official Working Groups:**

Trade Promotion
Human Resources Development
Fisheries
Tourism
Regional Energy Cooperation
Industrial Science & Technology
Telecommunications
Transportation
Marine Resource Conservation
Trade & Investment Data Review

**This is the only area where a formal process now exists to channel participation by NGOs.

Expert Task Forces

called "economies" rather than nations, that no national flags would be flown, and that Taiwan would use the alias "Chinese Taipei." Mexico and Papua New Guinea were added in 1993, and Chile was accepted a year later. By the time of the Manila meeting, 11 other countries were petitioning for membership, including Russia, Vietnam, and India.

The present roster accounts for 40 percent of the world's population, 46 percent of its exports, and 56 percent of its production. APEC includes the world's largest economies—the United States and Japan—as well as many of its fastest growing ones. Korea, Taiwan, Hong Kong, and Singapore have seen per capita income rise at an average rate of almost 7 percent per year during the past three decades. Indonesia, Malaysia, and Thailand have

Some supporters see the future of the world trading system in APEC . . .

grown at an average annual rate of 6 percent over the past decade. And China's economy grew at 10 percent in 1995, its fourth straight year of double-digit growth.

As APEC grows, it is continually redefining itself. What began as a set of meetings among foreign and trade ministers has mushroomed to include the 10 working groups shown in the diagram on page 11. APEC is sometimes called an "ad-hocracy." It has not created its own huge pool of in-house experts, because participants want to avoid what they regard as the deadening effects of a rule-bound bureaucracy. In this connection, APEC supporters sometimes point to the European Union (EU) and speak of "Euro-sclerosis." Instead, APEC seeks advice from ad-hoc task forces, as well as from groups of economists, business people, and government officials. At the APEC forum in 1993, U.S. President Clinton added substantial weight to this ad-hoc approach when he invited his fellow heads of state to a casual gathering on Blake Island off the coast of Seattle, Washington. Meeting in seclusion and studied informality, the leaders pledged themselves to deepening their "spirit of community." The spirit of this first APEC leaders' meeting was encouraging but perhaps unconvincing, given the region's multiplicity of cultures and political systems, its ubiquitous trading frictions, and its territorial conflicts.

Indonesia's President Suharto repeated the Blake Island formula in 1994, when he played genial host to the region's leaders at Bogor Castle. Suharto, an army general who came to power nearly 30 years ago in a coup that left hundreds of thousands massacred, is a good symbol of the challenges that confront APEC's "spirit of community." Even so, leaders emerged from their retreat with a sense of economic—if not political—common ground. That summit produced the most specific goal to date: to achieve free trade throughout the vast Asia-Pacific region by the year 2020, although industrialized countries are supposed to reach the goal by 2010. In Osaka, Japan, in 1995, leaders agreed on an "action agenda" with two parts: measures for easing restrictions on trade and investment, and a plan for building cooperation in international development. The first part of the agenda deals with a fairly conventional range of trade issues, such as lowering tariffs, reducing market barriers, standardizing customs procedures, and streamlining visa procedures for business travel. But the less-publicized second part ventures into deeper water, to attack problems that underlie regional inequities. It calls for such measures as an analysis of regional labor markets, the sharing of ideas on how to encourage private investment in infrastructure projects, and the transfer of new energy technologies.

Progress on the second—development—part of the agenda has thus far been largely a matter of "nuts and bolts" projects, which are put together by the working groups. By the time of the Manila meeting, 320 joint activities were underway, including regularly updated reports on telecommunications regulations in each economy, a Who's Who of fisheries inspectors, and a database on small business statistics. Increasingly, these projects are inspiring government-industry seminars, training sessions, and international exchanges.

For the first—free trade—part of its agenda, APEC's approach has been to seek progress not through painstaking negotiations, but through peer pressure. In Manila, for example, each country put forth its own non-binding plan of action. Delegates learned of China's pledge to allow foreign securities firms to establish branches on its territory by 2000. They heard Singapore vow to break up its telecommunications monopoly by 2000, and the Philippines promise to reduce import tariffs to 5 percent on everything but agricultural products by 2004. There was a set of collective agreements as well. All members agreed, for instance, to contribute to a customs and tariff database which is supposed to be available on the Internet sometime this year.

The aggregate effect of these plans should be to accelerate the push for free trade well beyond the schedule that member nations have already committed themselves to at the World Trade Organization (WTO), the 128-member body set up in Geneva by the General Agreement on Tariffs and Trade (GATT). And in fact, the Manila agreement that got the most media attention was a decision to press the WTO to accelerate its own schedule. APEC has asked the WTO to eliminate by 2000 most tariffs on information technologies, such as computer chips or software.

In pursuit of its vision, APEC has been courting industry at the highest levels. Hundreds of executives were lured to an APEC Business Forum last year in Manila, where President Ramos, exulting in what he called a "sea of happy CEO faces," exclaimed: "Before APEC, it was business that linked the region." Academic economists also haunt APEC. The forum's free trade blueprint was laid out by the ad-hoc Eminent Persons Group, an assembly of independent "wisemen," many of them PECC economists. Led by C. Fred Bergsten, Director of the Institute of International Economics, a Washington-based think tank, the group met from 1993 to 1995. Its vision of a diverse, competitive membership committed to "open regionalism" (an interest in lowering trade barriers for non-member states) was calculated to secure a global role for APEC. In a recent issue of *Foreign Affairs,* Bergsten argued that global free trade could make all countries richer by spurring competition, and could save regional trade organizations such as the EU and NAFTA (the North American Free Trade Agreement between Canada, the United States, and Mexico) from becoming hostile blocs. APEC's approach, in Bergsten's view, puts it "in a strong position to assume leadership of the global trading system."

Is APEC Accountable?

APEC's leadership potential is exactly what worries many of its critics. In the Philippines, for the first time in APEC's history, criticism from the "third sector"—nongovernmental organizations focused on environmental and social problems—reached a thunderous volume. NGOs had tried to make themselves heard at the 1994 APEC meeting in Indonesia, but were denied a permit to meet and had to relocate to Thailand. At the 1995 forum in Japan, NGOs drew closer to the process by gathering in Kyoto, one hour by car from the official meetings in Osaka. In Manila, four parallel forums confronted the official meetings with tactics ranging from pickets to a policy dialogue. The direct successor to the Kyoto conference, the Manila People's Forum, criticized APEC on several fronts but made its biggest headlines when the government interfered with its plans to highlight regional human rights problems. Among the speakers invited to the Forum was the Indonesian activist José Ramos-Horta, who recently won the Nobel Peace Prize for his crusade against human rights violations in East Timor, which Indonesia invaded in 1975. When the Philippines refused him entry, it created a media furor. Two other NGO conferences condemned APEC in its entirety; one of these was organized by labor unions and held in an abandoned factory to symbolize the effects of economic globalization on workers. Finally, representatives of a huge network of Philippine NGOs managed to discuss their concerns directly with President Ramos.

As I watched events at the Manila People's Forum unfold, I was reminded of an observation made by U.S. scholars Robin Broad and John Cavanagh in their book on the Philippines, *Plundering Paradise.* They likened Filipino activists to a local dessert called *halo-halo,* an unlikely mélange of ice cream, ice, fruits, gelatin, and corn—ingredients that "take on a surprisingly enticing flavor when combined. Like *halo-halo,* in union these groups become something more than the sum of their parts." In Manila, Filipino NGOs combined with their foreign counterparts to create something of a deluxe halo-halo of pub-

> *. . . and so do some critics, who question APEC's accountability.*

lic concern about APEC—about what they saw as the forum's lack of transparency and the consequences of APEC-led free trade for human rights, women's rights, the welfare of workers, cultural survival, and environmental health.

Among these skeptics was New Zealand law professor Jane Kelsey, who cited the lack of regular channels for citizen input as evidence that APEC is the most "antidemocratic, secret, invisible and inaccessible" trade regime yet devised—far more so than NAFTA or the EU. Walden Bello, a professor at the University of the Philippines, pointed out that the United States is supporting APEC as part of its campaign to open markets and reduce trade deficits with Asian countries. He and some of his colleagues fear that the U.S. brand of rapid, "cowboy-style" trade liberalization would benefit global corporations at the expense of local enterprises. Broad and her husband Cavanagh, who has written a book on multinationals, coauthored a speech in which they noted that of the 100 largest economic units in the world, only 49 are countries; 51 are corporations. Many APEC skeptics, echoing Kelsey's point, argued that the multinational corporations promoted by APEC are even less accountable than APEC itself.

Concerns about globalization were perhaps most vividly expressed by Ian Fry of Greenpeace Australia, who took off his shoe to make his point: "This is an example of globalization," he said. "Somewhere in Brazil or Australia, erosion is caused by grazing cows to produce the leather for my shoe. A river in maybe Thailand was polluted by the manufacturing of the rubber sole, and it was put together by cheap labor in China. You see why this shoe was cheap: I did not pay for the environmental and social damage that was caused by its production."

Given regional trends, these concerns are not just matters for academic debate. APEC countries contain 10 of the world's 15 largest cities: Tokyo, New York, Mexico City, Shanghai, Los Angeles, Beijing, Seoul, Jakarta, Osaka, and Tianjin. If India succeeds in its membership bid, Bombay and Calcutta will be added to that list. Increasingly from Los Angeles to Tianjin, urban demand for water is competing with agricultural needs. Disease and social problems associated with urban crowding are likely to grow more acute in many of the region's cities, and urban pollution is generally worsening. The World Health Organization ranks Xian, Shanghai, Guangzhou, Bangkok, Kuala Lumpur, Seoul, and Manila among the worst cities in the world for air pollution. In the countryside, rapacious deforestation continues apace. Asia is losing forest area more rapidly than any other region in the world; one study has estimated that a continuation of present trends would eliminate all of the region's remaining tropical timber in less than 40 years.

The region also has a gargantuan appetite for fossil fuels. It is home to the top two greenhouse gas emitters, the United States and China, as well as Japan, which ranks as number four. APEC energy ministers have noted with alarm that by 2010, regional electricity demand is projected to increase by 50 to 80 percent. Present energy consumption is thought to be growing by around 2.2 percent per year, compared with only 1 percent for the industrialized nations of the Organisation for Economic Cooperation and Development (OECD).

One type of pollution—toxic waste—is actually being brought into the region as a form of trade. Recycling plants in Thailand and the Philippines, for instance, accept shipments of electronics scrap or lead-acid batteries from the United States, the world's largest producer of hazardous waste. Studies done by Greenpeace have shown that many of these facilities are not equipped to deal with the material safely. A United Nations report has documented instances of "South-South" trade in toxic trash as well: Singapore, for example, has shipped hazardous waste to Thailand. And while there is growing international trend toward banning "North-South" trade in toxics, no such effort is underway for "South-South" trade. Given the rates of development in the Asia-Pacific, that could be a loophole with enormous potential.

Building an Environmental Agenda

There are signs that APEC is preparing to address at least some of the concerns raised by its critics. The environment is especially likely to get attention, since there seems to be an emerging consensus that environmental degradation is a drag on the region's economic development. Among the most visible signs of hope in this connection have been the announcements of the leaders themselves. Unlike more formal summits, where communiqués are usually hammered out well ahead of time, APEC leaders' statements can still surprise. Their initiatives

on free trade, for example, are the stuff of diplomatic legend: in 1993, APEC leaders spurred the closure of the contentious "Uruguay Round" of negotiations on the GATT, and in 1994 they made headlines with their vow to achieve free trade in the Asia-Pacific.

On the environmental front, several leaders, including Canada's Prime Minister Jean Chrétien, the Philippines' President Ramos, and U.S. Vice President Al Gore, have been promoting a vision of "sustainable development" since that first leaders' meeting at Blake Island. Following the 1996 conference, a Philippine newspaper noted that the leaders' declaration—sprinkled with phrases like "giving a human face to development"—read "more like a United Nations document than a statement by the world's most powerful and promising economies committed to free trade."

And there's growing evidence that the leadership pronouncements on sustainable development are not merely some sort of "greenwash." Environmental awareness appears to be seeping into a broad range of APEC activities, although it's still too early to look for much in the way of concrete achievement. In 1994, for the first time, environment officials were pulled into the orbit of APEC conferences. But rather than delegate environmental concerns to a single body, leaders have asked all of APEC's organs to report on their work towards the "overarching goal" of sustainable development. That requirement has had a practical effect on a wide range of working group activities. The transportation working group, for instance, is now producing an inventory of the region's oil spill preparedness. The fisheries working group is training local farmers in sustainable shrimp culture, and the economics committee is attempting to analyze how population and economic growth will increase the demand for food and energy, as well as the pressures on the environment.

APEC held its first major "sustainable development" conference in Manila this past July, as a lead-up to the November summit. Delegates managed to agree on three general goals for top priority: sustainable cities, cleaner industries, and a sustainably managed marine environment. There was no agreement to give a similarly high profile to many other critical areas. For example, agriculture and forestry failed to make it onto the list. Logging, subsidies for domestic crop production, and other politically sensitive issues are making these areas stumbling blocks in APEC's trade discussions too. They have not even been given their own working groups (see "Guide to APEC's 'Ad-Hocracy'"). But participants hope that a partial and pragmatic environmental agenda will still allow for progress. Current efforts are focused on how these goals can be used to "add value" to existing environmental accords.

The potential of the cleaner industries initiative has been championed by Greg Mertz, Senior Counsel for Trade and Environment at the U.S. Environmental Protection Agency. According to the EPA, the widespread adoption of already existing cleaner technologies could yield major progress in a wide range of industries, including textiles, pulp and paper, electronics, and petroleum refining. For example, in electronics manufacturing—a rapidly expanding sector that is already a focus for APEC—toxic solvents can threaten factory workers, and communities in general if the ground water becomes contaminated. In the United States, the industry has responded to these problems with a set of innovations, such as better air filters in factories, and redesigned production processes to eliminate the need for certain chemicals. If these technologies were in global use, they could greatly advance international efforts to counter persistent organic pollutants.

Bergsten's group of economists had used the "value added" approach on a much more basic level as early as 1994. The group recommended the sharing of environmentally friendly technologies, advancing the principle of internalizing environmental costs (as Greenpeace's Fry was suggesting), promoting environmentally sound development projects, and harmonizing environmental standards which could affect such areas as air and water quality.

The standards issue has captured the imagination of Lyuba Zarsky, who directs the Berkeley-based Nautilus Institute for Security and Sustainable Development, a think tank that has taken the lead in researching APEC's environmental agenda. Zarsky argues that in any given industry, businesses competing for the largest markets tend to work with roughly similar environmental standards—usually the lowest standards that will meet the demands of those markets. And policy makers, generally focused on the short-term needs of their national industries, are often reluctant to upgrade standards unilaterally. Such a move, they fear, could divert scarce investment dollars or increase costs of production. APEC, Zarsky thinks, could break this impasse. She believes that APEC's primary goal should be to set high environmental benchmarks, which could be continually revised upwards. She sees such an opportunity, for instance, in the sustainable cities goal set in Manila. APEC could ensure that a host of standards affecting cities—including' auto emissions, energy efficiency, and water treatment—are harmonized in ways that promote not only commercial but also ecological objectives. The same approach might allow for progress in the marine initiative as well. Zarsky thinks that APEC might be able to set standards for coastal management—a move that might help save rapidly disappearing mangrove stands and reduce land-based marine pollution.

Given the dismal environmental trends that afflict the region—and the power that many of the biggest and dirtiest industries have over national governments—APEC's future as an environmental boon is hardly assured. But many analysts regard "the APEC way" as the best available strategy. It is clear, in any case, that heavy reliance on the enormous WTO is probably not a prescription for success. In December 1996, the WTO's Committee on Trade and Environment, which had been locked for two years in disagreements between richer and poorer countries, finally delivered a weak report that did little to put international trade on a more sustainable footing. And the WTO's general effectiveness in Asia is still uncertain, because China's application for membership has not yet been accepted.

Regional trade agreements seem to offer more immediate opportunities for progress. The obvious precedent is NAFTA, which was the first trade agreement among countries of widely varying income levels to include environmental provisions. All three of the nations involved pledged not to lower their environmental standards to attract investment, and to enforce their own environmental laws while still adhering to free trade rules. During the NAFTA negotiations, critics of the agreement argued that NAFTA would tend to shift production from Canada and the United States to Mexico, where environmental and labor standards are easier to flout, and in some respects, those predictions have proved accurate. But much of this movement might have occurred even without NAFTA, and the agreement's supporters argue that the treaty's environmental and labor side agreements succeeded in wringing some benefit from the inevitable. Even if NAFTA were an unqualified success, however, its rule-bound approach would probably prove impractical in the immense Asia-Pacific region, where economic and cultural disparities are even greater than in North America. The APEC way, with its focus on cooperation, attempts in effect to make a virtue of necessity.

NGO Apathy

Over the next 15 years, growing energy demand in the Asia-Pacific region will probably require an investment of some $1.6 trillion in energy infrastructure. Much of this money is expected to come from the private sector through "build-operate-transfer" agreements, in which private companies build and operate powerplants; governments guarantee them a return on their investments; and the facilities are eventually incorporated into local electric utilities. The APEC energy working group is already attempting to educate officials in several countries on the potential of solar technologies. But at present, it's the big, wealthy fossil-fuel and nuclear industries that are winning the infrastructure bids. It would be possible to identify a similar predicament on almost any environmental front in the region. And APEC's growing ability to increase trade and investment is almost certainly going to make those predicaments worse, unless APEC's environmental agenda begins to gather force quickly.

Probably the only way to build an effective social and environmental agenda for APEC is to engage "third sector" NGOs. That's why the Manila NGO conferences were such an encouraging development. The conferences may serve as a useful precedent for NGOs elsewhere in Asia—even NGOs from countries that discourage such activities may be able to participate in international forums. Efforts at Manila began at a fairly advanced level because some Philippine NGOs had already forged a working relationship with the Ramos administration on sustainable development policies. At the helm of this movement is Nicky

Perlas, director of the Philippine Center for Alternative Development Initiatives. Perlas says the biggest political achievement that he has seen during his 25 years in the environmental movement came last September, when Ramos authorized a plan known as "Philippines Agenda 21." Named after the famous plan of action produced at the Rio "Earth Summit" in 1992, the document was created with NGO guidance, and it attempts to reconcile economic development with the need to stabilize the country's various ecosystems. It takes precedence over the country's more conventional economic plan, "Philippines 2000," which has been circulating in one form or another since Ramos came to power in 1992. (Currently, at least 17 countries have their own Agenda 21s.)

It was clear during the Manila forum that Ramos was taking his commitment seriously. At one point, in the midst of his duties as host to the heads of state assembled at Subic Bay, Ramos helicoptered back into the city to meet with some 150 NGO representatives at the presidential palace. The meeting, which had been arranged by Perlas and his colleagues, was intended to be a half-hour discussion of sustainable development. But it lasted over two hours. Ramos, who has announced a slew of initiatives to transform the Philippines into a "green tiger," seemed to be listening to the NGOs with real interest. (Presumably, since the Philippines has a single-term presidency, he is not seeking future votes.) Afterwards, he marked up the NGO declaration with instructions to his cabinet ministers and assured the group that their concerns would be conveyed to the prime ministers and presidents awaiting him in Subic. And indeed, much of the sustainable development language in last year's APEC documents apparently came from Ramos' meeting with the NGOs.

Despite the successes at Manila, most of APEC's "nuts and bolts" work is done between summits—not during them. Even among those NGOs following the summits, few pay attention to the forum the rest of the time, and that limits their influence. Another impediment is the novel structure of APEC itself. The Nautilus Institute's Zarsky says that both NGO and government officials often "simply don't know where or what to grab on to." Zarsky has encountered the problem first-hand, while traveling around the region engaging her counterparts in APEC-related dialogue. Her efforts landed her—quite by chance, as she tells the story—on the official U.S. delegation to that first ministerial meeting on sustainable development last July. "When I asked if they had made any arrangements for NGO participation, they invited me on the spot!" At the November summit, Zarsky's director of environmental programs, Jason Hunter, summed up the confusion when he said with undisguised puzzlement, "the government people are looking to us for help."

Another major obstacle to building a "third sector" in APEC is the curious apathy of most potential U.S. participants. Even though the United States is teeming with environmental NGOs, few have taken an interest in APEC. Rodrigo Prudencio, who coordinates the trade and envi-

ronment program at the National Wildlife Federation, laments the common U.S. tendency to see APEC in terms of NAFTA—to assume that since APEC isn't getting the same kind of continual high-level political attention that NAFTA got, it isn't going anywhere. But of course, NAFTA is a treaty. APEC is not, and making it work requires a very different sort of effort. Prudencio fears that the failure to make this distinction is keeping U.S. NGOs offstage, waiting for a kind of political moment that may be many years off.

Danny Kennedy, a former adviser to Greenpeace Australia, calls the lack of interest among powerful U.S. environmental groups "pitiful," given the urgent need for watchdog activity. A good example, says Kennedy, involves APEC energy ministers and the forum's Regional Energy Cooperation working group, all of whom are being watched by an NGO coalition organized by Australia's Climate Action Network. The working group is attempting to encourage heavier investment in renewable energy. But Australia is trying to use its influence as the current "shepherd" of this working group to promote its low-sulfur coal exports—a fact publicized by the NGO coalition.

Outside the NGO community, APEC continues to gather strength. Maurice Strong, the Canadian businessman who chaired the Earth Summit, recently pointed out a fact that is obvious but easy to forget: the key environmental stewards are not environmentalists, but the government and business leaders who manage the world's economies. These elites are already well represented in APEC, where they are influencing various unpublicized "technical" decisions—decisions that will eventually exert a profound influence on the region. This year, for instance, the energy working group will begin to discuss harmonizing energy efficiency standards for appliances; those standards will help determine the region's energy demand. Also this year, the transportation working group hopes to reach a consensus on automobile manufacturing standards. According to Kennedy, the working group is considering whether to make U.S. auto emissions standards the regional norm. But in the United States, car exhaust remains a major source of air pollution; "freezing" standards at current U.S. levels might actually increase the regulatory obstacles to further improvement.

Vancouver, Canada will be the venue of the leaders' summit this November, and Canada has already begun to host a formidable series of preliminary meetings. The schedule includes, for example, high-level conferences on energy and the environment. Another conference will explore the relationships among a set of basic trends: food demand, economic growth, energy needs, environmental problems, and population growth. (For more information, see the Web sites below.) Last year, Canadian officials pledged to look more closely into the environmental consequences of the region's growing economic integration. These meetings present an important opportunity to hold them to that promise, and to strengthen APEC's environmental agenda. That opportunity is not likely to repeat itself in the following year, since Malaysia, APEC's 1998 host, does not have a strong NGO tradition.

Perhaps the most urgent problem humanity faces is the task of reconciling the global economy with the natural world that ultimately sustains it. It is not yet clear what role APEC will play in the search for a solution. But given the size and wealth of the Asia-Pacific region, there is little hope of succeeding without it.

———————

Molly O'Meara is a staff researcher at the Worldwatch Institute.

Resources

APEC Secretariat, 438 Alexandria Road, #14-01/04, Alexandria Point, Singapore 119958, telephone: 011 65 2761880, fax: 65 2761775, Internet: http://www.apecsec.org.sg.

Nautilus Institute for Security and Sustainable Development, 1831 Second St., Berkeley, CA 94710, USA, telephone: (510) 204-9296, fax: (510) 204-9298, Asia Pacific Regional Environment Network on the Internet: http://www.nautilus.org/aprenet.

Yoichi Funabashi, *Asia Pacific Fusion: Japan's Role in APEC* (Washington, DC: Institute for International Economics, 1995).

ANALYSIS

Multinational Corporations: Saviors or Villains?

by Nancy A. Bord

Look at the labels on the clothes you are wearing, at your children's toys, at the containers for your appliances. More likely than not, they will read: Made in China, or India, the Philippines, Guatemala, or Ecuador.

Over the last several decades, an increasing number of unskilled and semiskilled manufacturing jobs have moved from the developed industrial economies of countries in North America and western Europe to the developing economies of countries in South and East Asia, Latin America, and the Caribbean.

What are the implications of this movement for companies, for workers, and for countries? Are multinational corporations exploitive villains who take advantage of low-wage workers in developing countries who toil long hours in often dangerous and unsanitary working conditions?

Or are the operations of multinational companies from postindustrial countries a boon to developing nations—providing jobs, investment capital, technology; and training in

management skills, all of which accelerate economic development?

Last year, the media spotlighted allegations by labor activists about the working conditions under which clothing endorsed by television personalities Kathie Lee Gifford (for WalMart) and Jaclyn Smith (for Kmart) and basketball player Michael Jordan (for Nike) was manufactured.

To take the Gifford example, allegations said that the TV host's line of women's clothing was made by Honduran youths aged 13–15 who labored in sweatshops from 8 A.M. to 9 P.M. Monday through Friday and from 8 A.M. to 5 P.M. on Saturday for 31–39 cents an hour.

But the situation surrounding the children and their "sweatshops" was more complex than had been portrayed, according to the Washington-based Economic Policies Institute. What critics—and the media—failed to note was that the prevailing average wage in Honduras was 16 cents an hour, a 70-hour work week was normal, and child labor was an unfortunate economic necessity for

many families to get by, according to the institute.

Moreover, since Wal-Mart summarily severed its ties with the Honduran clothing factory; it is not known whether the children were left without a job and what overall economic impact Wal-Mart's action had on the families and communities involved.

WHY THE CONTROVERSY?

As we all know, in the mass media—many of which are themselves multinational corporations—negative events make the news. Stories of mistreatment, especially involving children and animals, are much more newsworthy than stories about steady progress and improvement. It is an all-too-common human trait to focus on the one or two negative examples that stand out from the hundred positive ones.

In addition, Americans have a highly ambivalent view of big business, especially multinational corporations, and are all too ready to believe the worst of them. Content studies of crime and espionage stories on U.S. television over the years since the demise of the Soviet empire show scenarios of businessmen as villains and corporate greed as a principal motive more often than any others.

In the final analysis, we Americans, in a nation reputedly founded and built by "underdogs," often take a secret—or not so secret—pleasure in seeing our largest and strongest institutions derided.

But rhetoric and horror stories aside, is it possible to rigorously determine whether, on balance, multinational corporate operations in developing economies are a "good" thing, and for whom? Statistics on this issue-satisfying the criteria of relevance, accuracy, precision, and timeliness—are difficult to obtain. (This is not to say, however, that governments, trade associations, and transnational institutions, such as the UN, OECD, and World Bank do not produce such statistics in vast quantity.)

Anecdotal evidence is, of course, idiosyncratic and tainted by its source and purpose. Arguments at any level of abstraction are understood and interpreted in light of one's particular perspective. Nonetheless, as the accompanying table shows, it is possible to consider the issue of multinational corporate involvement in developing economies within a systematic, analytical framework.

The first step in assessing the implications of multinational operations in developing countries is to identify those affected in both the corporation's home country and the host country. Next, one can categorize the effects of a multinational as advantageous or disadvantageous in the near term and longer term based upon accepted precepts of developmental and social-welfare economics.

In this simplified model, six key entities are likely to be affected by the actions of multinational corporations abroad. Three of them are in the corporation's home country and thus not directly the focus of this analysis.

In the host (foreign) country; the most direct and immediate effects are felt by host-country workers. Thanks to the foreign corporations, they have jobs and salaries and sometimes even pensions and benefits. Many of these employees in developing countries were previously farm workers. Many are experiencing employment and receiving wages for the first time.

Of course, the wage rates paid in developing countries are not the same as those received by employees in the corporation's home country. After all, the competitive advantage of developing countries is their less costly unskilled and semiskilled labor. Absent the wage differential in developing countries, the multinationals would be less inclined to locate operations there.

MULTINATIONALS' EFFECT ON ECONOMIC GROWTH

The host country's economy begins to be affected by multinational operations as more workers with wages are able to both consume more and save more. The newly employed groups contribute to their country's economic base, increasing its per capita gross domestic product, one of the prime indicators of economic growth.

Foreign corporations also enhance economic growth in the host country through the ripple effects of their dealings with suppliers of goods and services there. Depending on regulations and laws governing foreign direct investment in the host country, foreign multinationals may be required to pay local taxes of various sorts, employ local managers and professionals, obtain permits, or even have a local partner. All these elements contribute directly to the host country's economic development.

The vast majority of Western multinationals with operations in developing countries are eager to train and promote local employees to supervisory and management posi-

tions. This cannot be accomplished instantly, however, but rather is an intermediate-term effect. Over time, a cadre of middle-income middle managers with a vested interest in sustaining and expanding their economic opportunities is created.

Some multinationals also contribute to their host country's infrastructure by building housing for their workers and schools for their workers' children, as well as undertaking various projects resulting in improved transportation, utility services, and sanitary conditions for the host country's citizens.

The host country's governing regime may regard development of a middle class as a mixed blessing. If the country's social structure and political culture are still quite rigidly stratified and if the governing regime is authoritarian, development of a middle class comprising middle managers and prosperous tradesmen and merchants may be perceived as a threat.

Fortunately, most developing-country political regimes, even those as repressive as China, recognize the value of economic development and the contributions of multinational companies in stimulating and fostering economic growth. A prosperous economy can contribute to maintaining a regime and to political stability. This in turn attracts more foreign direct investment.

IS FOREIGN DIRECT INVESTMENT NECESSARY?

Developing economies, by definition, do not generate sufficient investment capital to fuel their own growth. Many were colonies of western European or Asian countries and, even after achieving political independence, continued to be to some extent economically dependent on their former colonial masters. Some became de facto wards of the World Bank or other transnational lending agencies.

Some erected high tariff barriers. Others were (and a few still are) hos-

Multinational Corporations in Developing Countries

Advantages and Disadvantages

Affected Entity	Advantages		Disadvantages	
	Near Term	**Longer Term**	**Near Term**	**Longer Term**
Host-Country Workers	◆Enhanced employee status ◆Regular wages	◆Improved economic status	◆Adjustment to corporate working style ◆Possible sweatshop conditions, by Western standards	—
Host-Country Economy	◆Less unemployment ◆Improved GDP	◆Increased economic growth ◆Increased social welfare	◆Possible inflation	—
Host-Country Government, Politics, Social Structure	◆Public relations value of foreign direct investment	◆More affluent, better-educated electorate ◆More open, democratic regime	◆Can solidify power of repressive regime	◆Altered economic structure could threaten regime
Home-Country Employees	—	◆New skills and broader employment options	◆Possible temporary job loss	—
Corporation	◆Less costly workforce ◆Broader product distribution network	◆Improved profits ◆Expanded market access	◆Expenses of start-up abroad	◆Management of dispersed operations
Home-Country Economy	◆Increased integration of global economy	◆Corporate growth ◆Trade expansion	◆Possible temporary rise in unemployment	—

tile to foreign direct investment and restrict the activities of foreign corporations. These countries are a small and dwindling minority.

Nations that close their borders to foreign investment, or abuse such investment when it arrives (through property expropriation or profit-repatriation restrictions), are finding themselves left behind in the global marketplace. Contrast the rate of economic growth in the Asian "tigers" (Hong Kong, Singapore, South Korea, and Taiwan) over the last decade with, say, those in Latin America. Or compare the Czech Republic and Hungary with Russia

and the other countries comprising the former Soviet Union.

Most of Africa is still so far behind, so impoverished, and so politically unstable that foreign direct investment by multinational corporations, except those focusing on natural resource extraction, is generally unrealistic in the near term.

The countries whose economies are advancing most rapidly appear to be those that treat foreign direct investment as a shortcut to prosperity and a better life for their people.

Multinational corporations are not likely to invest in countries lacking the rule of law and protection for

private property. Indices of economic freedom, which rate countries on key elements of their economic and regulatory climate, provide ample evidence of the relationship between increasing economic growth and an environment favorable to direct investment by multinational corporations.

A WIN-WIN SITUATION?

If the evidence of the benefits of multinational corporations' investment in developing economies is so clear, why is it necessary to restate the obvious? Two reasons have al-

The vast majority of Western multinationals with operations in developing countries are eager to train and promote local employees to supervisory and management positions.

ready been presented: the Western media's penchant to dramatize the instances of apparent exploitation, and the American tendency to be ambivalent about big business.

Another factor is the lack of understanding about the dynamics of economic development. After all, America's development to a major world economic power was not accomplished overnight. It required over 100 years. And America's economic growth, lest we forget, was also attributable to the investment of foreign multinationals.

The advantages of multinational operations in developing countries, both near term and long term, far outweigh the disadvantages for all affected parties (see the accompanying table). While the host-country workers and economy are most directly affected in the near term, effects on the host country's government, politics, and social structure require a longer time to percolate through the system.

In some countries, depending upon the existing regime's openness and the regulatory climate for business, a growing middle class of more

affluent, educated managers is a positive phenomenon.

For multinational corporations and their home country employees, there may be temporary unemployment as lower-skilled jobs move abroad. For many who lose jobs, however, this phenomenon presents opportunities to acquire new skills and move in new directions.

At the macro level, industrial and economic restructuring in the home country may present short-term dislocations. But, as the recent experience of the United States has demonstrated, in a robust market economy such shifts stimulate productivity improvements, expanded markets, and trade.

The investing corporation obviously benefits, or else it would not have made a strategic business decision to move its operations abroad. Its start-up costs for facilities, training, and management in a developing country should soon be offset by improved profits and expanded markets.

ECONOMIC AND POLITICAL FREEDOM

The relationship between economic and political freedom has long been debated by academics and public-policy researchers. The eminent scholar Seymour Lipset has hypothesized a strong relationship between them, and overall experience of the last 50 years around the world has supported his thesis. Alexis de Tocqueville in 1835 noted the same relationship in his travels around America.

In those instances in which authoritarian regimes have shown dramatic growth, it has been because rulers have not tried to control the economy. But even in such regimes, over the long term, economic vitality and freedom lead to more liberal political re-

gimes. Illustrating this phenomenon are countries like South Korea, Argentina, Chile, and Kazakhstan (which has been becoming more politically progressive due to the need to accommodate the converging Western oil companies).

In the near term, however, foreign direct investment by multinationals in developing economies can often reinforce rigid, stratified regimes by simply making them more efficient. Multinationals seeking the advantage of lower-wage countries for their labor-intensive routine manufacturing tasks tacitly agree to conform to the country's existing rules and mores. Their executives deal with existing political parties and their leaders.

Thus, in the near term, investment by multinationals can perpetuate regimes dominated by entrenched elites. Policies of these regimes may not be conducive to promoting the economic and political reforms needed for sustainable economic growth. Brazil, Indonesia, and China are recent examples of this type of regime.

By and large, then, for those of us living in open Western democracies, the spread of decision-diffuse, market-based economies around the globe, from South Africa to the Arctic Circle, bodes well for the future. The role of multinational corporations is key to this dynamic.

The operations of multinational corporations, along with enlightened governing groups, can stimulate growth and openness in developing economies. If they are successful, can growth and openness in politics and social structures be lagging far behind?

Nancy A. Bord, director of the Institute for World Trade and Global Management, has been a scholar at the Hoover Institution and Heritage Foundation public policy centers.

The great escape

How do you say goodbye to a currency board? The more stable the economy, the easier the answer

JUST as slimmers sometimes have their jaws wired shut to stop them from gorging, spendthrift countries find that abolishing their central banks can end the itch to print money. A currency board, which takes the place of a central bank as a country's monetary authority, operates on a simple principle: all currency in circulation and (usually) all of banks' reserves must be backed by foreign exchange. "Even if we have only eight kroons in circulation, we will have a D-mark in our vaults to back them," said Siim Kallas, the president of Estonia's central bank when it launched its currency board in 1992.

Estonia's currency board helped stabilise the Baltic country's economy. Hong Kong's, created in 1983, has kept the colony's currency steady despite the massive changes in China. Argentina's has put an end to decades of inflation. Their success has tempted others: Bosnia-Hercegovina and Bulgaria may introduce boards soon. But although the IMF's experts offer guidance about how to start up a currency board, economists have little experience of how to wind one down.

There are two easily distinguishable sets of reasons why countries may wish to abandon their currency boards—good ones, and bad ones. And the motive itself has much to do with whether a country can make the transition successfully.

For all its advantages, a currency board has inherent drawbacks. Precisely because the exchange rate cannot adjust, it reduces a country's ability to cope with shocks, such as a big change in commodity prices. A board can make a country vulnerable to inflation, because an inflow of foreign investment, which puts more foreign currency into the board's vaults, will automatically lead it to print more money. And in the event of a financial emergency a currency board has less freedom than a central bank to act as lender of last resort, because the board cannot boost the money supply to aid troubled banks. If a country on a sound financial footing wants to scrap its currency board for these reasons, it should be able to do so without difficulty.

ECONOMICS FOCUS

How? One way is to stop covering the monetary base entirely with foreign currency, and gradually move to a mixture of foreign currency and domestic government bonds. The currency board will come to look like a central bank with a commitment to a fixed exchange rate. Eventually, as more and more domestic bonds back the currency, the board can engage in open-market operations, buying and selling the bonds to nudge interest rates, just as central banks do. Estonia is trying to move in this direction.

Another possibility is to announce that the currency will no longer be fixed at a specific rate. In 1973, for instance, Singapore and Malaysia abandoned their currency-board systems by allowing their currencies to float. Both countries had stable economic policies and strong capital inflows from abroad. Their

Two Baltic tales

Sources: EIU; Deutsche Morgan Grenfell

currencies immediately appreciated instead of falling. In effect, they left the currency board from positions of strength.

But what about countries with more questionable motives? The subject is topical in another Baltic state, Lithuania, which introduced a currency board in 1994. In contrast to Estonia, the move did not have broad political backing. Lithuania's industry has been slower to restructure than Estonia's, and it has lost competitiveness as the real exchange rate has appreciated. Many businesses claim to be suffering.

These problems have been exacerbated by the fact that Lithuania pegged its currency, the lit, to the dollar. As the

dollar has strengthened against the currencies of Lithuania's main trading partners in Europe, the country's trade deficit has ballooned to nearly 10% of GDP. Worse, the government reacted ineptly to a banking crisis, and in doing so weakened the credibility of its currency board. Despite the rules, it bailed out two big banks in 1995. Outsiders suspect that a chunk of the currency board's reserves are pledged to prop up the banking system.

Shedding the straitjacket

Given these problems, it is clear that many Lithuanians would like to wriggle out of the currency board's disciplines. The authorities say that they would like to keep the fixed exchange rate but not the board itself*. After this year, it plans to back only 80% of its lits with dollars. This, it argues, would provide the monetary flexibility to bail out dud banks (and so reduce some of the speculative pressure against the lit). Then, in 1999 or later, it plans to switch the currency's peg from the dollar to a basket of currencies.

But it is not clear that the government has the credibility to make these fundamental shifts in exchange-rate policy without scaring investors and risking a big devaluation. This is because Lithuania has failed to accompany its currency board with other essential economic measures. At 2.5% of GDP the budget deficit is showing no signs of shrinking. Privatisation has been haphazard and there has been relatively little foreign investment.

It is slow progress on these fronts, as much as the details of the monetary regime, that have made Lithuanians think their economy will do better without a currency board. And yet the very things that make the board uncomfortable could make it costly to leave behind. If the government's economic programme had truly succeeded in stabilising the economy, the move to a more flexible central bank might pass unnoticed by both currency markets and the public. But if investors think that Lithuania is acting from a position of economic weakness, they may not believe the government's promise to keep the currency stable. Abandoning a currency board because the discipline is too painful is not a prescription for economic health.

---

*"Monetary Policy Programme of the Bank of Lithuania for 1997–1999," Bank of Lithuania, 1997.

Reining in the IMF

The Case For Denying the IMF New Funding and Power

by Marijke Torfs

AFTER DECADES OF OPERATING in relative obscurity, the IMF is taking center stage of public debate in the United States and throughout the world. Frantically running to the rescue of the recently beleaguered Asian economies, the IMF is throwing around unprecedented amounts of public money, bailing out rich country banks and imposing its traditional austerity programs upon 350 million people in Indonesia, Thailand, the Philippines and South Korea.

Coming on the heels of the Mexican bailout of 1995, the IMF's central role in the Asian financial drama represents a substantial expansion of the Fund's mandate and power. Originally conceived as an entity to provide temporary financing assistance to Western countries having trouble sticking to the fixed exchange rates of the post-World War II era (currencies then had a set value relative to the U.S. dollar, which was redeemable for a set amount of gold), the IMF redefined itself in the 1970s. It began providing short-term balance of payment assistance (aid when money is flowing out of a country at unsustainable rates compared to the incoming rate) to developing countries, in exchange for their imposition of strict "structural adjustment"—budgetary and monetary programs of austerity, combined with economic deregulation. Now the Fund is carving for itself an additional role as guarantor of the private international financial system, a *de facto* insurer of loans and foreign investment to industrializing countries. The insurance comes free for lenders, but the traditional high payment of austerity measures is exacted from debtor countries having trouble repaying loans.

To fill this new function, the IMF needs more resources. During its last annual meeting, the IMF's board of governors agreed upon a 45 percent quota increase, adding $90 billion to its $200 billion budget. The U.S. share of the $90 billion is $14.5 billion.

Marijke Torfs is director of the international department at Friends of the Earth, U.S.

But even as the IMF and its U.S. allies misleadingly claim that the Asian crisis makes it urgent that the Fund quickly receive an infusion of new capital, U.S. lawmakers are raising serious questions about the IMF's lack of clear purpose, its counterproductive adjustment programs, its penchant for bailing out big international banks and its excessive secrecy. (The urgency claim is misleading because the IMF already has allocated monies to Asia from existing resources, because the IMF has plenty of capital on hand and can raise more, and because the money from quota increases would go for purposes other than financial bailouts.

The increasing volume of criticism from Congress, the mainstream media and establishment economists follows almost two decades of condemnation of IMF austerity from labor organizations, environmentalists, poverty groups, church organizations and sustainable development advocates, as well as more recent criticism from right-wing groups which denounce financial bailouts as an improper interference in the market economy. Rising criticism of the IMF is leading some IMF backers to offer to "condition" U.S. money for the Fund, and some opponents seem satisfied that conditions can satisfactorily reform the IMF. There is a decade of experience that suggests otherwise, however.

MUTED VOICE, NEGLECTED VOTE

Since 1989, Congressional approval of funding for the IMF has been linked to legislative language requiring the U.S. executive director to the IMF to use "voice and vote" in order to promote specific policy and procedural changes at the institution. In 1989, the Congress urged the U.S. executive director to promote: 1) the addition to the Fund's staff of natural resource experts and development economists trained in analyzing the linkages between macroeconomic conditions and the short- and long-term impacts on sustainable management of natural

From *Multinational Monitor*, January/February 1998, pp. 21-23. © 1998 by Essential Information, Inc. Reprinted by permission.

resources; 2) the establishment of a systematic process to review in advance, and take into account in policy formation, projected impacts of each IMF lending agreement on the long-term sustainable management of natural resources, the environment, public health and poverty; and 3) the creation of criteria to consider concessional and favorable lending terms to promote sustainable management of natural resources. This last requirement specifically refers to the reduction of the debt burden of developing countries in recognition of domestic investments in conservation and environmental management.

In 1992, the U.S. Congress passed even more comprehensive legislation demanding the U.S. executive director regularly and vigorously in program discussions and quota increase negotiations promote the following:

- Programs to alleviate poverty and reduce barriers to economic and social progress, and to incorporate environmentally sound policies into Fund-promoted government programs;
- Policy audits;
- Policy options that increase the productive participation of the poor; and
- Procedures for public access to information.

In order to prevent any ambiguity about the interpretation of these overall objectives, the 1992 legislation provides a detailed list of specific policy recommendations. Among the policy changes were:

- All IMF programs should consider poverty alleviation and the reduction of barriers to economic and social progress;
- All Policy Framework Papers (PFPs) should articulate the principal poverty, economic, and social measures that borrowing nations need to address;
- The IMF should incorporate environmental considerations in all of its programs;
- The IMF should encourage nations to implement systems of natural resource accounting in their national income accounts;
- The IMF should assist and cooperate fully with the statistical research being undertaken by the Organization of Economic Cooperation and Development and the UN in order to facilitate development and adoption of a generally applicable system for taking account of the depletion or degradation of natural resources in national income accounts;
- The IMF should conduct periodic audits of all its programs, on a country-by-country basis, to determine whether the IMF's objectives were met and to evaluate social and environmental impacts; and
- PFPs and the supporting documents prepared by the IMF's mission to a country, among other documents, should be made public at an appropriate time and in appropriate ways.

While both laws were very specific in their policy recommendations and reporting requirements, this important congressional action did not lead to any real changes of IMF operations or policies. The only noticeable shift was reflected in the IMF's managing director's rhetoric, emphasizing the importance of achieving high quality growth without hurting people or the environment in all IMF programs. The IMF also changed the job description of one of its senior economists, Ved Ghandi, to include environmental issues.

Having an environmental expert at the Fund did not benefit the environment in any discernible way, either. In fact, Ghandi's main tasks seem to focus on writing papers explaining why the IMF should not be concerned about or engaged in environmental issues. After two years of analysis, Gandhi concluded that macroeconomic stability would lead to environmental stability but that sustainable environmental management was not critical for macroeconomic stability. In other words, in a well-managed economy, the environment will take care of itself; and taking care of the environment is irrelevant to economic well-being. While Gandhi has shifted from this position, the IMF continues to support the notion that microeconomic policies, such as environmental resource management policies, do not affect the macroeconomic outlook of a country.

Two years later, the experience was replicated in the area of labor rights. In 1994, the U.S. Congress attached the Sanders-Frank Amendment to the Foreign Operations Appropriation Bill, requiring U.S. executive directors to use voice and vote to urge international financial institutions, including the IMF, to:

- Adopt policies to encourage borrowing countries to guarantee internationally recognized worker rights;
- Promote compliance with key International Labor Organization (ILO) conventions, including those guaranteeing the right of association, the right to organize and bargain collectively, prohibitions against forced labor, a minimum wage, maximum hours of work and occupational safety and health protections; and
- Establish formal procedures to screen projects and programs funded by the institutions for any negative impacts on key labor rights.

The Treasury Department was supposed to report on its progress in promoting these reforms at the international financial institutions after one year. It took almost three years for the Treasury to send its report to the Congress. Instead of explaining why the U.S. executive directors had failed to promote any of the legislative requirements, the report offered ideas on how to begin the process of implementing the Sanders-Frank amendment. For example, the report provided an outline of what a possible screening process could look like. It also cited general steps the international financial institutions have undertaken to reform labor markets as evidence of efforts to guarantee internationally recognized labor rights.

It is hard to imagine a more cynical response from the Treasury Department. "Not all labor market reforms have to do with improved labor rights," notes Terry Collingsworth, general counsel of the Washington, D.C.-based International Labor Rights Fund. "Instead, many of these reforms contribute to the denial of labor rights."

Collingsworth summarizes the report as "lacking in any real, substantive action or assessment that address the express requirements of the law."

MONEY TALKS

Something fundamentally different took place in 1994, the same year the Sanders-Frank amendment was passed, however. Frustrated with the lack of IMF responsiveness, the U.S. Congress cut the proposed $100 million U.S. contribution to the Enhanced Structural Adjustment Facility (ESAF) by $75 million.

In a conference report attached to the bill, members of Congress expressed their hope that the IMF and its member countries would work with the U.S. government to open up the IMF to more public scrutiny. Congress urged the U.S. Treasury Department to push for reform of the IMF's disclosure policies. Congress asked for the release of several IMF documents to the public including the Recent Economic Developments and program documents. Other IMF documents are owned by the countries themselves, and their publication depends on the willingness of the national government. But since most of these documents are prepared by IMF staff and are critical for understanding of Fund programs, the legislation required the IMF to strongly encourage governments to make these documents available to the public. These documents include: Article IV Consultations, Letters of Intent and Policy Framework Papers.

But the conference report did more than just urge these reforms. It strongly suggested that future funding for ESAF would be withheld until the IMF made the desired reforms. "To determine when and whether to recommend the remainder of the $100 million requested by the Administration for ESAF, consideration will be given to the progress made on the disclosure of the above information."

In contrast to all previous legislative efforts, the 1994 legislation did result in identifiable reforms. The IMF made the REDs publicly available and began posting summaries of the Article IV consultations on the Internet. IMF management also agreed, in 1997, to an independent review of ESAF programs to be conducted parallel to the IMF's own ESAF review. While the independent review has not yet been published, early statements of the reviewers have been critical and IMF management has promised to release an uncensored version of the reviewers' report.

The disclosure reforms have been progress, but not a panacea. While these documents provide a flavor of the nature of the program, even economists such as Jeffrey Sachs are unsatisfied with the progress. In one of the many editorials written by Sachs related to the Asia crisis, he states that the IMF is only paying lip service to "transparency." Sachs complains that the IMF provides virtually no substantive documentation of its decisions as the documents are shorn of the technical details needed for serious professional evaluation of the programs.

CURBING THE CASH

Many, not least those in IMF managerial positions, have criticized the legislative strategy to change the IMF. Opponents argue that the IMF is a multilateral institution which has to reflect the priorities of all its member countries. It is not appropriate, the argument runs, to use the U.S. legislative process to open up the IMF to public scrutiny or to force it to deal with social and environmental issues.

Unfortunately, the IMF has not given the public any other choice. People in borrowing countries do not have the same opportunity to influence the Fund, and neither do their elected governments.

Meaningful public participation in shaping borrowing country programs is currently not possible. The IMF's Articles of Agreement state that IMF mission people shall only interact with representatives from finance ministries or central banks. Even if finance ministries allow public consultation, crucial details of IMF programs remain confidential. With limited knowledge of the program details, the population in borrower countries—the ones to [be] affected by IMF-imposed policies—cannot seriously participate in policy formation. In most cases, even national parliaments have little choice but to "endorse" an IMF agreement without serious discussion, input or understanding of the programs.

The enormous leverage of the IMF over democratic institutions in borrowing countries was made plain in South Korea's presidential elections late last year, as the Fund insisted that all presidential candidates endorse the IMF bailout agreement.

In the United States, but also in a growing number of other industrialized countries, the public does have a voice in and can affect policy decisions of their governments. The United States is one of the few countries that offers public hearings on the operations of all mutilateral institutions financed by the public. During these hearings, non-governmental organizations (NGOs) from around the world have testified about the devastating impact of IMF programs. At the request of U.S. members of Congress, NGOs have provided input in the development of IMF reform language. These IMF reform initiatives reflect the concerns of people around the world.

If the IMF would provide serious avenues of communication with the public, perhaps advocacy groups would not have to resort to the legislative strategy of denying the Fund money. Until then, curbing the cash is the only way the public can be heard.

Unit Selections

Key Points to Consider

❖ Doing business outside the United States is different from doing business inside. In what ways is the foreign environment different from the domestic environment?

❖ Political risk has always been a part of international business. What approaches are North American multinationals using to deal with these risks?

❖ What has been the effect of international trade on labor?

 **Links**   **www.dushkin.com/online/**

These sites are annotated on pages 4 and 5.

For centuries most American businesses focused on the domestic markets. There were many reasons for this. The first was that during the 1800s the United States was probably the most rapidly developing country in the world, a huge continental market, limited only by the Atlantic and Pacific Oceans. This was true until the end of World War I, when the United States, for the first time, became the world's leading industrial nation. But distances between countries seemed greater than they do today, and communication was not as swift or sure. In addition, most Americans tended to have at least a partially isolationist outlook on the world. There were exceptions, notably in mining, agricultural commodities, and oil. The time between World Wars I and II was also marked by the worldwide Great Depression of 1929–1939. After World War II, the United States stood alone as the great industrial power. It was not really until the 1970s that the United States received notice, in the form of the first gasoline crisis, that its position in world economics had changed.

While many U.S. firms did extensive business outside the country, in the early 1970s these arrangements represented only about 6 percent of the total business in the United States. But, by the end of the 1980s, this figure was close to 33 percent. This means that nondomestic business activity matters greatly to U.S. companies. What goes on in Europe and the Pacific Rim has a direct impact on what happens on Wall Street as well as Main Street, U.S.A.

Doing business outside the United States is different from doing business within the country. First of all, there is the monetary problem. Every country has a different currency, banking system, and regulations affecting the financial system. Currency fluctuations can play havoc with the assets and profits of a firm.

Economic and socioeconomic forces also play a role. While the cold war is over and the United States and its allies won, it does not mean that doing business in Singapore is just like doing business in Denver. True, with a few minor exceptions such as Cuba and North Korea, capitalism is rapidly becoming the preferred method of organizing an economy. However, that organization will not necessarily be a clone of the system in the United States. There will be Indonesian capitalism, Chilean capitalism, and Hungarian capitalism, just as there is American capitalism, British capitalism, and Japanese capitalism. Each system will be based on the same general principles, but each will be different, with its own unique twists.

One factor that is going to have tremendous impact on international trade is the need to develop infrastructure in the developing world, and to maintain appropriate infrastructure in the developed world. Asia alone is expected to have over $1 trillion in infrastructure needs in the foreseeable future. Add to this the maintenance and modernization needs of the developed world, plus Latin America and Africa, and it is clear that there will surely be no shortage of work for contractors and engineers who are willing to go into these markets.

Among the fascinating aspects of the global environment are the differences in culture and ideas, as well as the many similarities. Human beings have a wide variety of answers to seemingly mundane, everyday questions. Customs and culture often play a role in how successful organizations will be when dealing in a foreign market. What may be rude and offensive in one society may be accepted or even expected behavior in another. Understanding these differences and why they are important can be the key to success in any market. "Can Multinational Businesses Agree on How to Act Ethically?" And if so, what will they come up with?

The political environment also plays an important role in international trade. Some countries are more politically stable than others. Nationalization of foreign assets is not unheard of, and corporations have little or no recourse when their assets are suddenly appropriated by the government. History teaches that this is a real risk. Learning to analyze and deal with this risk is something that multinationals have to do, as discussed by Robert Samuelson in "Trade Free or Die."

The laws of many nations when dealing with world trade are in the process of developing. Industries are now international in scope. The world is a market for small, as well as large, businesses. Illegal business practices are being identified because their cost is huge. Different laws in different countries concerning the same issues can contribute to confusion and misunderstanding, as discussed in "Antitrust Regulation across National Borders."

Labor is another important aspect of the trade environment. Different countries have different attitudes and rules concerning labor and its relationship to the economy, government, and corporations. For example, in the United States it is common for the relationship between labor and management to be adversarial, while in Germany, representatives from the labor unions often sit on the boards of their employers. The only thing that is certain about labor is that workers now compete in an international environment. No country has a corner on highly skilled labor, and if workers are going to be competitive in the future, they must have the skills necessary to succeed in the worldwide labor market. Some governments actually support some of the less than ethical business practices of some organizations, as may be seen in "Wanted: Muscle." The consequence of the global economy on labor is also discussed in "Global Economy, Local Mayhem?"

Finally, the environment for international trade will be highly competitive. Global markets mean global competitors and global standards. Successful organizations are the ones that can change and adapt to meet the competition. Not being able to change will, by definition, spell disaster for any organization. Flexibility and adaptability, instead, will be the keys to effectiveness in the coming world business environment.

INTERNATIONAL
MONETARY
ARRANGEMENTS

Is There a Monetary Union in Asia's Future?

BARRY EICHENGREEN

During 1995–96 the yen-dollar exchange rate endured a cycle of violent fluctuation. From 100 yen at the beginning of 1995 the dollar fell to 80 yen in April. At that point worried central bankers in Japan, the United States, and Europe intervened and halted the dollar's decline. The U.S. currency then trended sharply upward, most recently breaching the 120-yen barrier in late January. Concern for the strength of the yen was replaced by worries about its weakness: alarm grew that an undervalued yen would fan conflict over the U.S.-Japan current account balance and make life difficult for Japanese firms that import components from East Asian suppliers.

There is no question that this cycle created problems for both the Japanese and U.S. economies. It discouraged international trade by forcing firms to hedge exchange risk by purchasing "cover" in the forward market. And it created special difficulties for a Japan seeking to restructure and streamline a depressed economy. An exchange rate of ¥80 intensified the pressure on Japanese exporters of manufactures. The problems experienced by the tradables sector deepened the distress of financial institutions holding claims on manufacturing firms. The economy's deflationary crisis was thus compounded by the yen's appreciation in

Barry Eichengreen is professor of economics and political science at the University of California, Berkeley. This article is adapted from the introduction to the Japanese translation of his International Monetary Arrangements for the 21st Century (published in English by Brookings in 1994).

1995. And while depreciation in 1996 relieved the domestic profit squeeze, the yen's volatility complicated investment planning. Japanese producers may be discouraged from developing sustainable outsourcing strategies and shifting production to other parts of East Asia. The sudden improvement in competitiveness may distract producers and policymakers from the search for a permanent solution to the structural problems of the Japanese economy.

Looking for a Quick Fix

The 1995–96 yen-dollar dustup elicited the predictable demands for international monetary reform. If the major industrialized countries that make up the Group of 7 could only agree to establish a new system of pegged-but-adjustable currencies or exchange rate target zones, observers argued, these painful exchange rate fluctuations could be avoided. And if the seven could not reach agreement as a group, then the countries whose currencies were being affected should establish a bilateral target zone. Thus, we have heard repeated calls for the establishment of a target zone for the yen-dollar rate or a common basket peg, surrounded by fluctuation bands of plus-and-minus 10 percent, for nine East Asian currencies (those of China, Hong Kong, Indonesia, Korea, Malaysia, the Philippines, Singapore, Taiwan, and Thailand).

The matter, unfortunately, is not so simple. Stabilizing exchange rates by establishing a new system of pegs, bands, or target zones would require significant compromises of domestic policy autonomy. Intervention by central banks is effective only if it sends credible signals of future shifts in monetary and fiscal policies—that is, when there is no conflict between domestic and international economic policies.

But in today's world, conflicts between domestic and international economic objectives are inevitable. The removal of controls on international capital movements and the development of modern information-processing technologies over the past several decades permit billions of dollars to be traded across borders at the stroke of a key. The domestic policy independence that capital controls once afforded national monetary and fiscal authorities has become a thing of the past. Currency traders, no longer limited by controls, are free to attack an exchange rate as soon as they begin to suspect that the government is less than totally committed to defending it—a practice that can greatly increase the cost of defending the currency peg. With the end of the Cold War and the disintegration of dominant political coalitions in countries like Italy and Japan, governments are necessarily fragile and hesitant to put the domestic economy through the wringer to defend the exchange rate at any cost. Weak governments find it infeasible to pursue the international economic policies needed to maintain a durable currency peg.

Thus schemes to peg the dollar, the yen, and the deutsche mark against one another, as had been the practice until the Bretton Woods international monetary system collapsed in the early 1970s, will prove unavailing. Exchange rates between these currencies will continue to float against each other.

> Monetary unification banishes exchange rate volatility by abolishing the exchange rate. But it requires the participants to share responsibility for their common monetary policy.

prepared to take drastic steps to limit exchange rate volatility. In some cases they have done so by replacing their central banks with currency boards. This approach has been used by countries with exceptional problems with inflation and financial stability, such as Argentina and Estonia. A parliamentary statute or constitutional amendment requires the board to tie the domestic currency to that of a major trading partner. Argentina's currency board can issue a dollar's worth of currency only when acquiring a dollar of reserves, effectively pegging the peso-dollar exchange rate at one to one. Currency traders do not question the monetary authorities' commitment to the currency peg, since the latter are required by law to defend it. But a currency board leaves the monetary authority little leeway to act as a lender of last resort in the event of problems in the banking system. And once the inflationary crisis has passed, countries find it hard to eliminate their currency board and reacquire monetary flexibility without exciting fears of a return to the bad old days. A person with an overeating disorder may be inclined to padlock the refrigerator and throw away the key, but he may regret the extremity of the step once starvation sets in.

Another solution to the problem of exchange rate instability is a monetary union, like that the members of the European Union are currently seeking to establish. Monetary unification banishes exchange rate volatility by abolishing the exchange rate. But it requires the participants to share responsibility for their common monetary policy. Conveniently for the small open economies of Europe, the larger partner they wish to join in monetary union, Germany, may be prepared to compromise its monetary autonomy in return for reacquiring a foreign policy role in the context of a European Union foreign policy.

Small Countries, Big Problem

For the United States and Japan, large countries that remain relatively closed to international transactions, this arrangement, while painful, is bearable. For small open economies, where a larger share of production is typically sold on international markets, the dislocations caused by exchange rate swings can be excruciating. Because the financial sector is small relative to global financial markets, a shift in market sentiment or in interest rates in the United States can elicit a flood of capital inflows that leads to a dramatic real appreciation or massive outflows that cause the exchange rate to depreciate alarmingly.

Whether these small open economies are in Europe, Latin America, or East Asia, they find it exceedingly difficult to live with exchange rate fluctuations. They are thus

A Single Asian Currency?

The question for the 21st century is whether analogous monetary blocs will form in East Asia (and, for that matter, in the Western Hemisphere). With the dollar, the yen, and the single European currency floating against one another, other small open economies will be tempted to link up to one of the three. But the linkage will be possible only if accompanied by radical changes in institutional arrangements like those contemplated by the European Union. The spread of capital mobility and political democratization will make it prohibitively difficult to peg exchange rates unilaterally. Pegging will require international cooperation, and effective cooperation will require measures akin to monetary unification.

The day when the countries of East Asia including Japan will be prepared to create a single Asian currency (or, for that matter, when the countries of the Western Hemisphere are prepared to join the United States in a monetary union) remains far away. The political preconditions for monetary unification are not in place. Operating a monetary union requires some pooling of political responsibility. History provides very different prospects for this in Western Europe and East Asia. Proponents of European integration can trace their antecedents back for hundreds of years. Jeremy Bentham advocated a European assembly, Jean-Jacques Rousseau a European federation, Henri Saint-Simon a European monarch and parliament. By the middle of the 19th century, intellectuals like Victor Hugo could speak of a United States of Europe. In the 1920s, the Pan-European Union lobbied for a European federation and attracted the support of Aristide Briand and Edouard Herriot, future premiers of France. Konrad Adenauer and Georges Pompidou, two leaders of the postwar process of European integration, were members of the Pan-European Union. The ideal of European integration is intimately connected with the liberal and democratic principles of the European Enlightenment and has roots in centuries of European history.

East Asia, in contrast, lacks a comparable tradition of political solidarity. It lacks a Jean Monet or Paul Henri Spaak to speak for regional integration. In part this reflects the ideological distance between China's communist government and market-oriented regimes elsewhere in East Asia. By contrast, in postwar Western Europe, variants of the social market economy were embraced by virtually all the members of the present-day European Union.

At a deeper level, East Asia lacks a Benthamite-Rousseauian-Saint Simonian heritage of collective democratic governance through integration. As Peter Katzenstein puts it, "the notion of unified sovereignty . . .central to the conception of continental European states, does not capture Asian political realities." Not only in China do the regions resist the attempts of the center to exercise its political will through the operation of political and legal institutions. The idea of a centralized state with a monopoly of force that regiments its citizens through the superimposition of a common set of institutions is a European conception, not an Asian one. Asian civil society is structured by ritual, ceremony, and economic networks as much as by force and law.

Consequently, integrationist initiatives in Asia have proceeded not through the creation of strong supranational institutions but by establishing loose networks of cooperation. It is revealing that the Asia Pacific Economic Cooperation forum, which is essentially just a consultative body, has succeeded where initiatives to create smaller, more cohesive Asian analogues to the European Economic Community or the European Free Trade Association have not.

Gazing far into the 21st century, one can imagine the development of a single Asian currency analogous to the Euro, the prospective single European currency. In a world of open international capital markets and politicized domestic policy settings, that will be the only alternative to floating exchange rates. As the economies of East Asia grow still more open and interdependent, pressure will build to work toward this goal. But as yet the political preconditions are not in place. An Asian monetary union is at best a very distant prospect.

Asia Sets a New Challenge

Knowledge and technology are making clients far more demanding

Henny Sender

Hong Kong

It used to be that private banking evoked images of vast sums of money discreetly passed to Swiss bankers over cups of tea. The recipients, the fabled gnomes of Zurich, would then be expected to manage it on a discretionary basis, placing it in the most conservative investments in the safest harbours. Preservation of principal was as sacred a creed as confidentiality. And once a year, the client would receive a report, once again over tea, and the reassurance that his money was still safe.

Private banking has changed a lot. About the only thing that the traditional image has in common with the way private banking is done today is the tea, secrecy and the adherence to the belief that clients are unhappy when they lose a part of what they hand over. Private banking is now hi-tech. It's all about the latest structured products: complicated derivatives strategies that enable clients to place bets on any financial instrument in the world. And if they want to exchange a bit of the upside for a guarantee that their principal is protected, that's fine too.

Client contact has moved far from the genteel, infrequent chats of the past as well. Now private bankers have to carry mobile phones; on stormy days in the markets, they can expect calls inquiring about the value of positions on an hourly basis. Clients may be interested in long-term relations, but their preference these days is for short-term products. "Every month, I have to come up with new products," says F. W. Wong at Citibank in Hong Kong. "The time horizons are getting shorter."

Conversations with the new generation of private bankers such as Wong or HSBC's Kenneth Sit require calculators and a fine mind. The talk is of such arcane products as market-linked deposits, contingent premium currency options and convertible money-market units. "They know all the products," says Wong. "What they want is the best price. They want information, but never blind advice."

To be sure, there is still the rainy-day money, the funds that guarantee security. Banks like BZW still pride themselves on the more traditional approach. One of Austrian-based Creditanstalt's main comparative advantages is that Austria still has banking secrecy laws. But more and more, it's entertainment as much as security that clients seek, according to Paul Giles, head of private banking at Creditanstalt in Hong Kong—entertainment and leverage.

Traditionally, the European private banks sold service and discretion. Now that private banking is more the province of the giants, it is about products and lending clients the money to double their bets. Smaller banks can't really play the game any more.

The enthusiasm for taking bets has only been partially qualified by adverse experience. In 1994, many private investors were badly hurt when the United States Federal Reserve raised interest rates, notes Chew Mee Foo Kirtland, a managing director with Chase Manhattan Private Bank in Singapore. Since, then, she says, "Principal protection and managing the risk of capital erosion has become much more important."

The leader in this transformation of the business is Citibank. As with other areas such as retail, Citi has used its technology to design products and trades that can be applied worldwide. And it has brought them to Asia with flawless timing, just when the second generation of the region's wealthy families was coming back from the U.S. with their MBAs and a familiarity with hi-tech finance.

Clients all over the globe have their own preferences. Europeans tend to like bonds and are more obsessed with preservation of capital. Americans are generally uncomfortable with currencies. But Asians have a view on everything—just as long as the returns are there.

"Our clients have created wealth," says Paul Brown, chief executive for Asia at Barclays Private Banking. "They are less interested in discretionary management. They do their own asset allocation; they make their own calls."

Private banking is big business in Asia—and becoming bigger. It still clings to the image of secrecy, though. Except for bragging that all customers have to satisfy the bankers on their sources of funds (to dispel charges of money laundering), bankers prefer to maintain their usual discretion on such matters as the size of money under management.

Three years ago, Chase Manhattan did its own survey and concluded that the size of the Asian market was $650 billion. But during the past three years, most private bankers in the region say their asset sizes have doubled or even tripled.

In any case, since private banking is a perverse business, it thrives on political risk. There are plenty of Asian capitals where political jitters are on the rise, and such tremors reach the private bankers first. Even in islands of stability, such as Japan, prospects are becoming brighter.

Tokyo used to be the most sterile of locations for private bankers. High taxes meant that private banking was more the fiefdom of accountants than bankers. The Ministry of

HONG KONG
Questions of Trust

When Li Ka-shing established a Cayman Islands trust not long ago, many of the territory's private bankers gave a collective sigh of relief. For years the community has hesitated to bring up the subject of trusts with their Hong Kong clients. To do so was to allude to two of the Great Unmentionables: mortality and the even more delicate subject of ceding control.

"In the West, people are prepared to talk mortality," says Jonathan Hubbard, executive vice-president of HSBC International Trustees' Hong Kong branch. "But here, they dance around the issue."

The dancing is now getting less circular, though. There are a number of reasons for both the delay and the sudden popularity of the device.

For one thing, trusts are a convenient way to help minimize taxes. But in Hong Kong, unlike virtually everywhere else in the world, taxes have never been a problem. Precisely because the taxes here are so reasonable, there was never a reason to try to put ownership of assets either here or elsewhere anywhere else. "Hong Kong has always been such an *easy* place to hold domestic assets," says Hubbard summarily.

No longer. As 1997 approaches, the jitters which may not always be apparent on the surface of money-driven Hong Kong are beginning to be picked up by the delicate antennae of private bankers. Political protection is becoming a concern.

No legal document in the world can offer immutable protection for assets located in Hong Kong. But more and more private bankers report that clients are considering transferring ownership of overseas assets out of Hong Kong via trusts. If ownership of overseas assets is transferred," adds Hubbard, "no future government can interfere."

In addition, friendly Hong Kong also allows local assets to be held through offshore trusts; in other Asian jurisdictions, such as Indonesia or the Philippines, Hubbard points out, property can only be held onshore.

It isn't only politics which is driving the new popularity of trusts. There are personal factors as well: Wealth is being inherited now from those who generated it, and frequently their heirs understand the benefits of financial planning.

"Here people sit on money," says Thomas Petrig, senior representative for Union Bancaire Privee in Hong Kong. "There are cases where the person has passed away and nobody knows where the money is."

Then of course, this being Asia, the question of inheritance is almost as delicate as that of control. The family structure is frequently more complicated; there are second families, lovers, offspring to be provided for. And there are relatives who are most emphatically *not* to be provided for. "If you don't like your son-in-law, say," he adds, "trusts are a good way to have him out of the picture."

Petrig notes that trusts can minimize family disputes because they are harder to overturn than wills. Moreover, trusts also provide for confidentiality for the most complicated relationships; wills, in contrast, are a matter of public record.

Not everyone is a champion of the idea, though. Some private bankers recommend private family companies, say in the British Virgin Islands, instead. "No public record. Cheap and cheerful," says Paul Giles, head of private banking for Creditanstalt in Hong Kong. "Trusts are unpopular. When you talk about the idea of a trustee, and explain that they have to pass title of the factory in Kowloon or the house on the Peak to the trustee, they cease being receptive to the idea."

There is also the worry that courts may overturn trusts. In Hong Kong, for example, dependents have the right to claim benefits from the estate regardless of the disposition of assets in the trust.

If the clients are jittery, how about the bankers themselves? Hubbard estimates that only about 10% of his clients want to move their account administration from Hong Kong. But for Giles at Creditanstalt, the proportion is almost reversed.

Private bankers have always understood paranoia. It is at the heart of their business. "Our Hong Kong-domiciled accounts are going down rapidly," he says. "By next year, less than 10% will be here."

Henny Sender

Finance has always thrown a disconcerting wall of regulations around the business, with an eye, say the private bankers, to discouraging it.

The idea was that good Japanese don't send their money abroad—and the reality was that, even if they did, they were likely to lose it as the yen appreciated anyway. But now foreigners have new freedom with which to seek business in Japan, and old notions that private banking somehow undermined patriotism are beginning to fade—though slowly. Stephen Church, director of private banking at Lazard Japan Asset Management, is targeting his marketing efforts at potential clients in the Kansai area around Osaka, where attitudes have long been more open-minded than in the tradition-bound capital.

Asia has more and more of the world's wealth. Private banking is now part of the rising banker's career path. And Asia, in short, is reshaping the way the rest of the world thinks about the business.

Africa's New Dawn

High risk and lack of credit make trade financing in sub-Saharan Africa difficult to obtain. But short-term loans through commercial banks and long-term investment funds are growing as its markets develop.

By G. Alisha Davis

When businesspeople think of Africa, they are likely to recall images of Rwandan refugees fleeing civil war, rather than the bold strides many governments are making in liberalizing their economies. Even when they do associate business with the continent, their perception tends to be an area with high risks and low—or at least unimpressive—rates of return.

Many foreign firms, particularly US companies, consider Africa their lowest-priority business region, or ignore it altogether. Even many multilateral banks, traditionally the most active financial institutions on the continent, are backing away. Africa, perhaps the area that needs it most,

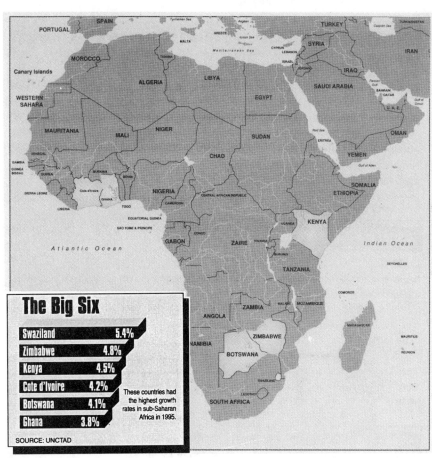

The Big Six

Swaziland	5.4%
Zimbabwe	4.8%
Kenya	4.5%
Cote d'Ivoire	4.2%
Botswana	4.1%
Ghana	3.8%

These countries had the highest growth rates in sub-Saharan Africa in 1995.

SOURCE: UNCTAD

is the only place where lending by regional multilateral development banks is declining, falling from $5.2 billion in 1994 to $4.8 billion in 1995.

"When Americans look out across Asia and Latin America, they see potential trading partners. When they look out across sub-Saharan Africa, they see potential aid recipients," said the late Commerce Secretary Ronald H. Brown as he opened trading at the stock exchange in Abidjan, Cote d'Ivoire, during the five-country tour of the continent he conducted last year to promote US trade and investment. "That view has to change."

Although sub-Saharan Africa cannot match the booming "Asian tiger" economies of the Far East in attracting foreign investment, observers say it is not a market to be ignored. If businesspeople take a closer look, they will find that, in addition to South Africa, which attracts the lion's share of investment, lesser-known countries such as Zimbabwe, Kenya,

The Ten Largest Sub-Saharan African Stock Exchanges

Country	Exchange Established	Local Currency	# Of Listed Stocks	Established Stock Mkt. Capitalization
Botswana	1989	PULA	12	338
Cote d'Ivoire	1976	CFA Franc	26	520
Ghana	1990	CEDI	20	1,943
Kenya	1955	Kenyan Shilling	54	1,770
Mauritius	1989	Rupee	45	1,520
Nigeria	1960	Naira	180	1,300 (est.)
South Africa	1887	Rand	637	243,000
Swaziland	1990	Lilange ni	4	330
Zambia	1994	Zambia Kwacha	8	222
Zimbabwe	1946	Zim Dollar	76	3,900

SOURCE: FCA CORP.

Where We're Spending Our Money

US Foreign Direct Investment in Sub-Saharan Africa (in millions)

Country	1983	1994	1995
South Africa	$900	$1,013	$1,269
Nigeria	478	322	595
Cameroon	253	228	258
Liberia	181	197	229
Kenya	104	134	190
Ghana	117	143	170
Zimbabwe	127	144	150

SOURCE: BUREAU OF ECONOMIC ANALYSIS

Botswana and Cote d'Ivoire provide attractive investment opportunities.

"Investment in Africa is still incredibly risky," observes Jill Insley, a financial analyst at ABN-AMCO in San Francisco. "But, as with all new markets, the opportunities are very good as well."

Many Asian firms are already finding that out; the continent is attracting increasing amounts of aid, trade and investment in transportation, telecommunications and energy from the Far East and Arab Middle East.

Banking On Success

Deciding you want to invest in or export to Africa is easy. Getting the money to finance your project is another matter. International lending has changed dramatically during the past decade due to many OECD governments and large companies migrating to bond markets. Bank facilities, however, still prevail for financing in Africa where, in many cases, bonds are not yet a viable option because of the high perceived risk in the region.

"Exploring financing opportunities within sub-Saharan Africa is something you don't take lightly," warns Ken Bruce, director of the trade underwriting desk at Pryor, McClendon, Counts & Co., a Philadelphia, PA, investment banking firm that has been active in trade finance to Africa since 1985, making it a veteran in a region that is only recently seeing investment activity. "There will be successes, and there will be failures."

One of the biggest problems US businesses face in initiating trade with Africa is financing—namely, a lack of credit and risk protection. Larger firms that invest in Africa, such as Coca-Cola, General Motors and AT&T, have the available cash required for equity financing, but small and midsize companies face the difficult task of raising the money.

"The first wall these companies run into is the Export-Import Bank of the United States," states Mr. Bruce. Due to government-wide policy decisions concerning the credit-worthiness of many African countries, legislative prohibitions and various repayment issues, the Ex-Im Bank is prohibited from providing trade financing for US exports to most African nations.

As for commercial banks, many are not active in sub-Saharan Africa, and those that are place significant restrictions on loans. "We have a big overhang of debt that many of the [African] governments owe us, so we are not increasing our per-country exposure on a long-term basis," notes Maurice Johnson, a vice president at Citicorp in New York. Last year, Mr. Johnson founded Citicorp's Africa Trade Finance Facility, which provides nonrecourse financing for US exports to Africa. "Our activity in the region is pretty much limited to

short-term financing. Almost everything is done on confirmed letters of credit, and virtually everything is short-term unless you've got export credit agency support."

Types Of Financing

Although many banks are hesitant, it is possible to get financing in sub-Saharan Africa. For example, the Ghana Cocoa Board, a state-owned organization based in Accra that oversees cocoa exports, secured im-

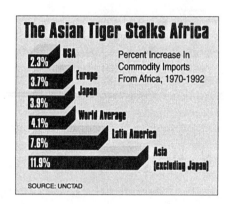

The Asian Tiger Stalks Africa

Percent Increase In Commodity Imports From Africa, 1970-1992

USA	2.3%
Europe	3.7%
Japan	3.9%
World Average	4.1%
Latin America	7.6%
Asia (excluding Japan)	11.9%

SOURCE: UNCTAD

proved terms in September from international commercial banks on its $275 million trade finance facility, ranking it one of the biggest African pre-export financing deals on the syndicated loan market. A total of 43 banks, including Citibank International, Sumitomo Bank and Rabobank International, participated in the deal.

Regional Lending By Development Banks
(percent change, 1989 to 1993)

Latin America	40%
Middle East/ North Africa	30%
Asia	15%
Sub-Saharan Africa	-20%

SOURCE: DEVELOPMENT BANK ASSOCIATION, INC.

"It definitely shows that for deals where the financial structure is not weakened, banks are willing to see [profit] margins continue to fall," says Robert Halcrow, head of syndications at Rabobank International in London.

Most banks like Citicorp require a trade letter of credit issued by the importer's bank on behalf of the importer and advised by the exporter's bank in favor of the exporter. Another option is a bill of exchange, essentially a promissory note or invoice signed by both parties involved in the trade

and, usually, a bank. The exporter can obtain financing by discounting the bill with a bank for an amount equal to the face value of the bill less interest costs and fees.

Bills of exchange that are guaranteed by a bank can also be negotiated in the forfeiting markets. In Africa, forfeit receivables almost always consist of deferred payments under letters of credit. According to ABN-AMCO's Ms. Insley, amounts typically range from $1 million to $50 million, and maturities range from one year or less (short-term) for most of sub-Saharan Africa, to two years in Ghana, Kenya and Zimbabwe, three to five years in North Africa and up to eight years in South Africa.

Factoring is similar to forfeiting because it involves assignment by an exporter of receivables on a non-recourse basis against an advance payment. Mr. Johnson explains that the process at Citicorp can involve reassigning receivables to a correspondent factor agency in the importer's country, which pays the exporter and then collects payment from the importer.

If, for example, a US company wanted to export goods to Africa, it would ship the goods and then sell the invoice to a third-party factoring agency for less than the full value. Thus, the exporter would be assured of immediate payment, and the factoring agency would assume the risk, much as in forfeiting. Unlike forfeiting, however, factoring does not require a bank guarantee, can be used by small exporters and covers small amounts and maturities.

Although Africa has not yet been active in the $20 billion international factoring market, Andre Ryba, a senior banking official with the World Bank in Washington, DC, predicts the region will become far more important in the next century as an

Sub-Saharan African countries in which Ex-Im Bank support is not available:

Angola, Burkina Faso, Burundi, Cameroon, Central African Republic, Chad, Congo, Djibouti, Equatorial Guinea, Gambia, Guinea-Bissau, Liberia, Madagascar, Malawi, Mali, Mozambique, Niger, Nigeria, Rwanda, Sao Tome & Principe, Senegal, Sierra Leone, Somalia, Sudan, Tanzania, Togo, Zaire and Zambia

SOURCE: EXPORT-IMPORT BANK OF THE US

arena for trade and investment. When this happens, the foreign firms that have patiently expanded their roles and developed regional knowledge bases and marketing networks from years of trial and error will be in the best position to exploit Africa's economic opportunities.

Funding Through Funds

Many international fund managers are beginning to see just that. In the past few years, Africa has been home to some of the world's top performing stock markets. A number of investment houses have responded by launching Africa-specific funds. They include Morgan Stanley's Africa Investment Fund, Baring Asset Management's Simba Fund and Regent's Undervalued Assets Fund. In December 1995, the Simba Fund raised $30 million, which, although short of the $50 million hoped for, indicates the new interest in African stocks.

"The fund is looking for long-term growth for stocks in Africa and is aimed at export-oriented companies," explains Iban Ortuzar, investment analyst at London-based Baring Asset Management. "This is an attempt to avoid any possibility of losses due to exchange controls through currency devaluations."

The spread of the Simba Fund illustrates how uneven private investment in Africa is as a whole. South Africa receives the majority of investment, with 40 percent of the portfolio; Central, West and North Africa receive 10 percent each and East Africa gets only 5 percent.

"When people talk about investing in Africa, I think 80 percent of them really mean South Africa," says Tew Jones, research director at Fund Research, a consulting firm in London. "But there are 25 other African stock markets, too."

Mr. Tew argues that because of the economic changes many African governments have made in the past decade, Africa is now ripe for private and foreign investment. "In the past, [there were] essentially socialist governments, [which instituted] high protective tariffs that were not conducive to investment and economic growth. That is changing," he explains. "Today, you are looking at governments that have grasped the nettle of capital investment as a means of driving their economies forward and making them grow."

But not everyone predicts as bright a future for African economies as the analysts selling funds to investors. Most banks still offer only short-term financing; long-term funds for private investment, although gaining steam, have yet to explode. The fact is, Africa continues to become more marginalized in the global economy. With varying degrees of enthusiasm, many African governments have readied themselves for foreign investment, but little change will take place until the rest of the world catches on. Many Middle Eastern and Asian countries are waking up to the opportunities in Africa. European and US companies would do well to remember the early bird gets the worm.

Global Transfer Of Critical Capabilities

Henry P. Conn and George S. Yip

Effective human resource processes and other means, coupled with hard work, help transfer the capabilities so crucial to the success of foreign operations.

In the last decade or so, multinational companies from around the world have eagerly embraced globalization and have striven to develop and implement worldwide strategy By now we all know how difficult this process is. Numerous barriers stand in the way of successful globalization. Some companies, however, have been spectacularly successful in taking their proven approach and replicating it across a range of markets. Examples include Toyota and Motorola worldwide, Disney in Japan, and, more recently, IKEA in Europe and the United States. Some companies have kept certain core aspects of their approach and significantly modified other aspects to suit local positioning; McDonald's in Asia Pacific (with common business systems but cuisine adjusted to local tastes) and Sears, Roebuck & Co. in Mexico (upscale image relative to mass merchant positioning in the U.S.) attest to this. Nevertheless, the business press is replete with examples of companies that have stumbled badly in transferring an approach proven in one market to other markets—Disney in Europe, Volkswagen in the U.S., and numerous companies in Japan, to name only a few.

Establishing, supporting, and leveraging foreign ventures is the essential building block in the globalization process. Yet failure can be more common than success, particularly in really tough markets such as Japan and China. In this article, we report that the effective international transfer of critical capabilities constitutes the single most important determinant of foreign venture success. We draw this conclusion from a study of the experiences of 35 major multinational corporations (MNCs) in establishing 120 foreign operations. We also discuss the means for achieving successful transfer of critical capabilities, focusing mainly on the role of global human resource processes.

Much has been written about how to go about developing and compensating managers to compete globally. Our study is, however, one of the first to make the statistical link between effective global human resource processes and superior corporate performance.

Variations In The Performance Of Foreign Operations

What causes some companies to succeed in globalization and others to fail, particularly at the level of foreign operations and subsidiaries? To investigate this and other questions, we structured our research using the framework in **Figure 1.** Industry globalization drivers, such as internationally common customer needs, global scale economies, barriers to trade, and global competitive threats, influence the worldwide strategy companies try to implement, as well as the organizational structures they adopt to enable that strategy. The automobile and computer industries, for example, face much stronger globalization drivers than most segments of the food or apparel industries. And strategy and organization reinforce each other in their effects. Witness Asea Brown Boveri, whose ac-

From *Business Horizons,* January/February 1997, pp. 22-31. © 1997 by the Foundation for the School of Business at Indiana University. Reprinted by permission.

claimed use of global strategy depends on its careful structuring of head office and subsidiary roles.

But however good the strategy and organizational structure, other key factors—particularly critical capabilities, people, management processes, and culture—intervene to affect implementation. The path to superior performance lies through these gatekeepers, which can accelerate, slow, or even derail the journey.

The Role of Critical Capabilities

We suspected that the effective transfer of critical capabilities would be a major contributor to success. These capabilities (sometimes called core competencies) are now widely recognized as essential to competitive advantage. In globalizing, therefore, MNCs need to be able to transfer the most critical capabilities within and between their networks of international operations.

McDonalds' tremendous overseas success has been built on the corporation's ability to rapidly transfer to foreign entrepreneurs the capability of operating the entire, complex McDonalds' business system. Hong Kong's luxury hotel chains—The Peninsula Group, The Regent, and Mandarin Oriental—are in the process of a similar transfer as they expand globally. Although the hotels have attained success in the rest of Asia rather quickly, winning over the United States has been tougher. But at least one transfer has succeeded: In fewer than four years since start-up, the Peninsula in Beverly Hills, California has established itself as perhaps the premier hotel in all the Los Angeles area. This success springs in great part from the Peninsula's ability to transfer the right critical capabilities, especially its immaculate service, while adding other local requirements, such as a "stare-and-be-stared-at" swimming pool setup complete with cabanas for Hollywood negotiations.

In the automotive sector, exchange rate volatility and local content considerations have driven many Japanese manufacturers to push once "sacred" value-added design/development activities into their foreign market subsidiaries. Nissan, Toyota, and Honda have all pursued strategies whereby major elements of vehicle development are performed by in-country design teams. For those procedures that remain centralized, such as body engineering, there is heavy cross-fertilization of ideas resulting from temporary staff transfers as well as shared computer databases and telecommunications linkages.

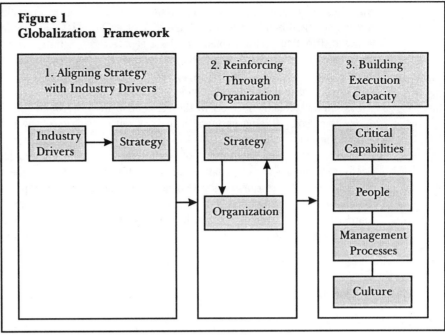

Figure 1
Globalization Framework

1. Aligning Strategy with Industry Drivers
   - Industry Drivers → Strategy
2. Reinforcing Through Organization
   - Strategy → Organization
3. Building Execution Capacity
   - Critical Capabilities
   - People
   - Management Processes
   - Culture

In much the same way, aerospace manufacturers Boeing and McDonnell-Douglas have increasingly shifted value-added design and manufacturing work to "alliance" partners. This process, known as "offset" (in which partner design/manufacturing resource expenditures are offset, or used as payment for project equity commitments), is largely the result of efforts by the air-frame manufacturers to defray the enormous expense of developing new aircraft and to favorably influence potential foreign customers (hoping, for instance, that JAL, ANA, and JAS will be more inclined to purchase from them if Kawasaki Heavy Industries has a significant level of design and manufacturing effort in the project). Typically, the foreign venture partner is most interested in receiving exactly the critical process/technology skills that a company such as Boeing designates as proprietary. However this issue is resolved, the success of the project rests on Boeing transferring the required skills and process knowledge to the foreign partner.

Defining Critical Capabilities

In our experience with clients and research participants, we have found the concept of "core competencies" to be ill-understood in practice—despite extensive academic discussion on the topic in recent years. Are core competencies "things we do well"? Activities that are unique to the company? Sources of competitive advantage? Some examples can illustrate the difficulties faced by companies trying to align their organizations on solid definitional ground.

General Motors, Toyota, and Volvo all know how to set up distributorships in markets outside their home base of operations, so none can claim a core competency in this regard. However, the lack of an effective distribution network could well be a significant source of competitive disadvantage. Accordingly, as a "thing we do well," the ability to define, structure, and manage distribution networks effectively across multiple country markets in the automotive industry is a "cost of doing business" activity, albeit a highly important one.

Likewise, the mere "uniqueness" of an activity clearly provides insufficient grounds for supporting a designation as a core competency. Companies and entire industries—food service, data management outsourcing, contract inventory replenishment—have been founded with the intent to off-load "non-core" activities that, although potentially "unique," do not pass a value threshold of an activity in which the company must invest its own resources.

Finally, a source of "competitive advantage," though important to maintain and develop, may have little actionable value for the thousands of employees comprising the global organization. Coca-Cola's manufacturing infrastructure in Southeast Asia, funded by the U.S. government and later turned over to the company, provided Coca-Cola with a significant cost advantage in the region. However, this asset is region-specific and therefore of limited relevance to other country operations. It is also lacking in "animation," or the intrinsic ability of a process/knowledge "asset" to be nurtured, redefined, extended, transferred, and so on.

By definition, the term "critical capability" conveys that we are dealing with capabilities (discrete, meaningful, actionable, animate) that are critical (providing sustainable advantage, highly leverageable) to the corporation. Throughout our research, we have spoken to companies about critical capabilities as defined by their business and organizational competencies as well as various forms of intellectual property, such as patents, trademarks, software technology, and other non-patented but exclusive technological products and processes. Superior value is created when the business, organizational, and technological skills of a company are enhanced by or interwoven with key asset "nuggets" (such as brands, patents, and the like). In this regard, some examples of critical capabilities might include:

- Image branding/high-end merchandising
- Rapid commercialization of new technology
- System-wide franchise quality management
- Design for low-cost manufacturing

Collecting And Analyzing The Data

To investigate our framework, we developed a questionnaire structured to collect data from three levels of a company—the corporate CEO, the head of a line of business, and the heads of foreign operations or subsidiaries. **Figure 2** summarizes the topics we addressed at each level. We then recruited 35 major MNCs from North America, Europe, and Asia Pacific (listed in **Figure 3**), and asked each company to select two lines of business and identify three diverse countries it had entered within the last 5 to 15 years for each line of business. The country operations also had to vary in performance and be continentally or regionally dispersed.

The companies responded by identifying 120 foreign operations. About 70 percent of these op-

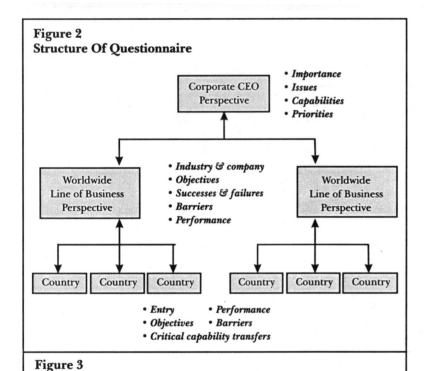

Figure 2
Structure Of Questionnaire

Corporate CEO Perspective
- *Importance*
- *Issues*
- *Capabilities*
- *Priorities*

Worldwide Line of Business Perspective
- *Industry & company*
- *Objectives*
- *Successes & failures*
- *Barriers*
- *Performance*

Worldwide Line of Business Perspective

Country Country Country   Country Country Country

- *Entry*   *Performance*
- *Objectives*   *Barriers*
- *Critical capability transfers*

Figure 3
Companies in the Study

North America HQ	Europe HQ	Asia-Pacific HQ
Amoco	Altana	BHP
Amway	Ansaldo	Canon
AMP	Barilla	National Australia Bank
Baxter International	Danfoss	Telstra
Dow Chemical	Fiat	TNT
Du Pont	Finmeccanica	
Eaton	Jotun	
Federal Express	Kværner	
FMC	Lafarge Coppée	
General Motors	Montedison	
Molex	Olivetti	
Pittston	Pirelli	
PPG	Volvo	
Rockwell		
Tektronix		
Tenneco		
Xerox		

erations were in developing markets in Asia, Latin America, and Eastern Europe, and the rest were in the United States, Canada, and Western Europe. On average, the companies had nine years of experience in these overseas ventures, and in total we collected more than 600,000 data points.

We measured the transfer of critical capabilities and most other variables, such as the effectiveness of the global processes for human resources, by asking respondents to rate these variables on a scale from 0 (not at all effective) to 10 (completely effective). To supplement the data collected from the questionnaires, we conducted personal interviews with 16 CEOs and 22 senior executives at the line of business head offices and country operations. We used correlation co-efficients and multiple regression to estimate the relationships between variables. We also compared the characteristics of foreign operations that were "winners" with those of the "losers."

How The Foreign Operations Performed

One primary measure, Expected versus Actual Performance, was obtained by asking each Line of Business (LOB) head to rate the company's performance in each country relative to the firm's expectations at the time of entry. A rating of 100 meant that expected performance was equal to actual performance. This measure allowed direct comparison of performance across industries and countries, and correlated highly with such traditional measures of performance as sales growth and market share.

The foreign operations varied greatly. Fewer than half had performed satisfactorily relative to expectations at the time of entry. Moreover—and not surprisingly—the spread in performance decreased with the years since entry. This was because the poorest performers were closed down and the companies had time to fix other poor performers.

Successful Transfer Has The Strongest Effect On International Performance

We examined a wide range of factors that might affect the success of foreign ventures. These included the extent of globalization strategy, the fit of this strategy with globalization drivers, organization structure, barriers to entry, entry objectives and strategy, use of performance measures, human resource practices, and localization of strategy and management. But the effectiveness in transferring critical capabilities was far and away the most important in affecting performance. On average, a 20 percent improvement in transfer ef-

fectiveness was associated with a better than 7 percent improvement in performance.

In addition, high performers (the upper third of our sample) scored 22 percent better than low performers (the lower third of our sample) in transfer effectiveness. If the average performer were able to improve its capacity to transfer critical capabilities to the level of the highest performer in our study, the performance improvement would exceed 15 percent. Average transfer capability among all participants was 6.8 on a scale of 0 to 10.

Several of the comments made in the interviews were:

• "If only we knew what the company knows" (a country manager).

• "what parts of the past do we want to use as pivots of the future?"

• "The firm does practice the shared services concept in North America, but not in Europe, though we are looking at this now."

CEOs Want To Improve Critical Capabilities

As could be expected, the CEOs repeatedly identified critical capabilities as being among the issues for which their companies most needed improvement. These are shown in **Figure 4.** As one CEO put it, "It is still a matter of debate, inside and outside our group, as to whether a large company can be effective in leveraging its critical capabilities when entering a market like, say, China." Another CEO saw no easy solution:

In terms of leveraging our knowledge across and around the Group, we do not have any simple solutions. We try and get our people around the

---

Figure 4
Identified Areas Most In Need Of Improvement

Strategic capabilities

• Fully exploiting worldwide capabilities
• Acting on changing globalization drivers
• Making moves against competitors around the world

Organizational capabilities

• Developing talent and leadership for innovation and renewal
• Leveraging global capabilities effectively
• Structuring for optimal global performance

Management process capabilities

• Nurturing global management talent
• Transferring best practices
• Stimulating transfer of critical capabilities

Figure 5

Type of Critical Capabilities Identified and Percentage Of Respondents Listing Each

CEO	Line of Business	Country
		Sales management - 41%
Product development - 67%	Product development - 53%	Product development - 39%
	Low-cost manufacturing - 53%	Low-cost manufacturing - 32%
Brands and products - 33%	Marketing - 29%	Marketing - 20%
Partnering skills - 30%		Brands - 20%
Low-cost manufacturing - 29%		Channel - 20%
Customer service - 22%	Customer service - 29%	Customer service - 9%
Sales management - 13%	Sales management - 26%	

world to work on common problems.... [T]hese may be common issues or ones common to a business across countries.

A third said, "We are mediocre, though improving in the exchange of know-how and best practices in manufacturing processes. The CEOs also recognized the competitive imperative to strengthen critical capability transfer. As one stated, "Early on, [our competitor] globalized their R&D capability, giving them a serious advantage."

But some CEOs are beginning to find solutions. Said one of our respondents, "(We are) establishing a more comprehensive and practical 'Corpus of Doctrine' reflecting the Group's experience in, and approaches to, strategy, marketing, operations, analysis, and reporting ... to facilitate know-how transfer."

Many Critical Capabilities Identified

Figure 5 summarizes the critical capabilities identified by each level of management. CEOs in particular

identified the general categories of new product development and technology as their companies' most critical capabilities. Aspects of these included design for manufacturing, time to market, patents and intellectual property, and technology in general. Other critical capabilities, in order of frequency, included partnering and alliance skills, low-cost manufacturing, customer service, product life cycle management, hiring and developing international managers, information technology, speed and flexibility, and quality management. Many of these capabilities were related to each other. One CEO said, "We have three interlinked capabilities: negotiating, developing contracts, and building relationships."

LOB heads were proportionately less concerned about new product development, but it still topped their list. Predictably, they saw operational issues as relatively more important, including capabilities in low-cost manufacturing, marketing, customer service, quality management, sales management, brands and products, channel management, product life cycle management, and hiring and developing global managers. The critical capabilities can also be very specific to individual industries. An LOB head of a mining company said, "Our critical capabilities are the ability to estimate the prospects for significant reserves and the ability to correctly assess political risks in the regions in which we operate."

The trend toward operational concerns was even more marked for country managers, although new product development was still a major concern. Other critical capabilities at country level were similar to those of the LOB heads.

The dispersion of activities in Figure 5 is noteworthy. Although differences in industries, product markets, and other factors clearly account for some of this spread, there still appears to be widespread confusion around what constitutes a critical capability.

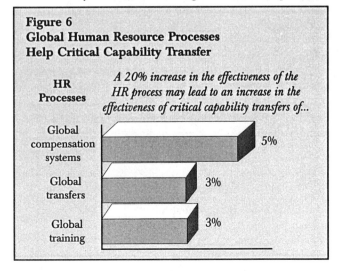

Figure 6
Global Human Resource Processes
Help Critical Capability Transfer

HR Processes	A 20% increase in the effectiveness of the HR process may lead to an increase in the effectiveness of critical capability transfers of...
Global compensation systems	5%
Global transfers	3%
Global training	3%

For example, "new product development" is defined at too high a level to be meaningful and actionable. Better definitions might be "rapid commercialization of new technologies" or "industry-leading styling."

Mismatch Between Management Levels

Within individual firms, the level of alignment was less than might be expected from the above picture. CEOs and LOB heads were each asked to identify six critical capabilities. On average, and even with a generous interpretation of similarity, only 2.1 of their selections matched. When country heads were asked to name three critical capabilities, on average only 1.6 of these could also be found in the LOB list. Given this low degree of alignment, it is not surprising that these firms had difficulty determining exactly what critical capabilities to transfer.

Although the respondents did not agree on what comprised critical capabilities in their companies, we were able to establish that the transfer of those capabilities was the most important factor in the success of foreign operations through the statistical analyses relating such transfer to performance. In other words, we did not have to ask respondents directly whether they thought critical capabilities affected performance, but could deduce that from correlation and regression analysis.

Human Resource Practices As The Key Method For Enhancing Transfer

Certain human resource practices, we found, had a high correlation to the successful transfer of critical capabilities: global compensation systems, transferring managers from country to country, and having worldwide training systems. A 20 percent increase in the effectiveness of each of these processes may lead to an increase of 3 to 5 percent in the effectiveness of critical capability transfer (**Figure 6**).

At the same time, the use and effectiveness of these processes were all relatively low-in the 3 to 6 range out of a possible 10 (**Figure 7**). Companies faced many problems in this area. One CEO commented, "People from central 'X-state' [location of company HQ] are very loyal, but they do not like to move." Another CEO said, "I have worked in the international area for almost 40 years. There is no greater need than identifying and nurturing talent for local markets. All U.S. corporations have the same problem."

Some firms were beginning to force international experience. "To reach a certain manage-

ment level," said one CEO, "it is mandatory to have 'out of country' experience." Other firms were working hard on the problem; one was putting together a skills matrix across its global operations and addressing how to take "a 25-year-old and develop him (or her) into a global manager [via, e.g.,] three functional careers, three geographic careers, and at least two business unit careers." Summarizing this issue, another CEO said, "My top globalization issue is people development and building a learning organization."

The low degree of global coordination of HR processes is not surprising, because country managers have the greatest autonomy in this area. The respondent country managers had more local autonomy in decisions about human resources (7.9 out of 10 overall) than about physical assets, technology, or capital (**Figure 8**). Among different types of HR processes, country managers did indeed have the lowest auton-

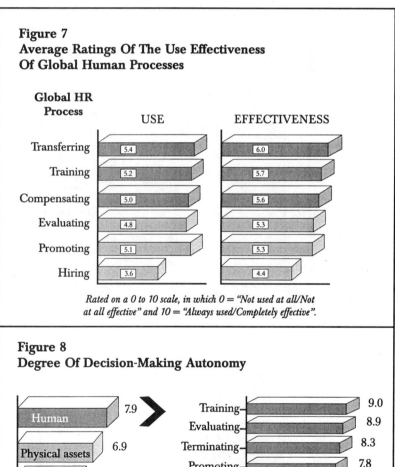

Figure 7
Average Ratings Of The Use Effectiveness Of Global Human Processes

Global HR Process

	USE	EFFECTIVENESS
Transferring	5.4	6.0
Training	5.2	5.7
Compensating	5.0	5.6
Evaluating	4.8	5.3
Promoting	5.1	5.3
Hiring	3.6	4.4

Rated on a 0 to 10 scale, in which 0 = "Not used at all/Not at all effective" and 10 = "Always used/Completely effective".

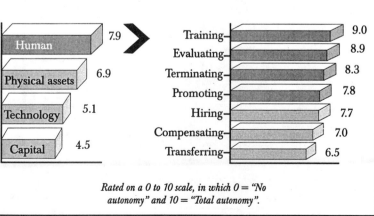

Figure 8
Degree Of Decision-Making Autonomy

Human	7.9
Physical assets	6.9
Technology	5.1
Capital	4.5

Training	9.0
Evaluating	8.9
Terminating	8.3
Promoting	7.8
Hiring	7.7
Compensating	7.0
Transferring	6.5

Rated on a 0 to 10 scale, in which 0 = "No autonomy" and 10 = "Total autonomy".

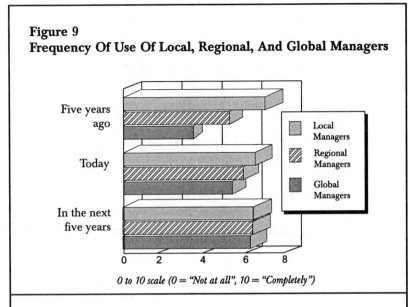

Figure 9
Frequency Of Use Of Local, Regional, And Global Managers

0 to 10 scale (0 = "Not at all", 10 = "Completely")

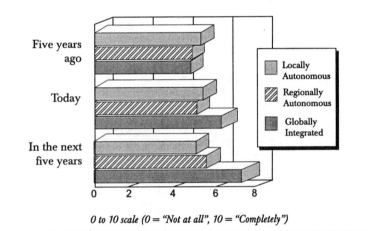

Figure 10
Frequency Of Use Of Management Processes

0 to 10 scale (0 = "Not at all", 10 = "Completely")

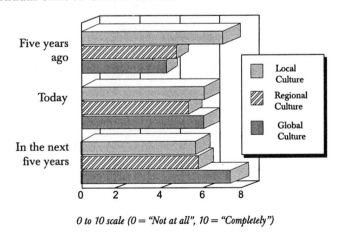

Figure 11
Gradual Shift to Global Culture

0 to 10 scale (0 = "Not at all", 10 = "Completely")

omy in transferring personnel (6.5). But this relative lack of autonomy was more than offset by very high levels in training (9.0) and evaluating (8.9).

Consequently, head office managers can exert only limited influence on global strategy execution and capability transfer when most types of HR decisions are beyond their control. Again, MNCs face the dilemma of a need for local autonomy versus a need for global coordination.

Need For More Global Managers

The companies surveyed certainly recognize the need to change their HR processes. For instance, they all plan to increase the use of global managers relative to local managers (shown in **Figure 9**). The executives we interviewed made many telling comments:

- "We have to find a way of managing the free flow of talent and necessary skills around the world with the objective of building a competence-based organization."
- "The single most important issue is creating internationalists."
- "The limiting factor for our growth is human capital."
- "How do we seed the samurai, and how should we manage the development and transfer of excellence?"
- "[The company] now insists that its top 50 managers have both international and cross-functional experience."

Global Management Processes Also Help Make The Transfer

In addition to international human resource processes, global management processes in general helped the transfer of critical capabilities. Overall, a 20 percent increase in the use of global, as opposed to regional or local, management processes may lead to a 3 percent increase in the effectiveness of critical capability transfer. The use of global management processes is relatively low today. But companies plan to do much more in this regard and lessen their use of local management processes (**Figure 10**).

In commenting on the problem, one CEO said, "We fragment the understanding, focus, delivery, and leveraging of our critical capabilities through our information systems, patterns of communication, career paths, management reward systems, and processes of strategy development." Proposing a solution, another CEO said, "We need to weave our critical capabilities into the corporate strategic themes for, and across, each of our business's plans and budgets."

Global Culture Plays Key Role

Having a global company culture, rather than regional or local cultures, also plays a powerful role in the transfer of critical capabilities. We found that a 20 percent increase in the extent of having a global culture may lead to a 4 percent increase in the effectiveness of critical capability transfer. Several quotes highlight this effect:

• "A global culture is denationalizing operations and creating a system of values shared by managers around the globe."

• "Culture is the value-setter and lubricator."

• "We get what we measure. We need to change our performance measuring and compensation systems to encourage sharing and teaming."

• "Establishing a common culture across the division is also a key globalization factor."

• "We are more transnational or global than [our competitor] because we grew up as a result of many acquisitions, each with its own culture."

As with global human resources and other management processes, the companies were gradually shifting from a local orientation to more of a regional and international orientation. Within the next five years, and compared with five years ago, the companies planned to reverse the dominance of local culture relative to global culture (**Figure 11**).

Other Methods Of Transfer

We also asked country managers about three key methods for transferring critical capabilities: rotation of staff, dedicated global teams, and management meetings. As shown in **Figure 12**, these methods averaged a rating of only 5.2 (on a scale of 0 to 10) in use for transferring critical capabilities from headquarters or other units to a country operation. They rated an even lower average of 4.4 for transfer from country operations to headquarters or other units.

When asked about other methods of transfer, the country managers identified many different mechanisms. Some entailed the sharing of information: written communications, memos to share lessons, newsletters and magazines, release of information, data transfer, and information technology. One CEO said, "Designing and installing an effective global IT network is critical if we are to keep in touch, share, and deliver the best—internally and to our customers." But technology will not be the sole answer. An-

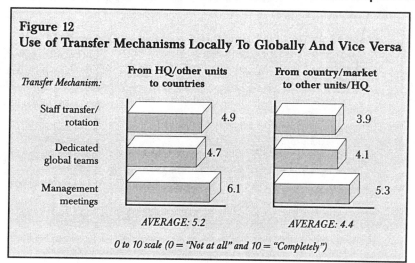

Figure 12
Use of Transfer Mechanisms Locally To Globally And Vice Versa

Transfer Mechanism:	From HQ/other units to countries	From country/market to other units/HQ
Staff transfer/rotation	4.9	3.9
Dedicated global teams	4.7	4.1
Management meetings	6.1	5.3
	AVERAGE: 5.2	AVERAGE: 4.4

0 to 10 scale (0 = "Not at all" and 10 = "Completely")

other CEO commented, "I do not see a cybernetic revolution ahead in addressing the issue of knowledge (including best practice) sharing."

Other transfer mechanisms related to training and education, and included training at home country operations, business academies, dedicated courses, and top-down training and implementation. Coordination mechanisms comprised cross-sector umbrella teams, a global executive committee that met monthly, application segment teams, and a global customer management process. As one CEO put it, "We have started the formation and use of 'Country Councils' whereby they bring the managers of the different businesses in a country together to share views but without getting tangled up in the details of each other's business."

Direct involvement by HQ also was cited. This took the form of strategy reviews, country visits, and central and regional control. Both technical support and head office support in general were also mentioned. Centers of excellence are also being used. One CEO mentioned, "We may try and use a 'Centers of Excellence' approach for technology and best practice." Finally, simply having a customer focus or market focus could also be of help.

Incentives For Adapting Or Sharing Critical Capabilities

Some companies provided incentives for adapting or sharing critical capabilities. Rewards to local managers for adapting corporate critical capabilities to the local market included:

• management incentive programs and other financial rewards;

• recognition programs such as corporate quality awards; and

• praise and recognition in performance appraisals.

One company went so far as to have specific performance objectives defined for implementing capabili-

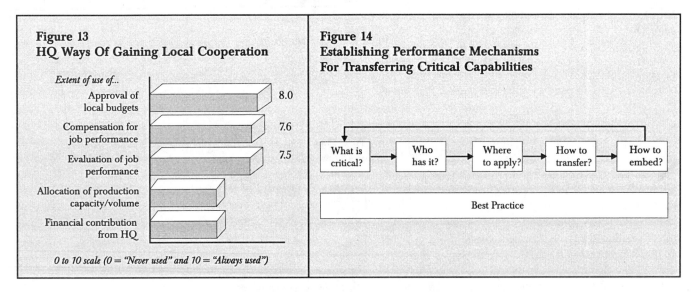

Figure 13
HQ Ways Of Gaining Local Cooperation

Extent of use of...

Approval of local budgets	8.0
Compensation for job performance	7.6
Evaluation of job performance	7.5
Allocation of production capacity/volume	
Financial contribution from HQ	

0 to 10 scale (0 = "Never used" and 10 = "Always used")

Figure 14
Establishing Performance Mechanisms
For Transferring Critical Capabilities

What is critical? → Who has it? → Where to apply? → How to transfer? → How to embed?

Best Practice

ties worldwide. Similar, though fewer, rewards were given to local managers for sharing capabilities from their country with headquarters or other units. Being recognized for their local capabilities seemed to be particularly motivating.

Many firms, however, had no specific incentives. And many local managers recognized the operating and strategic benefits of adapting corporate critical capabilities without additional reward. In actuality, there may often be significant disincentives to transfer, such as when a disproportionate level of resource investment must be borne by the capability "source" unit vis-à-vis the "recipient," or in the midst of political concerns about helping a future rival for promotion.

Methods Of Gains Cooperation

Many companies used direct mechanisms not only for the transfer of critical capabilities, but also for gaining the cooperation of country managers in global and regional strategies. Of the methods we asked about, approval of local budgets was at the top of the list–rating 8.0 in the extent of its use (**Figure 13**)–followed by compensation for job performance, evaluation of job performance, allocation of production capacity and volume, and financial contribution from headquarters. Executives also mentioned various other methods, some of which were formal (global policy directions, strategy integration systems, approval of strategic plans, capital authorization, global customer management, business management councils, international project organization, personnel selection) and some informal (training and follow-up, seeding personnel, esprit de corps, personal contact and relationships, and constant international networking).

These direct and indirect methods of headquarters control can be seen as counterweights to the autonomy enjoyed by country managers. Percy Barnevik,

the CEO of Asea Brown Boveri (not a participant in this study), frequently proclaims the high degree of autonomy given to local managers in his company. Less publicized is the fact that ABB's head office managers use the allocation of production volume as a powerful weapon to gain compliance. Most of the industries, such as power generation systems, in which ABB's businesses participate suffer from excess capacity. Moreover, in a given line of business, ABB usually operates factories in more than one country. Getting a production order thus makes a huge difference in whether a local ABB manager will make his or her budget for the year. So ABB's head office may speak softly but it carries a very big stick! Most MNCs have similar secret weapons for influencing the hearts and minds of their local managers.

If you truly want to be successful at globalizing your company, you need to establish permanent mechanisms for the transfer of critical capabilities. Start with understanding what is critical in your industries and lines of business. Then create and improve those capabilities, identify and recognize the sources and carriers, identify which types are needed in which countries, transfer and adapt them there, and embed them into your foreign operations.

Of course, a continuing feedback and learning loop is essential; **Figure 14** summarizes this process. Many of the executives in our study have pointed out what is needed:

• "We know our critical capabilities but have not done a good job in defining, communicating, and installing them."

• "We must be more explicit, exhaustive, and rigorous in communicating, educating, and practicing our critical capabilities."

• "Developing the understanding of how to transfer the lessons learned from one market to another [is crucial]."

• "View the company as a competence-based organization that delivers highest market impact through leveraging best practices worldwide."

You also need to recognize that HQ is no longer the owner of critical capabilities. Instead, it is increasingly a facilitator of their transfer. Critical capabilities may be created, adapted, and transferred by many different units: headquarters, line of business, country operation, business process, centers of excellence, teams, or a shared service center. Putting it all together can mean creating a multilevel spider web of transfer capabilities. As the CEOs put it:

• "We have now decided to change from informal networking to a formal comprehensive way of capturing, measuring, and installing best practices around our world.... In fact, it's not a choice, but a *must* if we are to be a leader."

• "In terms of leveraging our knowledge across and around the Group, we don't have any simple solutions.... [W]e try to get people from around the world to work on common problems.... [T]hese may be common issues or ones common to a business across countries."

• "Our focus is on the management and development of the intellect, information, and tools for tailoring, flexing, leading, and differentiating."

• "A virtual HQ is rapidly replacing a 'solid center HQ' as competence centers and responsibilities are spread across the network into the operating units."

Returning to the overall framework for this study, we can see that the global transfer of critical capabilities constitutes an essential step in moving from globalization potential to realized international competitive advantage. Even in light of the many ways to effect this transfer, in every case managers will have to work very hard to make it happen.

References

Christopher A. Bartlett and Sumantra Ghoshal, *Managing Across Borders: The Transnational Solution* (Boston: Harvard Business School Press, 1989).

Andrew Bartmess and Keith Cerny, "Building Competitive Advantage Through A Global Network Of Capabilities," *California Management Review*, Winter 1993, pp. 78-103.

Joseph H. Boyett and Henry P. Conn, *Maximum Performance Management: How To Manage And Compensate People To Meet World Competition*, 2nd ed. (Lakewood, CO: Glenbridge, 1993).

Joseph H. Boyett and Henry P. Conn, *Workplace 2000* (New York, Dutton, 1991; Plume 1992).

Gary Hamel and C. K. Prahalad, *Competing For The Future* (Boston: Harvard Business School Press, 1994).

J. K. Johansson and George S. Yip, "Exploiting Globalization Potential: U.S. And Japanese Strategies," *Strategic Management Journal*, October 1994, pp. 579-601.

Michael E. Porter, "Changing Patterns Of International Competition," *California Management Review*, Winter 1986, pp. 9-40.

C. K. Prahalad and Yves L. Doz, *The Multinational Mission: Balancing Local Demands And Global Vision* (New York: Free Press, 1987).

C. K. Prahalad and Gary Hamel, "The Core Competence Of The Corporation," *Harvard Business Review*, May-June 1990, pp. 79-91.

Joseph L. Raudabaugh, "Asian Investment: Lessons From The Japanese Experience," *Planning Review*, January-February 1995, pp. 38-40.

George Stalk, Philip Evans, and Lawrence E. Schulman, "Competing On Capabilities: The New Rules Of Corporate Strategy," *Harvard Business Review*, March-April 1992, pp. 57-69.

George S. Yip, *Total Global Strategy: Managing For Worldwide Competitive Advantage* (Englewood Cliffs, NJ: Prentice Hall, 1992).

Henry P. Conn is a vice president of A. T. Kearney, a global management consulting firm based in Chicago, Illinois.

George S. Yip is Adjunct Professor at UCLA's Anderson Graduate School of Management. This article reports on a study conducted by A. T. Kearney. The authors thank the many companies who participated in the study, and the many A. T. Kearney staff members, as well as Professor Phil Smith of Michigan State University, who worked on it.

Scaling The Great Wall: The *Yin* And *Yang* Of Resolving Business Conflicts In China

David Strutton and Lou Pelton

A philosophy of push and pull, compete and cooperate, may sound contradictory to many Americans, but it is the basis for attaining success in doing business with the Chinese.

There has always been an air of mystery about China, a land so remote from the United States in terms of distance and culture that Americans still refer to it as the Far East. Lately, however, East has been meeting West ever more frequently as China has become the world's hottest business opportunity. The country is so attractive that U.S. firms by the boatloads are making the strategic decision that they *must* be there. Too often, though, their understanding of China and its business practices is seriously limited. As a result, many American companies risk becoming marginalized there.

Consider the experiences of the U.S. pioneer companies in China. Coca-Cola, Otis Elevator, and Occidental Petroleum entered the country as soon as they gained permission from the Chinese government. Coke established a preemptive market position that has yielded formidable competitive advantages. The company succeeded in executing distribution strategies in a country with significant infrastructural problems because it first developed business relationships with local enterprises. Otis and Occidental, however, along with AT&T, Bethlehem Steel, Bechtel Group, Caterpillar, and many others, have not been so fortunate. They have had to close offices and even retreat from China after fumbling with local partners or for similar reasons. Hence, having Chinese partners does not guarantee successful market entry or subsequent expansion. Instead, the events of the last decade suggest that having contracts represents the start, not the end, of real negotiations.

The domestic business community's disillusionment with China has spread, as illustrated by a *Fortune* magazine cover featuring the byline, "First Prize, One Contract in China; Second Prize, Two Contracts" (Kraar 1996). Global alliances generally succeed only when the goals on which they are based remain acceptable to all parties in the face of naturally arising conflict. Unfortunately, amid repeated cultural clashes, strategic harmony among American and Chinese partners has often proved illusory.

From *Business Horizons*, September/October 1997, pp. 22-34. © 1997 by the Foundation for the School of Business at Indiana University. Reprinted by permission.

U.S.-Chinese Business Alliances: Relevant Issues

Managers from American firms interested in China should do two things before taking the plunge. One is to travel to the top of any skyscraper in Shanghai, Beijing, or Sichuan and enjoy a view that makes wallets throb. Shanghai alone has some 2,000 cranes working, more than are currently used in all of North America. The second is to accept as an idea whose time has come the notion that China can teach Americans a thing or two about business. The Chinese culture offers many insights that transcend Western business fundamentals.

This sentiment is especially germane when it comes to resolving conflict within U.S.-Chinese business alliances. International business people invariably run the risk of managing as if they were captives of their native country's culture. But an especially noxious cultural arrogance has frequently injured American business interests in China. Western expatriates there often seem unwilling or unable to compensate for their cultural limitations. Their exposure to the local culture is usually confined to rather stilted social encounters or shielded employer/employee relationships. Such detachment does not serve strategic ends; ignorance is never blissful when the subject is international business.

True assimilation can be achieved only when one's interactions with foreign cultures demonstrate that they must be considered equal to one's own culture. Time and again this lack of understanding has proven a telling shortfall for American managers in China, particularly because one never really negotiates contracts there; rather, personal relationships are negotiated. The Chinese even have a word to describe these relationships: *guanxi.*

At first blush, the *guanxi* concept hardly appears as though it should trouble American managers. For nearly a decade, relationship marketing has held sway as a dominant Western paradigm. But the nature of business relationships in China differs dramatically from Western analogues. When asked about the presumably cooperative *guanxi*, one Chinese expert laughed and replied, "I can't think of organizations where infighting is more rife" ("Business in Asia..." 1996). Not surprisingly, American firms attempting to manage relationships in China have regularly found that the nature of their expertise and power, and how both may be wielded to resolve alliance conflicts, has dramatically changed.

Clearly, the means by which alliance relationships are developed and sustained in China are acquired skills. Unfortunately, they are also competencies many American managers have yet to master. As John Platt, president of U.S.-based Agriglobal, put it, "Forget about your product and how good it is. [First] develop a relationship...." (Murphy 1996). Those who have worked there also understand that alliance conflict is endemic to China. Understanding how best to negotiate conflict resolutions is therefore crucial. But to negotiate successfully, American representatives must realize how the local culture influences the incidence and resolution of conflict in China. Otherwise, in light of their home field advantage, Chinese negotiators will routinely exploit U.S. firms.

Some readers may think this is too harsh an indictment. But the argument follows from two factors: the profit motive and the nature of Chinese culture. First, the Chinese understand that their market boasts two attractions irresistible to U.S. business interests: a market of 1.2 billion consumers and a vast land full of natural resources. Together, these assets provide sufficient bait to ensure that healthy numbers of Western firms will always be competing for a piece of the market and can thus be played off against each other. In 1995, for instance, China successfully played off General Motors against Mercedes Benz over which company would provide the most technology in return for the right to manufacture and market in China for fixed periods of time. Both corporations ended up giving China sophisticated technology with which to design and build new models.

Second, the Chinese expression *Shang chang ru zhan chang* translates literally as, "The marketplace is a battlefield." The statement reflects how the Chinese view the importance of success in the business world. They are culturally conditioned to believe that their nation's economy influences its survival and well-being as surely as does the outcome of a battle. Armed with what they see as an understanding of the true nature of business competition, they call it and act it as they see it. It is such American concepts as competition (a sort of cooperative competition) that Chinese have difficulty grasping.

Two methods exist for American managers to negotiate resolutions to *guanxi* conflict. The right way is to use negotiating principles consonant with the cultural expectations of their local partners. The wrong way is to negotiate in various states of relative cultural ignorance and insensitivity. China expert Randall Stross (1991) describes the gap between the two nation's cultures as "gargantuan, almost geological, in nature."

To this end, our discussion blends ancient historical precedent with current marketplace examples to illustrate where critical cultural differences lie. Recommendations regarding how American managers can use a knowledge of these differences to their advantage when negotiating conflict resolutions are also offered. The discussion is derived from the Chinese *Bing Fa*[1] (military strategy) literature, personal interviews with representatives of American firms who have or have had Chinese operations in China, and the personal experiences of the authors. Because of the occasionally judgmental nature of the discussion, some American sources have requested and been granted anonymity.

An American Manager in China: Parable or Paragon?

Behold the American expatriate manager. An awkward creature, his life in China is marked by uncertainty, resistance, and struggle. Often he wobbles from one activity to the next, sometimes soaring high, at other times crashing into unanticipated ceilings. Too often he is conspicuously unaware of harbingers in the Chinese environment or the unintended consequences of his actions. Even success stories such as Coca-Cola have fallen prey to such missteps. Years passed before Coca-Cola's managers accepted that the nature of the Chinese environment precluded their controlling their distribution in China as easily as they controlled their advertising.

When resistance arises, the manager tends to overreact through either aggression or inertia. Disagreements frustrate him and leave him vulnerable. His comfort zone is narrow because he usually thinks in black and white. Dualistic thinking is a two-edged tool, and like all tools it can be useful. Wielded carefully, it helps managers organize their knowledge and solve routine strategic problems. If managers never swing a two-edged sword, they procrastinate and act indecisively. Indeed, most global business relationships are dualistic, featuring varying degrees of success and failure.

Unfortunately, dualistic perspectives also contribute to the archetypical American illusion that things must be one way or the other. Managers who view phenomena this way may miss the full range of opportunities available to them. Indeed, the American tendency toward dualistic thinking can wreak havoc in alliances with the Chinese. It radically oversimplifies the nature of business relationships in China, splitting the

> "PepsiCo pushed back hard and saved the Shanghai location, But less than a year later, when chicken prices surged in Japan, Chinese suppliers shipped KFC's chicken orders to Japan, leaving many restaurants with no meat."

organizational marketplace into two groups, usually "us" and "them." This can lead American managers to take nationalistic positions. Among may Americans, a kind of "China exhaustion" appears to have taken firm hold. From this juncture, they need take just a few small steps to proclaim *their* actions as just, rational, or defensive, while considering the actions of *others* as inhuman, unjustified, or aggressive. But this leaves too little latitude in terms of entry strategies or post-entry behaviors.

Those who manage in black and white can either be cooperative and trusting after entering China or build walls of self-protection. Open arms have their place in human interaction, but in Chinese business alliances they can lead to victimization. Thugs are indeed doing business in China–literally. The case of a Corning Inc. consultant stabbed to death in a five-star Shanghai hotel prompted many domestic firms to hire bodyguards and investigators to "check out" their prospective partners. Still, most conflicts in China are played out in the domain of promises made and broken. Clenched fists promise short-term security, but they also foreclose much of the attractiveness inherent in building the kinds of sustainable relationships that can allow U.S. firms to avail themselves of China's market opportunities.

Because conflict in Chinese business alliances arrives in all shades of intensity, managers' conflict resolution strategies should be highly variable. Dualistic thinking precludes such fine adjustments. When concentrating on either passive or aggressive extremes, making the precise adjustments essential to sustaining U.S.-Chinese alliances will prove difficult.

Achieving Negotiating Symmetry: The Dove And The Serpent

A *Bing Fa* maxim says, "Combine in yourself the dove and serpent, not as a monster but as a prodigy." This adage reflects the essence of *yin* and *yang*, and may provide an antidote for the American tendency toward dualistic thinking. U.S. firms entering alliances with Chinese partners should view their situation as if they were standing on one side of a door and the Chinese partner on the other side. The door swings freely in both directions. When relationships conflict, only two movements are available to either partner: to push or pull the door. Pushes are *yang* movements; they are direct and active. Pulls are *yin* movements; they are receptive and yielding. Whether alliance relationships in China can be sustained or strengthened in the face of conflict depends in part on the interplay of these forces.

Suppose the Chinese partner decides to "attack" its American counterpart by pushing the door. If the U.S. firm meets this push with a push of its own, it has responded symmetrically. In symmetry, *yang* meets *yang* or *yin* meets *yin*. In purely symmetrical encounters, strength is useful, but only in the short run. If the American firm can push back harder on the door than its Chinese counterpart, it wins. But such victories will be short-lived, because Chinese partners will try to even the score. Recently, PepsiCo's most profitable KFC restaurant was told to move and make way for a subway. PepsiCo pushed back hard and saved the Shanghai location. But less than a year later, when chicken prices surged in Japan, Chinese suppliers shipped KFC's chicken orders to Japan, leaving many restaurants with no meat. When both parties respond symmetrically to conflict, escalation is inevitable. As Gandhi summarized the sequence, "To punish an adversary merely initiates a new cycle of violence."

Symmetrical actions fall short even as self-defense strategies in China. U.S. managers tend to assume that the stronger their push, the better the result. So they attack the door with a mighty burst of power. But in China, extremes often lead to opposites. Likely as not, Chinese partners will withdraw their opposition (for now) in the face of a strong attack. Momentum then carries the U.S. firm crashing to the floor because it loses its equilibrium. Sun Tzu called this the "weakness of strength."[2] Begin pushing, and American firms often discover pushing assumes a life of its own. A large multinational's power can actually become a liability in such a market as China.

Of course, symmetrical conflict resolution strategies have value. They can set limits. They can even become necessary for survival. When cornered in China, American firms may have no option but, as Ian Murphy (1972) suggested, "to drive a spear into the throat of the dragon."

The alternative strategy is a complementary response. This involves yielding, seemingly nonresistant actions. When the door is pushed by one partner, the other pulls it open. When using complementary responses to conflict, strength becomes less important. Cultural sensitivity, a sense of timing, strategic and intellectual flexibility, and knowing what can be given up without compromising a firm's integrity become essential. The Chinese believe one key to resolving conflict lies in the ability to harness the motion inherent in an aggressor's attack. This is called "fighting without fighting" and involves compensating for weaknesses by yielding in harmony with attacks. Chinese business people know that proper timing can cause aggressors to lose their balance and become vulnerable to counterattack.

Complementary responses exploit the natural limitations of attacks. Consider that the force of any punch is restricted by human physiology. When striking at a point close to or removed from the aggressor's body, blows lose their effectiveness. Most attacks are weak, then strong, then weak. Such natural limitations

should be understood by Americans when negotiating conflict resolution in China, if only because their counterparts will appreciate them.

In defense, attacks should not be engaged in the midst of their natural power range. Instead, U.S. managers should act selectively, nipping conflict early or retreating to act later after the attack's power fades. Selective nonresistance can allow American managers to lead, control, or reverse conflicts initiated by their Chinese partners. Attacks must be given someplace to go. Rather than countering their positions, the path of adversaries should be cleared through acceptance, inquiry, and encouragement. This response will disarm Chinese partners, leaving them flat-footed and wondering what happened to the resistance expected from Westerners.

The Atlantic Richfield Co. followed such a tactic. After dozens of oil companies had already given up on China, Arco discovered a small natural gas field. With local cooperation, the firm decided to build a pipeline through South China to ship the resource to Hong Kong. While the pipeline was being bridged ashore, a grove of trees "miraculously" appeared, blocking the way, and Arco was asked to pay to "transplant" them. Refusal would have shut down the project. Instead, keeping its eye on the larger prize, Arco complied, and is now reaping a 20 percent return on its investment.

When on the offensive, American negotiators must recognize the danger of extending beyond their inherently limited range of influence in China. Headlong attacks are as dangerous as are tentative, halfhearted movements. Extending beyond a firm's natural range compromises balance and invites risk. When conflict arises within Chinese business alliances, U.S. firms should "push the door" only when the push reflects intentional striving toward a worthy objective. But as a company approaches the limits of its strength, it must again exercise extreme caution.

Understanding *yin* and *yang* forces yields the greatest advantage when it is used in dynamic combinations. American managers in China should master improvisational transitions from *yin* to *yang* or *yang* to *yin* as conflicts unfold. Because opportunities and

> "Too much yang, and firms cannot rein in their power; they become aggressive and domineering. Too much yin, and they fail to accomplish goals; the Chinese will capitalize on their weaknesses."

threats are always changing, such dexterity is a key skill. When conflict arises, managers should remain balanced between *yin* and *yang* responses. They should be predisposed to neither, but capable of each; they should be, as Zen masters exhort, "capable of striking or embracing with either hand."

Miyamoto Musashi (1982) once noted, "An elevated spirit is weak and a low spirit is weak." The lesson: Achieving balance is essential for defense, creativity, and relationship building in the face of conflict. Too much *yang*, and firms cannot rein in their power; they become aggressive and domineering. Too much *yin*, and they fail to accomplish goals; the Chinese will capitalize on their weaknesses. The value of achieving negotiation balance may appear obvious, but it too can be carried to extremes. Without under-standing Chinese culture, U.S. firms could "split the difference" on every conflicted issue and fail to optimize their positions. Negotiators must be balanced about achieving balance. Merely knowing *yin* and *yang* is necessary but not sufficient to ensure negotiating success in China.

Culturally Based Negotiating Guidelines

The Chinese believe conflict and harmony lie at opposite ends of a continuum. To understand one phenomenon, individuals must know the other. Business conflict is part of the Chinese culture; opposition to things American is normal there. As

Culturally Based Guidelines For Negotiating Business Conflict Resolutions In China

1. *EXPAND YOUR CULTURAL COMFORT ZONE.*

Underlying Chinese Value: "Learn something from 5,000 years of Chinese history."–Jiang Zemin
Implications for American Managers Who Are Negotiating Conflict Resolutions in China:
  a) Embrace the unusual as normal.
  b) Get rid of any misplaced sense of (American) cultural arrogance.
  c) Seek all forms of knowledge about China's history and culture.
  d) As a result of this cultural immersion, seek to absorb strategic thinking unconsciously. Then strive to accept the mental "thrust-and-parry" associated with strategic thinking as a natural part of human interaction in China.

2. *LAST THINGS FIRST.*

Underlying Chinese Value: "*Reng Qing,* the belief that the human element should never be removed from business affairs."–Confucius
Implications for American Managers Who Are Negotiating Conflict Resolutions in China:
  a) Learn that not having goals in the face of Chinese conflict may be worse than not being able to achieve them.
  b) Welcome conflicts as an opportunity for creative expression within the context of the business relationship.
  c) Learn how to create obligations (in one's Chinese counterparts) through gestures or actions that cost little. Also, learn when and how to subtly call the debt due. In short, learn the essence of *Reng Qing.*

3. *ANTICIPATE CONFLICT.*

Underlying Chinese Value: "He who excels at resolving difficulties does so before they arise. He who excels in conquering his enemies triumphs before threats materialize."–Sun Tzu

Implications for American Managers Who Are Negotiating Conflict Resolutions in China:
  a) Learn that active measures should be taken in anticipation of conflict rather than dispassionately waiting for disagreements to arise.
  b) Learn that the opportunity to act in China turns on the ability to make small adjustments or corrections in advance of significant disagreements.
  c) Learn to separate essential (hard-boundary) issues or concepts from nonessential ones, and do not allow hard-boundary issues to be violated by Chinese partners.
  d) Learn to specify hard-boundary issues or concerns to Chinese counterparts very early in the relationship; otherwise, doubts may arise.

4. *DO NOT RESIST RESISTANCE.*

Underlying Chinese Values: "Travel where there is no enemy."–*Bing Fa* • "Understand your adversary thoroughly, and lead him to where he is without fault."–Chuang Tzu • "Become your opponent."–*Bing Fa*
Implications for American Managers Who Are Negotiating Conflict Resolutions in China:
  a) Accept Chinese resistance to Western business practices.
  b) Learn to maintain organizational flexibility (except with respect to hard-boundary issues) in the face of conflict; then strive to blend with and redirect attacks.
  c) Put yourself in your opponent's place, consider his goals, and develop empathy toward him.
  d) Work toward a solution that allows each party to achieve what it desires.

5. *RETREAT GRACEFULLY.*

Underlying Chinese Values: "Retreat is another form of advance. Good men do not fight losing battles."–*Bing Fa* "If I can fight and

William Safire (1997) remarked, this opposition is grounded in part in a "contempt for American greed; the Chinese are convinced that U.S. politicians and business leaders will do anything, or put up with anything the Chinese do, for a buck." No matter what American companies do in China, someone will find it controversial.

Sustainable, mutually beneficial business relationships in China will therefore be accessible only to firms that fight well and in accordance with Chinese "rules." The absence of either skill exposes outsiders to double jeopardy; not only will conflicts continue to rage, but expatriate managers will be victimized in the process. U.S. firms entering China may not be interested in fighting, but fighting will be interested in them.

American managers' troubles with conflict in China have not resulted from a lack of pugnacity. Rather, they have generally followed from a lack of knowledge of Chinese history and martial arts. Americans often describe Chinese behavior as unprofessional and inconsistent, when in fact Chinese business people study and follow an even more definite set of rules. Derived from their knowledge of history, these rules are brought to bear in *every* aspect of their lives. The study of history is far more intensive among Chinese business people than among their Western counterparts. The system of examination is critical for advancement in many jobs. Subjects of inquiry are generally the human mind and how historical events illustrate universal principles at work. Chinese learn that all elements of life are intercon-

win, I fight. If I cannot fight, I will escape."—Ancient Chinese schoolchild adage

Implications for American Managers Who Are Negotiating Conflict Resolutions in China:

a) Develop alternatives for every negotiating response expected from the Chinese and create exit strategies for each business negotiation.

b) When original positions are knocked down, compensate as gracefully as possible and retreat slowly toward hard-boundary issues.

c) Accept that U.S. firms in China will sometimes find it necessary to accept temporary defeat, and attempt to preserve strength for other days (and future conflicts).

6. UNDERSTAND THE ROLE OF DECEPTION.

Underlying Chinese Values: "Offer the enemy a bait to lure him; then feign disorder and strike him." • "Pretend inferiority and encourage his arrogance." • "Do not gobble proffered baits."—*Bing Fa*

Implications for American Managers Who Are Negotiating Conflict Resolutions in China:

a) Do not idealize Western traditions of openness and fair play while in China.

b) Be aware of the likelihood that deception will be used in China. These illusions are likely to assume the form of "hiding the truth," "showing false strength," or "bait and switch" tactics.

c) Reserve a place for illusion in one's own business practices in China, but use the tactic sparingly, selectively, and properly.

7. GIVE YOUR OPPONENT FACE.

Underlying Chinese Value: "Gentleman call attention to the good points in others; they do not call attention to their defects."—Confucius

Implications for American Managers Who Are Negotiating Conflict Resolutions in China:

a) Acknowledge opponents' potential for future excellence.

b) Remember that taking away an opponent's face is perhaps the worst tactical error that can be made in China.

c) Always acknowledge the value, dignity, and position of one's adversaries. Whenever possible, feed their self-worth.

d) Remember that if your firm is the selling partner in a Chinese business alliance, it operates under a culturally induced obligation to defer to the buying partner.

8. IN DEATH GROUND, FIGHT.

Underlying Chinese Value: "In death ground, fight"—Sun Tzu

Implications for American Managers Who Are Negotiating Conflict Resolutions in China:

a) When encountering a worst-case scenario, recognize the danger.

b) Quickly and accurately analyze the direct threat to your firm's survival in China.

c) Integrate all available resources and energies into a single, focused ("zero-doubt") strike at the heart of your adversary.

d) Use this sort of "zero-doubt" negotiating style only when absolutely necessary.

nected. The wisdom that guides generals in battle is thought to be the same wisdom by which business people should exercise power. Clearly, to achieve the harmony desired from conflict resolution efforts, American managers should execute their negotiation strategies based on guidelines taken from Chinese cultural values. These guidelines are outlined in the sidebar and discussed below.

1. Expand your cultural comfort zone. This should be the first rule for U.S. managers in China. Having an expanded cultural comfort zone makes negotiators better fighters, able to tolerate higher levels of adversity and ambiguity while retaining their composure. It also increases their range of strategic options. Wider experiences contribute more latitude to maneuver and act creatively, which in turn allows a greater sense of control, confidence, and objectivity.

Conflicting business relationships in China may follow few rules that are apparent to "culturally challenged" negotiators. Every opponent is unique, every attack is by definition unpredictable. Any and all knowledge of Chinese culture is therefore valuable, not only for practical self-defense but also as a source of creative inspiration and empathy. As knowledge grows, so will American negotiators' stockpile of personal and nonpersonal connections to the culture. American business people should become xenophilic managers, embracing the unusual as normal.

No need exists for Americans to cower in the shadow of an ancient civilization. But regardless of the criticism American managers might have of Chinese ways, they must acknowledge that China is the world's oldest civilization. It survived when other civilizations vanished. Now it is reasserting its position of importance in the international community. And few, if any, international relationships can be more important to American business people than those established in China.

American strategies should learn and accept that Chinese business partners will be difficult, cunning, and deceptive–but take comfort from knowing that some of our traditional allies often act the same way. American managers should accept that Asian partners will demand to make up some of the rules, a role primarily dominated by U.S. firms since the 1940s. Chinese believe that American expatriates' misplaced sense of cultural superiority has long been among their worst characteristics. President Jiang Zemin personally admonished Bill Gates to spend more time in China and "learn something from 5,000 years of Chinese history" (Engardio 1996a). The workaholic Gates took him up on the offer, riding bicycles in Beijing, flying a kite at the Great Wall, and boating up the Yangtze River.

By being immersed in Chinese culture, one absorbs strategic thinking unconsciously and learns to embrace the mental thrust-and-parry as a natural part of human interaction. Americans would do well to study and adopt (to some extent) the Chinese habit of strategic thinking, but they should not attempt to become too Chinese in their behavior. Being a good American business person is clearly preferable to being a poor imitation of a Chinese business person. Well-mannered individuals who exhibit respect for the culture, even though they may make occasional blunders, will be better received than Chinese "experts" whose self-assurance borders on arrogance. This was apparently the case with Arabica Roasters, Inc. Staurt Eunson, co-owner of the small, entrepreneurial coffee company positioned to serve expatriate customers, made sure "his first move was to understand the [local] culture" (Yang 1996). He apparently understands the premise underlying this first guideline: that merely learning about Chinese business people's actions without grasping their underlying cultural motivations will not greatly help Americans successfully conduct business with them.

2. Last things first. When alliance conflicts arise, American negotiators should, in a broad sense, already know where they wish to go and why. Not having goals in the face of conflict may be worse than not being able to achieve them. Goals provide focus and bring order; they prevent negotiators from leaping about impulsively.

Targets reflected within these goals should be precise but flexible. Because China is a nation in flux, wise objectives today might prove fool's errands tomorrow. American business people also understand that vague targets are notoriously difficult to hit–abstractions offer no benchmarks. But in China a reason exists for alliance goals to be a bit nebulous. This is because Chinese cultural values are profoundly influenced by a Confucian concept called *Reng Qing*. Translated literally as "human feelings," *Reng Qing* dictates that the human element should never be removed from business affairs. Although the ideal is an informal and unselfish give-and-take among people, in reality accounts are kept very strictly. In China, flexible objectives have their place.

When American negotiators encounter resistance, their culture has taught them to label it a "problem"

> *By being immersed in Chinese culture, one absorbs strategic thinking unconsciously and learns to love the mental thrust-and-parry as a natural part of human interaction."*

that can be "solved" through strategies or technology. By contrast, Chinese negotiators often welcome conflicts as opportunities for creative expression. American managers should thus understand that they are surrendering little to chance by reaching agreements according to the *Reng Qing* custom of leaving many details open to interpretation. In fact, if they are skillful they can incur obligations in their Chinese counterparts that will lead them to grant more generous terms informally than they would be willing to grant in a detailed, goal-driven, Western-style contract.

The "trick" is to create an obligation through a gesture that costs little and then subtly call the debt due when your adversary can only repay it with a more valuable concession. A delicate touch and perceptiveness are required. Rather than focusing on conflict as something to get rid of, American negotiators should concentrate on something they would like to bring into being: a *strengthened relationship*. Boeing has managed to do just that in the face of continual conflict with its partners, and most of China's 32 airlines have remained loyal to the company.

Western economic history may repeat itself in Asia. But history is more likely to fly off in non-linear, uncharted directions. American negotiators cannot slavishly adhere to Western politico-economic models in China. Today's Chinese conflicts should be managed in accordance with today's needs, and resolved with an eye toward tomorrow's possibilities.

3. Anticipate conflict. Sun Tzu counseled, "He who excels at resolving difficulties does so before they arise. He who excels in conquering his enemies triumphs before threats materialize." The lesson: By anticipating conflicts in China, measures can be taken ahead of time rather than dispassionately waiting for disagreements to arise. Conflict can then be addressed more easily while it is new and relatively pliable.

Unfortunately, whether because of fear, ignorance, or time differences, U.S. firms in China often delay their responses to conflict. By then, relationships have had time to polarize and the negotiators must wield extremely high levels of skill or power just to break even. China is, after all, a nation about which Boston businessman Garrison Rousseau observed, "The difference between China and other places is that in China, you can't get things done even when you have paid bribes" (Lee 1991). The ability to anticipate and take action turns on a talent for making small adjustments or corrections in advance of significant disagreements. This, in turn, demands paying attention to the smallest details associated with the relationship. Trends should be studied and embryonic changes noted.

Few limits exist on how early firms should act. It depends on an understanding of the role that "pre-designated limits" can play in sustaining relationships. American negotiators enter China knowing what their inviolable issues are and how they will react if such niches are violated. Hard boundaries should be established in some areas, soft boundaries in others. Where soft boundaries exist, partners can be given the benefit of the doubt. With hard boundaries, situations are rigidly cast. If the boundary is breached, the violating party is subject to sanctions.

Active conflict resolution processes should begin with self-knowledge and end with an informed partner. The process demands that American firms first separate essential concerns from nonessential ones. Vital interests are maintained at the center of attention; they form a nucleus protected by a strong boundary. These limits should then be clearly communicated to Chinese alliance partners; otherwise, doubts may arise. American and Chinese cultures have divergent views of territory, so substantial confusion and conflict can be preempted by educating partners about organizational limits and how rigidly they are set.

> "American negotiators have no duty to judge Chinese behavior. Disapproval is of no consequence; what matters are the creativity, intelligence, and quality of their response."

Lying idle during tranquil times is wrong. Chinese business people have been taught from an early age that agreeable futures are always created in the present. American managers would do well to recall the same. Companies that fight the little fight today in China should be more likely to avoid the big fight tomorrow. Occasions when alliance partners have to engage in active battle may then be refreshingly rare.

4. Do not resist resistance. American managers must understand that when negotiating conflict resolutions in China, their local partners can never be wrong (unless they are encroaching on a hard boundary). Americans often become upset when meeting resistance. This is understandable (to Westerners), but such responses are irreverent when doing business in China. Like it or not, resistance to Western business practices will exist.

Once this principle is accepted, American negotiators can more readily accept whatever opposition comes their way. Chinese adversaries are capable of all kinds of behaviors, some rational, some apparently outlandish by Western standards. Masachika Onodera, an executive at Sakura Bank Ltd., notes how requests such as "Why don't you set up a school?" or "Why don't you take care of the funeral (of a retired person)?" often prove the norm rather than the exception. This follows from the "iron rice bowl" philosophy–cradle-to-grave welfare benefits and lifetime employment–that still prevails in China. But American negotiators have no duty to judge Chinese behavior. Disapproval is of no consequence; what matters are the creativity, intelligence, and quality of their response.

The *Bing Fa* advises, "Travel where there is no enemy." Expatriate managers should consider the value of this sentiment. When conflict occurs, they generally widen their stance and harden their position. But if an organization's flexibility is regained, its negotiators can blend with and redirect an attack. The American partner's position might be adjusted so that it closely parallels that of the local partner. It would then enjoy a position from which it can redirect an attacker's momentum.

Imagine a boulder rolling down a mountain. If a man tries to stop it directly he'll be crushed. But if he runs alongside it and nudges it, he will be safe. Business conflict in China is like this rock. When it begins rolling downhill, American negotiators should maintain their integrity while making subtle adjustments in the rock's position and movement. Of course, contact must be maintained with hard-boundary organizational interests even as ground is surrendered to the boulder.

This ground-giving process requires that negotiators understand the experiences of their counterparts. Once negotiators see through a rival's eyes, blending efforts will be more effective. With more empathy, negotiators can more easily move parallel with the flow of the attack and make small adjustments in its course. Chinese alliance partners recognize this as well. The wisdom of Chuang Tzu has taught them to understand one's adversary thoroughly, and "lead him to where he is without fault" (Tzu and Merton 1965).

Before entering important negotiations, American managers should carefully consider what objectives follow from their "hard boundary" issues. They should visualize all the people who will participate in the meeting, then put themselves in each one's place and consider all the respective goals, as well as any objec-

> "By Western standards, literally anything can happen in Chinese conflicts. Negotiators must create alternatives for every business expectation and exit strategies for every negotiation."

tions that might be raised to their agenda. Managers should prepare to disarm the opposition and not enter negotiation until they are absolutely sure of the direction sought for the meeting. This approach, known in the *Bing Fa* as "becoming your opponent," breeds an empathetic understanding of adversaries and their objectives. American tractor maker Paccar, Inc. used similar "blending" tactics to overcome the objections of its Chinese counterparts, and has now started a successful truck-making operation in China. Solutions that give all parties what they want often become more apparent when this tactic is used–solutions that would have remained hidden if the American managers had focused narrowly on a one-sided agenda.

5. Retreat gracefully. When negotiators too readily accept mistakes or poor judgments, their performance suffers. But when they see mistakes as the enemy, negotiators become inflexible–and are more likely to receive the harsh blows they were trying to avoid in the first place. As usual, the ideal relationship in China is paradoxical. Errors can be both friend and foe to negotiators.

By Western standards, literally anything can happen in Chinese conflicts. Negotiators must create alternatives for every business expectation and exit strategies for every negotiation. If their initial thrusts are knocked down, they should compensate as gracefully as possible and return to their hard boundary positions. As one American consultant in China said, "In tough negotiations in China, you can retreat but you can't let yourself be steamrolled. You have to hold strong at some point." He quickly added, "Please don't quote me."

Graceful compensation involves a smooth transition from original to alternative positions. The process should be open-ended. Planning for failure and retreat is a simple act of foresight. Doing so honors the unpredictable nature of the Chinese marketplace. Given the context of Chinese business relationships, continually refining one's views represents the essence of intelligence. Chinese alliance partners understand this. They have inculcated the *Bing Fa* maxim, "Retreat is another form of advance. Good men do not fight losing battles." To attain ultimate victory (market share, technological advantage, customer intimacy) in China, companies may need to accept a temporary defeat and, by escaping, preserve their strength for other days and other conflicts. American firms should learn that no disgrace is associated with changing soft-boundary objectives in China.

One fear of many American companies entering joint ventures is that their arrangements could cause them to lose valuable technology. And indeed, sustaining successful market entry may well require American firms to give up such valued assets as technology. But, says Paul Cheng, head of Asian mergers and acquisitions at BZW Asia Ltd., "Protection of technology is a lost cause. In a competitive [Chinese] environment, even if you don't want to give away your technology, somebody else will—in order to get into that particular market" (Miller 1995). Microsoft, itself a celebrated victim of Chinese piracy, decided in 1996 to share portions of its proprietary technology with some two dozen strategic tie-ups among government ministries, local computer makers, and universities. Its reasoning: Microsoft is in China for the long run and this action will build closer relationships.

6. Understand the role of deception. According to Sun Tzu, a battle may be won by "offering the enemy a bait to lure him, then feigning disorder and striking him." *Bing Fa* texts agree that the essence of successful warfare is deception. Victory is to be achieved through any means, and deception of the opponent plays a vital role in the strategy of war. Although Western history features numerous examples of deception. Americans still tend to idealize a tradition of openness and fair play. Skill in deception has never seemed a heroic quality to them. When applied in business settings, the word "deception" raises strong negative connotations among most Americans, thereby tending to make U.S. negotiators naïve and vulnerable to Asian strategies of deception (remember Pearl Harbor). The ability to mislead an opponent has always been seen by Chinese as admirable. Chinese are clearly not without honor, but such ethical distinctions are cultural. American managers should thus enter conflict negotiation only after they are conversant with what are (by Western standards) Chinese ways of deception and guile.

The art of Chinese deception, say Hamilton and Strutton (1994), involves two basic tactics. Hiding the truth is a tactic of concealment that potentially might be used to prevent alliance partners from learning the true extent of one's capabilities or the true nature of one's intentions. The "real" may be concealed by showing false strength or false weakness.

Showing false strength is a tactic of deterrence or bluffing. Organizations can show false strength by embellishing actual market positions or exaggerating strengths. Though popular, this strategy has serious flaws. Success hinges on an opponent's rationality; the strategist is betting that a reasonable opponent will avoid the prospect of a forceful counterstrike by withholding attack. But showing false strength might actually prompt assaults; some Chinese business people prefer to attack strength.

Showing false weakness (disclosing the false) is also a common Chinese tactic. Here, strategists construct scenarios in which their organizations will be perceived as less than they actually are. Sun Tzu advised, "Pretend inferiority and encourage his arrogance." This tactic can be useful in that many

negotiators—particularly Americans—may lack the motivation to crush the weak.

When taking advantage of apparent weakness, American firms may be walking into a trap. If an opening appears enticing, be wary. If an opportunity seems too good to be true, it probably is. Consider the value of Intel CEO Andy Grove's motto, derived from his extensive business experience: "Only the paranoid survive." By following such a precept upon market entry, Intel is now doing more than just surviving in China.

So American negotiators should be aware of the likelihood that deception will be used. Once the possibility of its presence and the cultural rationale for its use is understood, deception is easier to counter. One Chinese business person said that the Chinese "study history and strategy not to practice deception on others, but to protect themselves from the deceptions of others." It appears, however, that someone must be practicing to deceive or there would be no need for protection.

> "Stripping an alliance partner of his face is perhaps the worst tactical error that can be made in China."

The use of deceptive practices will affect both parties to a *guanxi*. When creating a ruse, the deceiving negotiator's attention is likely to become fragmented, making it difficult to focus on a single objective. Maintaining a deception, which often involves a series of other deceptions, can easily become time consuming and debilitating. In most negotiations, American firms should practice honesty as the policy of choice. Still, when negotiating conflict resolution in China, firms should reserve a place for illusion; but it should be used sparingly, selectively, and wisely.

7. Give your opponent face. "Gentlemen call attention to the good points in others; they do not call attention to their defects. Small men do just the reverse"—or so said Confucius in *The Analects* (Giles and Tsieng 1970). In China, any verbal tactic that involves "trash talking" or denigrating any aspect of an opponent should be rejected out of hand. Opponents in conflicted relationships should be treated with sincere respect. This is not just a common courtesy; it is an imperative born of logic. Human beings and organizations are fundamentally unpredictable. Appearances deceive; partners may be far more capable than they initially appear. Current adversaries may acquire new knowledge, skills, or allies that will make them formidable enemies or impressive partners in the future. Clearly, then, the short- and long-term interests of

American business entrants will usually be best served by giving face to all Chinese opponents.

Americans should be enthusiastic in their dealings with Chinese interests, but they must avoid appearances of aggression. They should never attempt to resolve a conflict by making a demand and should never ask partners, "Do we have a deal?" Chinese business people will have great difficulty responding to an ultimatum. To acquiesce to such demands would cause them to lose face. Stripping an alliance partner of his face is perhaps the worst tactical error that can be made in China. In Asia, face is the reflection one sees in one's fellows' eyes; it embodies one's standing in the community. Face is valued immensely in China; losing it diminishes one's identity. Nothing is gained by taking another's reputation, even in complete victory. Instead, any possibility of a future relationship is destroyed.

The other side of this equation is to give face to adversaries. U.S. managers should acknowledge their opponents' value, dignity, and position; they should feed their self-worth. Such respect indicates cultural intelligence and, for American managers, represents a non-losing proposition. Negotiating processes can be moved along by making polite inquiries as to whether a counterpart needs any information to make a final decision. Selling partners are expected to be deferential to buying firms. To act otherwise is considered rude.

Often, Americans believe respect for opponents is a sign of weakness. They believe "warriors" should be supremely confident, and that recognizing opponents' skills, power, or worthy positions reflects the attitude of a loser. Chinese alliance partners, on the other hand, are unlikely to have pretensions of invincibility. All Chinese students learn the expression: "If I can fight and win, I will fight. If I cannot fight, I will escape." In conflicted relationships, they are quick to recognize their partner's potential for high performance or, at the least, for a lucky break. Such attitudes are another reason why the Chinese are such worthy adversaries (and business partners) for American firms.

8. "In death ground, fight." (wisdom of the *Bing Fa*) For years to come, American firms participating in Chinese strategic alliances will occupy vulnerable positions in a risky marketplace. Occasionally, foreign partners will do everything well—learn the culture, avoid foolish mistakes, assemble seemingly healthy relationships—and still have the rug pulled out from under them. McDonald's recently had its 25-year lease on a key Beijing location revoked through no fault of its own.

Surviving a worst-case scenario first requires recognizing the danger. No model exists for such situations because no two are alike. In all cases, though, survival may depend on a timely and accurate analysis of the direct and immediate threat to survival. Negotiators should then integrate all their energies into a single, focused strike, aiming at the jugular or the knees. Mental state is the determining factor. No amount of skill or logic can compensate for a lack of intensity or a failure to exercise the universal right to self-defense. Such conviction will earn a Chinese adversary's respect and may temporarily forestall disaster. In fact, the Chinese classics call "for using noncoercive measures when confronting a more powerful and determined enemy, but only as an expedient, until [the Chinese 'opponent'] could be sure of prevailing" (Cohen 1997).

At the end, then, American managers should revert to a zero-doubt, *dualistic* state. In the face of absolute crisis, a zero-doubt final negotiating position must be buttressed by dead serious, in-your-face logic. A zero-doubt negotiating thrust implies a perfect, black-and-white commitment to a principle or position. All power should be harnessed and unleashed. At this point, if other things are equal, the firm that is more unified will prevail. This principle holds at all levels, from simple verbal disagreements to full-scale conflict. The more "at one" an organization is, the better its chances for effective performance in the face of worst-case conflict.

In 1989, Motorola and Chinese officials reached an impasse over China's insistence that Motorola accept a joint venture partly owned by the Chinese—the usual arrangement for foreign investors. The deal was about to blow up, but Motorola reintegrated its efforts, stayed the course, engaged its Chinese counterparts in continuous dialogue, and attained the outcome it sought. Sometimes in China what appears to be a dead end is actually a corner that needs to be turned.

A zero-doubt negotiating style should only be used when necessary. It is a short-term solution that easily leads to overextension and defeat if used beyond the initial crisis. Zero-doubt, by definition, means no opportunity exists to revise the strategy. Over the longer run, of course, zero-doubt stunts learning, prevents flexibility, and obstructs creative relationship-building efforts.

Many businesses face a considerable need to develop successful strategic alliances with Chinese partners. To do otherwise would forfeit incredible market opportunities. After entering such relationships, U.S. managers have a legitimate right to exercise some influence in China and protect what is legitimately their own. It is also logical for them to attempt to expand their original niche. But U.S. firms also must respect the ongoing need to exhibit restraint, moderation, and cultural humility.

As conflicts arise, American managers should take victories where they can be found; however, there is no point in aspiring to domination or long-term security. Neither outcome is likely to occur. American firms should content themselves with partial power and partial influence. By participating in the game without attempting to dominate it, foreign market entrants can enjoy a lengthy run. Western business people do not need to rule the Chinese to thrive in their market.

At century's end, the American style of capitalism seems to have emerged as the envy of the world. So why has it proven so easy for Chinese to get the better of American business people in many transactions? The answer, again, is culturally bound. Most Americans picked up their habits of thought in a world that has enough for everyone. In such a land, honesty, fair play, and generosity are more highly valued than the ability to wring every advantage out of every transaction. Chinese, for the most part, were educated in a school where no such luxuries existed. Now U.S. business people and their Chinese counterparts are meeting at the crossroads of these cultures.

But cultures do not have to continue to divide the nations, or make one nation vulnerable to the tactics of the other. Many of the negative outcomes described above can be avoided when Americans develop a better understanding of how to resolve disputes in accordance with Chinese cultural values. No U.S. firm will win its negotiations all the time. But after learning how to mollify conflicted relationships, American companies will secure the chance to do business with the same partners over the longer haul. This, in turn, ensures an opportunity for *guanxi* partners to engage in "give and take" over time.

The *yin* and *yang* of relationship marketing in global settings is that effective competitors usually must be effective "cooperators." Effective cooperation first requires that trusting relationships be established between the parties involved in global alliances. American firms operating in China should similarly strive to achieve such trust with their partners—even though it may be decades in the making. The alternative is that Chinese businesses will have little reason to feel committed to any mutual cause involving American partners.

Notes

1. Because the Chinese believe the marketplace is a battleground and that life is a series of battles, they also believe that mastering military strategy is essential for success. Asian leaders and common folk alike have always placed a great importance on studying the classical Chinese treatises on military strategy, known as the *Bing Fa*. Literally hundreds of such texts exist. *Bing Fa* principles are commonly applied to all affairs of daily life and thus exercise a profound effect on Chi-

nese culture. In fact, Johnston (1997) describes the Chinese culture as a "strategic culture."

2. Sun Tzu wrote *The Art of War*, the most reputable book of Chinese military strategy in existence. All translations of his work are quoted from Wu (1990).

References

Annual Report on National Accounts, Economic Research Institute, Economic Planning Agency, Tokyo, Japan (1996).

William Beaver, "Levi's Is Leaving China," *Business Horizons,* March-April 1995, pp. 35-40.

Richard Bernstein and Ross H. Munro, *The Coming Conflict With China* (New York: Knopf, 1997).

Business in Asia: The Search for the Asian Manager," *The Economist,* March 9, 1996, pp. 3-26.

Chin-ning Chu, *The Asian Mind Game* (New York: Maxwell Macmillan International, 1991).

Mark Clifford, "Coke Pours Into Asia," *Business Week,* October 28, 1996, pp. 72-76.

Warren I. Cohen, "China's Strategic Culture," *The Atlantic Monthly,* March 1997, pp. 103-105.

Confucius, *The Analects of Confucius,* L. Giles and Y. Tsieng, eds./contrs. (New York: Heritage Press, 1970).

Deng's China: The Last Emperor," *The Economist,* February 22, 1997, pp. 19-21.

Pete Engardio, "Microsoft's Long March," *Business Week,* June 24, 1996(a), pp. 52-54.

Pete Engardio, "The Relentless Pursuit of *Guanxi*," *Business Week,* September 30, 1996(b), pp. 124-125.

Jerry Flint, "In Good Times, Prepare for Bad," *Forbes,* July 1996, p. 46.

Aaron L. Friedberg, "The Problem Across the Pacific," *Wall Street Journal,* March 5, 1997, p. A17.

Mahatma Gandhi, *Mahatma Gandhi: His Own Story,* C.F. Andrews, ed. (New York: Macmillan, 1930).

Carl Goldstein, "A Delicate Balance," *Journal of Business Strategy,* November-December 1996, pp. 41-43.

Baltasar Gracian, *The Art of Worldly Reason* (New York: F. Ungar Publishing, 1960).

Erik Guyot and Diane Brady, "Banker's Death Highlights Risks for Business in China," *Asian Wall Street Journal,* September 23, 1996, p. 2.

J. Brooke Hamilton III and David Strutton, "Two Practical Guidelines for Resolving Truth-Telling Problems," *Journal of Business Ethics,* November 1994, pp. 899-912.

Philip R. Harris and Robert T. Moran, *Managing Cultural Differences,* 3rd ed. (Houston: Gulf, 1991).

Murray Hiebart and Lee Matthew, "Pirates or Police?" *Far East Economic Review, 158,* 28 (1995): 25.

Chamers Johnson, "Breaching the Great Wall," *The American Prospect,* January-February 1997, pp. 24-29.

Alastair Iain Johnston, *Cultural Realism: Strategic Culture and Grand Strategy in Chinese History* (Princeton, NJ: Princeton University Press, 1997).

Joseph Kahn, "The Pioneers: Certain Companies Want to Be First In When a Country Opens Its Doors," *Wall Street Journal* (Special Supplement: World Business), September 26, 1996, p. A12.

Lou Kraar, "First Prize, One Contract in China; Second Prize, Two Contracts," *Fortune,* Dec. 11, 1995, p. 28.

Dinah Lee, "A Billion Customers, A Thousand Blunders," *Business Week,* July 15, 1991, p. 16.

William A. Miller, "The Far East," *Industrial Week,* June 5, 1995, pp. 37–42.

Ian P. Murphy, "It Takes *Guanxi* to Do Business in China," *Marketing News,* October 22, 1996, p. 12.

Michael Murphy, *Golf in the Kingdom* (New York: Viking Press, 1972).

William Safire, "China's 'Princelings' Play it Smart," *International Herald Tribune,* February 14, 1997, p. 18.

Karl Schoenberger, "Motorola Bets Big on China," *Fortune,* May 27, 1996, pp. 73–76.

Miyamoto Musashi, *A Book of Five Rings* (Woodstock, NY: Overlook Press, 1982).

C.S. Smith and M.W. Brauchli, "To Invest Successfully in China, Foreigners Find Patience Crucial," *Wall Street Journal,* February 23, 1995, p. A1.

Randall E. Stross, *Bulls in the China Shop, and Other Sino-American Business Encounters* (New York: Pantheon, 1991).

Hung-Chao Tai, *Confucianism and Economic Development: An Oriental Alternative* (Washington, DC: Washington University Press, 1989).

C. Tzu and T. Merton, *The Way of Chuang Tzu* (New York: New Directions, 1965).

U.S. Bureau of the Census, *Statistical Abstract of the United States: 1995,* 115th ed. (Washington, DC: 1995).

Jiu-long Wu, ed., *Sun Tzu Art of War* (Beijing: Military Science Press, 1990).

Anne Yang, "All the Coffee in China," *Chinese Business Review,* November-December 1996, pp. 47-49.

David Strutton is the Acadiana Bottling Professor of Marketing and the J.W. Steen Professor of Business Administration at the University of Southwestern Louisiana, Lafayette, Louisiana. **Lou Pelton** is an associate professor of marketing at the University of North Texas, Denton, Texas.

Prospects for consensus on global
business ethics principles.

Can Multinational Businesses
Agree on How to Act Ethically?

by RONALD E. BERENBEIM

I N HIS DISSENT in *Lochner v. New York* (1905), Oliver
Wendell Holmes gave definitive expression to the belief that it is possible to construct a workable system
for governing a diverse community. In words that presaged
nearly a century of constitutional change, he thundered
that "a constitution is made for people of fundamentally
differing views." Pressing the argument further, Justice Holmes insisted that societies can and must avoid the pitfalls
of ideology to construct a system of rules and processes
for governing people of many cultures, regions, and yes,
even "values" can be added to that list. What else is a
constitution but a system designed and built to function
in that way?

The foundation of Holmes' boundless confidence in
constitutionalism was his belief that a self-governing community derives its laws naturally through experience. Earlier, in his Harvard series of lectures on The Common Law,
Holmes argued that "the life of the law has not been logic:
it has been experience. The felt necessities of the time,
the prevalent moral and political theories, intuitions of
public policy, avowed and unconscious, even the preju-
dices which judges share with their fellow men, have had
a good deal more to do than the syllogism in determining
the rules by which men should be governed."

These words have considerable resonance for companies competing in a global economy. A workable consensus regarding business principles, practices, and procedures
that are applicable to situations that arise in radically different societies is now viewed as a matter of "felt necessity." It is also evident after a half-century of ideological
warfare that a successful effort to reach agreement on
common principles of business conduct will be derived
more from "experience" than from the application of

"prevalent moral and political theories" [or] "intuitions of
public policy."

A corollary to that proposition is that governments are
limited in their ability to promote agreement regarding
global standards of business conduct. In contrast, practitioner commissions have, within the last decade, enjoyed
demonstrable success in encouraging serious discussion
and formulation of guidelines for best practices. For example, the response to the Cadbury and Vienot corporate
governance reports suggests that a committee of peers may
have greater potential than a governmental commission to
generate interest and incentives for companies to focus on
best practices.

In its search for global business ethics principles, practitioners and interested parties should examine four subjects: 1) standards of conduct for the business professional;
2) global standards of corporate conduct; 3) essential host
country conditions for profit-making activity; and 4) protocols for operating in host countries where minimal
standards are not met.

STANDARDS OF CONDUCT FOR
THE BUSINESS PROFESSIONAL

The first step in the articulation of global business ethics
principles is the recognition that ethical decision making
is a key responsibility for a growing percentage of the
work force. The complexity of tasks and issues confronted,
the diversity of cultures in which companies engage in
business (within and outside the borders of their own
countries), the need for continuous learning, and limited
supervision challenges individual workers to be moral
legislators.

Even as work has developed a larger ethical component, the institutions to which society looks to develop
the moral imagination have diminished in importance. In
the United States, the town meetings and voluntary asso-

*Ronald E. Berenbeim is director of Global Business Ethics
Principles Working Group at The Conference Board.*

From *Business and Society Review*, Number 98, 1997, pp. 24-28. © 1997 by Blackwell Publishers. Reprinted by permission.

ciations that de Tocqueville so admired have ceased to play the vital role that they once did in helping people to become morally articulate. While it is worth noting that we live in an era of religious revival (nowhere more evident than in the United States), it is primarily in the office that people are confronted with the choices that will enlarge or diminish their moral capacity.

Within the last 10 years, business institutions have begun to acknowledge a role that they did not welcome and with which they were not at first entirely comfortable. Corporations are learning organizations and ethical literacy is part of their curriculum. Employees have responded in a curious way. No doubt many of them resent the new demands of ethics training and review of conduct statements, but, at the same time, the professional associations in functional specialties such as human resources and purchasing to which many belong have developed statements of professional conduct and accountability. In addition, a growing number of corporate employees are already subject to the well-established ethical requirements of law, accounting, and increasingly, medicine.

"It is primarily in the office that people are confronted with the choices that will enlarge or diminish their moral capacity."

Despite the influx of workers trained in traditional professions, the most common professional degree for managers remains the Master of Business Administration (MBA). As a result of curriculum changes, recent and prospective graduates of leading business schools are now well versed in legal and ethical methodologies for resolving problems on a case-by-case basis. At a minimum, the current expectation is that an MBA can recognize an ethical problem and the interests affected by the outcome, has acquired the analytical skills necessary to deal with this kind of conflict, and can apply methodologies to formulate a rule for dealing with recurring situations.

Senior executives and most of the people that their companies are recruiting are now comfortable with the language of ethics. Of the four major subject matter areas in the search for global ethics principles, it is easiest to reach a consensus on standards of individual accountability. After all, it is a fairly undemanding exercise for companies to tell their employees that they are expected to act in accordance with the highest standards of honesty and care and that they will suffer severe consequences if they do not. The challenge is to make these exhortations meaningful. Companies that do not have ethical performance standards, criteria for the political or legal environments in which they do business, and protocols for operating in countries where the environment makes it difficult to function ethically will force employees to

choose between complying with ethical requirements or achieving business performance objectives.

In addition, many of these employees will belong to professional associations that have their own proposed rules of conduct which may, in certain instances, raise serious questions regarding individual business decisions. While such situations cannot be avoided, there is a need to discuss how the risk of conflict can be minimized.

GLOBAL STANDARDS OF CORPORATE CONDUCT

All major business enterprises (even those that do not pursue business outside the home country) now compete in a global arena. Efforts to develop global standards of corporate conduct have achieved some degree of consensus with respect to appropriate subject matter (e.g., corruption, environmental responsibility, product safety and quality), but, of course, the actual standards with respect to these areas are a matter of serious debate.

The most difficult analytical problem in this area (and a critical element in determining standards) is the issue of accountability to stakeholders. The requirement (or lack thereof) to balance competing stakeholder claims is a critical issue because, with the exception of corruption, the growing consensus as to appropriate subject matter reflects an implicit acknowledgement of stakeholder claims other than those of the shareholder.

In this discussion the law creates more confusion than clarification. Jurisdictions vary considerably in their prescriptions to officers and directors for the balancing of stakeholder claims. For example, in the United States alone, there are states that have stakeholder statutes that permit varying degrees of consideration of the economic impact on local communities of the sale of the company. Other states, notably Delaware, where a significant number of U.S. companies are incorporated, have no such statutes. And, of course, U.S. law and that of other countries differ considerably with regard to the obligations of officers or directors to show moral restraint in situations where maximizing profit may inflict injury on nonshareholders who have an important relationship of dependency with the company.

Ultimately, widespread acceptance of corporate conduct standards will depend in significant measure on the degree of acceptance accorded to the emerging corporate governance model for global companies. The interest in a global corporate governance template is driven in large measure by the need for uniformity in standards of board accountability, performance measures, and disclosure requirements in world capital and consumer markets. Unavoidably, the demand for corporate accountability to investors will also generate a broader discussion as to whether corporate acknowledgement of nonshareholder interests remains primarily a matter of strategic necessity or rises to the level of a moral, or even legal imperative.

In comparison with the analytical difficulties of formulating global standards, issues encountered in implementation and monitoring are somewhat less formidable, but they are by no means easy. The fundamental problem is simply stated. Companies have legislative and enforcement mechanisms for the development and implementation of rules of conduct. As processes go, legislation is

---

"Does acknowledgement of nonshareholder interests remain primarily a matter of strategic necessity or does it rise to the level of a moral or even legal imperative?"

---

malleable; enforcement is oppositional. Legislative success requires inclusion and mutual forbearance to achieve a consensus that is somewhat less than each individual party had hoped to obtain. Legislation is an effective method (perhaps the most effective) for reconciling conflicting cultural norms and giving expression to them in a single rule.

In contrast, enforcement demands obedience and, significantly, in this context, a willingness on the part of community members to report the infractions of others. Indeed, there may be no historical example of effective enforcement of a rule that did not have a substantial degree of voluntary compliance combined with a significant amount of citizen cooperation in identifying rule breakers. A law that can be enforced through voluntary compliance alone is unnecessary. Alternatively, where significant member or citizen cooperation in enforcement is not forthcoming, the state or organization would lack the means or the will to obtain compliance because it would require nothing less than tyranny to do so.

The foregoing formula exposes the difficulty that global companies encounter in the promulgation and enforcement of rules. No matter how inclusive a company's legislative process is, it is not representative in any real sense. In addition, enforcement of rules of conduct for global enterprises invariably requires compliance systems in cultures where there is intense hostility regarding the need for any citizen involvement in the identification of wrongdoers. If the employees also think that the rule is pointless, the compliance effort is doomed.

ESSENTIAL HOST COUNTRY CONDITIONS FOR PROFIT-MAKING ACTIVITY

No company can hope to comply with the rules for itself or its employees in environments where the absence or the breaking of such rules is a necessary condition of profit-making activity. You cannot say to a country manager, "Don't do this, don't do that, now here are your goals for Country X where all of our competitors do this and that. I don't want to hear any excuses if these objectives are not met." Under those circumstances, either rules

will have to be broken or ambitious goals will not be achieved.

The way to avoid this kind of impossible situation is to build a consensus among practitioners for enforceable rules and follow with an effective enforcement strategy. The example of the Foreign Corrupt Practices Act (FCPA) is a case in point. Although it would be more satisfying to punish the person who demands the bribes than the company that pays it, obtaining legal prohibitions in the major industrial countries and targeting the companies that bribe rather than the local citizens who demand payment is likely to have greater impact. Of course, both efforts are needed, but success is possible by focusing primarily on the supply side. After all, if no one paid bribes, before long, insistence on them would become less frequent.

Still, there may be practices that are so endemic (in some countries, bribery may be one of them) that they endanger a company's profit-making activity. There are two reasons why a country's failure to meet threshold legal and political requirements can compromise the profitability of a venture:

First, the absence of the fundamental elements of a civil society such as an independent judiciary, enforceability of contracts, and protection of intellectual property deprives companies of the minimal assurance that functioning capitalism requires to assure the reliability of transactions.

"There does seem to be some movement in the direction of corporate standards for host country moral minimums."

Second, the credibility and legitimacy of companies that aspire to global stature is significantly undermined when they do business in countries where the local regimes engage in conduct that traduces the rights of their people. To cast the matter in a more positive light, some companies are now more sensitive regarding human rights issues. It is an open question as to whether these concerns rest on principle or on a belief that such high-profile public statements are a source of competitive advantage in other markets where the company does business. Regardless of the motive, there does seem to be some movement in the direction of corporate standards for host country moral minimums. Just exactly what these minimums are with respect to due process and human rights protections is open to discussion. There does, however, appear to be a growing acceptance that they do exist.

The formulation of minimal standards has been further complicated by the argument that such initiatives show insufficient respect for host country cultures—or, as the proponents like to say, "values." One could just as easily argue that these self-appointed advocates also show a lack of respect for the complexity and richness of their own civilizations. In the case of Asia, the most prominent instance in which this specious argument has been advanced, the authoritarian interpretation of Asian tradition has been challenged by Amartya Sen and Simon Leys who have recently demonstrated what one would have thought a likely point that no one else had the wit to make—Confucian Analects are at least as contradictory as Platonic Dialogues. One example will suffice: "When Zilu asks him 'how to serve a prince,' Confucius replies: 'Tell him the truth even if it offends him.' "

Still, there is something even more odious about the rhetoric of "Asian values." Its condition for acceptance is the very patronizing attitude that it criticizes. No American would regard a country's current government as the apotheosis of its civilization. Is the Italian government the distilled essence of the culture that gave us Dante, Michelangelo, and Verdi? Even the Italian prime minister, one of the more estimable individuals to hold that post in some years, would make no such claim.

Of course it is important to recognize and respect the disparate values of the many different communities in which a company does business. Arguably, the best way to do so is through participation of representative members of all affected communities in a global effort to achieve consensus on minimum standards and to identify areas of difference in which it is important for companies to demonstrate awareness, flexibility, and tolerance with regard to local beliefs and customs.

PROTOCOLS FOR OPERATING IN COUNTRIES WHERE MINIMUM STANDARDS ARE NOT MET

Both corporations and their critics have tended to regard withdrawal as the only appropriate response where host countries fail to meet minimum civil law or human rights requirements. When confronted with the alternative of pulling out of or remaining in a country which the company has already identified as offering a good business opportunity, the argument often evolves into a debate over whether withdrawal or continued engagement is the most effective way to pressure rogue political regimes into more acceptable behavior.

More often than not, converting the discussion into a choice between sanctions and engagement results in the wrong argument about the wrong issues. Even countries that attempt these exercises in sovereign behavioral modification usually wind up confronting the stubborn fact that the course of a nation's history is seldom affected (except possibly at the margins) by external forces. Sea changes in political, economic, and legal systems are invariably the product of internal rather than external pressures.

Rather than limiting the potential responses to the two extremes of sanctions and engagement, sophisticated global companies now look at a broader range of issues in assessing the prospects that a host country offers for business success. If appropriate weight is given to factors such as the honesty of local officials, the enforceability of

contracts, protections for intellectual property, and the rights of local citizens, it is likely that fewer companies will have to choose between withdrawal or continued participation in an unattractive host country. They simply will not be there in the first place.

For those companies that do find themselves in a host country that fails to meet minimal standards, the focus should be on the company's needs and not the outcome that is most likely to bring about an improved situation. The important questions to ask are whether the weakness of civil society endangers prospects for profit in the host country market; or, if being tethered in the public mind to repressive host country regimes will have an impact on profitability in other markets. Finally, as a growing number of companies have mounted efforts to define core principles, decision makers must ask whether continued engagement in certain countries will breed a lack of respect for those principles and, in so doing, will weaken the company's institutional fabric.

THE SEARCH FOR GLOBAL BUSINESS ETHICS PRINCIPLES: PROSPECTS FOR SUCCESS

Until recently, we have not thought much about global business ethics principles because it was not necessary to do so. For nearly 50 years the cold war limited opportunities in much of the world for U.S., Canadian, European, and Japanese companies. It was difficult to find a corporation that could claim to be truly global. The cultural factors that Justice Holmes would acknowledge are unavoidable considerations in the formulation of general principles for "people of fundamentally differing views" were safely ignored in authoritarian countries whose rulers were guided by the prospect of their personal gain and the West's strategic and geopolitical priorities.

For example, 30 years ago, most, if not all, U.S. and European companies had limited business prospects in what was then known as Czechoslovakia and enjoyed highly favorable opportunities in Iran. Today, there is no East or West as such. Achieving some degree of consensus regarding the Czech Republic's business conduct standards and those prevalent in the rest of the advanced industrial world is not a matter of serious concern. At the same time, after nearly two decades of isolation, the day may be at hand when global companies can again compete in Iran. And the terms of Iran's reemergence requires careful thought.

The Iranian example underscores the importance of global business conduct principles. Business practice now plays a critical role in defining the terms of engagement between nations. The effort of global companies to reach consensus regarding the rules that govern their competition will go a long way in determining how effectively the world of the twenty-first century can accommodate people of fundamentally differing views.

Us and Them

The gospel is that we must be sensitive to cultural differences to succeed in a multicultural environment.
Don't swallow that gospel whole.

By Lívia Markóczy

As we increasingly find ourselves in multicultural environments, we are told—often we tell ourselves—to be ever more sensitive to the power of cultural differences.

We've been told that American management is deeply rooted in the culture of the frontier and individual freedom, while Japanese management is deeply rooted in a collectivist national spirit. The story goes that there are fundamental differences between "us" and "them" in how we perceive business environments, threats, and opportunities; the role of management; the value of cooperation; the importance of maintaining dignity (or "face"); and so on.

It's a nice story, and its claims are often supported by impressions, amusing anecdotes, and even research, but some hard questions should be asked:

- Are its claims so common because they are correct?
- If they're incorrect, why are they believed?
- And, finally, if national cultural differences don't matter as much as is often claimed, can we ignore them?

My own feeling, to put it plainly, is that national cultural differences are overrated. How can I justify such a bold claim? First, I must "unconvince" you of conclusions that you either have experienced or have likely heard about.

Take a look at the two lines in the familiar Müller-Lyer Illusion shown above. Although you may perceive—like most people the world over—that line (a) is longer than line (b), you can quickly confirm that they are the same lengths. Even armed with that knowledge, however, line (a) still appears longer than line (b). Just as some fact about the human mind causes us to misperceive the relative lengths of those lines, some cross-cultural fact about the human mind leads us to exaggerate cultural differences. Just as we know to be extra careful when looking at the figure, we must learn to proceed with caution when looking at cultural differences.

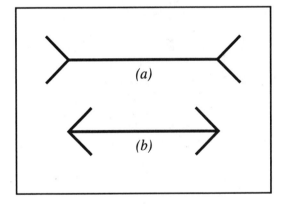

Again and again, psychological experiments have shown that when we view behavior from someone of our own culture, we treat it in a rather mundane manner, but when we view the identical behavior from someone of another culture, we attribute deep cultural explanations for it. In one experiment, American MBA students shown a video of a white American manager (actually an actor) behaving in a particular way were asked to evaluate him. They rated him in fairly normal ways. When a similar group of students were asked to rate a Japanese manager (another actor) be-

LÍVIA MARKÓCZY is senior research fellow at the Cranfield School of Management in the United Kingdom.

From *Across the Board*, February 1998, pp. 44-48. © 1998 by The Conference Board, Inc. Reprinted by permission.

having in exactly the same way as the other manager, they began to argue about how different Japanese management was. This is just one of many examples that social psychologists have used to show that we automatically and subconsciously look for and exaggerate differences based on nationality.

Recycled Impressions

Some studies have reported the importance of national differences based on expatriate surveys or interviews. Such studies usually contain delightful anecdotes and often insightful analysis into the differences.

Ultimately, however, these studies are like demonstrating that line (a) in the figure is, in fact, longer than line (b) by asking people which line appears longer. It may be a very important fact that people *see* one line as longer than the other (or see large and important cultural differences), but the *actual* lengths of the lines cannot be determined by majority vote.

Psychologically, the most overwhelming factor of cultural identification is language. It is also the means of cultural transmission, and, upon learning a second language, almost everyone soon concludes that you can only understand the other culture if you know its language. The "Whorf Hypothesis" (named after 1950s amateur linguist Benjamin Lee Whorf)—that grammatical facts and categories of the particular language you speak influence (or even determine) the way you think—is republished year after year, and has often been used to argue for cultural differences. Some articles in leading management journals attribute differences in Polish and English management more to the differences in the respective languages than to the 40 years of communist rule in Poland.

The problem with the Whorf Hypothesis is that it evaporates whenever linguists and anthropologists take a closer look. Sometimes "facts" about the language disappear, as in the case of the alleged 80 Eskimo words for snow. (When examined, English and most Inuit languages have about the same number of words for snow.) Or the argument proves to be circular: (1) People who talk differently think differently; (2) how do we know they think differently? (3) Well, they talk differently! My native language, Hungarian, does not use separate words for "she" and "he," but I assure you that Hungarians are as conscious of

the differences between the sexes as anyone else.

Those who pursue this sort of linguistic speculation too often fail to notice that their own language may contain the same exotic features they report in the foreign language. Some have tried to make a case about a difference in the Japanese mentality by pointing out that one of the words used in Japanese for "unusual" can also mean "foreign." That may or may not be an interesting fact, but as an argument for a different mentality it is outlandish. Only a stranger to the subtleties of English could advance such an argument.

Seeing Differently Or Seeing Different Things

In one series of studies, businesspeople in China and America were surveyed about how they see business. They found that Chinese managers thought that government support was more important for success than American managers did. Thus it was reported that Chinese and American managers have inherent cultural differences—different ways of seeing. But if one is willing to question the conclusion even slightly, the more obvious (and mundane) explanation for the difference immediately leaps out: Government support probably *is* more important for success in China than in the United States.

Some of the better work in management literature about cultural differences suffers from what I call the "spectrum illusion." If you were to blind yourself to every color except green, you would see a whole spectrum of differences in shade, from yellowish-green to blue-green. If, however, you saw the entire visible spectrum from red to violet, green would make up a small slice. And if you saw the spectrum from radio waves to X-rays, green would be a minuscule band in the middle.

One of the best ways to identify national (or any) differences is to blind yourself to other factors. Look for national differences by taking perfectly matched samples from national cultures, and see if you find differences. Careful studies conducted this way have found differences, and there is good reason to believe that what these studies have found is genuine. But they cannot tell us whether those differences are substantial, just as no one can say whether the difference between yellowish-green and blue-green is substantial.

A Hungarian manager and an American manager may have a different set of beliefs, but that difference may pale next to the varying views of a production manager vs. a marketing manager in the same organization. In some firms, I have found barely measurable differences along national lines, while the differences along functional lines were substantial. But I never would have found this if I only looked at differences based on nationality. I had to look for both kinds of differences, and then compare them.

Although I have been pointing out flaws, a great deal of work on national culture in management is very well-conducted. Most studies use a variety of methods so that a single flaw in one doesn't invalidate the whole study. But given our natural tendency to exaggerate national differences, we all need to exercise more skepticism about the importance of cultural differences. This means looking for flaws in work that reports such differences. And since management scholars are as vulnerable to the temptation to overrate national differences as anyone else is, we must take an especially hard look at this work.

Tempest in a Coffee Cup

Even if cultural differences are imagined or exaggerated, they should not be ignored. Imagined cultural differences can play as big a role as real ones; they will exist in any organization that has a workforce from different countries.

When I was conducting a study of organizations in Hungary with mixed-nationality management teams, I fell victim to the exaggeration of differences. As I went from manager to manager in Tungsram, a GE-owned lighting company, I had the feeling that the Americans didn't know how to treat a guest. After each meeting with an American, I walked away feeling that I was somehow unwelcome, despite the fact that some of the Hungarian managers were positively frightened. (One of the first things said to me by many of the Hungarians I spoke to was, "Who sent you to me?" I had more difficulty winning the trust of the Hungarians than the Americans.)

After reflecting a bit on why I found the Americans rude, I noticed that all of the Hungarians offered me coffee, while only one of the Americans did. I immediately started to speculate that the Americans had a more "down to business" attitude, while the Hungarians were more "people- and relationship-oriented." Perhaps that speculation is correct, but maybe it is because Americans drink less coffee than Hungarians. Or maybe Americans drink coffee at certain times of the day. (I met the one American who offered me coffee at 8:30 a.m.) Maybe offering coffee to office visitors is an arbitrary fact about Hungarian culture.

The Hungarian/American Continental Divide

For the most part, Americans as well as citizens of other nations tend to exaggerate cultural differences. But sometimes differences—however small—can have a real impact; we shouldn't brush off those that genuinely exist.

A lot of my work has dealt with Hungarians and Americans, and I've come across a few broad-based differences that may matter for management. Be advised that not all of these are based on solid difference; many are changing rapidly as the Hungarian economic system changes.

Short-term vs. long-term view. Counter to the standard stereotypes, Hungarians tend to advocate a long-term view of the organization, while the Americans stressed the short term. Of course, the organization in which I saw this most strongly was suffering tremendous losses at the time and had an American parent. So the Hungarians were, in effect, advocating the continued subsidy of a loss-making entity—the standard practice under socialism.

Zero-sum perception. Some Hungarians appear to see all business transactions as "zero-sum games," in which it is possible to win only if someone loses. This may lead to some added temptation to cheat in deals. Also, a failure to understand the difference between zero-sum and non-zero-sum games makes people vulnerable to pyramid schemes. The extent to which people buy into such schemes may be an indicator of how well people see the difference between zero-sum transactions and real business. Hungary suffered far less from these than Romania, which, in turn, suffered far less than Albania. It is tempting to say that the more exposure people have to a functioning market, the less vulnerable they are to zero-sum thinking. My view (based on impression, not research) is that in Hungary the problem has radically diminished in the past seven years.

Jobs are for earning a living, nothing more. Surveys have shown that under socialism in Hungary, people saw their jobs as merely something they had to do for money, not as something they could identify with. Note, however, that this could be a consequence of doing mind-numbing work in corrupt organizations that produce little of value. This sentiment may pass quickly. —L.M.

Maybe Americans don't enjoy the way coffee is made in Hungary. Maybe it was a statistical fluke.

The deep, culturally significant explanation was the one that came instinctively to mind, but once I forced myself to look for mundane explanations, they seemed at least as plausible as the deep cultural one. While I can't rule out the possibility of a fundamental difference in mind-sets, I should explore the mundane possibilities first.

Although my feeling that the Americans were slightly insensitive was probably based on a misperception on my part, the feeling was real. This real feeling, based on an imaginary difference, may very well have influenced my own behavior. I may have then been slightly colder than I otherwise would have been. It is then possible that the person who hadn't offered me coffee (which I would have refused anyway) would have sensed my coldness and responded in kind. This could cycle into a deep (and real) division. Just because the actual cultural difference may be small or even imaginary doesn't mean that it won't have real and substantial consequences.

At Compack Douwe Egberts, a Hungarian manager told me that the Dutch were mismanaging because they didn't understand Hungarian culture. Monday, March 15, was a holiday that year, and as a Hungarian manager explained, "[The Dutch] wanted to put this working weekend on the 12th–14th, which would have destroyed our holiday. They thought that this was the best arrangement for us, since we can then relax on Monday. This, however, shows that they do not understand the Hungarian culture and mentality."

Maybe this does show that the Dutch didn't understand the Hungarian mentality. But perhaps it showed only that the foreign managers—many there without families—had little better to do during this weekend. They could've expected the local managers to do the same, forgetting that the locals probably would like to spend the holiday with their families or had other uses for a block of three free days. Although this was inconsiderate of the foreign managers, it turned out to have nothing to do with not understanding the "Hungarian culture and mentality."

There may be important job-related differences between the expatriate and the local, but those differences often arise more from the nature of being an expatriate and being a local than from national culture. Accusations of fundamental inability to understand each other's mentality, however, can quickly escalate.

Enough Is Already Too Much

Armed with the knowledge that cultural differences are often illusory, we must still remain sensitive to people's perception of them. We can't just declare that we won't care about the differences. The arrogance of that stance would fall clearly into the stereotype of the "cultural imperialist." Learning each other's language is always an important step, as is trying to avoid nationality-based cliques. These steps are obvious.

Trying to show respect for a culture by following some of its behaviors is a far riskier strategy. There is a special danger when, for example, people from a developed country are working in a less developed one. An American trying to display a taste for Romanian folk dress might see himself as being culturally sensitive and open. A Romanian might simply consider it condescending.

Reflecting on the attitudes toward the fictitious African country Rimalia in the 1992 novel *Le Premier Siècle Après Beatrice* (The First Century After Beatrice), Lebanese writer Amin Maalouf makes this point: "I remember meeting a Rimalian academic who now missed the time when people spoke of 'a civilizing mission'; at least then it was still admitted that everyone was civilizable, even if only in theory. More pernicious, according to him, was the 'attitude which consists of proclaiming that everyone is civilized, by definition, and to the same degree, that all values are equal, that every human being is a humanist, and that, consequently, everyone must follow the path prescribed by his roots.' The young man hid his anger behind a veil of cool ironic ridicule: 'Formerly, we had to put up with contemptuous racism; nowadays we suffer from respectful racism. Indifferent to our aspirations, gushing over our gaucheries. . . .' "

While it is important to make an effort to learn each other's language, even here care should be exercised. English speakers who make a concerted effort to pronounce my name "correctly" or "the Hungarian way" may think that they are showing respect for me or my culture, but it can be (and often is) perceived as showing me my place and insisting on accentuating my differentness.

The sad thing is, there simply may not be a correct amount of cultural sensitivity. Whatever amount is sufficient to demonstrate openness and a desire to understand may already be seen as condescending to the individual. Enough may already be too much.

In the face of this, there are only two things that I can unequivocally recommend. First, with any sensitive interaction, consider both whether you are behaving in a way that is not sufficiently culturally sensitive and whether it is so culturally sensitive that it is condescending. Recognize (and accept) that your behavior might have to fail on both counts. Second, when you sense a cultural division, look first for a mundane, ordinary explanation before attributing the cause to deep cultural differences.

This is hardly a magic formula for managing and utilizing cultural diversity. It does, however, have the advantage of being based neither on illusion nor wishful thinking. There is also a pragmatic upshot to all of this: Deep cultural differences of incommensurable mind-sets are largely unresolvable. Once something has been identified as such a difference, nothing can really be done about it.

Ordinary misunderstandings and differences, however, can usually be resolved by ordinary means. Just as it makes sense to think of horses and not, say, zebras when you hear hoofbeats, it makes sense to look for tractable explanations for various problems before attributing the problems to some intractable cause.

Managing among cultural diversity will still remain something that requires care and thought, but it should be *careful* thought. We must move away from a culture of *culture* in which we attribute everything to deep, mind-shaping cultural differences, and more toward viewing individuals as individuals.

Government And National Parliaments

HOW RELEVANT IS ECONOMIC GLOBALIZATION AND REGIONALIZATION IN THE NEXT MILLENNIUM

Address by ROY MACLAREN, *High Commissioner for Canada*

Delivered to the 552nd Wilton Park Conference on the Role of Government and Parliament, West Sussex, England, February 23, 1998

That the direct role of national governments in a broad range of public policies has declined during the past decades seems incontrovertible. They increasingly share power with nongovernmental organizations, both national and international. The myriad of reasons for this—some of which combine both cause and effect—can be readily identified. What cannot be so readily identified are the implications for national legislatures. Among the reasons for the reduced centrality of legislatures which arise from burgeoning globalization are, in no particular order:

1) the ease of travel and other forms of communication, contributing to the rapidly growing globalization of trade in services, creating in turn a growing homogeneity of popular taste, gradually and unevenly we are all moving toward a world of consumer dominance rather than producer dominance, a new horizontal world which legislatures find far less easy to scrutinize and regulate;

2) information technology which transcends borders, collects and manages information independent of governments, facilitates electronic commerce and the further spread of transnational corporations and international standardization and regulation of business practices, values and nomenclature; hierarchies are being replaced by networks;

3) private capital flows now far exceed the value of trade in goods and services, the result of technology which is transferring financial influence from governments to an international marketplace; the global economy forces national governments into fiscal responsibility; basic economic decisions are made in and by the global economy rather than by legislatures;

4) the end of the Cold War or, as one wit famously put it, the end of history; or at the least the end of po-

litical history and the beginning of economic; the decline in the testing of national policies by legislatures against the omnipresent threat of latent nuclear hostilities, leaving only one superpower to which a degree of exceptionalism may apply, but replacing even there the primacy of defence, that single area of public policy to which legislatures could always lay undisputed claim;

5) the challenge of legislatures to cope with a new range of threats that respect no political boundaries: environmental degradation, narcotics, crime, corruption, terrorism and poverty to name but a few; the increasing blurring of what is foreign and what is domestic policy;

6) the parallel transfer of powers of decision-making and regulation upwards to supranational organizations—political, social, military but especially economic—and downwards to local authorities in an attempt to satisfy local aspirations to retain a range of tribal distinctions and traditions; international decision-making is seen as contributing to what has been called the "democratic deficit" of powers moving from elected assemblies to unelected international organizations;

7) widescale privatization of state enterprises which has reduced substantially the ability of governments to involve themselves in commercial decisions, thereby further limiting the relevancy of legislatures. Government fiscal disciplines, intended to eradicate budgetary deficits, lessen the ability of legislatures to attempt to manipulate economies through official spending;

8) the growth in influence of minorities or special interest groups—a common if not fully explained social phenomenon—imposes a certain paralysis in legislative action, sometimes at the expense of the common good. The current cliché, "political correctness," implies new awareness of

From *Vital Speeches of the Day*, May 1, 1998, pp. 425-428. © 1998 by City News Publishing Company, Inc. Reprinted by permission.

minority interests that vote seeking politicians assiduously court.

Much of this has major implications for the "relevancy"—to use that overworked word of legislatures today and tomorrow. Allow me to expand a little on one or two examples from the foregoing. Costly social programmes have everywhere been scrutinized and frequently reduced or even eliminated. An indirect result is that legislatures no longer continually pass judgment on their scope, duration or cost, at least to the degree that they did when they were major elements in national fiscal policy. Or to take another fiscal example: military policy and expenditure has always been regarded as the exclusive prerogative of national legislatures. So it is today, but military budgets are now almost everywhere substantially lower than they were in the perilous days of the Cold War. And so it is with development assistance, a result in part of the ending of the Cold War and a parallel disillusionment with the effectiveness of such transfers. The inclination now is to transfer the development role to the marketplace, to the private sector, and away from legislatures. All this and much else has resulted in a search for regulation at the international rather than the national level. As I said a moment ago, there is a parallel transfer of powers, of decision-making and regulation upwards to supranational organizations—political, social, military but especially economic—and downwards to local authorities in an attempt to satisfy local aspirations.

Some or all of these dynamic factors have led to two broad and quite contradictory conclusions. One school of observers contend that all these factors underline the need for the development of international rules and supranational organizations that can make and enforce rules for the global economy. The opposite school of thought argues that globalization—in the words of Karl Marx—will lead to the withering away of the nation state. Powers traditionally seen as the prerogative of sovereign states are being dispersed up, down and sideways, creating not a world government but rather global governance. One observer has contended that "a new world order is emerging, with less fanfare but more substance than either the liberal internationalist or new medievalist visions." The state is not disappearing, it is disaggregating into its separate, functionally distinct parts. These parts—courts, regulatory agencies, executives, and even legislatures—are networking with their counterparts abroad, creating a dense web of relations that constitutes a new, transgovernmental order . . . one that is more effective and potentially more accountable than either of the current alternatives. Liberal internationalism poses the prospect of a supranational bureaucracy answerable to no one. The new medievalist vision appeals equally to states' rights enthusiasts and supranationalists, but could easily reflect the worst of both worlds. Transgovernmentalism, by contrast, leaves the control of government institutions in the hands of national citizens, who must hold their governments as accountable for their transnational activities as for their domestic duties.

None of this—if indeed it is happening to the extent that the observer whom I have just quoted suggests—is necessarily in conflict with the development of international rules and institutions. Indeed, the "networking" at the sub-national level can help to provide the surveillance, monitoring and indeed eventually control of supranational entities.

Membership in any international organization—at least in any rules-based organization—necessarily involves a transfer of powers, a derogation of sovereignty, as traditionally conceived. And any derogation of sovereignty reduces traditional responsibilities of legislatures through the transfer of powers to the international organization. For example, membership in the European Union or in NATO or in the United Nations all limits to some degree the role of national legislatures, but in no sphere is this more evident than in the economic. It is patently obvious that participation in a free trade area or more especially in an economic union brings not only economic benefits but also limitations on the powers and responsibilities of national assemblies. This will be evident to any member of the European Union, but perhaps less evident than the impact of regional groupings is the transcendent impact of the World Trade Organization. Let us spend a few minutes on the example of the World Trade Organization as an example of an effort to reconcile globalism with a degree of national legislative responsibility.

The predecessor organization of the WTO, the GATT, was in letter a quite different organization than the WTO—at least in its formative years. To reassure the ever-vigilant U.S. Congress that its constitutional right to make trade law was not apparently infringed, the proposed international trade organization was eschewed and instead the General Agreement was cast in terms of a contract to which the Contracting Parties had freely entered and from which they could equally freely depart. There were rules of sorts, but their enforcement was decidedly within the purview of the Contracting Parties themselves. Today's World Trade Organization is quite another matter: it has many more agreed rules, more sophisticated and more comprehensive, but even more important is that it has an effective procedure for their enforcement, complete with panel reviews and a process for the appeal of their decisions.

This is revolutionary stuff. But perhaps we should not be surprised that it is primarily in the economic sphere that such reduction in the relevancy of legislatures is occurring. The Cold War era was essentially political; the post-Cold War era is essentially economic. The United Nations remains mired in assumptions of fifty or more years ago that the essence of the post-war comity of nations would be voluntary international co-operation by sovereign nation states. By contrast, the new World Trade Organization and several regional groupings are predicated on a system of rules which, if violated, offenders can be sanctioned. This, however, is not some blind commitment to supernationalism, but rather the national impact of moving toward one global market. If there is to be a single global market, facilitated by electronic commerce, then it would seem to follow that there should be one set of rules for all players.

The formulation and acceptance of global rules would be a complex enough challenge, fraught as it necessarily is with implications for the relevancy of national legislatures. Two additional complexities, however, immediately arise. First, if the implementation of trade and investment rules has been shifting from national legislatures to international organizations and if electronic commerce can readily transcend borders, who governs the governors? Can or should national legislators have any real role in the formulation, implementation and surveillance of international rules? If so, how? Second, globalization of trade and investment has necessarily rendered the WTO a very different animal from the old GATT. The elimination of border restrictions, the traditional role of the GATT, remains a vocation for the WTO, but increasingly the barriers to global free trade are recognized as residing in domestic regulation. If these domestic barriers are to be reduced or eliminated, then the WTO will increasingly enter fields—as the European Union has so preeminently done—that have been long regarded as the exclusive preserve of legislatures. Trade and investment in services and in agriculture are two obvious examples where the international and national priorities may conflict, but questions of trade and the environment and labour standards are not far behind—as NAFTA has already demonstrated. In the North American Free Trade Agreement, rules regarding labour and environmental standards were incorporated, a major step in international regulatory reach, prompted in part by the international networking of nongovernmental organizations.

In foreign and domestic policies the trend lines may now appear obvious enough, but the debates in the WTO can certainly be expected to become increasingly lively as national interests, emphasized by local legislatures, encounter the transcendent nature of global trade and investment liberalization.

The new global economy has many facets, but one of the most important changes has been at the level of ideas—the emergency of a remarkably broad international consensus that free market forces are the best prescription for economic growth. The end of the Cold War marked a triumph of this philosophy. There is a growing recognition among all countries that prosperity must be market-driven. Nations who erect trade barriers in a fruitless effort to preserve existing structures can look forward only to a faster decline. Underlying this is the dizzying pace of technological change. Semiconductors, fibre optic cables and communication satellites are weaving together a seamless world. Programmers in India are keeping the accounts for physicians in Texas. Internet customers can plan vacations, conduct banking and download products which never need to pass scrutiny at the border. The result is that whole areas of economic activity are becoming decoupled from time and space.

The speed of technological change has also contributed to an important characteristic of globalization—one which has caused a good deal of anxiety. I refer here to the massive structural change which is occurring throughout our economies. New industries are being spawned while old ones decline. Competition has grown ever fiercer as markets are deregulated and companies jostle for a global position. The result is a sometimes uncomfortable pace of change but also the creation of greater prosperity. As the economist Schumpeter noted, one of the hallmarks of capitalism is "creative destruction"—a constant churning which renews and rebuilds economic structures to ensure their ongoing vigour.

That brings me to another point about the new global economy—the opportunity which it presents to spread more widely the benefits of economic growth. In today's multi-polar world, economic power is becoming increasingly dispersed. As globalization deepens, the lines between the industrialized and the developing world are becoming blurred. As we link our economies—through wire, cable and satellite beam, and through an ever-swelling flow of trade and investment—we are also linking together global interests into a common future. As Richard Cobden said in 1857, "Free trade is God's diplomacy and there is no other certain way of uniting people in the bonds of peace."

But what does all of this mean for the international trading system? Globalization has brought a new agenda to the international trading system—an agenda which has expanded dramatically the scope and complexity of trade policy. Not so many years ago, trade negotiations tended to stop at the border. They were largely about reducing tariffs or bringing rules-based disciplines to bear on other border instruments such as quotas or anti-dumping duties. But today the trade policy agenda has as much to do with the regulation of domestic industries as with what happens at the border. Paradoxically, as our economies have become more international, trade policy and trade negotiations have in a sense become more domestic.

The process of moving trade policy from outside to inside the border has been going on since at least the Tokyo Round of the GATT and even earlier. But it took a quantum leap forward in the Uruguay Round, as we dealt with issues such as trade in services and intellectual property. The process will intensify further as the multilateral trading system addresses a challenging new agenda: trade and investment, trade and competition policy, trade and environment, trade and labour standards.

As we expand the ambit of international trade rules, we also place new demands on the WTO dispute settlement system. This system is generally regarded as one of the most important successes of the Uruguay Round. We put in place a single undertaking so that all disputes, regardless of subject matter, would benefit from the new rules. We agreed on tighter time frames and more automaticity to ensure that Panel reports would be accepted and respected. And we created a new Appellate Body.

The vibrancy of the WTO is particularly evident in this new dispute settlement system. No other multilateral institution is so active or so successful in resolving international disputes. The number of dispute settlement cases has increased significantly under the WTO, but this should not be taken as a negative sign. It has not happened because the international trading system is today somehow in worse shape than it was before. To the contrary, it is because countries now have more faith in the global system and in its ability to resolve trade problems. Legislatures have been willing to transfer upwards to a supranational organization the right to make, implement and monitor international rules in areas where not many decades ago national rules largely applied.

The WTO dispute settlement system is without equal in the field of international law, driven in part by the desire of governments to protect that increasingly large stake which their citizens have in international trade and investment, despite the occasional charge that a system that works on consensus like the WTO cannot possibly succeed in today's world. Yet how else would an international organization that increasingly deals with domestic policy make decisions? Is it likely that a democratically-elected legislature would legislate unpopular changes if its representatives had been "outvoted" at the negotiating table? I think of the consensus rule much as Churchill thought about democracy; it's the least unsatisfactory approach available.

So the vital life signs of the multilateral trading systems are strong. We can look forward to the WTO's continued success. For example, the next challenge will be to conclude, by the end of this year, a complex set of negotiations on financial services—which, incidentally, will be another example of an international trade agreement having a significant impact on domestic regulation. Looking ahead over the next few years, we shall see a number of negotiating timetables come together as the result of the built-in WTO agenda.

There is already agreement that another round of agricultural negotiations will commence by the end of 1999. This in itself will entail a major negotiation but, based on the Uruguay Round experience, it is unlikely to be successful if it remains limited to agriculture. In any event, there is also a commitment by the end of the decade to reengage a broad negotiation on trade in services. At the same time, we shall grapple with how to follow-up on the pioneering WTO working groups on the related questions of trade and investment and trade and competition policy. One can already see a critical mass of issues which need to be treated simultaneously, as we move the multilateral trading system toward the next millennium. This has already led some to suggest the possible need for a new round, a "Millennium Round," of multilateral trade negotiations.

I have not said much about regional trading arrangements and their impact on legislatures and traditional concepts of sovereignty. I have not because some of what I have said

about the multilateral trade organization applies holus bolus to regional arrangements—of which there are now so many and at such varying degrees of sophistication. Some, like NAFTA, parallel the WTO itself in having a dispute settlement procedure of real substance, others like APEC and Free Trade of the Americas are still at an embryonic state. And the European Union, being a single market and an economic union, is in a class by itself. Representatives of the Union will be able to discuss the far-reaching implications for national legislatures of a union which is now so advanced that it has its own parliament. This development can hardly be unexpected; again, as in the WTO, legislatures have voluntarily surrendered some of their traditional powers so as to capture more benefits for their citizens.

I said at the beginning a word about the "exceptionalism" that applies to the sole remaining superpower. In international relations this expresses itself in a variety of ways. The United States Congress, in the cases of both NAFTA and the WTO, hedged about its acceptance of their dispute settlement procedures with qualifications that in practice may amount to little, but were necessary to salve the unease of a legislature uniquely sensitive about any derogation of its sovereignty. But this exceptionalism has not in fact impeded the seemingly relentless trend to the transfer of traditional legislative responsibilities from the national to the multilateral level. This apparent trend has led one observer to offer the inconclusive and consciously contradictory comment that, "States feel they need more capable international organizations to deal with a lengthening list of transnational challenges, but at the same time fear competitors. Thus they vote for new forms of international intervention while reasserting sovereignty's first principle: no interference in the domestic affairs of states. They hand international organizations sweeping new responsibilities and then rein them in with circumscribed mandates or inadequate funding. With states ambivalent about intervention, a host of new problems demanding attention, and NGOs bursting with energy, ideas, and calls for a larger role, international organizations are lurching toward an unpredictable, but certainly different, future."

Unease about the role of unelected officials in decision-making in Brussels is evident among members of the European Union. But this unease is certainly not limited to Europe. "Globalization" has given rise globally to concerns about who can assert a democratic scrutiny of transnational activities. The way forward in the economic field, broadly speaking, appears to be the endorsement by legislatures of rules negotiated internationally and the provision for global review of their application. In other fields of human endeavour, the impact of globalization is even less clear and the response less certain. But one can take hope from conferences such as this that we shall, collectively, evolve new or additional institutions that will accord with the challenges and opportunities of transnational developments and with the expectation of citizens that democratic governance will be preserved.

Pat Buchanan and the illusions of protectionism.

Trade Free or Die

By ROBERT J. SAMUELSON

I.

In many ways, the timing of Pat Buchanan's plea for more protectionism could not be worse. The American economy is humming along, with unemployment around 5 percent since late 1996. If more than two decades of trade deficits have crippled us, the consequences are not immediately obvious. Not only is the economy of the United States now the strongest among advanced societies, but American companies still remain formidable, if not always dominant, competitors in many critical industries: computers and software; aerospace; biotechnology; communications and entertainment; banking and finance; business consulting; and medicine. The auto and steel industries—once given up for dead—have recovered from fierce foreign competition.

The coexistence of extraordinary prosperity and constant trade deficits is a paradox to be explained, but Buchanan ignores it. Reading him, you would not know that the United States is in a mighty boom. The temptation, then, is to dismiss his book as irrelevant. That is not a good idea. An all-but-announced Republican presidential candidate in 2000, Buchanan is a born-again protectionist, who sees his conversion as a harbinger of a broader shift among the public. "The Young Turks of the New Conservatism who would capture the Republican Party for Barry Goldwater in 1964 and Ronald Reagan in 1980 [were] free traders," he writes. "I know, because I was one of them." His hopes of a protectionist revival are not preposter-

ROBERT J. SAMUELSON writes a column for *Newsweek* and The Washington Post Writers Group. He is the author of *The Good Life and Its Discontents: The American Dream in the Age of Entitlement* (Vintage).

ous, regardless of the fate of his own candidacy. In a weakening economy, the message could play. Fears of an overseas job drain can be exploited; and working-class Democrats (Reagan Democrats) can be wooed with promises of greater job security. A populist majority might one day rally to economic nationalism.

Until now, of course, protectionism has been a political flop. Every politician who has tried to ride it to the White House has failed: John Connally in 1980, Richard Gephardt in 1988, Ross Perot in 1992, Pat Buchanan in 1996. It's worth trying to understand why. A common theory is that protectionism does not have much of a constituency. It is good rhetoric, but in the end it does not attract many voters, because not many Americans would benefit from import restrictions, especially if they resulted in retaliation against American exports. The raw numbers seem to confirm this. In 1997, for example, imports equaled only 13 percent of the economy's output, or Gross Domestic Product, and this was nearly offset by exports, 12 percent of GDP. Such figures suggest that protectionism has only a tiny constituency.

Buchanan, by contrast, argues quite plausibly that trade politics must be seen in a broader context, and that the free-trade consensus that arose after World War II has been crumbling for decades. It rested on three pillars, he says, each of them now weakened. The first pillar was a general sense that American industry was invincible; but that confidence shattered in the late 1970s and early 1980s, when many venerable American companies (Ford, Caterpillar, U.S. Steel, Xerox, Intel) came under siege from foreign competition. The second pillar of the postwar period was the cold war: greater trade with our allies promoted their prosperity (it was said), and this inoculated them against communism. The end of the cold war obviously dispensed with this argu-

ment. And the third pillar was the once-common belief that protectionism (and the Smoot-Hawley tariff) had been a major cause of the Great Depression. But memories fade, and much modern scholarship discounts protectionism as a major cause of the Depression.

The correct implication is that protectionism could again find a large following. The present optimism of Americans masks a deep uneasiness about the global economy that, once today's boom ends (as it will), could reemerge. We face a collision between an instinctive nationalism and the relentless expansion of global markets. Just because protectionism is not a desirable response does not mean that every protectionist grievance is bogus. Many of its complaints are clearly true: burgeoning global trade and investment do erode national sovereignty and self-sufficiency; and they do threaten some industries and workers; and they do create divided loyalties for American companies between enhancing profits and preserving American jobs.

It would be unnatural if Americans did not worry about these developments. Moreover, the economy's exposure to

The Great Betrayal: How American Sovereignty and Social Justice Are Being Sacrificed to the Gods of the Global Economy by Patrick J. Buchanan (Little, Brown, 376 pp., $22.95)

global competition is greater than the raw trade statistics indicate. In 1997, for example, imports accounted for only about 13 percent of American car and truck sales. But the entire auto industry faces global competition, because imports could capture almost any individual sale; and foreign car firms now produce here. The same is true of many industries. Global competition doesn't yet affect a majority of workers, but its impact—real and psychological—extends beyond an isolated minority.

Polls also find Americans to be ambivalent about trade. A CBS survey in late 1996 asked whether trade was good or bad for the country. The response was that 69 percent said it was good and 17 percent said it was bad. But a *Los Angeles Times* poll a few months earlier asked whether imports should be restricted to "protect American industry and jobs" or rejected "to permit the widest choices and lowest prices." The response: 63 percent favored restrictions, only 28 percent didn't.

It is easy to imagine a recession and a huge trade deficit fueling protectionism. Or a general isolationist drift could infect trade policies. One sign of how weak the free-trade consensus has grown is that the hostility is not confined to one party. Both Democrats and Republicans have protectionist wings. Three decades ago, this was unthinkable. Buchanan's audience is not economists or academics. It is the political class, and the editorial boards, and the opinion-makers. Despite its poor logic, his case has a glib allure. Protectionism has been so disreputable for so long that its opponents have grown complacent. They have not candidly acknowledged possible conflicts between free trade and foreign policy goals. And if they don't wake up, they could lose the argument by default.

II.

One thing is certain: the case for free trade cannot honestly be made on the basis of heritage. The greatest virtue of Buchanan's book is to remind us that America has mostly been a protectionist nation.

The political culture is certainly receptive. The godfather of protectionism was Alexander Hamilton, whose "Report on Manufactures," written in 1791, urged a protective tariff to nurture industry. To Hamilton, American "wealth . . . independence and security" depended on "the prosperity" of manufacturing. "Every na-

tion," he argued, "ought to endeavor to possess within itself all the essentials of national supply." The Tariff Act of 1789, which imposed duties of 5 percent on many imports, was the second law passed by Congress. Later tariffs went higher, and they stayed high for most of the nineteenth century. With the exception of slavery, they were the largest source of conflict between North and South.

The Tariff Act of 1828—the Tariff of Abominations—almost triggered secession. It imposed an average duty of 62 percent on 92 percent of the country's imports. The South Carolina legislature subsequently declared it and a revised tariff "null, void." A secessionist crisis was avoided in 1833 only because Congress agreed to reduce the tariff to 20 percent over ten years. In general, the South, a big exporter of cotton and a big importer of manufactured products, detested high tariffs. The North, with a larger manufacturing base, adored them.

One reason that tariffs stayed high was their role as the federal government's main source of revenue for most of the century. (The Civil War was the major exception.) But they were also kept high to protect industry. In the 1830s and 1840s, the Whig Party—headed by Henry Clay—urged national economic development through internal improvements (roads, harbors, bridges) and high tariffs. Lincoln, an early Whig, generally supported high tariffs.

Protectionism was often equated with patriotism. Listen to Justin Morrill, a Republican senator from Vermont who entered Congress as a Whig in 1855, and was among the most steadfast guardians of high tariffs until his death in 1898: "Free trade abjures patriotism and boasts of cosmopolitism. It regards the labor of our own people with no more favor than that of the barbarian on the Danube or the cooly on the Ganges." Buchanan enthuses over such flag-waving. He argues that high tariffs enabled America to become the world's great industrial power in the nineteenth century.

During the last half of the century, many individual tariff rates hovered around 50 percent, and the average tariff (on dutiable and non-dutiable items alike) was about 30 percent. They stayed high partly to repay the huge national debt run up during the Civil War. (The federal debt rose from $65 million in 1860 to $2.8 billion in 1866.) But there were other rea-

sons for the persistence of the tariffs. They were blatant protectionism and fervent nationalism.

A historic reversal was accomplished by Cordell Hull, Roosevelt's secretary of state, who shepherded the Reciprocal Trade Agreements Act of 1934 through Congress. This law transferred much of Congress's power to set tariffs to the president, who could negotiate mutual tariff cuts with other countries. A former senator from Tennessee, Hull had long believed that trade fostered goodwill among nations. And the Depression produced a backlash against protectionism. The backlash continued after World War II. In the 1940s, the United States helped to create new global institutions to prevent the return of '30s protectionism and deflation. These included the International Monetary Fund, which would make short-term loans of foreign exchange, generally dollars, to countries with big trade deficits (the idea was to preempt competitive currency devaluations or protectionism); and the General Agreement on Tariffs and Trade, which would negotiate and police tariff cuts and international trade rules.

Trade also quickly emerged as a central weapon against communism. The Japanese needed to trade to buy basic raw materials (food, fuel, minerals). "Japan cannot remain in the free world unless something is done to allow her to make a living," President Eisenhower said. Otherwise, "it is going to the Communists." For Europe, trade succeeded the Marshall Plan as a recovery strategy from war. In trade negotiations, American officials often made more concessions than they received. In 1954, the State Department proposed unilateral concessions on roughly half of all Japanese imports, from glassware to optical goods to cars. Hardly anyone—the textile, apparel, and shoe industries were major exceptions—felt threatened, because American industry and technology were so dominant.

In 1962, Congress passed John F. Kennedy's Trade Expansion Act, authorizing new trade talks, by huge margins (78–8 in the Senate and 299–125 in the House). As a 23-year-old editorial writer for the *St. Louis Globe-Democrat*, Buchanan was caught up in the fervor. Passage of the Trade Expansion Act, he wrote, was a "thumping administration triumph" that could "become the most potent cold war weapon in the free Western arsenal. . . ." Although he thinks expanded trade was then justified, he says that Americans went overboard. Free trade is not just an idea, Buchanan argues; it is a false religion that "holds out the promise that if we follow the gospel of free trade, paradise can be created on earth." Buchanan contemptuously quotes the nineteenth-century French economist Frederic Bastiat: "Free trade means harmony of interests and peace between nations. . . . We place this indirect and social effect a thousand times above the direct or purely economic effect."

On this, Buchanan is more clear-eyed than many free-trade enthusiasts. It is true that trade cemented America's cold war alliances, but this does not mean that trade can take us the next step—to universal peace and goodwill. What held the cold war alliance together was the cold war. It is dangerous to generalize from this experience; and a lot of history warns against viewing trade as a shield against war. Before World War I, Germany and Britain were major trading partners. Germany also traded heavily with Russia, Holland, and Belgium—and attacked them all.

Trade does not just bind countries together; it also arouses suspicions. In the 1980s, many Americans wrongly feared that the country would be taken over by the Japanese. Canadians feel constantly assaulted by American trade and culture, and so (to a lesser extent) do Europeans. Nationalism endures and endures; and although the tensions and conflicts rarely end in war, trade is not an automatic pacifier.

III.

What trade has going for it, of course, is economics. The most astonishing thing about Buchanan's book is that, although it is ostensibly about economics, it almost never engages in genuinely economic thinking. For Buchanan, the decision to expand or to restrict trade is mainly a political choice. Thus he ignores lower communications and transportation costs (container ships, transoceanic telephone cables, jets, satellites, and, now, the Internet) as driving forces; and as the cost of doing business across borders goes down, the demand to do business—including political pressures to permit it—goes up.

Neither Buchanan nor anyone else can repeal this relationship. Certainly countries can prevent trade by shutting themselves off from the world (as China did until the late 1970s), but it is harder and harder to do with surgical precision.

With trade comes travel, and modern communications, and global finance. Controlling the process has proven arduous even for the countries (such as Japan) most determined to do so.

This is one reason why more and more countries have embraced the global economy across a broad range of industries and activities. The other reason is that the potential economic gains of doing so have become self-evident. Buchanan treats the process mainly as a zero-sum game: one country's gain is another country's loss. If this were true, there would not be much global trade and investment. When losers recognized their losses, they would withdraw. Trade would occur mainly as a consequence of sheer economic necessity—countries importing essential raw materials (fuel, food, minerals) or goods produced only in a few countries (commercial jets, for example); or as a consequence of coercion—the strong compelling the weak to trade on disadvantageous terms, an informal neocolonialism. Otherwise trade would wither.

What is true, of course, is that individual companies or individual workers can lose in trade. General Motors can lose to Toyota; Hitachi can lose to IBM. But what is bad for a company or an industry is not necessarily bad for a country. Moreover, domestic competition causes more job losses than trade. Consider, for example, the job losses counted by the consulting firm Challenger, Gray & Christmas. Between 1993 and 1997, it found almost 2.5 million job cuts by American companies. The top five industries were: aerospace and defense, 270,166; retailing, 256,834; telecommunications, 213,675; computers, 212,033; financial services (banking, brokerage houses), 166,672; and transportation (airlines, trucking companies), 136,008. None of these cuts involved global trade. The causes ranged from defense cutbacks (aerospace) to new technology (computers). But Buchanan wishes to leave the false impression that, but for trade, the economy would be far less turbulent and harsh.

Given Buchanan's ignorance of economics, it is no surprise that his history, too, is badly warped. To suggest that the vast industrialization of the late nineteenth century, and America's rise as the world's most powerful economy, owes a great deal to protectionism is absurd. In the last half of the nineteenth century, the American economy benefited

from a virtuous circle. Railroads expanded dramatically. Between 1860 and 1900, the miles of track rose from roughly 30,000 to more than 200,000. Lower transportation costs expanded markets. In turn, this encouraged investment in new manufacturing technologies that lowered costs through economies of scale. Industrial output soared for all manner of consumer goods (clothes, shoes, furniture), for farm implements, for machinery. Larger markets and lower costs fostered new methods of retailing and wholesaling: the mail-order house Sears, Roebuck was founded in 1891.

None of this depended on protectionism. Some basic technologies (steelmaking, railroads) originated in Europe. And the United States also imported another vital ingredient of growth: people. In each of the century's last four decades, immigration averaged more than 5 percent of the nation's population. As for trade, it grew as the American economy grew. Between 1870 and 1890, both imports and exports almost doubled. The decisive limit on imports was the ability to export (as it is for most countries), not high tariffs.

Tariffs may have protected some American industries, but any effect on the overall economy is exaggerated. Suppose there were no tariffs; some companies might then have faced cheaper imports. To survive, American companies would have had to cut prices; and they could have done so by reducing wages. In this era, wages were what economists call "flexible": employers cut them when they thought that they must or they could. Between 1866 and 1880, annual wages for nonfarm workers actually declined 21 percent. But this did not mean lower living standards, because prices dropped even more. Over the same period, purchasing power for average workers rose 23 percent.

The point is that a country's capacity to achieve economic growth lies mainly in its own people, values, resources, and institutions. Trade supplements this in many ways. The simplest is comparative advantage, as it was classically conceived by David Ricardo. Countries specialize in what they do best, even if one country could produce everything more efficiently than another. Suppose the United States makes both shoes and supercomputers more efficiently than Spain. We need 100 workers to produce either one supercomputer or 1,000 pairs of shoes annually; and Spain needs 1,000 workers to make a supercomputer and 200 workers to make 1,000 pairs of shoes. Total production of computers and shoes will still be greatest if each country concentrates on its strength (shoes for Spain, computers for us) and trades with the other to satisfy its needs: America will have more supercomputers and shoes, and so will Spain.

Much trade of this type occurs. The United States imports shoes, toys, and sporting goods; it exports bulldozers, computers, and corn. Trade's greatest benefits, though, may transcend comparative advantage. Not everyone has to reinvent the wheel or the computer chip. Technologies, products, and management practices that have been developed abroad can be deployed at home. In theory, these gains can occur without a country opening itself to trade. Information can be stolen; products and processes can be imitated. In practice, however, it is much easier if a country is open.

For commercial or technological insight does not derive from a single dazzling flash. It consists in thousands upon thousands of small details. It encompasses how things are made, distributed, sold, financed, repaired, and replaced. The more isolated a country, the harder it is to come by all the details. Whatever its tariff rates, the United States in the nineteenth century was open in this critical sense. Its people traveled freely abroad; immigration was large; merchants were eager traders; and industrialists borrowed ideas from wherever they could.

These same processes also operated after World War II. All countries could (in theory) tap the same international reservoir of technologies, products, and management systems. Yet some countries did better than others, which was a reflection of their practices and policies. Despite mercantilist tendencies, Japan enthusiastically embraced trade; it systematically imported (via licensing agreements) foreign technology; and it routinely studied American management. The combination of high saving and proven investment opportunities propelled great economic growth, averaging about 10 percent a year in the 1960s. Countries that were more shut off (China, the former Soviet bloc, India) fared less well. And only when other Asian societies began imitating Japan did their economic growth accelerate.

This explains why poorer countries should now like trade. It has helped lift millions of people in Europe and Asia from abject poverty. But what's in it for us? Trade

can help to erode a country's relative economic superiority, and for the United States it has contributed to such an erosion. As other countries advanced rapidly, our dominance of the early postwar decades was lost. But this history cannot be undone. To preserve our position, we would have needed to be ruthlessly protectionist in the 1950s and 1960s: a policy that deliberately aimed to restrain the economic progress of Europe and Japan. But this would have been unwise, and even Buchanan does not contend otherwise. To long for our superiority of the 1940s is an exercise in nostalgia. Still, what is not true, then or now, is that trade impoverishes us. It is not depressing our living standards. It is elevating them. Trade may enable poorer nations to catch up, or to grow faster than we do; but this does not cause us to slow down. It is not a zero-sum game. We gain, too.

Competition is one way. Many countries now make and trade the same things, so comparative advantage doesn't really apply. Japan makes and trades cars, computer chips, and telephone switching centers; and so do the United States and Germany. The result is bigger markets that enable efficient producers to achieve greater economies of scale by spreading costs across more buyers. Prices to consumers drop. Boeing, Microsoft, and Caterpillar all have lower unit costs because they are selling to a world market. Domestic competition also intensifies. Imports compel domestic rivals to improve. Chevrolets and Chryslers are now better and more efficiently made because Americans can buy Toyotas and Hondas. In many industries—cars, copying machines, and machine tools, to name a few—American firms and workers have had to adapt to the best foreign practices and technologies.

What haunts free trade is the specter that all production will flow to low-wage countries. Yet this does not happen, for two reasons. First, low-wage workers in poor countries are usually less productive than well-paid workers in rich countries. In 1995, Malaysian wages were almost 10 percent of American wages; but the productivity of Malaysian workers (output per hour worked) was also about 10 percent of American levels, according to Stephen Golub of Swarthmore College. Companies shift production abroad, Golub main-

tains, only when relative productivity exceeds relative wages. If Malaysians earn and produce 90 percent less, there is no advantage in moving to Malaysia.

Second, when developing countries export, they earn foreign exchange (mostly dollars) to import—and do so. The global market for pharmaceuticals and software could not exist without the global market for shoes and shirts. In practice, developing countries' trade with advanced countries is fairly balanced, whether in deficit or surplus, as the table below shows. It gives developing countries' manufacturing trade with advanced countries as a share of their GDP. (The data is from Golub.)

Trade With Advanced Countries 1995 Percent of GDP			
	Exports	Imports	Balance
Brazil	1.7	3.1	−1.4
China	8.8	7.7	+1.1
India	3.8	3.3	+0.5
Indonesia	6.4	8.7	−2.2
Korea	12.3	13.9	−1.6
Mexico	19.3	16.8	+2.5

On economic grounds, then, the case against trade is puny. Gains dwarf losses. Still, the puzzle remains: If trade is good for us, why do we run massive trade deficits? We must (it seems) be doing something wrong if we regularly import more than we export. Well, we aren't. The explanation is that our trade accounts are incomplete. They omit a major American export which—if it were included in the reckoning—would bring our trade flows closer to balance. That American export is money.

The dollar serves as the world's major money: a means of exchange, a store of value. It is used to conduct trade and to make investments. In 1996, countries kept 59 percent of their official foreign exchange reserve in dollars; the next largest reserve currency was the German mark at 14 percent. Multinational companies keep accounts in dollars. So do wealthy individuals. In some countries, where people distrust the local money, dollars circulate as a parallel currency to conduct everyday business. Indeed, the Federal Reserve estimates that more paper dollars (the folding stuff) exist outside the United States than inside.

The United States provides the world a service, in the form of a fairly stable currency. To pay for this service, the world sends us imports. It is a good deal for us: every year Americans buy 1 or 2 percent more than we produce. This is the size of our current account deficit, a measure of trade and other current overseas flows (such as tourism and freight).

The concept here is the old idea of seigniorage: the profit that a government earns when it can produce money at a cost less than its face value. If a government can print a dollar for 5 cents, it reaps a 95 cent windfall when it spends that dollar. Similarly, the United States reaps a windfall when the world uses our money. The transfer occurs through the exchange rate; the world's demand for dollars holds the dollar's exchange rate high enough so that we do not balance our visible trade. (A high exchange rate makes imports cheaper and exports more expensive.) But for many reasons—intellectual laziness, theoretical messiness—most economists have not applied seigniorage to the world economy.

That is too bad. If they did, we would see that the trade debate's main symbol—the nagging trade deficit—does not symbolize what it is supposed to symbolize. It does not show that we are becoming "uncompetitive," or that we are "deindustrializing," or that we are "losing jobs" abroad. In any single year, shifts in the trade balance may reflect temporary factors. Stronger or weaker growth abroad will affect demand for our exports; stronger or weaker growth here will affect our demand for imports. Changes in technology or exchange rates may alter trade flows in particular industries and products. Yet the continuous trade deficits of the United States do not reflect any of these things. They reflect the world's demand for dollars. Perhaps that demand will someday abate (Europe's single currency, the euro, may provide an alternative global money); and if it does, the American trade account will swing closer to balance. For now, though, it is virtually condemned to deficit.

If we acknowledged this, much of the present trade debate would disappear, because the presumed goal of a "good" trade policy—a trade balance or a trade surplus—would be seen as unrealistic and probably undesirable. Instead, the debate over the economics of trade is simplistic and distorted. The supporters of free trade claim that it creates jobs; the opponents of free trade claim that it destroys jobs. Although both are true for individual workers and industries, they are usually not true for the economy as a whole. We could have "full employment" if we

didn't trade at all; and in a workforce of nearly 140 million people, the number of net jobs affected by trade (jobs created by exports minus jobs lost to imports) is tiny. Trade's true advantage is that it raises living standards.

IV.

The trouble is that the trade debate should concern more than wages or jobs. Buchanan's political appeal lies in his unabashed nationalism, and he is correct that we do not trade for the benefit of the British or the Brazilians or the Chinese. Trade needs to be connected to larger national purposes, and free-traders have grown lax about making such a connection. They are too eager to reduce the debate to a technical dispute over economic gain and loss. Although Buchanan engages in the same exercise—and reaches the wrong conclusion—he is much more willing to cast trade in terms of advancing broader American interests, preserving our national identity, and maintaining our moral values. A lot of this patriotic chest-thumping is nothing more than rhetorical flourish. And yet Buchanan is actually onto something.

Since World War II, American trade policy has made two central assumptions. The first, inherited from the Depression, is that protectionism destabilizes the world economy and that free trade stabilizes it. The second is that free trade enhances American security interests. Both notions were once right, but times have changed. Matters are now more ambiguous. A big outbreak of protectionism would still harm the world economy. Too much economic activity depends on trade for it to be cut painlessly. Yet deepening economic ties among countries—"globalization"—may also create instability. As for trade and security, they were fused by the cold war. Our main trading partners were military allies, and they generally embraced democratic values. Now trade has spread to some countries that do not share our values and to some countries that one day might be adversaries (China and Russia, most obviously).

What has gradually disintegrated is the postwar convergence among economic, strategic, and moral interests. Global economics has raced well ahead of global politics, creating potentially dangerous instabilities that are only barely perceived and may not be easily subdued. Commercial interests may increasingly conflict with security interests or moral values. If

we decide, for whatever reason, not to trade with India or China, other countries will probably fill the void. The possibility is hardly theoretical. After India's recent nuclear tests, the United States immediately imposed sanctions; but most other countries—Japan was an exception—did not. There are other examples involving Iran, Libya, and Cuba. Commercial rivalries can undermine security alliances: If our "allies" aid our "adversaries," are they truly our allies?

The very expansion of global commerce has also raised economic interdependence to a new level. Until now, the "world economy" has been viewed less as an organic whole than as the sum of its parts. It is the collective consequence of individual economies whose performance (though affected by trade) mainly reflects their own strengths and weaknesses. This may still be true, but it is less so. The growing connections among nations—through trade, financial markets, computer systems, people flows—may be creating an independent beast whose behavior affects everyone and is not easily controlled by anyone. Asia's economic crisis is surely testing the notion that growing "globalization" can boomerang. South Korea, Thailand, and Indonesia all borrowed too much abroad; Japanese, European, and American banks lent too much. Excesses went unchecked by either local or international governmental supervision. Economic growth in all these countries has now plunged. There are spillover effects, and this could portend future crises.

Protectionism's best case is that it might insulate us against potential global instability. We would sacrifice somewhat higher living standards for somewhat greater tranquility. But this is not what protectionists have in mind; and if it were, it would be hard—maybe impossible—to achieve.

Consider Buchanan's program. He would impose sliding tariffs on countries reflecting his likes and dislikes. Europe would be hit with a 15 percent tariff; Canada would be spared if it adopted our tariffs (otherwise foreign goods would pour into the United States via Canada). Aside from a 15 percent tariff, Japan would have to end its trade surplus or face tariffs that would do so. Poorer countries would face an "equalization" tariff to offset their lower wages (such tariffs could go to 90 or 95 percent).

The result, Buchanan says, would be "millions of high-paying manufacturing jobs for all our workers—immigrant and native-born, black and white, Hispanic and Asian— . . . and trade and budget surpluses as American workers find higher-paying jobs and contribute more to Social Security and Medicare, deficit reduction and tax reduction." Well, not exactly. If the program worked as planned, it would repatriate low-wage jobs making toys and textiles and eliminate high-wage jobs making planes and bulldozers. Overseas markets for American exports would shrink, because countries that could not sell to us could not buy from us. And it is extremely doubtful that Buchanan's program would work as planned. He ignores floating exchange rates: if we raise tariffs by 15 percent, other countries' currencies may fall by 15 percent, leaving import prices unchanged.

Moreover, anything like Buchanan's plan might also create so much uncertainty that it would depress global economic growth. Companies might not invest in the United States—to make toys or textiles—because they could not be sure that high tariffs would not be repealed or neutralized by exchange rates. Yet companies might not invest elsewhere, because they could not know whether the tariffs might work or, if they did not work, whether they might inspire higher tariffs. All countries would suffer from lower investment and growth.

The point is that global commerce has become so widespread that it cannot be wrenched apart, short of some calamity. It is increasingly hard to find major American companies (trucking firms, railroads, or electric utilities, perhaps) that do not have major overseas stakes, either through trade or investment. Coca-Cola sells 70 percent of its beverages outside North America; McDonald's has almost half its 23,000 outlets in foreign countries; Intel derives 56 percent of its revenues abroad. The quest for global markets is one of the economic hallmarks of our times. The recent announcement of the Chrysler/Daimler-Benz merger emphasizes the point. To the extent that people like Buchanan try to frustrate it, they will simply inspire more ingenious—and probably more inefficient—ways for companies and investors to try to evade new barriers.

Even more daunting is the inclusion in the global trading system of countries that do not qualify as either allies or adversaries. We are, in effect, taking a colossal gamble that our commitment to greater trade will turn out for the best. This gamble rests on two pious hopes. The first is that trade, by tying countries closer to each other, diminishes or eliminates the prospect of war among them. Countries that trade are too interdependent to take up arms against each other. Again, Buchanan is properly skeptical of this; what he might also have said is that we could be far more threatened by a modernized China or Russia than by countries that exist in self-imposed economic isolation. One obvious aim of Chinese trade is to transform its military into a world-class force. In theory, American policy prohibits the export of potentially defense-related technology. In practice, controlling "dual use" technologies (those that have both civilian and military applications) was difficult even in the cold war. It is much more so now.

The other (related) pious hope is that greater trade abets prosperity, and that the entire process builds a new middle class, which in turn leads to the triumph of democracy and respect for individual liberties. As nations become more like us, the dogma says, they will be less antagonistic. In some countries, this has happened. Yet surely there is no logical or mechanical connection between growing trade and the creation of genuine democracies. Political progress does not automatically follow economic progress. A less inviting possibility is that rapid economic growth will subvert traditional political and social systems without immediately creating viable, open alternatives. Nor is it inevitable that all democracies will be friendly with each other. Americans too easily think—this erroneous assumption has characterized all recent administrations, from Reagan to Clinton—that we can find a formula for cloning our beliefs and our institutions in foreign cultures.

None of this seems to matter much now. The world is generally at peace. America is prosperous. People easily overlook the contradictions and the inconsistencies. Yet these abound and, in more stressful times, they could bubble to the surface. The more countries blend economically, the more their values and their political systems collide. What we consider normal and desirable, other countries often consider abnormal and undesirable. To some extent, differences will persist: if McDonald's wants to do business in Russia, it will have to conform to Russia's laws and customs. But to some extent,

differences will erode: if Russia wants McDonald's, it will have to accommodate that company's needs and demands. How are these conflicts to be mediated? And, if the world economy if becoming an organic whole, how are collective problems or crises to be prevented or mitigated?

The answers are not obvious. Except in the crudest sense, a market is not just the meeting place of buyer and seller. It is a framework to conduct ongoing business. It is a political, social, and cultural phenomenon, as well as an economic one. It requires laws, customs, and understandings to foster the certainty that is needed for investors and enterprises to risk capital and to make forward commitments. A market is a system to deal with common conflicts. All nations build market frameworks, for better or worse. A global economy requires its counterpart. Not surprisingly, then, more global commerce has meant more global rules. These now apply, in some form, to banking, insurance, communications, air travel, government procurement, copyright protection (for everything from CDs to software), the environment, and health and safety.

These rules go well beyond the standard stuff of trade policy: tariffs and quotas. Not surprisingly, Buchanan attaches an inflammatory label to this process. He calls it world government. But the label is accurate. We are haphazardly building a crude world government, in a fragmented and piecemeal fashion. To flourish, the world economy probably needs more of it. There are many ideas. One recent proposal would create global accounting standards so that investors can more easily compare companies across borders. Much of this makes economic sense, and the United States has led the process. We have urged global rules to "open up markets," curb industrial subsidies (which might hurt our companies), and make government procedures more "transparent" (to limit discrimination against our firms).

Not surprisingly, many countries resent these rules as intrusions, as violations of their sovereignty. We are (it is said) trying to Americanize the world, to foist our values and our institutions on others. Interestingly, many Americans also deplore the process, because even though we have taken the lead in crafting these new global conventions, we don't run them unilaterally. We are (it is said) surrendering our sovereignty to global bureaucrats.

And indeed we are. Here is the nub of the matter. The ultimate promise of ever-greater global commerce is a universal contentment based on a spreading addiction to material well-being. Prosperity has a tranquilizing effect. It dulls the dangers of undiluted nationalism. People increasingly lead the same lifestyles: drinking Coke, driving Toyotas, conversing on the Internet. All this numbs national differences and permits a growing overlay of international agencies and authorities needed to regulate the global economy. Countries see that they have a common stake in cooperation. There are disagreements and conflicts, to be sure, but they are small-time, and they substitute for larger human tragedies of war and poverty.

This is the underlying moral logic that justifies the commercialization of the world, though hardly anyone puts it quite so forthrightly. It is a seductive vision that can draw much inspiration from the ex-

perience of the last half-century. Over this period, the world economy has been a spectacular success. It has helped power an enormous advance in human well-being. Free trade has triumphed to an extent that hardly anyone could have foreseen at the end of World War II.

In the end, however, the vision is almost certainly false. Just because people watch the same movies and eat at the same fast-food outlets does not mean that they have been homogenized. National identities are not so easily retired. For good and ill, ethnic and religious differences show a remarkable ability to survive the march of material progress. National affections and animosities endure; and combined with the terrible and unpredictable potential of modern technology, they preserve humankind's capacity for ordinary trouble and unimaginable tragedy.

The world is fusing economically more than it is fusing (or will ever fuse) politically. We have created a system that requires ever-greater amounts of global cooperation, because it generates new and unfamiliar forms of international conflicts. One day, perhaps, the irresistible force of world markets may meet the immovable object of nationalism. Protectionism and isolationism are not so much agendas as moods, and countries—including the United States —might react to domestic disruption and international disorder by blaming foreigners and trying to withdraw from a global system on which most nations now increasingly depend. Buchanan has inadvertently identified the dilemma, but he has done exactly nothing to resolve it.

By ELEANOR M. FOX

Antitrust Regulation Across National Borders

THE UNITED STATES OF BOEING
VERSUS
THE EUROPEAN UNION OF AIRBUS

There was a certain irony when President Clinton threatened in July to go to the World Trade Organization if the European Union moved against Boeing's acquisition of McDonnell Douglas. ◆ "I'm concerned about what appears to be the reasons for the objection to the Boeing–McDonnell Douglas merger by the European Union," the president said, "and we have some options ourselves when actions are taken in this regard." The president was apparently referring to retaliatory trade sanctions against Europe, such as putting U.S. tariffs on European planes.

There was a brisk run up to the brink. High U.S. officials, up to and including the president, called or met with high officials in Europe to force a retreat. At the eleventh hour the Europeans did back down (or did they?). They let the merger proceed, but on two important conditions: Boeing would give up exclusivity on long-term supply deals, and Boeing would license to its competitors—that is, Airbus—McDonnell technology developed with U.S. government funding.

Just another trade case with a fairly happy ending? So the press and popular view would have it. Indeed, in the popular view this was a festering trade war triggered by European Competition Commissioner Karel van Miert, who was determined to protect Europe's subsidized Airbus from the competition that would be waged by a stronger Boeing. Europe took the first shot by threatening to ground the merger. In the name of its honor, its standing, and its economy, the United States had to fight back.

Eleanor M. Fox is Walter Derenberg Professor of Trade Regulation at New York University School of Law.

But wait a minute. Is something wrong with this picture? Is this not the merger of two of the last three firms in the highly concentrated commercial jet aircraft market? Is this not the administration that has threatened to sue Japanese glass makers for keeping American exporters out of Japan; that has sued two Swiss companies for merging in Switzerland; and that has (though I should not say it in the same breath) signed into law the Helms-Burton bill that penalizes foreign countries engaging in business in Cuba? Is this the administration that has temporized with the European Union's proposal for internationalizing antitrust on grounds that antitrust issues do not belong in the WTO, lest U.S. sovereignty get compromised? Is Boeing–McDonnell Douglas not an antitrust case, or has antitrust gone the way of politics?

In the aftermath, few Americans or Europeans believe that the Boeing affair was anything other than political. Most Americans believe the skirmish was a game of the Europeans to protect their champion Airbus. Most Europeans believe it was a game of the Americans to protect their champion Boeing.

Can it be that Boeing–McDonnell Douglas was a serious antitrust case dealt with in good faith on the merits by the expert agencies on both sides of the Atlantic and that the problem was one not of offensive intrusions meriting retaliation but of slightly divergent law in need of sympathetic links? Yes, it can be; and that is my thesis.

Can it be that the Boeing affair was a serious antitrust case dealt with in good faith on the merits by the expert agencies on both sides of the Atlantic?

It is worth comparing the law of the United States with the law of the European Community, examining the divergences, and asking how Boeing–McDonnell Douglas might have been an antitrust case, start to finish, rather than a trade war.

Two Sets of Laws

The U.S. and EU authorities reached different conclusions on the competitive effect of the merger. Why? Cynics find it obvious. The Federal Trade Commission's allowing the merger promoted the U.S. champion, and the European Community's challenging the merger promoted the European champion. But this simple, obvious answer is almost surely wrong. Each set of experts appeared to apply the law on the merits.

This was possible both because there was an arguable question of fact and because of differences in the law.

The question of fact involved a prediction: was McDonnell Douglas still a competitive force in commercial jets? Would it ever again, on its own or with a new parent, be able to make and sell fleets of jets to the commercial airlines?

The [FTC] answered no. It was apparently unable to uncover or discover a willing purchaser for the commercial jet assets of McDonnell Douglas, and McDonnell Douglas, on its own, had no prospects of making and selling next-generation fleets. The European Commission apparently disagreed as to McDonnell Douglas's effect in the market-place—as did one of the five commissioners of the FTC. The divergence of opinion was not suspect; reasonable people could differ.

When the FTC found that Douglas (the commercial aircraft division) was competitively insignificant, this meant the end of the U.S. inquiry. But in Europe the Commission

had another string to its bow, because of the different tilt to its law.

U.S. merger law is consumer oriented. The inquiry is whether the merger will make consumers worse off, as by raising the price of jets to the airlines. If McDonnell Douglas was not a competitive force to be reckoned with, there was no antitrust problem.

EC law is concerned not only with consumers, but also with unfair competitive advantages of dominant firms. Thus, not everything turned on the prospects for Douglas.

The cases are eclectic and contain hidden tensions. In some cases, where no competitor is threatened by a merger, the decision may focus on efficient market competition and consumer impact. In others, where competitors may be disadvantaged, the decision may postulate a predatory scenario with the prospect that the dominant firm will squeeze out its competitors and ultimately charge monopoly prices to consumers.

So it was with a case called *de Havilland,* which is cited by Europeans as authority for *Boeing*. ATR, a joint venture owned half by France and half by Italy, sought to buy Canadian de Havilland from its parent, Boeing. The merging firms made commuter aircraft. De Havilland was in poor financial condition and needed a subsidy from Canada to survive. Canada welcomed the acquisition, and Canadian antitrust authorities cleared it. But the European Commission enjoined the deal because the dominant joint venture gained a fuller line of commuter aircraft, which would so disadvantage the competitors (the Commission said) that they would be squeezed from the market, to the ultimate harm of consumers.

The parallels to Boeing–McDonnell Douglas are striking. Moreover, this winter and spring Boeing entered 20-year exclusive contracts with three big airlines. To the FTC, these contracts were a separate matter from the merger, though they could be anticompetitive since they fenced Airbus out of 11 percent of the market. To the EC, these contracts were an integral matter, since Boeing's already dominant market share would increase as a result of the merger, and the effect of the fencing out—the unfair competitive advantage—was accordingly magnified.

In the EU, Boeing–McDonnell Douglas may have been an easy antitrust case. And just because Airbus was a European favorite did not mean that the merger was not anticompetitive.

Avoiding The Next Trade War

There are two ways to look at the Boeing–McDonnell Douglas problem. One view is the antitrust perspective. The other is the national trade policy perspective.

The Boeing affair unfolded from the national trade vantage. Here is how it looks from the antitrust perspective.

First, we accord each agency the presumption of dispassionate application of the rule of law, unless proved otherwise.

So doing, we observe: one authority has examined a merger and closed its investigation. (This act, incidentally, has no legal consequence. If, for example, the airlines believed that the merger was power-creating, they could and still can sue in U.S. courts.) The other authority has identified an antitrust problem under its law, and the merging parties have agreed to a solution that is satisfactory to that authority. A routine, colorless tale, this, much less riveting than the drama of a trade showdown.

The antitrust view is also the liberal trade policy perspective. That is so because the liberal point of view accepts the divergences of systems of law and tries, in the event of tension, to find linking or sympathetic solutions.

From the antitrust and liberal point of view, one would recognize the problem as an international (not national) one and would give deference to the autonomy of states to intervene against effects in their territory. Only in the event of a true conflict would there be need for a higher principle.

Some might argue that there is always a conflict when one nation's law is permissive and the other nation's law is proscriptive and both laws apply to the same transaction. A tension, yes; but not a conflict requiring one nation to abstain from using its law to protect its citizens from harm.

To be sure, there are costs to tolerance of diversity. Unless and until (if ever) there is a world law for international transactions, this is a cost we choose to bear.

Nonetheless, there are principles that can make nations' laws more sympathetic with one another, conferring on them aspects of open architecture and minimizing unnecessary costs of divergence. For example, nations could adopt the following four rules for transactions that could inflict antitrust harms across national borders.

1. Nations should apply their antitrust laws without discrimination.

2. Nations should not allow "national champion" interests to trump competition interests.

3. If nations pursue noncompetition objectives in antitrust cases, such as national security or a clean environment, they should do so transparently.

4. Political officials should neither provoke nor threaten trade retaliation against nations that have credibly applied their antitrust laws.

Politicians should leave antitrust to the experts.

CHINA

Rule by Law

As parliamentary chairman Qiao Shi pushes for legal reform, delegates to the National People's Congress will be watching for signs of a split between him and party chief Jiang Zemin.

By Matt Forney in Beijing

In the same Great Hall of the People where the Communist Party held its funeral for patriarch Deng Xiaoping four days earlier, China's rump parliament opened on March 1 with the promise of two weeks of muted debate. The country's new "collective leadership" is enjoying its honeymoon period, and nobody, including the parliament's prickly chairman, Qiao Shi, is expected to pick a spat.

That doesn't peg this annual National People's Congress session as insignificant. Qiao has structured the meeting around legislation which could have an impact on everyone from political dissidents to the People's Liberation Army to residents of China's most populous city.

For the past five years Qiao has staked his career on legal reform—albeit without threatening party authority. And he is expected to push his reform ideas in his closing remarks scheduled for March 14. That in itself could pressure President Jiang Zemin, who as the designated "core" of the Communist Party is considered by many to be above the law. Although critical eloquence is quickly swept from the floor of the Great Hall, Qiao has striven to shed the congress's image of a rubber-stamp.

Observers will scrutinize Qiao's every word for evidence of a split with Jiang. Back in 1989, Qiao turned down the position of party secretary-general that Deng eventually awarded to Jiang. Since then, few leaders other than Jiang's associates from his power base of Shanghai have lent him their unambiguous support.

"Premier Li Peng doesn't go out of his way to give Jiang face, but he gives it when it's necessary," says a Western diplomat and veteran NPC-watcher in Beijing. "Qiao doesn't give it even when it's necessary." This year, however, Qiao's opening comments included what was for him a rare reference to Jiang as the "core." Last year he avoided that obligatory fillip until his closing words.

The most progressive legislation on the docket would eliminate, at a stroke, an entire category of political dissent. Barring the unexpected, delegates will vote on March 14 to delete a 17-year-old list of "counter-revolutionary" statutes from the nation's criminal law.

This is not a human-rights breakthrough, however, and it won't lower the prison population. State prosecutors already prefer charging dissidents with criminal offences, such as leaking state secrets. And most of the doomed counter-revolutionary statutes have already been rewritten to find a new home in the State Security Law of 1993, which covers:
• "Plotting or carrying out activities for endangering state security together with organizations, institutions or individuals outside the country."
• "Establishing social organizations or enterprises or business institutions" which endanger state security.

• "Publishing or disseminating written or verbal comments" that threaten the state—a statute clearly aimed at curtailing dissidents' contact with foreign journalists.

One of the most prescient critics of transferring counter-revolutionary clauses to the State Security Law was Wang Dan, who served three-and-a-half years in prison for his role as a student leader during the 1989 Tiananmen uprising. In 1994, Wang noted that the law was self-defining: the kind of action that harms state security is "an action harmful to state security"—a tautology that covers almost any critical utterance. Wang predicted that Beijing would stop charging dissidents with counter-revolutionary crimes, and instead charge them with endangering state security.

Wang predicted his own fate. Last October, a three-judge panel sentenced him to 11 years in prison for "conspiring to subvert the government" by publishing overseas and writing to foreign groups. He was sentenced according to both the counter-revolutionary statues *and* the state security law. "Wang's was a bridge verdict spanning the transition from laws on counter-revolution to those on state security," says Robin Munro of Human Rights Watch/Asia.

One thing to watch: the Tiananmen uprising of 1989 is still officially "counter-revolutionary turmoil." But the phrase loses its foundation if a crime by that name no longer exists—which could facilitate a reassessment of the uprising. "The term for the turmoil is political, not legal," says Chen Guangzhong, former president of the Politics and Law University in Beijing who helped draft the new criminal law. "But," he admits, "it could add impetus for a reassessment."

Other significant legislation would give China a legal basis to invade Taiwan. The National Defence Law, drafted by the Central Military Commission, mandates army "crackdowns on any attempts to seek independence and separate the motherland," said Defence Minister Chi Haotian last year. Chi immediately added the need to "keep on the high alert against the activities of Taiwan independence elements." China, therefore, could insist on "rule of law" as it scrambles the jets to attack its "renegade province."

The law also directs the PLA to quell unrest in Tibet and largely Muslim Xinjiang province in the far west. Soldiers haven't opened fire on Tibetans since 1989, but did so in the Xinjiang hotspot of Yining only last month. China insists 10 people or fewer were killed; Muslim separatists put the figure at more than 100.

The defence law will also put the 3-million-strong People's Liberation Army under the explicit control of the Communist Party. That, of course, has been standard policy since the communists came to power and established their dictatorship of the proletariat in 1949. Less than three hours after Deng Xiaoping died on February 19, China's top generals swore "to obey the leadership of the Communist Party Central Committee." The problem is, China's constitution holds that the armed forces "belong to the people" and report to the State Military Commission, which in turn subordinates itself to the National People's Congress. The party garners no mention.

The debate may sound academic. It is not. Last year, literary critic Liu Xiaobo was sentenced without trial to three years in a labour camp for demanding party chief Jiang Zemin's impeachment. Jiang, he wrote, had violated the constitution by insisting that the party controls the military. Any first-year law student would observe that the accusation, although politically sensitive, was correct.

Neither the changes to the criminal law nor the new defence law are expected to elicit much debate from delegates. On the year's most hotly contested issue, however, delegates are being handed a *fait accompli*.

The delegates will be asked to approve the State Council's elevation of China's most populous city, Chongqing in mountainous Sichuan province, to the status of a province. The move strengthens Beijing's control over Sichuan by wrenching a major industrial city away from the provincial capital, Chengdu. It also enables Beijing to more closely monitor resettlement of 800,000 people in greater Chongqing who must move to higher ground before the Three Gorges dam project is complete in 2009.

Chengdu officials are enraged by the decision, though silently. Bureaucrats in the city refused requests to be interviewed on Chongqing's status. In the unlikely event that delegates reject this decision, it would be the first time an NPC vote has changed state policy.

Last year, Chongqing for the first time received its resettlement funds directly from Beijing, instead of through Chengdu. Beijing has already promised more this year. Chongqing officials estimate that 20,000 bureaucrats in Cheng-du who used to administer Chongqing's affairs are now redundant. Beijing has already appointed Chongqing's de facto mayor, instead of approving Chengdu's appointment, as was past practice. Chongqing has even designed new licence plates for its cars.

Still, no deep divisions within the NPC are expected over the new slate of laws. With memories of Deng's funeral still fresh, nobody wants to send the first ripples from a rocking boat. In all likelihood, serious legal reform will wait for future congresses.

LABOUR

Wanted: Muscle

ILO seeks more power to police workers' rights

By Shada Islam in Brussels

Just four months ago, Asian governments were claiming victory in their debate with the West over workers' rights. Many countries in the region have long viewed Western attempts to link trade and labour issues as nothing more than protectionism disguised under a moral cloak. So they were jubilant when the World Trade Organization decided at its December meeting in Singapore that it was best to let the International Labour Organization deal with the matter. Though the ILO monitors the application of global labour rules, it has no power to enforce them.

But those who thought the issue was safely buried are having to think again. United States President Bill Clinton has just unveiled a "code of conduct" for American companies that is designed to curb labour abuses in Asian and other developing countries. Firms that sign on—at the moment they include Nike, Reebok and Liz Claiborne—promise to stop employing young children, to pay the minimum wage established by local law and to recognize the right of workers to associate freely and bargain collectively.

More significantly, the ILO is demanding greater powers to police workers' rights worldwide. The organization's director-general, Michel Hansenne, wants governments to sign a new declaration next year giving it greater powers to promote "core" labour standards, such as freedom of association, collective bargaining and bans on forced or child labour and sexual or racial discrimination.

Hansenne wants to plug a key loophole in the present system, under which countries can escape ILO scrutiny in some sectors simply by not ratifying the related conventions. It's a tactic Asian—and Western governments too—have often used: Bangladesh, Pakistan, Thailand and Indonesia haven't put their names to the ILO convention prohibiting gender discrimination. Pakistan, India and Bangladesh haven't ratified the convention setting a minimum age for workers, and Malaysia hasn't ratified the convention banning forced labour.

Hansenne's plan is to have a new declaration annexed to the ILO constitution that would make the core principles binding on all members, regardless of whether or not they have ratified specific conventions.

Asian trade officials in Geneva say they're ready to take a closer look at Hansenne's proposal—but under certain conditions. "The important thing," says Pakistan's ambassador in Geneva, Muneer Akram, "is that the declaration is implemented in a nondiscriminatory and universal manner. In no way must this be linked to trade." Another Asian trade official in Geneva, meanwhile, stresses that instead of trying to get a new declaration, the ILO should try to get more countries to ratify the existing core conventions.

Some analysts believe Hansenne's proposals don't go far enough. "The real problem is that the ILO has no power to take action against countries which flout its rules," says Willem van der Geest, research director at the Brussels-based European Institute for Asian Studies. On the other hand, he says, there's very little the agency can offer countries that do adopt good labour practices.

ILO officials argue that even though they don't have an army at their disposal, "moral pressure" is effective. In recent years, says Francis Maupain, the agency's legal adviser, complaints about curbs on freedom of association in the Philippines, Sri Lanka, India,

Pakistan, Indonesia and Malaysia have led to changes in local laws. "The publicity given to these cases was reasonably effective in ensuring compliance with ILO rules," says Maupain.

As for rewards, Hansenne is pressing for a ground-breaking new system under which the ILO would give its tag of approval to countries that can prove they're respecting fundamental labour rights and freedoms. Maupain says current voluntary codes and "no sweat" labels given by sectors and companies to allay concerns about workplace conditions are "chaotic and selective." For instance, he says, they may cover concerns about child workers, yet ignore gender discrimination.

Asians are likely to balk at the idea of "global social labels." Their main concern is that by making the proposal, the ILO is getting involved in trade issues. Says Akram: "We can't accept any connection between trade measures and labour standards. By talking about social labels, this proposal seems to be bringing the trade-labour link back on to the international agenda through the back door."

The ILO's experts, however, argue that a strengthened supervisory role for the agency is probably Asia's best guarantee against unilateral trade measures, consumer boycotts and the confusing proliferation of voluntary social codes and labels. "Asian countries stand to lose the most through the trials by accusation" conducted by Western consumers and trade-union groups, insists the ILO's director for information, Michel Barton. Once they've looked at the pros and cons of a global social label, he says, most Asians will realize that it makes good business sense.

Global economy, local mayhem?

Rioting strikers in South Korea, France, Argentina and elsewhere are not a sign that "globalisation" is a disaster

IT LOOKS like a delicious irony, and the enemies of global capitalism are pouncing gleefully upon it. Having grown rich on exports, South Korea, the erstwhile tiger, has suddenly come to resemble famously arthritic countries such as Germany and France. Its economy is still growing at a healthy 6% or so. But its president believes that its future prosperity depends on making its labour market more flexible, helping (says he) its firms to compete better internationally. New laws that would make workers easier to fire have provoked bitter clashes and strikes over the past few weeks. Now that even the tigers are being clawed, say globalisation's critics, is it not plain that the ever-freer international flow of goods and capital, and the competition it unleashes, ends up by hurting workers everywhere? "Why should workers bear the brunt of globalisation pain?" huffs a columnist in the *International Herald Tribune*.

The events in South Korea do contain a moral about globalisation, but it is not this one. If anything, the intellectual case for believing that open economies and flexible labour markets are net creators of wealth and jobs has been growing increasingly strong. Since 1993 even the European Union has paid lip service—though little else—to the idea of labour flexibility. What South Korea underlines is that most governments have so far done an inept job of explaining the issues to their voters.

To many workers, especially those previously in secure employment, the "flexible labour market" is a euphemism for freeing employers to cut wages and abolish jobs at will. The trade unionists who have taken to the streets all over the world argue that the only beneficiaries of this sort of flexibility are the big companies that scour the world in search of places where desperate people are willing to work for less money, and in worse conditions. In this view the "Manic Logic of Global Capitalism" (the subtitle of the latest populist tome on the subject) is to make people beggar their neighbours by turning their own country into a sweatshop.

Yet to portray the impact of globalisation and the case for flexible labour markets in this way is a travesty. The growing integration of the world economy has in general been an engine of mutual enrichment. Indeed, there could be few better illustrations of this than South Korea itself. Far from making it into a sweatshop, globalisation—in the form of access to overseas markets—has hoisted South Korea's wages by an average of 15% a year for ten years. Over the same period South Korea has become not only a fast-growing market for the products of the rich world but a big overseas investor and employer in its own right.

Why, then, do the critics of globalisation continue to strike such a responsive chord? It is human nature to fear change—and the instinct of many trade unionists to oppose it. But part of the answer stems from a misunderstanding. The point of a flexible labour market is not to win some global ugliness contest for jobs (the bulk of foreign investment by multinationals anyway flows between rich countries, in search of markets, not to poor ones in search of cheap labour). It is to enable your own country to react quickly to change—technological and otherwise—by switching people and resources swiftly from declining industries to growing ones.

Again, South Korea is an excellent illustration. Its new labour laws are not designed to staunch a flight of manufacturing jobs abroad; with virtually full employment, that is hardly South Korea's problem. The changes are needed to release the *chaebol*, its big conglomerates, from a trap: unable to sack people, they have been forced to diversify into businesses about which they know nothing, simply to find berths for surplus workers. A freer labour market would help the *chaebol* to focus their activities and boost productivity. Small firms should benefit, too. Until now, the conglomerates have grabbed all the brightest workers for themselves.

Claims about the virtue of flexible labour markets are not just theory, to be taken from economists on trust. A huge worked proof exists in the contrast between America's ability to create a net 8m jobs since 1991 and the European Union's loss of nearly 5m. Moreover, it turns out that much of America's new employment has consisted not of the deadbeat "McJobs" some expected but of good jobs in new industries, especially in services; the reward, in other words, for running an economy capable of listening to the signals of the market and adapting fast to new technology.

Perspective, please—and consent

How are governments to persuade nervous workers of these truths? Certainly not by pretending that the vast changes under way in the world economy will claim no victims at all. The jobs of many unskilled workers in the rich world may indeed migrate. German companies expect to employ at least 300,000 more people abroad in the next three years—mainly in the lower-wage countries of Central and Eastern Europe. But these dislocations need to be put into perspective. Germans have gained far more than they have lost from the emergence of a great new market to their east; and they have lost more than they have gained by allowing rigid and expensive labour laws to stifle the creation of new jobs at home.

It will, naturally, always be hard for governments to persuade workers to trade their immediate job security for a vague promise of future opportunity. Different societies will strike the balance in different ways. But the other moral from South Korea is the folly of trying to free up labour markets without popular consent. You might expect South Koreans, richer than ever and basking in full employment, to feel less threatened than anxious Frenchmen and Germans by ideas for changing employment law. But, quite rightly, they turn out not to want controversial legislation thrust down their throats in a manner reminiscent of their country's authoritarian past. Affluence, it seems, breeds democrats; just another benefit, as it happens, of rampaging global capitalism.

GLOBAL DEREGULATION

IN THE NEW GLOBAL ECONOMY, FREEDOM FROM EXCESSIVE REGULATION IS A STRONG ASSET. JAPAN IS MOVING IN THE RIGHT DIRECTION. GERMANY AND FRANCE AREN'T, AND THEY ARE PAYING THE PRICE.

A CENTURY AND A HALF AGO MILLIONS of German peasants crossed the ocean to find new homes in the Americas. They were fleeing a rigid social and economic system and seeking opportunity for their children.

In the 1990s it is German industry that is emigrating, and for many of the same reasons that drove the ancestors of so many of today's Americans from their old homes.

German industry has lost none of its technological and managerial prowess, but products made in Germany are becoming increasingly uncompetitive in cost. The latest survey by the Institut der deutschen Wirtschaft shows that, on average, industrial labor now costs $31.76 an hour in western Germany and $20.82 in the eastern part, versus $20.26 in France, $14.63 in Britain and around $17.50 an hour in the U.S.

Since there is no way that German workers can be worth 55% more than U.S. workers, the conse-

quences are predictable. National statistics are not available for the number of jobs that German companies have created abroad, but the picture is clear at the company level, as our table (*see next page*) shows. Nearly every day reports tell of expansion in the U.S. or abroad by a German company. The latest: Bayer Corp., the U.S. subsidiary of German Bayer Group, which announced last month it planned investing a further $6 billion in the U.S. by 2000.

It is not merely the level of wages that is driving these good Germans away from their homeland. The corporate restructuring that has made U.S. industry so much more competitive in the past decade and a half is almost impossible in Germany. Blame the unions in part. Blame the stuffy German business establishment, too.

The attempted $5 billion hostile takeover of Thyssen by Gerhard Cromme, chairman of Fried. Krupp-

Hoesch, was immediately blocked by the powerful steel industry union, IG Metall, with the backing of the opposition Social Democratic Party. The proposed takeover made economic and operational sense.

But it wasn't just that the unions were against the deal. That it was hostile aroused the opposition of much of the German business establishment. The deal was right, but it wasn't polite. But this hostile takeover would have been a done deal in the U.S., or even the U.K. Not in Germany.

Instead of an outright merger, the two companies will combine their steel operations. Thyssen's threatened managers will run the merged steel operation. And to win a union okay the companies had to agree not to lay off more than a handful of people for at least three years. The combination will do little to reduce overcapacity in the German steel sector or to make the new operation world-competitive.

A few weeks earlier, in Germany's coal industry, union diehards and their political allies won an even more smashing victory. In an effort to reduce Germany's budget deficit, Chancellor Helmut Kohl's Christian Democrat-led coalition proposed to reduce the $5.24-billion-a-year subsidy for Germany's out-of-date coal industry. This subsidy is equal to $61,650 a year for every one of the 85,000 German mining jobs. It would be cheaper to retire most of

German industry is fleeing Germany. Why?

Deutsche hegira

By Howard Banks

the work force on full pay than to keep them digging.

The Kohl government didn't propose eliminating the subsidy. It merely proposed cutting it by reducing the 85,000 work force to 25,000 by 2003. Mass marches by egg-throwing union mobs, backed by local opposition politicians, forced the Kohl government into a humiliating cave-in. It will leave the work force at 39,000 miners, and the subsidy per job will increase to $87,000 a year. German coal today costs around $180 a ton, versus around a $65-a-ton world price.

Construction workers, too, took to the streets in Bonn, still the seat of national government, to protest job cuts. Once again protest worked: The Kohl government caved in here, too, agreeing to pump another $7.5 billion into construction projects.

Much of the business establishment is hardly more progressive than the unions and politicians. Dieter Vogel, chairman of Thyssen, called Cromme's unwelcome bid for his company "Wild West tactics"— code for vulgar, American-style behavior.

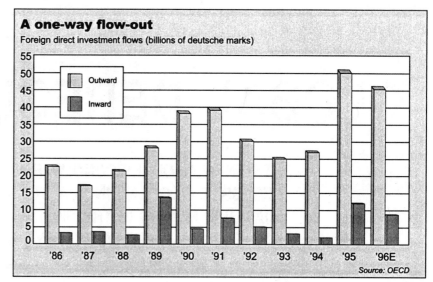

A one-way flow-out
Foreign direct investment flows (billions of deutsche marks)

Source: OECD

DAVID LADA/FORBES

Since the mid-1980s German industry has been a major investor outside Germany. But foreign firms, turned off by Germany's high costs, have largely shunned the country as a place to invest.

In Germany it is still difficult and costly to fire anybody. The workweek is restricted, with overtime rates being paid after 37.5 hours, 35 hours in the metals industry. And long paid vacations, averaging six weeks, plus liberal sick leave (which leads to high absenteeism) means that Germans work much less of the year than American or British workers.

Germany is paying a terrible price for this refusal to change. German unemployment is now running at around a 12% unadjusted rate and seems to be on a rising trend. When labor is overpriced, employers will shop elsewhere.

Even this unpleasantly high number disguises the real level of joblessness in Germany. Government-funded training schemes are mostly little more than disguised unemployment insurance. This and early retirement probably add another 4% to 5% to Germany's real unemployed.

To keep the jobless quiet, the government supports them with high benefits. With at least one child, the unemployed can collect 57% of their former income indefinitely, tax free, with more for the first six months on the dole.

Around 1988, when U.S. corporate restructuring was at its height, German companies began to invest abroad (see chart, above). Until then, German companies had done little direct investment abroad in comparison with companies in most large, industrialized countries, especially the U.S. and the U.K. Now the Germans are catching up.

While the U.S. was sending money and jobs overseas, foreigners were sending money and jobs to the

Is this any way to run an economy?

Company/business	1985 Employment			1995 employment		
	German	foreign	% foreign	German	foreign	% foreign
BASF/chemicals, pharmaceuticals	87,292	42,881	32.9%	63,715	42,850	40.2%
Daimler-Benz/cars, trucks and aerospace	257,538[1]	62,427	19.5	242,086	68,907	22.2
Henkel kGaA/chemicals	16,006	15,015	48.4	14,684	27,044	64.8
Hoechst/chemicals, pharmaceuticals	61,642	118,919	65.8	39,108	122,510	75.8
Krupp/steel	59,978	7,424	11.0	49,112	17,240	26.0
MAN Group/capital equipment	52,264[2]	8,513	14.0	45,085	11,418	20.2
Mannesmann AG/machinery	77,174[1]	32,280	29.5	78,015	41,660	34.8
Metallgesellschaft/materials	21,384	3,458	13.9	18,571	4,870	20.8
SAP/software	749[3]	191	20.3	4,345	4,851	52.8
Siemens/electrical and electronic	240,000	108,000	31.0	211,000	162,000	43.4
Veba/energy and transport	68,689[1]	5,361	7.2	125,158	24,930	16.6

[1]Figures are for 1986. [2]Figures are for 1987. [3]Figures are for 1988.

Since 1985, with the exception of SAP and Veba, these big German companies have cut jobs at home—absolutely and relatively—while creating thousands of new jobs in other countries.

U.S. as well. It was a two-way flow. In Germany's case the flow is all one way—out. Thomas Hatzichronoglou, a noted expert on global business trends with the Organization for Economic Cooperation and Development, says that foreign firms with operations in Germany are cutting back there. "In 1991 foreign affiliates in Germany employed 963,000 people. By 1994, the latest detailed survey we have, that was down to 799,600, and from what we know that number continues to fall," he says.

The resulting unemployment explains why Germany is having such trouble reducing its public sector budget deficit sufficiently to meet the 3% deficit target for European monetary union in the Maastricht Treaty. The German Bundesbank has reported that the deficit in the first two months of this year was a third higher than the target rate. Germany's finance minister, Theodore Waigel, has appealed to the rest of Europe to be generous about (i.e., turn a blind eye to) his inability to meet the Maastricht targets.

There are other factors adding to the cost of Germany's job crisis.

In the end, the unions and politicians will have to bow to economic reality. Until then, German business will vote with its feet.

During the U.S. restructuring period in the 1980s, the Reagan Administration slashed taxes and went for high growth. The resulting job creation, especially among small, fast-growing firms, helped cushion the loss of jobs from restructuring. Germany has no such crutch. Economic growth is slow—coming off a recession, it is just creeping at 2% to 2.5% this year, after 1.4% in 1996. And Germany is still only talking about cutting taxes.

Germany and other European Union countries are trying to create a common currency. An odd feature of the single-currency process is that if Germany doesn't make it into the European Monetary Union on time, the deutsche mark will rise as investors holding other European currencies sell them and go back to the mark (and the dollar and yen) as safe havens. The last thing that German industrialists want is a stronger mark, which will make even more of their exported production uncompetitive.

Germany is by no means going down the drain. In the end the unions and the politicians will have to bow to economic reality and loosen the legal and customary straitjacket in which German industry operates. Until that happens, German business will continue to immigrate to more hospitable climes. "Change is coming to Germany," says Jürgen Dorman, chairman of the board of management of Hoechst AG. "But it will take longer than in America."

USA LOOKS AT THE WORLD

Controlling Economic Competition in the PACIFIC RIM

The Big Three economic powers in Asia—China, Japan, and the U.S.—must learn to cooperate economically, politically, and militarily if prosperity is to succeed in this burgeoning marketplace.

by Charles W. Kegley, Jr.

As ASTONISHED lenders and investors surveyed the wreckage from the chain-reaction near-collapse of Asia's currencies and markets, their former smug self-confidence began to fade. The spread of Asia's economic flu throughout the globalized marketplace has provoked widespread anxiety about the prospects for a 21st century of peace bolstered by prosperity through free trade in a borderless, integrated international economy. The financial typhoon amidst contagious currency devaluations, budget deficits, and bankruptcies has exposed the logical flaws underlying the megalomania during the 1990s' string of boom years. Now, in the face of crisis, the basic fault lines and vulnerabilities in the unmanaged trade and monetary system have been exposed. Policymakers worldwide have ample reasons to fear the future. The economic foundations of peace in the Pacific Rim are precarious and, without Asian regional stability, there

Dr. Kegley, Associate American Thought Editor of USA Today, is Pearce Professor of International Relations, University of South Carolina, Columbia.

exists little chance for the interdependent international political economy to remain stable.

The challenge of building a more stable institutional architecture for order must be faced if the future is to be prosperous and peaceful. The obstacles to cooperation must be confronted collectively to overcome nations' natural temptation to bolster exports at one another's expense. To avert the disaster of another competitive round of "beggar they neighbor" policies that was the tinderbox for the 1930s Great Depression which ignited World War II, the leading powers must overcome their divisions and work together or their national economies will implode. In a globalized economy where states only can help themselves if they help their rivals as well, *all* have a clear stake in the collective management of collective problems. Still, history does not inspire much confidence that parochial impulses can be resisted. How, then, should the pitfalls and prospects for a prosperous and peaceful future be envisioned?

Any understanding of the prospects for the Pacific Rim, and the globe in general, must begin with a sense of history. As British statesman Winston Churchill once ob-

served, in looking to the future, the further back one looks, the further ahead one can see. To find an informed basis for grasping the major challenges that should be faced by the Big Three economic powers in Asia (China, Japan, and the U.S.), one should follow his advice by looking at long-term historical trends and learning from their lessons.

A second analytical axiom for viewing the future is that there exists a tight interface between the political and military preconditions for continued economic growth in the Pacific Rim. A synergistic, interactive interrelationship has developed among economics, politics, and military security, which can not be meaningfully separated. Peace is a precondition for prosperity, and inspired diplomacy to manage economic competitors' trade relations in the global market is, in turn, a precondition for lasting peace.

What are the long-term problems of the past and the core contemporary circumstances that most will affect the future? First, the U.S. still is a military superpower and an economic giant. It once was said that when the American economy sneezed, the rest of the world caught a cold. That

From *USA Today Magazine*, May 1998, pp. 22–25. © 1998 by the Society for the Advancement of Education. Reprinted by permission.

assertion no longer is quite true, but the globalization of trade means that the impact of changes in the American economy continue to reverberate throughout the world.

A second feature of today's global realities lies in how the law of gravity applies in international relations. In the historical evolution of the global political economy, as in nature, what goes up must come down. That natural phenomenon pertains to the U.S. It now is recognized widely that, although the recent Japanese economic upheaval has interrupted that nation's ascendancy, Japan and China's economic growth will resume over the long term. China and Japan enjoy massive trade surpluses and hold vast reserves of foreign currency. Their own currencies are not challenged immediately, and, banking crises in Japan notwithstanding, both nations continue to cut into the U.S. share of world output. The American share peaked after World War II at almost 50%, but steadily has slid since.

Simply put, the U.S. is in decline relative to its two Pacific Rim economic rivals. Without a doubt, the next superpower contest will be between the U.S. and China. The question is not if, but when, China will surpass the U.S. as the leading economic power in the world. More problematic is if and how long it might take a recovering, restructuring Japan to challenge U.S. economic supremacy as well. Whatever the timetable, current economic trajectories suggest that a major power transition likely will occur in the early 21st century, with three great powers wealthy enough to project military might throughout the region.

This leads to a third unfolding trend. In the likely new 21st century global distribution of power, military and economic might increasingly will be diffused. In contrast to bipolarity, where two superpowers held a preponderance of strength compared to all other countries, the multipolar state system of the future appears destined to contain three roughly equal great powers: China, the U.S., and Japan. The changes from this power transition promise to be profound, creating a new hierarchy with the Big Three at the top of a tripolar regional pyramid.

Such a reordering of the global economic pecking order raises important questions about future military and political order in the Pacific Rim and the world at large. Which powers might align with one another? Will these alignments be seen as a threat by others and stimulate the formation of counteralliances? Can a security regime be built to prevent the rise of such rival trade blocs and military coalitions primed for war on the economic and, perhaps, even military battlefield? To frame an answer, let us return to Churchill's advice that prophets need good memories and look at some additional facts surrounding the advent of a new multipolar Pacific Rim.

"Conflict over political and territorial issues remains much in evidence. While there have been mutual gains made through foreign trade, geostrategic military differences in the interests of the Big Three have not disappeared."

The diffusion of strength among the world's three economic powers demands attention because, in history, some forms of multipolarity have been more peaceful than others. For instance, the multipolar system of antagonistic blocs that developed on the eve of World War I proved particularly explosive. When many great powers split into rival camps, there is little chance that competitors in one policy arena (for example, trade) will emerge as partners somewhere else (say, defense), so as to mitigate the competition. Rather, the gains made by one side will be seen as losses by the other, ultimately causing minor disagreements to grow into larger face-offs from which neither coalition is willing to retreat. Since the international system of the early 21st century probably will be dominated by the Big Three extremely powerful states whose commercial and security interests are global, it is important that they do not become segregated into rival blocs.

Aside from the danger of trade wars and armed conflict, the security threats of the Pacific Rim future will include such challenges as interdependent monetary affairs, environmental degradation, resource depletion, internal rebellion by minority ethnic populations, the rising tide of refugees, and the cross-border spread of contagious diseases through increased contact, ranging from AIDS to multi-drug-resistant strains of tuberculosis. None of these regional problems can be met without substantial Big Three cooperation; they are transnational issues that necessitate not national, but global solutions. The threats on the ho-

rizon require a collective approach, at the very time when the accelerating erosion of national sovereignty is reducing states' control over their national fates and forcing them to confront common problems through multilateral diplomacy.

However, whereas the impact of these traditional non-military threats to regional welfare and stability promises to be potent, they do not necessarily mean geo-economics or ecopolitics will replace geopolitics. Conflict over political and territorial issues remains much in evidence. While there have been mutual gains made through foreign trade, geostrategic military differences in the interests of the Big Three have not disappeared. As former U.S. Secretary of State Lawrence S. Eagleburger has pointed out, the world is "returning to a more traditional and complicated time of multipolarity, with a growing number of countries increasingly able to affect the course of events." The primary issues are how well the U.S. can adjust to its decline from overwhelming preponderance, and how well China and Japan will adapt to their newfound importance. "The change will not be easy for any of the players, as such shifts in power relationships have never been easy," Eagleburger cautions. The challenge to be confronted is ensuring that Big Three cooperation, not competition, becomes institutionalized. At issue is whether the traditional politico-military and non-traditional economic security threats that collectively face the greater Asian Pacific will be managed through concerted Big Three action, to preserve the order that has made the extraordinary progress of the past three decades possible.

Multipolar future options

As power in the Asian Pacific becomes more dispersed, what can be done to prevent the re-emergence of an unstable form of multipolarity? How can the Big Three avoid becoming polarized into antagonist trade and military blocs and avert the use of currency devaluations and protective tariffs as competitive weapons? Three general courses of action exist: they can act unilaterally; they can develop specialized bilateral alliances with another state; or they can engage in some form of collective collaboration with each other.

Of course, each option has many possible variations, and the foreign policies of most great powers contain a mix of acting single-handedly, joining with a partner, and cooperating globally. History shows that what has mattered most for the stability of past multipolar systems has been the relative emphasis placed on "going it alone" vs. "going it with others," and whether joint action was defined in inclusive or exclusive terms.

Unilateral policies, though attractive because they symbolize the nostalgic pursuit of national autonomy, are unlikely to be viable in a multipolar future. The end of the Cold War has reduced public anxieties about foreign dangers. In the U.S., the collapse of the communist threat has led to calls for a reduction in the scale of foreign commitments. In Japan, the Asian financial crisis has prompted the declaration at the December, 1997, Asian Summit that its neighbors could not count on Japan to cushion the cascading economic collapse by opening its market for their exports. In China, echoes of enthusiasm for the Middle Kingdom assertively to chart an independent path can be heard growing more vocal. However, an isolationistic retreat from world affairs by any or all would imperil efforts to deal with the many transnational threats to regional security that require global activity and engagement, and this decreases the incentives for a neo-isolationist withdrawal from existing involvements abroad.

On the other hand, a surge of unilateral activism by any of the Big Three powers would be equally harmful. None of them holds unquestioned hegemonic status with enough power to override all others. Although the U.S. is unrivaled in military might, its offensive capability and unsurpassed military technology is not paralleled by unrivaled financial clout. The U.S. economy faces problems that constrain and inhibit the projection of American power on a global scale. (The U.S. remains the biggest debtor country in history and suffers from extremely low savings rates. Moreover, the American investment in infrastructure is the lowest among all the G-7 industrialized economies.) Given the prohibitive costs of shouldering the financial burden of acting alone, and given the probability that other great powers would be unlikely to accept subordinate positions, unilateralism will be problematic in a multipolar future. The Big Three countries will have to accommodate themselves to the need for internationalist roles so they can coexist and interact with each other.

An alternative to acting unilaterally is joining with selected states in a series of special relationships. On the surface, this option appears attractive. Yet, in a world lacking the stark simplicities of obvious allies and adversaries, differentiating friend from foe is exceedingly difficult, particularly when allies in the realm of military security are the most likely to be trade competitors in a cut-throat global marketplace. Instead of adding restrictive predictability to international affairs, a network of special bilateral relationships and internally active restrictive trade blocs would foster a fear of encirclement among those who perceive themselves as the targets of these combinations.

> "Creating a new Pacific Rim security structure that enlarges the circle of participation to include all the Big Three in collective decision-making will not be easy, especially in a climate of financial crisis and fear."

Whether they entail informal understandings or formal treaties of alliance, all bilateral partnerships have a common drawback: they promote a politics of exclusion that can lead to dangerously polarized forms of multipolarity, in which the competitors align by forming countercoalitions. For example, the formation of new Russo-Sino, Japanese-American, and Sino-American mutual defense agreements have elevated others' security fears. In much the same way, construction of a U.S.-Russian-European Union axis stretching from the Atlantic to the Urals, if institutionalized, greatly would alarm both China and Japan. The trouble with bilateral alliances and multiparty defense and trade coalitions is that they inevitably shun those standing outside the charmed circle. Resentment, revenge, and revisionist efforts to overturn the *status quo* are the predictable consequence. The freewheeling dance of balance-of-power politics typically produces much switching of partners, with some cast aside and thus willing to break-up the whole dance. Arms races fed by beggar-thy-neighbor trade and monetary competition almost always result.

Beyond forming special bilateral alliances, the Big Three have the option of cementing their mutual financial fate in the strengthening of the broad, multilateral associations and cooperative institutions they have created. Two common variants of this option are concerts and collective security organizations. The former involves regularized consultation among those at the top of the global hierarchy; the latter, full participation by all states in the region. A concert offers the benefit of helping control the great-power rivalries that often spawn polarized blocs, though at the cost of ignoring the interests of those not belonging to the group.

Alternatively, the all-inclusive nature of collective security allows every voice to be heard, but makes more problematic providing a timely response to threatening situations. Consensus-building is both difficult and delayed, especially in identifying a party to the regime aiming at overturning its rules or preparing for either parochial economic protectionism or, even worse, armed conquest. Collective security mechanisms are deficient in choosing an appropriate response to a challenger to order and in implementing the selected course of deterrent action as well. Since a decision-making body can become unwieldy as its size expands, what is needed to make multilateralism a viable option for the Pacific Rim multipolar future looming on the political horizon is a hybrid that combines elements of a Big Three concert with elements of collective security.

Assuring collective security

Throughout history, different types of multipolar systems have existed. Some of these systems of diffused power were unstable because they contained antagonistic blocs poised on the brink of trade or military warfare. History shows that the key to the stability of any future multipolar system in Asia lies in the inclusiveness of multilateralism. While not a panacea for all of the region's security problems, it offers the best chance to avoid the kinds of polarized alignment patterns that have proven so destructive in the past.

Creating a new Pacific Rim security structure that enlarges the circle of participation to include all the Big Three in collective decision-making will not be easy, especially in a climate of financial crisis and fear. When seen from today's perspective, however, there is no alternative but to try. The other options—unilateralism or bilateralism—have severe costs, because any of the Big Three is certain to look disfavorably on any great power's hegemonic effort to bully the others, or on an alliance between the other pair that defines its purpose as the third's containment. Restricting security protection and free-trade zones in a way that ostracizes and encircles one of the Big Three is a path to division and destruction of the very pillars of prosperity provided through open regional trade and agreements to facilitate exports.

The Big Three must not ever return to the days of a world divided in separate blocs, each seeking to contain the expansion of the other. Such a *realpolitik* response is likely to produce the very kind of polarization into competing coalitions that would benefit no one and corrode the cooperative trade links that provide the basis for lasting friendship. As countries connected by a web of economic linkages, there are material incentives for the Big Three to avoid policies that will rupture profitable business transactions, such as those that stigmatize any core player in the game as an enemy.

This is not to ignore the stubborn fact that trading relationships involve both costs and benefits. The rewarding aspects of commerce likely will be offset by fierce competition, breeding irritation, disputes, and hostility between winners and losers. In view of the differential growth rates among the Big Three and their anxiety about trade competitiveness in an interdependent global marketplace, their major battles of the future indeed are likely to be clashes on the economic front. Still, the Big Three have it within their power to avoid

armed combat among soldiers if they keep their aim set on the business of managing business instead of warfare.

A full-fledged, comprehensive Pacific Rim collective security system, dedicated to containing aggression anywhere at any time, may be too ambitious and doomed to failure. A restricted, concert-based collective security mechanism, though, could bring a modicum of order in a fragile and disorderly new Pacific Rim multipolar system, and provide the umbrella needed to allow the regional marketplace to contribute to continuing prosperity.

Whether the actions taken by a Pacific Rim concert-based collective security organization can succeed will hinge on how such a body is perceived and the ways members in it are treated. A Big Three consensus on the rules of trade and security regimes is imperative. It also is vital that each of the Big Three be accorded the equal

status it deserves in such multilateral institutions, and none be deprived of membership or equal power over decision-making in such organizations.

In this light, China needs to be included in the World Trade Organization and Group of Seven (and agree to abide by its rules for membership as Russia has done in its participation as the G-7's eighth member). Japan has to be seated on the United Nations' Security Council, and the enlarged NATO and European Union must define their agendas with greater sensitivity to the fears enlargement provoked in the minds of leaders in Tokyo, Beijing, and Moscow. Unity for a globalized, increasingly borderless world is the *sine qua non* to future prosperity and peace. The Big Three have special responsibilities to lead in fostering a unified collective spirit, not only in the Pacific Rim, but in the 21st-century global system.

Unit 4

Unit Selections

Key Points to Consider

❖ What are some things marketers can do to market more effectively on the international level?

❖ The challenge for managers is a changing international environment. How can managers strategically plan for success in the future?

❖ Why do East-West relations remain important?

❖ How can the international financial system be strengthened?

 **Links**   **www.dushkin.com/online/**

25. **International Marketing Review**
    http://www.mcb.co.uk/cgi-bin/journal1/imr/
26. **IR-Net**
    http://www.ir-net.co.za/
27. **Kitchener Business Self-Help Office: Seven Steps to Exporting**
    http://www.city.kitchener.on.ca/kitchener_import_export.html
28. **MELNET**
    http://www.bradford.ac.uk/acad/mancen/melnet/index.html
29. **Research and Reference (Library of Congress)**
    http://lcweb.loc.gov/rr/
30. **Telecommuting as an Investment: The Big Picture—John Wolf**
    http://www.svi.org/telework/forums/messages5/48.html

These sites are annotated on pages 4 and 5.

How Management Deals with Environmental Forces

Managers of international organizations have to deal with a changing and varied global environment. To be successful, managers cannot just sit back and wait for things to happen. Rather, they need to be proactive in their approach to the problems and opportunities associated with doing business on an international basis, and they need to find partners who can help them. Fred L. Steingraber reports on such approaches in "How to Succeed in the Global Marketplace."

One of the major tools that managers have to help their organizations become successful on the global stage is marketing, and in particular, marketing analysis. Managers need to realize that, while all markets have certain similarities, they are all different in their own way and each can pose different problems, as outlined in "Troubles Ahead in Emerging Markets." Many practices are different and many hurdles exist. In sales, communicating with customers can be difficult and demanding, even in an "integrated" market such as Europe.

An easy way for a firm to get into international trade is through import/export channels. Often, when a small firm first starts to engage in international trade, it is not due to any deliberate decision of its own. Instead, the firm may place an advertisement in an industrial magazine, have a booth at a trade show, or be featured in an article on the news. As a result, one day they happen to get an order from someone outside their domestic market. It may be a very small order that merely says, "Send us one of these; we would like to look at it!" That first small order is then frequently followed by a much larger order, and the small domestic firm suddenly finds itself doing business abroad. This can happen on either side of the equation, as an importer or an exporter. As time passes, the company's foreign business grows at a faster rate than does its domestic business, especially if it involves one of the more rapidly developing economies, and soon, a significant amount of business is being done overseas.

China, Eastern Europe, and the former Soviet Union have been especially difficult for firms. Certainly there is great opportunity in these markets, but there is also great risk, as seen by the recent developments in the Pacific Rim. Many people in these societies simply do not know how to operate in a developing capitalist system. Commercial laws have not been developed, and an understanding of the fundamental aspects of capitalism has not been achieved by much of the population, including important government officials, as well as quasi-capitalists, such as factory managers. International managers must be prepared for setbacks and disappointments before they will be able to experience success. Linda M. Randall and Lori A. Colkley describe this phenomenon in "Building Successful Partnerships in Russia and Belarus: The Impact of Culture on Strategy."

The monetary problem has always been of particular concern in international trade. Currency trading and fluctuations cause managers sleepless nights and terrible days. Some currencies of the developing world, in particular, are difficult to deal with. The rewards can be very high, but, unfortunately, so can the risks. Managers who engage in world trade need to develop a strong financial management system to deal with the financial aspect of their global business if they are going to be successful.

An additional factor that needs to be considered is that of production. A world economy means not only worldwide customers but worldwide production. To be competitive, organizations must be able to produce around the globe and to coordinate production for the greatest advantage. With the introduction of the North American Free Trade Agreement (NAFTA), firms in North America are not just American, Canadian, or Mexican, but North American, with an entire continent as their backyard. Production is global and "Erasing Boundaries: Globalization" is rapidly becoming the business of global organizations.

Organizations that are going to produce, distribute, and sell overseas must realize that they cannot do this without workers, the people who perform the necessary tasks for the organization's success. Generally speaking, labor relations are very different outside the United States. The relationship between union and management in Germany, for example, frequently involves a highly cooperative arrangement. On the other hand, in some less developed countries, child labor is common, and a living wage, let alone benefits, is as rare as a union organizer. This does not mean that organizations from developed countries should emulate all these practices but, instead, that they should select the best aspects.

International managers must learn to combine all these parts of the new global business environment. They must plan strategically to make good use of marketing, production, finance, and labor. They must learn to control this highly diverse and sometimes contentious brew by using the most modern management technologies available. Controlling a business on an international scale is certainly not easy, and new systems will be needed in the future for managers to be successful. Perhaps even new approaches to exactly what constitutes a company need to be considered as presented in "A Company without a Country?"

In conclusion, there are many challenges facing managers in the international environment. But, fortunately, they have at least some of the tools they need to deal with these challenges. The task will not be easy, and new problems and opportunities are certain to arise in the future. Managers will have to develop the necessary new tools to solve the problems and grasp the opportunities for success in the ever-changing international business environment.

How to Succeed in the GLOBAL MARKETPLACE

Getting ahead "requires patience, commitment, and an open-minded approach to how industries work and consumers think in other cultures."

By Fred L. Steingraber

DURING THE PAST DECADE, the distinctions between foreign and domestic companies have become increasingly irrelevant in every market. Advances in transportation and electronic technology have helped reduce the impact of distances and time zones and differences among political and monetary systems, tastes, and standards. Organizations such as the General Agreement on Tariffs and Trade (GATT) and emerging trade groups such as the European Union, North American Free Trade Agreement (NAFTA), and the Association of Southeast Asian Nations (ASEAN) are encouraging moves to accelerate the integration of commerce and trade still further. These changes have helped turn a world of distinctly separate nations, each with its own barriers, into a single global marketplace.

Global trade has tripled in the past 25 years. Customers—both industrial and consumer—are becoming global shoppers. Today, it is easier for a firm of any size to operate on a global scale.

There are a variety of reasons for a company to consider globalizing, including labor and material cost advantages and

Mr. Steingraber is CEO, A.T. Kearney, Inc., Chicago, Ill.

shrinking market barriers in every region of the world. However a company that operates only in its home market today just can't decide to be global tomorrow. No matter where the global adventure begins, it is inevitable that the firm will go through a gradual transformation on the way to becoming a timely global organization. We have analyzed the way companies choose and implement globalization strategies and developed a framework that describes the range of options and stages they can pursue and move through.

Essentially, globalization is the process of building, reinforcing, and leading an organization toward establishing and maintaining competitive positions across a set of geographically dispersed markets. Before a company decides to enter the global arena, it must consider a range of key factors: top-line opportunities, economic leverage, competition, decreasing transaction costs, and increasing interdependencies.

Top-line opportunities. A number of economies, especially in Asia, have grown large enough to support critical mass operations. As these economies continue to develop, customers will demand higher product quality and performance at world-class standards. Executives who think they can dump

obsolete technology and marginal-quality products and services into these markets will be bitterly disappointed.

Economic leverage. In some industries, it is essential to access world markets to leverage large capital and development investments in order to reduce unit costs to competitive levels. For example, this is required in semiconductors, pharmaceuticals. and telecommunications.

Competition. Other companies are not standing still, but are investing in world markets. Leaving them alone to reap the rewards of "safe sanctuary" in their home or other strategic markets is competitive suicide. If a German or Japanese manufacturer is a strong competitor, a good strategy may be to compete against that company on its own turf in order to cut off cash flow at the source.

Decreasing transaction costs. Tariffs, logistics, regulations, and non-tariff barriers are declining worldwide. These decreases in costs spell increased opportunities.

Increasing interdependencies. Different economies develop different resource endowments, and prospective investors are encouraged to formulate investment strategies that recognize the different strengths—and interdependencies—among countries. This could mean taking advantage of raw material re-

From *USA Today Magazine*, November 1997, pp. 30-31. © 1997 by the Society for the Advancement of Education. Reprinted by permission.

sources of one nation, high technology research skills of another country, and the highly skilled workforce of yet another.

Attaining economies of scale often accelerates globalization, but not all firms need to be globally pervasive to compete effectively. The important point is to recognize that each company has a unique set of markets and internal requirements that govern the pace of globalization.

Four stages of global development provide a framework for evaluating a company's global profile and identifying areas that require action:

• Stage I companies are *opportunistic exporters*. They domestically design and manufacture their products, which find their way to overseas markets through standard export channels. These companies have little or no presence or investment outside their home market. They make no efforts to differentiate their product or service geographically. Typically, a foreign agent or licensee handles their products once they leave the boat. Stage I companies export because they see an opportunity to leverage an underutilized asset and to test foreign markets on a valuable cost basis using existing technology.

• Stage II companies are *international enterprises*. The top executives of such companies generally are conversant in international business, but not yet fluent. They want to be in foreign markets and recognize the advantages of tailoring a product to them. They have personnel who travel abroad. Frequently, they employ expatriates and may engage local foreign advisers. Nevertheless, they typically pursue an evolu- tionary strategy to adapt local designs fully and are slow to manufacture in other countries and make major investments such as product modification, local manufacturing sites, and human resource commitments. These organizations tend to be "plodders" in their approach to localization.

• Stage III companies are *multinationals* with extensive experience in a number of markets (although they frequently are concentrated in cultures similar to their home country). They have established marketing, manufacturing, and/or research and development (R&D) bases in several foreign countries. Frequently, local nationals manage these foreign operations. They tailor products to local standards and local mar-

kets, yet still generate and maintain critical strengths in their home markets and roll them out to foreign subsidiaries.

• Stage IV companies are truly global. They are local players in a diverse mix of foreign markets and have extensive foreign experience tailoring products to overseas markets. They manufacture and/or conduct some technical development activities in foreign nations and fulfill all service needs locally. They have research and development in multiple regions of the world. They source financial requirements globally, and their stock may be traded on multiple stock exchanges.

These companies are country neutral, but they are at home and typically have a competitive advantage in their key markets. They have developed a highly interdependent and geographically dispersed organization that creates, maintains, and shares distinctive strengths throughout the company. Resources are fluid and exchanged efficiently among parts of the firm. They tend to be pacesetters or leaders in multiple locations, setting and influencing standards globally.

There is a correlation between companies ranked as more advanced in their global development and those reaping greater returns from their foreign investments. However, most firms are inconsistent in observing relevant guidelines to creating a global business, which keeps them from fulfilling all the Stage IV requirements and enjoying the related success that follows.

Companies need to become global so they can establish a defensible strategy and achieve higher earnings, faster growth, and greater return on investment promised by participation in the global marketplace. Effective localization is the starting point.

Localization is based on identifying and addressing the differentiated needs of customers in the local markets while leveraging the resources of the organization. Success in a foreign country requires that the company adapt local demands in product or service offerings, business processes used, and technology applied. Globalization is the result of successful localization, or a local building blocks strategy.

Whether a firm is destined to be a very good Stage II company in its global development or will strive to reach Stage IV, management must select carefully from among geographically dispersed local markets in which to leverage its competitiveness. This leveraging can include a range of activities such as sourcing, R&D, and manufacturing, as well as local marketing and distribution. It must manage each activity, supplier, facility, affiliate, and resource both as local operations and as part of a globally interdependent group of activities that work to help the company achieve a competitive advantage by leveraging its core compe- tencies or distinctive strengths.

Trailblazing global winners like Hewlett-Packard understand the need to leverage resources. To address the differences in Asian markets, Hewlett-Packard has introduced computer printers that print in Japanese, Chinese, or Korean. The corporation adapts the printers to local languages by leveraging its own worldwide resources, including a research lab in Japan and a plant in Singapore, plus joint ventures with software design and manufacturing companies.

Before diagnosing where an individual firm is and ought to be, it is well to remember that every firm does not need to be a Stage IV company. Companies can succeed and gain competitive advantages at any stage, depending on variables, such as the nature of their product or service, distribution strategy, cost structure, strategic alliances, and competitive environment.

Not every business is cut out to compete at Stage IV. One of the greatest limitations many find in trying to achieve the goal of globalization is the human resource factor. A lack of talent and experience and an immobile cadre of key executives will limit any company's ability to achieve success in globalization. Moreover, not every industry is optimized by truly global companies. Different industries and businesses need different strategies and time frames in terms of global development. In construction equipment, for instance, two major worldwide competitors control 70% of the world market. These firms do not need to behave like Stage IV companies in every way to maintain their competitive positions. They are probably Stage IV for customer service, but Stage II or III for other factors. Global scale is not an issue because bulldozers are not produced in huge production runs.

Some companies can do very well at Stage I and II, again depending upon their products and other factors. Louisiana-Pa-cific, a lumber firm headquartered in Oregon, took the first steps toward localization by tailoring its product to Japanese customers. The company took advantage of its export potential and is selling wood to Japan by the boatload. First, though, it talked to customers to find out what they needed. Louisiana-Pacific now makes 3' × 6' paneling that is favored by Japanese customers in addition to the standard 4' × 8' paneling, which is preferred in the U.S.

Another example of a firm pursuing carefully planned Stage I export strategies is Dean Foods, a $2,000,000,000 dairy and vegetable processing company based in Illinois. Dean Foods exports non-dairy powdered creamer and canned and frozen vegetables to Europe and Asia, but its strategy does not provide for operating production facilities overseas.

The firm's executives have decided they don't want to take on the problems of setting up complicated distribution systems in underdeveloped countries. They may find they can succeed as a fairly sophisticated Stage I company for many years.

Each business has to examine its key resources, recognize strengths and limitations, then select a realistic course for gaining and sustaining competitive advantage. Globalization is not an end in and of itself, but can be a means, in the best case, to achieving competitive superiority. If globalization does not serve that mission, it has no place in a firm's strategy.

Traveling the road to the global marketplace requires patience, commitment, and an open-minded approach to how industries work and consumers think in other cultures. The road is not necessarily paved with gold. Nevertheless, once a company reaches its optimal stage of global development, the corporate treasury should benefit.

A WORLD OF ADVERTISING

The way we do things in the United States may dominate world media markets, but it's not the only way. This new model shows how advertising gets delivered in other countries.

BY KIP D. CASSINO

The old concept of "international" as a good resting place for passed-over sales execs no longer applies. The need to understand the world's markets grows in importance every year. Media measurement is an important part of the understanding, especially for U.S. firms used to working with the relatively precise information available for North American markets. Until recently, media estimates for much of the rest of the world have been difficult or impossible to come by.

Less-developed nations lack good information for a good reason: they don't collect it with any regularity—if at all. But even some of the world's larger economies are less obsessed with data than Americans are. Most of the world's nations, for instance, don't pay the same attention to "sales" statistics as U.S. researchers would like. Employee counts and other sparse business information—much of it available only in hard-to-decipher local units—are all that's available.

That being said, sources do exist. The Central Intelligence Agency provides good data on telephones, radios, televisions, and communication-satellite use for literally every country in the world, and it updates its information annually. Circulation figures for the world's newspapers are published every year. The World Bank (among other sources) keeps reasonably good records of many national statistics—including per-capita incomes, literacy rates, imports, exports, and a variety of other information. Finally, many large industrial firms provide worldwide sales estimates. This assortment yields enough raw material to construct a useful picture of world media spending.

AdWorld is a model that estimates advertising spending for specific media in 130 countries, encompassing virtually all of the world's population. It offers usable estimates of global media spending that are "approximately right" rather than exactly wrong. On the consumer side, it contains estimates for television, radio, print, outdoor, cinema, point-of-purchase, promotions, direct marketing, catalogs, ad production, and other (includes public relations, sales-force training and support, marketing research, and online marketing). For business-to-business, it covers print, direct marketing, promotions, catalogs, trade show and exhibitions, distributor materials, and ad production.

PANORAMIC VIEW

In a world where more than $1.4 trillion will be spent to market goods and services this year, more than 90 percent of the total is concentrated in 28 nations—most of them in Europe, the Pacific Rim, and North America. This set of countries accounts for about 17 percent of the world's population. Adver-

Kip D. Cassino is principal of Ad Audit Services in Miami, Florida.

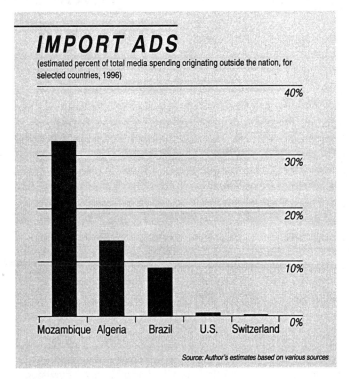

IMPORT ADS

(estimated percent of total media spending originating outside the nation, for selected countries, 1996)

Source: Author's estimates based on various sources

Nearly one in three media dollars targeted to residents of Mozambique comes from outside its borders. In contrast, virtually every dollar (franc, actually) spent on the Swiss originates in Switzerland.

tising spending per person ranges from a low of less than $1 in Laos to more than $2,100 for every man, woman, and child in Japan, the most intensely advertised-to population. These two Asian countries are geographic near-neighbors, but economically, they are light years apart.

About two-thirds of all media dollars spent around the world this year ($956 billion) will be spent to market consumer products and services. The rest ($478 billion) will be spent by businesses pitching their wares to other businesses. In developing economies, the ratios divert from this norm. Countries in the Middle East see nearly a 50/50 split between consumer and business-to-business marketing expenditures.

By itself, the United States accounts for over one-third of the planet's media spending—more than $479 billion, all told. But on a per-capita basis, the Japanese spend more to advertise consumer goods and services. "I'm not surprised," says Michelle Foster, head of marketing for Gannett Newspapers. "In Japan, everything's an ad."

AdWorld estimates that more than one-third of the world's total marketing expenditures ($508 billion) go for promotions rather than straightforward advertising. Efforts ranging from cents-off couponing, stocking fees, sweepstakes, and discounts to distributor rebates, finders' fees, and other costs of doing business in various national markets are the biggest single part of the world's marketing costs. This single category accounts for two in five global consumer-related marketing dollars, and three in ten business-related marketing dollars.

FIVE SNAPSHOT SEGMENTS

By dividing the world's nations into five reasonably equal-sized groups by population (quintiles), it is possible to get a sense of the level of international variation in media spending. The first quintile includes China and neighboring Vietnam and Laos, as well as Nigeria. These four nations are home to one in four human beings, but they receive less than 0.25 percent of world media spending. The average Quintile 1 resident is exposed to less than $3 worth of marketing expenditures during the course of a year.

A total of 43 nations make up Quintile 2, including most of Africa and central Asia. They collectively house 19 percent of the world's population and receive a little less than 1 percent of total advertising spending. India and Egypt dominate the 11 nations of Quintile 3, which comprise 20 percent of world population and a little less than 2 percent of media spending. Brazil, Mexico, South Africa, and the Russian Federation join 40 other nations in Quintile 4, which total 18 percent of the world's people and 6 percent of global media spending.

Western Europe, Canada, the United States, Argentina, Middle Eastern oil states, Israel, Japan, and the strong economies of the Pacific Rim combine in Quintile 5, where 17 percent of the world's people absorb more than 90 percent of all marketing dollars spent. An average Quintile 5 resident finds close to $1,400 worth of media spending in reading materials, broadcast entertainment, at work, and in the stores where he or she shops—524 times the amount of her Quintile 1 neighbor.

The following are examples of spending estimates from typical countries in each of the five quintiles.

Quintile 1: Vietnam

Vietnam's 71 million people own an estimated 7 million radios and 2.5 million TVs. Reported daily newspaper circulation is 1.2 million copies. But low levels of imports and one of the lowest per-capita incomes in the world means that marketing expenditures are concentrated in cities, where only one in five Vietnamese lives. No form of consumer media consistently reaches beyond the wealthiest one-fifth of the nation's population, which accounts for 44 percent of consumer spending. Outdoor advertising reaches the most Vietnamese—an estimated 14 million, followed by point-of-purchase materials, at 11 million.

Quintile 2: Kenya

Roughly one in four Kenyans lives in a city. Almost one in three is illiterate. Nevertheless, this African nation continues to show steady economic growth and a positive international debt balance. It has 1 radio set for every 33 people, and 1 TV for every 109. Newspaper circulation is slightly more than 1 million for a population of 25 million. As with Vietnam, only outdoor advertising reaches beyond the wealthiest 20 percent of Kenyan consumers.

GLOBAL MEDIA SPENDING

(estimated media spending in millions of U.S. dollars and percent distribution for selected countries, by category, 1996)

	Vietnam (Quintile 1)		Kenya (Quintile 2)		Egypt (Quintile 3)		Russian Federation (Quintile 4)		Singapore (Quintile 5)	
	Dollars	Percent	Dollars	Percent	Dollars	Percent	Dollars	Percent	Dollars	Percent
Consumer	$139.9	66.8%	$148.3	75.8%	$1,256.1	78.8%	$9,609.7	50.0%	$1,519.7	54.6%
TV	15.5	11.1**	15.2	10.2**	119.7	9.5**	718.4	7.5**	129.7	8.5**
Radio	0.8	0.6	0.2	0.1	4.8	0.4	123.0	1.3	67.0	4.4
Print	24.4	17.4	24.0	16.2	188.4	15.0	1,130.5	11.8	204.2	13.4
Outdoor	1.3	0.9	1.2	0.8	9.8	0.8	58.7	0.6	10.6	0.7
Cinema	0.2	0.1	0.2	0.1	1.2	0.1	7.3	0.1	1.3	0.1
Point of purchase	0.8	0.6	2.0	1.3	46.8	3.7	374.6	3.9	261.6	17.2
Promotions	79.7	57.0	88.7	59.8	727.9	57.9	2,773.0	28.9	535.7	35.3
Direct	7.2	5.1	5.5	3.7	30.3	2.4	324.5	3.3	66.3	4.4
Catalog	0.1	0.1	0.2	0.1	8.8	0.7	208.7	2.2	101.5	6.7
Ad production	9.1	6.5	10.9	7.3	113.8	9.1	341.4	3.6	73.4	4.8
Other*	0.8	0.6	0.2	0.1	4.6	0.4	3,559.6	37.0	68.4	4.5
Business-to-business	$69.5	33.2	$47.4	24.2	$337.5	21.2	$9,609.3	50.0	$1,262.7	45.4
Total media spending	$209.4	100.0	$195.7	100.0	$1,593.6	100.0	$19,219.0	100.0	$2,782.4	100.0

* Includes public relations, market research, and online.
**Percent of consumer media spending.

Source: Author's estimates based on various sources

TV accounts for a slightly larger-than-average share of consumer-directed media spending in less-developed countries, where it's accessible to a smaller but more upscale audience than in more-developed nations.

Quintile 3: Egypt

Egypt is the Middle East's most populous nation. Two in five Egyptians live in cities. Slightly more than half cannot read or write. One in 13 owns a radio, and 1 in 45 has a television—fed by the world through five satellite receivers. The

> *Even though Marx's and Lenin's theories depended upon the masses, only one in three Russians has access to a television or radio.*

nation circulates more than 2.2 million newspapers daily, to be read by 27 million of Egypt's 56 million people. In this nation, point-of-purchase and cinema advertising join outdoor advertising in reaching beyond the wealthiest 20 percent of the total population, which, however, accounts for 52 percent of Egypt's total consumer buying power, even more than in poorer Vietnam.

Quintile 4: The Russian Federation

Economies in transition make up much of Quintile 4, which includes the Baltic states, Georgia and the Ukraine, Poland, and the Czech Republic. The people in these nations are, in

many cases, even less used to the mechanics of free markets and application of marketing and advertising than their neighbors in less-developed Quintile 2 and 3 countries. Russia is no exception. Even though Marx's and Lenin's theories depended upon the masses, only one in three Russians has access to a television or radio. On the other hand, Russians are better-educated than people in less-developed nations, and a healthy 26 million newspapers circulate each day through a vast nation spanning six time zones. Furthermore, every form of media reaches beyond the most wealthy 20 percent of the nation's population, and outdoor ads are potentially seen by everyone.

Quintile 5: Singapore

Quintile 5 nations receive and create the vast majority of the world's advertising and marketing efforts. The entire populations of nations like Singapore, Japan, Australia, the United States, Canada, and most of Europe have access to every form of media. Singapore, for example, averages 2.2 radios per person, and enough televisions to supply more than one to each household. The average resident appears to read more than one newspaper per day, and only cinema advertising fails to potentially touch the entire population. Because Singapore's economy is dynamic beyond the size of its population, the

REACHING PEOPLE

(media spending per capita for top-ranking and bottom-ranking countries, 1996)

rank	country	per-capita media spending
1	Japan	$2,137
2	United States	1,861
3	France	1,845
4	Germany	1,593
5	Netherlands	1,517
6	Denmark	1,504
7	Belgium	1,357
8	United Kingdom	1,286
9	Hong Kong	1,180
10	Australia	1,166
126	Tanzania	$4.10
127	Vietnam	2.92
128	Nigeria	2.77
129	China	2.62
130	Laos	0.41

Source: Author's estimates based on various sources

At nearly $6, daily media spending directed at the average Japanese resident is 14 times greater than the amount aimed at the average Laotian in an entire year.

business-to-business segment makes up a relatively high percentage of total marketing expenditures for a Quintile 5 country.

The Environment Behind the Numbers

Each country's advertising and marketing environment is as unique as its people. Certainly more effort—and specifically, more directed effort—is targeted toward wealthier consumers and larger businesses in Quintiles 4 and 5 than in the rest of the world.

In the less-developed nations of Quintiles 1, 2, and 3, most people don't have contact with advertising until they enter a store with money in hand to make a purchase. Packaging and other point-of-purchase elements have an even greater effect on buying decisions when people haven't seen or heard advertising messages before they walk in.

On the other hand, advertising to the affluent market in such countries is relatively inexpensive, because they are few in number and easy to target. The polarity in media exposure and purchasing patterns in less-developed countries favors goods and services that are either very cheap or very expensive. Demand for mid-priced products, and the need to balance advertising reach with its costs, grows with personal income and creation of a visible middle class.

As a result, advertising to businesses in the less-developed economies of Quintile 1 takes up a disproportionate share of total media spending, an estimated 56 percent. As consumer disposable incomes rise, consumer advertising becomes pre-eminent, approaching 65 percent of media spending in Quintiles 2 and 3, and 71 percent in Quintile 4. In the wealthiest nations with the largest industrial economies, the pattern reverses slightly. Business advertising makes up about one-third of marketing expenditures in Quintile 5 economies.

In the United States, large-scale advertising began in newspapers, then spread to broadcast media as they became available. In Quintiles 1 through 3, where the press may be government-controlled, the reverse is often true. In these countries, outdoor advertising is often the dominant media choice for marketing low-cost consumer items. Upscale goods are sold through regional editions of western magazines read by a small literate population and via satellite-fed broadcast media to the few who are wealthy enough to own TVs.

In some cases, however, technological advances are making it possible to make vast inroads in a very short period of time, skipping some of the interim steps through which more developed economies have moved. Today, advertising trade journals discuss Indian TV satellite networks with the same fervor reserved in the past for Europe and the Pacific Rim. After all, people don't have to live in major cities to have access to satellite TV, and they don't have to be literate to watch it. Some advertisers and agencies are finding it worthwhile to help finance the continued development of media that bring their messages to people in less-developed countries.

In Europe and the United States, advertising and a free-market economy have created the most informed populations in history. Advertising-supported media bring entertainment, ideas, and news to literally everyone. Perhaps AdWorld is not as much a measure of marketing activity as it is a gauge of human horizons.

TAKING IT FURTHER

The AdWorld model depends on two major sources: the annual *World Fact Book* published by the Central Intelligence Agency and available from the U.S. Government Printing Office; and the World Bank's annual *World Development Reports,* published by Oxford University Press. Supporting information is provided by Editor and Publisher's *Year Book, Advertising Age International,* and annual reports of 200 large U.S. corporations.

The model consists of two independent databases. One compares advertising expenditures with advertising revenue and employees per area served. The second compares revenue from media companies with populations served. The results are compared and reiterated until a relatively close match (plus or minus 5 percent) has been achieved. The average of the two numbers becomes the AdWorld estimate. The same process is used in Ad Audit, which tracks and estimates media spending in U.S. metros, and is now available through Claritas, Inc. For more information about Ad Audit and AdWorld, call (305) 376–6166.

Asia's Next Tiger?

Vietnam is fraught with promise and peril for marketers.

by Clifford J. Shultz II and William J. Ardrey IV

Vietnam has come a long way since the 1986 decision by the Communist Party (CPV) to implement *Doi Moi*, or economic renovation. Its economy is humming along with near-double-digit growth rates and foreign investors line up to fund the choice projects for Vietnam's expansion. Abroad, Vietnam has achieved stable relations with its neighbors, reduced its military expenditures, and forged foreign policy successes with the Association of Southeast Asian Nations (ASEAN), the United States, and China.

These macroeconomic and foreign policy trends have spawned a boom economy. The Vietnamese government wants—indeed, desperately needs—this boom to continue, and Vietnamese consumers are increasingly unlikely to accept anything less than full integration into the global economy. As economic reforms create more wealth in Vietnam, more and more Vietnamese consumers are shifting from the grind of daily subsistence to the joys of consumption.

If Vietnam continues its drive to modernize, promising opportunities for marketing firms will continue to emerge. But peril accompanies this promise and marketing managers must have a keen awareness of the many factors that can predict success or failure in Vietnam.

War Wounds

Say the word "Vietnam" and myriad images come to mind. For most Americans, it evokes recollections of grisly war footage and boat people; for younger Americans, it conjures up Hollywood's depictions of the war. Rarely does one think of present-day Viet-

nam, a country of enormous natural wealth and limitless potential. Its natural assets include timber, fisheries, vast oil and gas reserves, a coastline longer than the one extending between Seattle and San Diego, and fertile soil that has enabled Vietnam to become the third-largest rice producer in the world. The nation's cultural wealth includes the traditions and historical sites of 4,000 years of national identity. Its people are industrious, cheerful, and very keen to join the consumer society. Yet Vietnam still struggles to be seen as a *country*, not a war.

Recently, Vietnam has been able to attract significant private investment capital and multilateral aid; the Ministry of Planning and Investment received license applications for $5.4 billion in 1995 and hopes to exceed $6 billion in 1996. With development aid came more private business. The World Bank financed a $2 billion highway and infrastructure project that brought big American companies such as Caterpillar, Morrison Knudsen, and others to Vietnam. Total investment of over $520 million from U.S. companies alone flowed into Vietnam by the end of 1995.

EXECUTIVE BRIEFING

Vietnam has evolved from one of the worst performing economies in Asia during the early 1980s, to winning the Euromoney Best Managed Economy Award in the '90s. Foreign investors, betting that Vietnam was serious about its economic reforms, rushed to penetrate this market. Some succeeded, many failed. Vietnam must now respond to the challenge of rising expectations by foreign investors while delivering increased variety and quality of goods demanded by its people. The transition from a command to a market economy continues to lurch forward, creating a promising but perilous marketing environment.

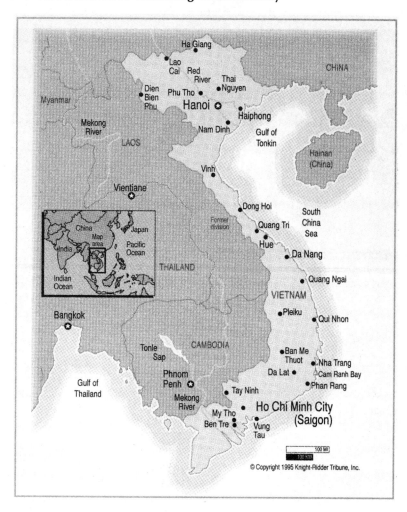

© Copyright 1995 Knight-Ridder Tribune, Inc.

Forward-thinking marketing managers look at Vietnam as a promising market; with 74 million consumers, it is the 13th largest in the world. Whether one is selling earth movers or soft drinks, airplanes or cosmetics, Vietnam is already a burgeoning market with considerable purchasing power. In 1994, the United States was a virtual nonplayer; by 1996, it was the sixth-largest investor. Nevertheless, Vietnam is not an "easy" market, nor is it one that lends itself to simple replications of successful strategies used in other parts of Southeast Asia or China. Vietnam is a market of inexplicable contradictions of the good-news, bad-news sort.

First, the Bad News

With all the hype over opportunity in Vietnam, it's easy to forget that this economic change is quite recent. Once isolated and totally dependent on dwindling aid from the Soviet-controlled Council for Mutual Economic assistance, Vietnam was unable to tap into Western capital and know-how until its withdrawal from Cambodia in 1989. In addition, as a re-

sult of the U.S.-led embargo and poor central economic planning at home, Vietnam still has an annual per-capita income under $400. And even though the *Doi Moi* policy has been successful to date, Vietnam's small but growing middle class counts on annual incomes of less than half the $2,600 of their upwardly mobile neighbors in China.

Vietnam remains a poor country with a physical, legal, and economic infrastructure that is still undergoing a massive overhaul. Economic reform was undertaken in reaction to the utter failure of the command economy to survive without Soviet assistance, not as part of a master plan for development as envisioned by other Asian "tiger" states. This overhaul was and still is administered by CPV and any ambition for doing business in Vietnam must consider that the country will continue to be a single-party state. Accordingly, regulations, laws, and licenses continue to be issued and enforced at the discretion of the CPV, which despite the reform movement, is not altogether comfortable promoting "market socialism," the term preferred by the CPV to describe a market economy administered in the shadow of socialist ideology. But the reform process does continue to lurch forward, albeit with numerous stops, starts, and more than a few steps backwards.

The result is that Vietnam is similar to a football field with moving goal posts—the rules always seem to change just when one is about to be profitable. This phenomenon is explained partly by bureaucracy, partly by government insecurities about administering a market economy, and partly by corruption. Despite the efforts of Prime Minister Vo Van Kiet to take a personal interest in streamlining licensing agreements and business procedures, generally, the bureaucracy and red tape in Vietnam remain daunting. So, while license applications for investment continue to grow, actual investment by foreign corporations in approved projects fell over 40% in the first half of 1996. Some foreigners have become especially wary of joint ventures with Vietnamese firms (usually state-owned), and the Vietnam News Agency has reported a trend toward wholly owned foreign projects.

Besides bureaucratic slowdowns and corruption, the CPV continues to coddle state-run enterprises and Hanoi intends to keep the state sector as the vanguard of the economy. Investment in infrastructure and the fledgling private sector remains relatively small. Virtually all investments to date have been in oil and gas exploration, fisheries, cash exports, or other big-ticket items, with state enterprises serving as the Vietnamese partners.

The private sector grew to more than $300 million in combined capital in 1993, with license applications for private businesses maintaining double-digit growth since 1993. But local private manufacturers complain of excessive taxation, lack of capital and resources, and government favoritism for foreign investments, especially joint-venture projects with the state.

Foreigners looking to create partnerships with a private Vietnamese company must be aware that the private sector receives lots of praise, but few useful resources in Vietnam. The state-run commercial banks, which account for almost 90% of bank assets, are heavily, if not exclusively, geared toward the state enterprise sector. Listings on the long-planned Vietnam Stock Exchange–and the exchange itself–have not yet appeared. Some 50 state firms have been ordered to begin "equitization," gradually selling small stakes into private hands.

Unfortunately, there is no secondary market for these equity stakes. Smaller private companies and foreign joint ventures already prepared for privatization have been discouraged from offering shares, and management buyouts and outright acquisitions have been frowned upon as well. By 1996, 5,000 of the 12,000 state-owned enterprises (SOEs) operating in 1993 were closed or merged as part of *Doi Moi*, but only five small state enterprises have "equitized" to permit private participation.

Medium-size firms also have felt the financial squeeze due to efforts by CPV conservatives to keep all assets in the hands of the state. From 1991–1995, Vietnamese state and private partners were able to attract foreign investors by offering land rights directly to foreign companies as an important part of the local partner's contribution to the capital of a new business venture. Before the controversial Decree 18/CP in February 1995, Vietnamese firms also were able to mortgage land-use rights for loans. And while repeal of this decree is still being debated in the National Assembly, for the time being, land use rights must be leased directly from the state. This places a significant burden on existing companies and new ventures attracting loans and foreign investments.

Individuals and small firms typically have been left out of plans for financial-services reform. If they can buy shares of equitized firms, they cannot trade them. The 62 foreign banks and bank representative offices in Vietnam are severely restricted in taking Vietnamese dong deposits, especially from Vietnamese citizens. The dong's present exchange rate is approximately 11,000 to 1 U.S. dollar. The Vietnamese government has development plans that require between $40 billion and $50 billion of investment, yet it can reasonably expect only half this figure to come from foreign sources. Government officials must mobilize domestic savings to fund the needed investments in infrastructure and key industries if they want to emulate the Asian tiger economies.

Without banking services from foreign banks, Vietnamese citizens and small private firms are left with

Important Political Developments Since 1992

➤The United States and Vietnam established diplomatic relations in 1995; Vietnam likely will be granted most favored nation status as a trade partner. The latest reports out of both Washington and Hanoi suggest this decision is not likely to be made before the end of 1997.

➤Vietnam joined ASEAN and is expected to join the Asia Pacific Economic Cooperation (APEC).

➤Constructive engagement with China, Vietnam's principal rival in the region, resulted in reduced military threats, exchanges of senior delegations, and an 80% increase in bilateral trade.

➤The Greater Mekong subregion–a trading zone of 200 million consumers from Vietnam, Cambodia, Laos, Thailand, and southern China–emerged. The subregion shares the costs and benefits of regional infrastructure and investment products, lowers trade barriers, and facilitates exchanges of goods and services. Vietnam, at the mouth of the Mekong, serves as the primary conduit to the entire region.

➤A 50% debt forgiveness negotiation with the Paris Club, and rescheduling and forgiveness of over $750 million in debt with the London Club, allowed Vietnam to tap the Eurobond market for needed capital.

➤Joint arrangements with Asian and Western governments and banking groups were established to reorganize and to reform Vietnam's ailing financial-services sector.

the state banking system. This system is set up to serve state enterprises and continues to have serious service delivery problems, such as the inability to clear checks between branches of the same bank. Even for a developing country, Vietnam has a low volume of noncash transactions and difficulty with checks and wire payments. In many cases, foreign firms must pay their employees–and settle payroll tax liabilities–in cash. Vietnam has one of the lowest deposit rates in the developing world, less than 25% of GDP. (Most countries average 75%, with higher rates in Asia.)

This is not surprising considering that local banks charge for withdrawals, an obvious disincentive to save in the formal banking system. Memories of high inflation and bank failures also impede progress. In the 1980s, state-run banks failed to honor withdrawals, informal credit cooperatives collapsed, and high inflation discouraged saving.

Alternative services and sources of capital have filled the vacuum created by state-bank shortcomings. Informal credit rings are flourishing, with more than $2 billion being hoarded outside the formal banking system in U.S. dollars, gold, or consumer goods such as liquor and durable goods that will hold their value over time. Viet Kieu (overseas Vietnamese) infusions

Vietnam: The Bad News

➤Inconsistent and frequent inexplicable policies that hinder all aspects of the transition from a command to a market economy, including the legal, banking, and accounting systems.

➤Persistent and expanding trade deficits, which ballooned from $60 million in 1992 to $2.2 billion dollars in 1996.

➤Growing overseas debt.

➤Burgeoning current account deficit, which hit an estimated 15.1% of GDP in 1995.

➤Stagnating foreign direct investment (FDI) realizations; while approval rates are soaring, actual realization of the projects is slowing, partly because of the frustrations presented by bureaucracy.

➤Inefficiencies of state-owned enterprises, as evidenced by little job creation and the failure to create value-added exports.

also play a role. Approximately 2 million Viet Kieu bring money into the country and/or send money to families and friends. Some private banks also have been established in Vietnam, with many turning a profit from trade finance. Financial-service reforms, however, still tend to ignore small enterprises and consumers, and the institutions generally are out of step with the standards required by serious players in a global economy.

All of these perils have taken the bloom off Vietnam's rose. Many investors who came with high expectations and hopes for quick results quickly had them dashed and departed Vietnam in search of the next investment Shangri-La. Michael Scown, a partner with Russin and Vecchi in Ho Chi Minh City and a former president of the American Chamber of Commerce in Vietnam, recently shared a growing sentiment among investors: "It has become increasingly apparent that investors will have to set more realistic goals, truly commit to projects and settle in for the long haul."

Now, the Good News

It would be easy for a marketing manager in charge of introducing and/or managing a product in Vietnam to become disheartened by the bad-news scenario. But for every investor who leaves, two more seem to fill the vacuum because the market is so promising. The macroeconomic reforms that resulted from *Doi Moi,* have controlled inflation, freed prices, promoted agriculture and export marketing, spurred foreign investment, and opened domestic markets.

Many of the problems in Vietnam are simply growing pains, which the central government is working to remedy. And, after a decade of reforms,

the direction, if not the pace of *Doi Moi,* remains focused on economic growth and expansion. Moreover, Vietnamese authorities increasingly are attempting to facilitate the foreign investment process. "We have shifted toward a market economy, says Tran Quang Nghiem, chairman of the Government Price Committee. "Now, we must modernize. This requires establishing a modern, integrated marketing, finance, and accounting system throughout the country and with links to external markets." To those ends legal, tax, and financial reforms have been proposed, and many desirable projects have had their license procedures "fast tracked" by the government. The economy continues to grow, inflation remains low, and some early foreign investors have begun to generate returns.

Recent political developments also should make investors optimistic. Vietnam has been at the heart of a region dominated for centuries by brutal conflict, but the climate in the last five years has arguably fostered progress on a sustainable peace and more-predictable economic growth than any time in the past 50 years.

Improved relations with the United States and China have been critical to Vietnam's economic success. Vietnam faces few external constraints on growth and can continue to reduce military spending in favor of infrastructure investment. Vietnam now boasts of trading relationships with over 100 nations. Once contentious with most countries outside the former Soviet bloc, Le Van Bang and Ha Huy Thong, Vietnam's ambassador to the United States and deputy consul, respectively, have on more than one occasion informed us that Vietnam's current foreign policy is to "get along well with everyone."

Vietnam continues to capitalize on its successful mix of domestic reforms and openness to foreign investment. Even though the country started its reform process nearly a decade after China, the Vietnamese have been able to catch up in the areas of agricultural reform, price reform, currency devaluation, and healthy growth rates for GDP and foreign investment. Similar to China, the Communist Party has remained in command, with the role of guiding the economy along the road to "marketization." In this regard, CPV is functioning much more like the single-party "capitalist" states in the region than the Stalinist regimes of the cold war. The Asian Development Bank and other sources predict 9%–10% annual growth rates, single-digit inflation rates, and exponential growth in consumption.

Marketing Environment

The bureaucracy can frustrate the most determined investors and the CPV does not yet fully embrace the private sector but, on balance, the macroeconomic and political changes coupled with pent-up consumer demand make a compelling argument for investment in Vietnam. Indeed, precisely because of the current uncertainty of the market, opportunities abound if investors understand the unique dynamism that is Vietnam. Investors who wait for optimal conditions will miss the proverbial boat. But where, exactly, are the opportunities right now?

Infrastructure

Because Vietnam is in the process of rebuilding a nation, there are many opportunities in infrastructure development. Seaports, airports, highways, water treatment facilities, buildings, dams, power stations, and other foundations to support a modern economy are being built or refurbished. Goods and services that abet the process—construction, telecommunications, and transportation supplies and equipment—are in huge demand, and investors have access to multilateral aid to fund the projects.

Export Markets

Many government policies, including tax breaks and export processing zones, encourage investors to initiate operations that facilitate export growth and development. Imports of heavy equipment, for example, often are duty free. Petroleum and minerals, aquaculture, and agriculture also are viable industries. Vietnam is beginning to demonstrate the ability to produce quality products in low-tech, labor-intensive, value-added industries such as textiles and furniture. With a redoubled effort to establish technology parks and R&D centers, and a commitment to maintain low wages, Vietnam hopes to compete in high-tech industries within a decade.

Consumer Markets

All types and brands of consumer products and services are rapidly diffusing throughout Vietnam. Popular brands familiar to Americans are beginning to dominate the clothing, electronics, household goods, and recreational beverage markets. Foreign brands are equated with quality and prestige, and consumers are willing to pay price premiums for them. This trend, while generally positive, also has some drawbacks because even though brand names are very popular among Vietnamese, brand *authenticity* is a secondary consideration. Consequently, one drawback is a booming brand-piracy industry, whereby the Vietnamese manufacture or distribute counterfeit items. Brands associated with pop culture, Disney characters, Ray Ban sunglasses, and Nike are just a few examples of popular trademarks that are frequently victimized.

Vietnam: The Good News

➤Annual GDP over the last five years has averaged 8.2%.

➤Inflation has dropped from 487% in 1986 to 12.4% in 1995, mainly attributable to tough government budgets.

➤Agricultural production has risen 7% annually and industrial production has jumped 13%-15% annually since 1988.

➤Reorientation of trade to a market-style economy doubled exports between 1992 and 1995.

➤Registered imports are up; unregistered imports smuggled in from Southern China and Thailand via Cambodia are *way* up.

➤FDI licensing approvals totaled $18 billion at the end of 1995, up 97% in 1995 alone.

➤Overseas direct assistance pledges remain healthy, with $2 billion pledged at the latest donor conference held in November 1995 in Paris.

A second drawback is concern by the CPV and domestic manufacturers that Vietnamese products are being squeezed out of the marketplace. Consequently, domestic producers have called on the government to protect industries such as cigarettes, beverages, detergents, and paper. The success of foreign products has been accompanied by a crackdown on "social evils" such as karaoke bars and many types of outdoor advertisements. While the government has not expected demand for popular brands or non-Vietnamese ideas to disappear, it has taken steps to avoid cultural disintegration and complete dominance by foreign products. For example, the government stipulates that ads for foreign products include copy in the Vietnamese language.

Government rhetoric, however, cannot affect the reality that the consumer is now king in Vietnam. Truly, there is no stopping or even slowing this revolution. Rising incomes, exposure to popular culture, product availability, and limited opportunities for other forms of recreation are making shopping and consumption popular pastimes. More specifically, trends affecting the shift toward a consumer culture include five basic factors: urbanization, family dynamics, emerging middle and upper classes, a foreign invasion, and the youth movement.

Urbanization. Vietnam is still an agrarian society with 80% of the population living in the countryside, but there is large-scale migration to the cities. This migration is the result of economic growth and opportunities afforded by extensive foreign investment in Hanoi, Ho Chi Minh City, Danang, Can Tho, Hue and Haiphong, and special economic zones such as Vung Tau. As part of this urbanization process, Vietnamese

EXHIBIT 1

Household possessions of durables

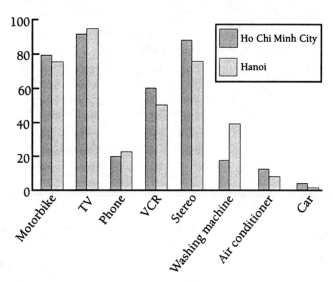

Source: 1996 raw data provided by SRG Vietnam

are increasingly exposed to the new consumption ethos found in the cities.

Family dynamics. Large families continue to share small houses, with urban households typically consisting of more than seven members. Although each family member earns only a few hundred dollars each year, household income more than exceeds expenses. Children live at home until marriage, contributing to the family income in addition to their own needs. Viet Kieu family members also contribute significantly by sending money or gifts. So, while individual purchasing power is modest, pooled resources by families create purchasing clout.

> An affluent population of teenagers in Ho Chi Minh City now has the wherewithal to obtain credit cards from foreign banks and purchase expensive imported consumer goods.

Emerging classes. Millions of Vietnamese now have disposable income. Official figures in Hanoi and Ho Chi Minh City indicate incomes now often approach and exceed $1,000, respectively. Our personal interviews indicate much larger, unreported and untaxed pockets of wealth springing up throughout Viet-

namese cities. A middle and even a small upper class is emerging. Many consumers or households now can afford relatively expensive items such as motorcycles, televisions, VCRs, stereo equipment, and washing machines; some can afford luxury items of all kinds, including automobiles, villas, and high-fashion products (see Exhibit l).

Foreign invasion. Many Vietnamese feel under siege with all the new products and advertisements. Furthermore, tourists and expatriates visiting or working in Vietnam bring new ideas, products, expectations, and demands. Hotels, transportation services, discos, newspapers, magazines, golf courses, promotion campaigns, and satellite TV all are intended to meet the needs of this growing "foreigner" market. But Vietnamese also are exposed to these new products, information, ideas, and values and, subsequently, are changing their expectations and demands.

Tabula rasa. The combined impressionable nature of youth and the flood of new ideas and products has created a segment of Generation X consumers in a very short period of time. The *tabula rasa* factor and the sheer size of the youth market is having a profound effect on Vietnamese society. Although still family-oriented and living under the shadow of socialist dogma, more than half of Vietnam's population is under age 20. To these consumers, the Vietnam War and the teachings of Uncle Ho are little more than a history lesson.

But then, who has time for history when one can work for a Western company; save a little money; buy the latest CD, a pair of jeans, and some fake Ray Ban sunglasses; and then cruise Le Loi Boulevard and Dhong Khoi Street on a new Honda Dream motor scooter? Anyone who has spent an evening trying to cross these streets will appreciate the accuracy of this description of the youth market. An affluent population of teenagers in Ho Chi Minh City now has the wherewithal to obtain credit cards from foreign banks and purchase expensive imported consumer goods. In addition to constituting a growing market in their own right, Vietnam's young are becoming opinion leaders for others.

These trends all indicate radical change, rapid market segmentation, and consumer clout. A decade ago there was only one segment: the destitute. Just a few years ago segmentation schemes differentiated consumers on urban-rural and North-South dimensions. More recently, age, access to Western or developed-market Asian ideas and products, one's marketable skills, and disposable income have become factors that predict consumption patterns. Although it should be noted that as in any transforming agrarian economy in which socialism and collectivism were the norm, there is a conservative element, particularly in Northern and rural regions, whose members prefer traditional or local Vietnamese products. Nevertheless, the sweeping trend is a society transforming to a consumer culture, and in the cities this transformation is occurring at an astonishing rate.

'Exit' Interviews

Vietnam is a promising market, but to succeed there, marketing managers must have more than a fundamental understanding of the classic 4Ps of the marketing mix. They must accept that Vietnam is a series of enigmas and seemingly illogical confounds. Management in Vietnam is as much art, nuance, and persuasion as science. We have conducted many exit interviews with investors—literally, interviews with investors at either Tan Son Nhat or Noi Bal airports exiting Vietnam because of failed projects. For the most part, those projects did not fail because of poor market demand for the goods or services, but because managers and investors simply could not come to grips with the arcane conditions of Vietnam's management environment. The emergent themes from those interviews, as well as from the success stories, are factors U.S. managers need to consider.

Move With the Goal Posts

Managers must accept that the goal posts in Vietnam will continue to shift, making it difficult to score. Asian investors and some Europeans seem much more willing to accept this fact and spend considerable amounts of time nurturing relationships with partners and government authorities. (Note too that these two entities are sometimes synonymous.) Consequently, they are able to predict and adjust to goal-post movements. More importantly, they often discover that because of their efforts to nurture relationships, the goal posts haven't moved at all for them.

As a case in point, the country manager for one European brewery was pleased to inform us that his firm would not have to remove or repaint its billboards in response to the social-evils campaign. He attributed this time and cost savings solely to his efforts to maintain a good relationship with government authorities. American investors, however, find it difficult to work solely on solid relationships and trust and want to ensure that all the legal issues are agreed upon before moving forward. If this strategy were not so counterproductive, it would be comical because the legal codes in Vietnam are either nonexistent or revised continually.

This is not to argue that one should abandon respect for laws and the legal process. To the contrary, understanding Vietnamese laws and Vietnam's legal system is very important. For example, favoritism toward

Americans and American brands is a powerful advantage that should not be underestimated. But Tanya Pullin, an attorney for Baker and McKenzie who has practiced in Vietnam, adds that "trademarks in Vietnam mean nothing unless they are registered in Vietnam." Trademark registration begets government protection. Despite problems with brand piracy, the government will crack down by closing bogus plants and fining purveyors of pirated goods *if* the pirated trademarks are registered.

Market research has been and always will be important in Vietnam.

Even the fundamental logic of "best product for the best price" means little in Vietnam. "We went to the Vietnamese government with a proposal for a new cement formula that was 30% better and 30% cheaper," says James Reany of International Trade Resources. "We even used Vietnamese laboratories to 'convince' them of our product's superiority. To make a long story short, there's a lot of building going on in Vietnam, but we're not part of it yet." So, investors and managers constantly struggle to balance home-country laws, Vietnamese laws, and social forces in addition to managing the marketing mix.

The moving goal posts make Vietnam an exceptionally challenging market. But there are good, recent examples of large and small firms that have figured out how to score. PepsiCo, typically second in market share in the cola wars around the globe, arrived in Vietnam five hours after the U.S. embargo was lifted. The company thoroughly researched all relevant aspects of the market and, in so doing, determined demand and found an optimal partner and appropriate manufacturing sites. PepsiCo kept the initial investment low, established quality controls, offered professional training and cash resources, and effectively used *Su Lua Cua The He Moi* ("The choice of a new generation") as Pepsi's promotional tag line.

In one year, this joint venture, in which PepsiCo holds 30% equity, had sales revenues of $33 million and a profit of $2.5 million. In two years, Pepsi outpaced local producer Tribeco to become the dominant brand in southern Vietnam (see Exhibit 2). In the process, PepsiCo solidified its relationship with the government by paying $6 million in taxes and employing 1,200 people. Procter & Gamble, Colgate-Palmolive, and the Coca-Cola Co. also are enjoying success. Companies providing a product or service that consumers can pay for *now* are doing well.

Small-firm success stories also are being written by a number of young, energetic entrepreneurs from the United States who are targeting newly emerging niche

EXHIBIT 2

Top five most frequently consumed soft drinks in Ho Chi Minh City

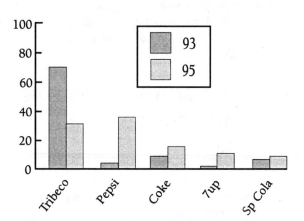

Source: 1996 raw data provided by SRG Vietnam

markets. From bamboo production and real estate brokerage to trading companies and language centers, these pioneers are making a mark in Vietnam. They all have some common threads: low overhead, flexibility, an ability to see opportunities where others only saw stumbling blocks, target focus, enthusiasm, and a sense of adventure. And they all made a total commitment: They moved to Vietnam, immersed themselves in the environment, learned the language, and made discoveries that enabled them to leverage their skills. Upon reflection, we concluded that the successful large multinationals exhibited many of these traits as well.

Pick the Right Location

Managing business affairs from outside Vietnam generally proves to be an unsuccessful strategy. Precisely where one should locate in Vietnam depends on the product line, target market and strategic interests, but a local presence and some official support are crucial. Ho Chi Minh City (formerly Saigon) is the largest, most cosmopolitan urban center and Vietnam's commercial hub. Given that it has only been part of a socialist economy since 1975, it also has a population more familiar with free enterprise. Not surprisingly, it is usually favored by foreign investors. (By the way, Saigon is still the preferred term among locals, but marketers would be well-advised to speak of Ho Chi Minh City when dealing with government authorities.)

There are other locations, however, that should not be overlooked. The Vietnamese government is eager to develop the North and the countryside, and often offers incentives to foreigners interested in in-

vesting in these areas. The Coca-Cola Co.'s decision to establish a joint venture in the North, for example, has helped to overcome its comparatively slow start in Vietnam and is considered a factor in Coke's popularity in the northern part of the country. Moreover, while the urban sprawl of Ho Chi Minh City may make it an attractive consumer market, rent and wage increases may make it less desirable for manufacturing. Consequently, special development zones such as Haiphong or Vung Tau, which also happen to be ports, may be more attractive sites for factories.

Research the Market

Market research has been and always will be important in Vietnam. But because of proliferating products/promotions and growing consumer sophistication, the dynamics of the market—and the research requirements—have changed considerably during the past three years. For many Vietnamese, attitudes and beliefs have changed. Understanding how they have changed is instrumental in determining how to manipulate the marketing mix.

Second, the competition across product categories has become much more intense. These changes collectively shape how one might now administer, for example, a promotions campaign. Unlike the early 1990s, the battle for many segments now is being fought on differentiation rather than awareness. Furthermore, where simple outdoor advertisements and P-O-P materials once sufficed, many managers will now have to consider the importance of other variables in the marketing communications mix.

> The Vietnamese have earned a reputation for being hard workers and as a population they enjoy one of the highest literacy rates in Asia.

Several market-research and advertising firms have established operations in Vietnam, but there still is no substitute for sending multiskilled employees there to examine market conditions thoroughly and to determine the viability of the product or service offering as well as the appropriate management of pricing, distribution, and promotion.

Invest in the Vietnamese People

No matter how great the demand for a product or service, if the organization to manage it is going to be larger than a mom and pop operation, employee selection, training, and management are critical. Fortunately, the pool size and quality of applicants for many jobs have increased impressively in the past three years. Younger Vietnamese are scrambling to learn English, computer skills, and marketing. Only three years ago, we were hard-pressed to find anyone who could operate a computer *and* speak English well. We found no one who had both of these skills plus a customer orientation. By comparison, we have associates who recently placed an ad in a Ho Chi Minh City newspaper for a clerical position that required some customer contact and received 1,500 applications–more than 200 of whom met or exceeded the qualifications.

The Vietnamese have earned a reputation for being hard workers and as a population they enjoy one of the highest literacy rates in Asia; they are also very keen to learn contemporary business practices and often prefer to work for American companies. The work force is still lacking middle managers, however, and this problem can only be remedied with substantial investments in corporate-sanctioned training.

> Problems especially relevant to Vietnam include the absence of qualified managers, poor infrastructure, and erratic improvements in the legal, tax and accounting systems.

Three More Ps

The initial reforms in Vietnam favored only well-capitalized or well-connected businesses that could build roads, export oil, or generate hard currency. But the country is opening up to marketing enterprises of all sizes and specialties. Vietnam's transformation has created a growing appetite among Vietnamese and the expanding foreign community for all kinds of goods and services. It also has links to other promising markets in the region. For example, its strategic location in the Greater Mekong subregion makes it possible for firms to enter Vietnam as part of a larger plan to market products to the 200 million consumers in this emerging trade bloc.

But as promising as the market may be, it is still perilous. Bureaucratic encumbrances and other constraints one would expect to find in any developing economy are inevitable. Problems especially relevant to Vietnam include the absence of qualified managers,

> Good contacts, understanding the market, incremental growth, and sound business practices that address the unique Vietnamese condition will pay off in the long term.

poor infrastructure, and erratic improvements in the legal, tax and accounting systems. Rent extractions and other forms of corruption by national and local authorities also are problematic; so too are occasional reactionary movements within the government as Vietnam makes its transition to a market economy. And now competition has become a factor, as many companies struggle to penetrate the market and establish brand dominance.

Any serious marketing manager in Vietnam should add "prudence," "patience," and "persistence" to the classic 4Ps of the marketing mix. In Vietnam, relationships take time to nurture and can be expensive to maintain. Favorable brand and company images must be built and cared for. Good contacts, understanding the market, incremental growth, and sound business practices that address the unique Vietnamese condition will pay off in the long term.

Although the Vietnamese government's policies can be confusing, the government has attempted to address problems that need longer term solutions. Even with 10% growth rates, however, it will be at least a decade before Vietnam joins the ranks of the tiger economies. But marketers would be well-advised to seize the day. Vietnam will eventually join them, and companies that enter the market now will gain an early foothold as significant players in Vietnam and the region as a whole.

Editor's Note: In April 1996, Cliff Shultz chaired a conference on "Markets and Marketing Opportunities in Vietnam." Cosponsored by the American Marketing Association, Arizona State University West, and the World Trade Center, it brought high-ranking Vietnamese government and business officials together with their American counterparts to address the current marketing environment in Vietnam.

About the Authors

Clifford J. Shultz II is Assistant Professor of Marketing at the Arizona State University West School of Management where he specializes in marketing, consumption, and policy in transition economies. Cliff was the first scholar invited to Vietnam to lecture on consumer research and regularly serves as a Visiting Scholar at Vietnamese universities and research institutes. He holds an MA and PhD from Columbia University and his Vietnam work has been published in the *Columbia Journal of World Business, Business Horizons, Contemporary Southeast Asia, Asia-Pacific Advances in Consumer Research, Marketing News, Journal of Commerce,* and *Research in Consumer Behavior* and is coediting a book on marketing and consumers in East and Southeast Asia. As a consultant for over 15 years, he has helped governments and industries on five continents manage their trade, development, and transition challenges.

William J. Ardrey IV is Senior Vice President and International Policy Analyst at Fiduciary Communications Group in New York. William is a frequent lecturer at the Marketing College of Ho Chi Minh City and has published Vietnam articles in *Business Horizons, Contemporary Southeast Asia,* and *Asian Wall Street Weekly.* He holds a bachelor's degree from the Georgetown School of International Affairs and an MA from Columbia University. He and Shultz have completed a monograph for the United Nations entitled *Enterprise Management in Transition Economies,* and William is currently writing a doctoral dissertation on Financial Services Marketing in Vietnam.

Acknowledgment

The authors wish to acknowledge the ASU FGIA, SRCA, and IIM programs, Nguyen Xuan Que and his associates at the Ho Chi Minh City College of Marketing; Ha Huy Thong, Nguyen Duy Khien; and Tom Vallely and the Harvard Institute for International Development.

Additional Reading

Chapman, Matthew (1996), *Vietnam: Transition Under Threat,* Hong Kong: Peregrine Securities.

Dapice, David O. and Thomas J. Vallely (1996), "Vietnam's Economy: Will It Get and Stay on the Dragon's Trail," research report, Harvard Institute for International Development, Cambridge, Mass.

Shultz, Clifford J. (1994), "Balancing Policy, Consumer Desire, and Corporate Interests: Considerations for Market Entry in Vietnam," *Columbia Journal of World Business,* 29 (Winter), 42-53.

Shultz, Clifford J., William J. Ardrey, and Anthony Pecotich (1995), "American Involvement in Vietnam, Part II: United States Business Opportunities in a New Era," *Business Horizons,* 38 (March/April), 21-7.

Shultz, Clifford J., Anthony Pecotich, and Khai Le (1994), "Changes in Marketing Activity and Consumption in the Socialist Republic of Vietnam," in *Research in Consumer Behavior,* 7, C. Shultz, R. Belk and G. Ger, eds., Greenwich, CT: JAI Press, 225-257.

The opportunities in emerging markets are huge. So are the risks.

TROUBLES AHEAD
IN EMERGING MARKETS

by Jeffrey E. Garten

Throughout the 1990s, financial investors, corporate strategists, and political leaders in the United States, Western Europe, and Japan have been intensifying their focus on emerging markets. Such companies as Morgan Stanley, General Electric, and Johnson & Johnson are placing enormous bets on these markets. The Clinton administration's export-promotion strategy is based on the premise that the most promising markets are not in Europe and Japan but in the so-called big emerging markets. And the U.S. approach is mirrored abroad as presidents and prime ministers from France to Japan make pilgrimages to China, India, Brazil, and elsewhere to hawk their countries' wares.

Emerging markets are indeed the new frontier. But like all frontiers, they present a mix of opportunity and risk. The question now is whether businesses and governments in the industrialized world are sober enough about the problems that lie ahead. I do not believe they are. There is considerable evidence indicating that the tides of capitalism, which

Jeffrey E. Garten is dean of the Yale School of Management in New Haven, Connecticut. His new book, The Big Ten: The Big Emerging Markets and How They Will Change Our Lives, *is published by Basic Books. Garten was undersecretary of commerce for international trade in the first Clinton administration and, before that, a managing director of the Blackstone Group, an investment-banking firm.*

rose so powerfully after the collapse of the Soviet Union, are poised to recede. This reversal may signal much more than the usual ebb and flow of political and economic progress in the developing world, and could amount to a fundamental disruption of the generally upward trajectory in so many countries.

What can governments and businesses in the developed world do in the face of such likely turmoil? The industrial-world member-nations of the Organization for Economic Cooperation and Development (OECD) must ask whether they are pushing enough for growth and trade liberalization. Multinational companies, meanwhile, can no longer leave foreign policy to politicians and bureaucrats. They must develop capabilities that will allow them to anticipate and respond to the upcoming disruptions in emerging markets. And they must remain open to opportunities for cooperation between private and public sectors in those markets. Such cooperation can improve the economic environment and mitigate the risks of doing business in developing countries.

The Clash of Capitalism and Democracy

Emerging markets do represent undeniable commercial opportunities. In the last decade, the ten big emerging markets—Mexico, Brazil, Argentina, South Africa, Poland, Turkey, India, South Korea, the ASEAN region (Indonesia, Thailand, Malaysia, Singapore, and Vi-

etnam), and the Chinese Economic Area (China, Hong Kong, and Taiwan)—have opened their markets to foreign investment and trade. The gross domestic product of the big emerging markets has been increasing two to three times faster than that of developed countries. At the same time, emerging markets have made genuine progress in reining in deficits and inflation, as well as in selling off bloated state enterprises to private investors. Of course, the measures taken have been uneven, and there is a long way to go in every case, but it is indisputable that Adam Smith's philosophy has won the day.

It should not be surprising, therefore, that long-term projections for market expansion have been optimistic. In 1995, the ten big emerging markets accounted for about 10% of the world's economic output. The U.S. Department of Commerce believes that percentage may more than double over the next two decades, as those countries boost their share of global imports from 19% to 38%. Private capital has been flowing to emerging markets in unprecedented amounts, rising 19% in 1996 to a new high of $230 billion. Enormous potential exists for further expansion: for example, whereas all emerging markets account for 40% of global production, they still represent only 15% of global stockmarket value.

Any optimistic reading of the future, however, is based on a critical assumption: the economic reforms that have been so impressive in the 1990s will continue more or less along a straight line. There are good reasons to doubt that developing countries will continue to liberalize at the pace of the last few years. The threat does not lie in a repetition of the financial shocks that have hit emerging markets (such as the peso crisis that struck Mexico in the mid-1990s). Today governments and financial institutions in the OECD are reasonably well equipped to respond to such events. The worrisome problems are of a different order of magnitude—going well beyond the ups and downs of the business cycle, the usual gyrations in countries undergoing difficult transitions, or the episodic political crises that have always characterized such societies.

Something deeper is at play in the late 1990s, the collision of two forces that have not coexisted before in emerging markets: free-market capitalism and democracy. The philosophy of Adam Smith is giving rise to powerful new pressures that have enriched many, created enormous social changes, and unleashed new political forces. But Thomas Jefferson's part of the equation is not working so well. Democratic structures in many emerging markets are either nonexistent or too weak to ensure the modicum of economic fairness necessary to sustain democratic capitalism. As a result, emerging markets may well lose some of the progress they have made toward regulating markets and creating the rule of law that is essential to any commercial regime.

Moreover, in previous eras of crisis, the companies and governments of the industrialized world essentially wrote off emerging markets and left them to fend for themselves. Now, however, foreign investors, creditors, and governments will not be able to walk away from trouble without damaging themselves. Companies in the industrialized world depend on overseas markets for both economies of scale and increasing profits. The countries in the developed world want the jobs at home that come with expanding exports. And many pension-plan investors are banking on the high returns that can result from investing in the developing world.

Threats to Reform

A number of emerging markets already are under severe pressure. In Mexico, the path to progress has some enormous obstacles along its way. True, the economic reforms of the 1980s and 1990s were impressive, even if the government badly mismanaged its currency devaluation at the end of 1994. Today the country appears to be on the road to recovery from the peso crisis: forecasters estimate growth in the range of 4% to 5% for 1997, and the nation's export economy is flourishing. But the current-account deficit is rising again. Mexico's external debt has grown from 35% of GDP in 1992 to more than 60% in 1996. High interest rates and taxes are strangling the middle class. The banking system borders on insolvency. In the recession of the past two years, 5 million Mexicans have been added to the 22 million citizens (one-fourth of the population) who already live in extreme poverty. And the government estimates that an annual growth rate of 6% is necessary to absorb the 1 million new entrants into the labor force each year—a rate that does not appear to be attainable anytime soon.

Mexico's ability to deal with those daunting problems depends on an effective government. The country has been ruled by the iron fists of the Institutional Revolutionary Party for more than 60 years, but the party has become arthritic and corrupt. It is incapable of acting as a safety valve for the wellspring of popular discontent in Mexico, let alone as a vehicle for implementing critical new policies necessary for a rapidly changing economy. The party is in fact resisting change, having recently overturned President Ernesto Zedillo's far-reaching proposal to open and modernize Mexico's political process.

Nevertheless, political change will come—if not peacefully then violently. Already, crime, kidnapping, assassinations, and guerrilla activity are on the rise, signaling both a mounting level of dissatisfaction and the inability of the public sector to maintain order. But even if a more open and representative government emerges, it will lack the experience and the underlying institutions—such as honest courts—to govern effectively in the short run. Initially, that government may be besieged by the accumulated demands of tens of millions of Mexican citizens who have felt disenfranchised. It also will have its hands full cleaning up the old system—getting a grip on widespread criminality and creating a rule of law that all segments of the population can respect.

In light of those pressures, future governments may put off liberalizing the economy and instead concentrate on the immediate welfare of ordinary citizens. A democratic administration could become more nationalistic and more protectionist than the existing oligarchy. It could take many years before Mexico restores its current trajectory, at least in the eyes of foreign companies and governments.

Consider also Indonesia, the largest Muslim nation and the fourth largest country in the world by population. As in Mexico, the political system there may soon be unable to cope with economic and social pressures. By any measure, Jakarta's economic performance has been strong. GDP growth has been on the order of 6% to 7% annually, non-oil exports have been growing, and billions of dollars of foreign investment have poured in. But the country is a powder keg waiting to explode. With the exception of China, no major country is more dominated by autocratic rule than Indonesia. The 75-year-old president Suharto, who has ruled since he came to power in the mid-1960s in a bloody coup, *is* the political system. The only

Two forces are colliding in the emerging markets of the late 1990s: free-market capitalism and democracy.

opposition allowed is government-approved parties that support the president. Any challenge is immediately squelched—by military force if necessary.

Enormous pressures are building below the surface. When the aging president leaves the scene, they are likely to explode. It is difficult to envision a scenario that will contain those pressures when there are no existing political institutions to modulate them aside from the apparatus that Suharto now dominates. The military will want to maintain order. The Chinese minority will want to maintain its wealth. Both will be challenged by the Muslims, who constitute the overwhelming majority of the population; by the labor unions, which have been suppressed; and by the students, whose activism has been outlawed.

In a politically repressive society, change usually does not come gradually; it bursts on the scene. Some recent events are telltale signs of Indonesia's possible fate after Suharto. Last August, for example, when government pressure suppressed the voice of the leader of an opposition party, the largest riots of the past two decades ensued, followed by a brutal military crackdown. Afterward, the government began a systematic persecution of other potential "troublemakers," including the leader of the largest independent labor union. He and several labor and student leaders are currently on trial for subversion, a crime punishable by death. In early 1997, a Muslim mob burned a Chinese temple as well as Christian churches. The alleged cause was a complaint by an ethnic Chinese trader that the call to prayer from a mosque near his home was too loud. The incident highlighted the seething ethnic rivalries and resentments that will play out in the open once Suharto departs. It's difficult to see how economic progress won't suffer.

What about countries that have better track records politically? Several of the big emerging markets have practiced democracy for years, but even those nations are struggling with political pressures stemming from economic change. In India, for example, Prime Minister P. V. Narasimha Rao's measures in the early 1990s to open the economy astounded outside observers. For nearly

half a century, India had been a closed economy wedded to socialism, and its sudden embrace of capitalism stimulated high levels of economic growth and trade as well as an influx of capital from abroad. But in the national elections of 1996, the Indian people jettisoned Rao's government. In its place emerged a coalition of 13 parties—an unwieldy assemblage that includes nearly every major and parochial interest group in the country, from communists to religious extremists.

Such a fractured group will struggle to make the hard political decisions that are necessary to continue economic liberalization—including massive reduction of subsidies, new infrastructure development, and labor reform. If India stands still because of political polarization—in fact, if it doesn't move ahead

Many underestimate the impact of the political dimension of change.

quickly—it faces a dire situation as popular expectations rise. India has a long way to go to overcome a host of problems such as food production that loses 30% each year to spoilage; an energy distribution system that loses 25% to leakage during delivery; crumbling roads, ports, and airports; and a primitive telecommunications sector. India is falling further behind its Asian rivals in economic reforms, a problem that may jeopardize its ability to attract foreign capital in the future.

Economic pressures also are straining South Korea's politics. No one can deny the progress that this country has made in the past several years on both economic and political fronts, but now it must move out of the ranks of emerging markets to join those that have emerged. It can no longer compete internationally with such countries as China and Brazil, where the costs of doing business are much lower. South Korea must move from a system founded on paternalism and authoritarianism to one based on democratic values, for there is no other way to unlock the initiative of the Ko-

rean people and create an economy flexible enough to cope with rapid technological change.

Nowhere are these challenges more evident than in the need to reform labor laws, which derive from an era when Korea was a military dictatorship. The challenge is to balance the ability of employers to control costs with a system of free collective bargaining. With no experience walking this tightrope, the administration of Kim Young Sam has badly mishandled the task. Last December, it passed legislation making it easier to lay off workers and postponing the right of labor to unionize until the year 2000. The laws were passed in a secret closed session with no pubic hearings and without the involvement of the political opposition. The unsurprising results were the largest strikes in South Korea's history. Today the government and the unions are still trying to work out a viable long-term settlement.

This bruising struggle is likely to make it more difficult to enact future reforms—reforms that are needed now more than ever. The country's GDP growth is slowing, the current-account deficit is soaring, and the Seoul stockmarket is at its lowest point in several years. Moreover, of all the major emerging markets, South Korea is the most hostile to foreign investment. And in the wake of the prolonged strikes, workers are especially sensitive to the issue of job security—which makes measures to open up the economy politically difficult. Such measures, however, are essential if the South Korean economy is to maintain its competitive position.

Other big markets are showing worrisome signs. In South Africa, President Nelson Mandela has not been able to bring about either prosperity or social justice. In fact, political wrangling within the ruling party has rendered it incapable of action, and critics fear that the nation is headed toward anarchy or permanent third-world status. In Brazil, the populist congress is resisting constitutional changes that would enable such reforms as large-scale privatization. In Argentina, unemployment has reached 17%, a level that is severely straining the ability of the ruling party—itself built around the labor movement—to streamline the economy any further. And in Turkey, economic reform has been all but taken off the table amid the election of the first Islamic government in the country's modern history.

Interpreting the Turmoil

There are several ways to account for the mounting pressures in emerging markets. One explanation is that many of the easier economic-reform measures already have been taken. A country's leaders can reduce tariffs from 300% to 50% more easily than they can reduce them from 50% to 5%; similarly, they can sell off the most viable government companies—such as the hard-currency-earning airlines—more readily than they can the money-losing steel plants. The first set of reforms can be enacted quickly: foreign and local investors respond positively, and foreign governments applaud. But the afterglow doesn't last long. Soon the domestic opposition organizes a counterattack, and those who haven't benefited from liberalization measures throw up roadblocks. Ordinary citizens, having heard about the magic of the marketplace, wonder why they can't get hot water or why the phones don't work. And top-level decision makers get worn out fighting battles over such questions.

In many emerging markets, the list of what still needs to be done is long. Market regulation is highly underdeveloped. Rigid labor laws need to be restructured. Limits on prices for energy and telecommunications discourage foreign investment. Government payrolls need to be pared down; at the same time, however, more skilled and experienced people need to be attracted to the bureaucracy. Expensive social-welfare policies need to be dismantled and rebuilt. The massive amounts of red tape that still interfere with normal business

transactions need to be slashed. And legal systems need to be strengthened.

But by far the biggest reason for anxiety about economic reforms is the political dynamics of the reforms themselves. Those who have embraced emerging markets with enthusiasm have failed to consider a number of factors: the political dimension of change, the difficulty of implementing massive transformation in a short period, and the lack of skills and institutions needed to manage democratic capitalism. In moving toward open political and economic systems simultaneously, emerging markets are on uncharted and precarious ground.

As economic liberalization in emerging markets replaces rigid control, a new more laissez-faire, but more sophisticated, kind of economic and commercial regulation needs to be put in place. Governments need to shrink in size while managing more difficult tasks more effectively—a trick even the leaders in Washington, Bonn, and Tokyo have not yet mastered. In the absence of such a new set of political arrangements, those who held power under the old regime end up in favored positions under the new one and simply increase their dominance and privileges. In addition, the

ment, let alone plan for essential long-term investments, and they are unable to deal with the popular demands critical to their legitimacy. Under those pressures, a new democracy sometimes drifts toward weak administrations and deadlock. At other times, the government moves in the opposite direction—toward the very dictatorial systems it replaced. Then comes a popular backlash, which reduces a government's ability to pursue the economic reforms that once constituted its primary mission.

These observations do not apply to every emerging market. Poland, for example, seems to have made an exemplary transition. In seven years, it has crated a mature democracy, achieved the highest growth rate in Europe, and reduced the share of GDP stemming from government-owned activity from 100% to 33%. Warsaw did have special advantages: it once had a very sophisticated economy, it has a highly educated population, and it was greatly helped by sitting on Europe's doorstep. Taking another tack, China has managed to combine rigid political control with gradual economic liberalization—perhaps because its system of political control is so highly developed, and because

In moving to open political and economic systems, emerging markets are on uncharted ground.

transition from a command to a market economy brings with it a hiatus of order that invites a serious increase in fraud and corruption. Leaders in emerging markets rarely have the skills and experience to make the transition smoothly.

On the political side, democracies are defined by more than just voting; they also require a complex infrastructure. Without the solid foundations of a professional civil service, a strong independent judiciary, and arm's-length regulators, the leaders of new democracies can spend all their time dealing with the pressure groups that emerge from an open economy. They cannot attend to the requirements of everyday manage-

its very size and economic potential is mesmerizing to foreign investors, who have made China the largest destination for foreign capital among emerging markets.

It would be misleading, too, to say that there are no other scenarios for Mexico, Indonesia, South Korea, and India than those described above. Political change in Mexico may come at a slow but steady pace at the municipal or state level. A more conciliatory military group may replace Suharto. South Korea may apply Asian-style discipline and determination, and persevere on the course of economic reform. India may muddle through. In the end, of course, it is not possible to predict with complete confidence the course of such profound and complex transitions.

Still, it is best now to be sober. The prevailing optimistic view of what will happen in key emerging markets underestimates the impact of variables that cannot be measured: frustration about missing out on the boom times and anxiety about the massive changes wrought by foreign investment and technology. Moreover, those who say that Mexico has always had pervasive poverty or that India has always progressed slowly are underestimating both the current pace of global change, which is new, and the impact of seeing and knowing what a better life is all about, which is now more possible than ever because of modern communications. This much is sure: the risks of setbacks in many big emerging markets are escalating. Over time, democracy and free markets can reinforce each other, but the journey will be precarious. And we are entering its most dangerous phase.

Pressure on the Developed World

A slowing of economic reforms in emerging markets would be a disaster for the industrialized world on several counts.

First, powerful trade and investment ties have made the emerging markets essential to the continued economic expansion of industrialized OECD countries. For example, exports have been responsible for about one-third of U.S. economic growth in the past few years, and already the ten big emerging markets account for a greater proportion of U.S. exports than the European Union and Japan combined. Exports to the big emerging markets have been equally important for both Europe and Japan.

The ability to increase exports to emerging markets is all the more important because those markets will be selling a growing amount to industrialized countries. The enhanced competitiveness of emerging markets stems from the economic reforms they have already undertaken, as well as from low wage rates and increasing productivity. In the

United States, for example, the average hourly wage in 1996 was $17.20. In South Korea, it was $7.40; in Taiwan, $5.82; in Brazil, $4.28; in China, 25 cents. And productivity in these markets will be greatly enhanced because of growing access to Western technology and supervision by foreign managers. To avoid unmanageable trade deficits and the flaring up of protectionist sentiments, the West and Japan will need to offset the likely increase of imports with their own exports. And that can happen only if emerging markets grow at a strong pace.

Second, the developed nations are counting on the growth of emerging markets to help finance pensions for their aging populations. The demographics are well known. People in the industrialized world are living longer, and there are fewer workers to support retirees. Public spending on pensions as a percentage of GDP in OECD countries is projected to soar from 8% in 1990 to more than 15% over the next 25 years. The easiest way to raise the financial returns on workers' savings is to look for a good portion of those returns in those areas where growth will be the fastest. In other words, it means looking for those returns largely in emerging markets.

Third, a slowdown in the growth of emerging markets may lead to destructive competition among governments in the developed world. Encouraged by the boom overseas, multinational companies, often backed by the financing and lobbying of their home governments, have already intensified their competition. Free and fair competition is to be welcomed, but the pressure on companies to win big contracts in emerging markets has led to bribery, violations of OECD trade-financing agreements, and escalation of political pressure by home governments on those awarding contracts. There is no sign that such competition will let up anytime soon,

because the contracts in question are of the utmost national importance to countries suffering from high levels of unemployment. It is not an exaggeration to say that rivalries in this arena are becoming major wedges between countries that were allies during the Cold War. Left unchecked, these contests could create major international tensions.

There also are larger dimensions to economic failures in the developing world. Borders in a number of emerging markets are contested, and civil wars in others are possible. The economic strains caused by slower growth and a reversal of reforms could exacerbate tensions in any of these hot spots. Setbacks in economic development also would hamper the countries' efforts to invest in environmental protection. And continued growth is the only way to

Multinational companies should not be mere bystanders to change.

boost the livelihood of hundreds of millions of people who are living in miserable conditions.

What Can Be Done?

There was a time, just a few decades ago, when the industrialized countries thought they could build democracies and capitalist societies by injecting massive amounts of foreign aid, making trade concessions, and providing technical advice. Following great disappointments with programs such as the U.S. government's Alliance for Progress in Latin America, ambitions about directing such transformations have been greatly deflated. In the last decade, OECD governments have either reduced aid or redirected it toward the poorest countries. The emerging markets in the meantime have entered the mainstream of the world economy, linking their fates not to other government's largesse but to private capital, foreign direct investment, and global trade. In 1990, for example, net financial aid to emerging markets was four times the flow of private capital. By 1996, that ratio was reversed: the flow of private capital was five times that of government aid.

In Malaysia, Motorola's and Intel's training programs have enhanced the skills of local workers.

If aid is not the answer, what can governments in the West and Japan do? They will need to manage their economies in a way that keeps the world economy buoyant and conducive to the expansion of trade. That will take some effort. The United States, the European Union, and Japan are all growing at a much slower rate than they have historically, and fiscal contraction is everywhere in vogue. Meanwhile, enthusiasm for trade liberalization seems to be waning; there is little appetite for new rounds of trade negotiations.

As for multinational companies, they should not be mere bystanders to political and economic change abroad. They can take steps to prepare for trouble. For example, they can apply higher discounts on earnings projections and diversify their activities rather than gamble on any one country or region. Managers can engage in serious contingency planning in order to cope with political and economic turmoil in emerging markets. They can improve their efforts to gather information on economic and social trends as well as on upcoming political decisions. In

addition, they can work harder at collecting information about which local businesses are in the best position to survive a prolonged transitional period and might therefore make good partners. Executives can sensitize colleagues and board members to conditions in a particular country or region so that new developments do not take them by surprise and cause ill-advised knee-jerk reactions.

Astute human-resource management also can make a difference. For the most part, plenty of capital is available to facilitate entry into the emerging markets. What is often lacking are managers who know how to operate amid uncertainty and instability—managers who appreciate local politics and cultures and can build the relationships that not only enhance today's sales but also act as a safety valve in turbulent times. How to recruit, develop, and train managers who can operate in emerging markets is the key question. Companies should make their best effort to obtain highly adaptable men and women from the local scene. In addition, they should learn as much as possible about the mistakes that other multinational companies have made. Finally, it is essential that companies provide courses to their managers on the history and the political and economic institutions of individual developing countries.

Companies also have an opportunity, sometimes in partnership with Western governments or the World Bank, to assist emerging markets in their quest for progress. From Brazil to Thailand, countries need sophisticated technical assistance. Merrill Lynch, for example, is helping public officials in India devise sensible regulatory policy for stock markets. In China, Aetna and Procter & Gamble are helping local schools and universities train and educate leaders who understand how capitalist economies work. In Malaysia, Motorola and Intel have instituted training programs to enhance the skills of local workers. Companies that establish deep local roots and show, by dint of example rather than empty rhetoric, that their strategies are aligned with the long-term goals of the host country stand the best chance of prospering. At the same time, such companies help keep up-and-coming countries on the track of economic and political progress.

To be sure, no one can predict exactly how economies and regimes will develop. The emergence of so many capitalist economies within a few years is unprecedented and holds great opportunities—as well as equally great risks. In the 1980s, experts failed to see the rise of Japan or that of the Asian tigers. They failed to predict the collapse of Mexico, Brazil, and Argentina in the 1980s or the implosion of the Soviet Union. When it comes to the future of big emerging markets, however, enough warning signals are flashing. The penalty for not recognizing them will be severe.

Not-So-Clear Choices

Should you export, or manufacture overseas?

By Russ Banham

ob Moog has a child's imagination coupled with killer business instincts. When the board-games company he created in 1985 sought growth through global expansion 2 years later, Moog faced the usual two options: export the product or manufacture it overseas for local distribution. Moog chose the latter.

"We decided for a number of reasons to manufacture our board game, '20 Questions,' in Holland for distribution throughout Europe," said Moog, president of University Games Corp. of Burlingame, CA. Moog's company started with a $20,000 loan and spent its first two years in a 20 ft. by 30 ft. room sublet from the father of Moog's former girlfriend, before blossoming into a $50 million-per-year, international company.

International sales make up 8 percent of University Games revenue. Moog predicts that international sales will rise to 35 percent in the next 3 years because of new overseas ventures. This year, the company expanded into Australia. Unlike the European ventures, however, Moog decided that it was more economical to import its products into Australia from the US manufacturing facility.

"Our anticipated initial sales in Australia just did not warrant a manufacturing operation there at this juncture," Moog said. "If sales pick up down the line, we may then examine local manufacturing."

Moog's dual strategy is not unique. One of the toughest questions a company confronts when pondering an international

sales strategy is: To export, or not to export?

While exporting is often the least risky method of selling overseas, it frequently involves significant transportation, logistics, and tax-related costs that may make it uneconomical when compared with foreign manufacturing.

On the other hand, foreign manufacturing, while potentially a more competitive way of entering an overseas market, has its own bugaboos. Political instability, fluctuating market conditions, and the huge capital costs to set up an overseas manufacturing operation are daunting challenges. Determining the best way to go often involves solving a perplexing conundrum. "It boils down to a tradeoff between classic cost-and-time considerations and eco-political factors," said Richard Powers, president of Insight Inc., a provider of management support systems based in Bend, OR.

With exporting, a company must evaluate the various modes of transportation that would be involved in getting the goods there, and how this relates to the cycle time of putting the product in the marketplace. Some products are time-sensitive; others are less so.

On the other hand, if a company determines that an overseas manufacturing operation best meets its needs, it must examine the eco-political factors involved, such as tariff and duty drawbacks and international tax issues. "It may be less expensive, given these factors, for a company to incur the logistics costs of exporting

than to risk the eco-political costs," Powers explained.

Trade-Offs and Traps

In addition to weighing these trade-offs, there are other related factors affecting the decision to either export or locate a plant overseas. To compete in their market, for example, some countries require that some form of local infrastructure be in place.

"Sometimes you run into government contracts where the only way to distribute a product in that country is to have it made locally," said Fred Ehrsam, vice president at Bain & Co., a Boston-based strategy consulting firm. "In China, for instance, you pretty much have to build something there in order to enter that market."

Certain products also dictate the international sales strategy to be taken. "If your company makes drinking glasses, you'll want to manufacture them in whatever country you plan to sell them," observed Scott Setrakian, a director in the San Francisco office of Mercer Management Consulting. "Drinking glasses, generally speaking, are pretty cheap to make and expensive to ship."

Political instability is another guiding force in a company's decision-making process. "If you want to sell in Russia, you're facing political instability as your biggest single operating risk," noted John Koopman, a principal in Mercer's Toronto office. "In Western Europe, this is not an issue. In Asia, there's a little risk, but in Russia it's a given." Other factors include time, the distance to the market, and price. Certain products require short lead times and, thus, may best be delivered via a locally manufactured plant. "This is where you get into issues like transportation costs, tariffs and duties, labor expenses, and how much it costs to build a plant," Ehrsam explained.

The maturity of a company's product affects this decision. A product expected to require design changes, for example, may not fit well with foreign manufacturing plans. "It's pretty hard to implement changes to a product when the product is fairly far removed from the product development and engineering people," Ehrsam continued. "Tactically, you want to be moving products offshore that are relatively stable."

Another factor is the skill of the labor force in the market being considered. "You have to question whether or not the labor pool—no matter how low-cost—can be trained to do the things you need," Ehrsam added.

Best Laid Plans

Perhaps the best way for many companies to enter a foreign market is to first export there, but with an eye toward building overseas in the future. "Exporting will give you a feel for the product and its market potential," Powers said. "Instead of jumping in the lake head first, exporting allows you to get your toes wet. It may cost more, but you're able to hedge your risks."

Such a strategy worked well for IPSCO, Inc. In the early 1980s, the Regina, Saskatchewan-based steel producer exported its steel pipe and flat steel to the United States from Canada—despite significant transportation costs. Once the company realized there was significant US demand for its products, it decided to set up shop there.

"Fundamentally it is very expensive to transport pipe steel from Canada to the United States," explained Mario Dalla-Vicenza, IPSCO senior vice president. "Unlike flat steel, which you're able to transport up to the maximum load-bearing capability of a railcar, pipe steel—because it is hollow—fills the volume of a railcar before it fills the maximum load-bearing capability. So, there's a fundamental freight cost disadvantage." To overcome this drawback and make the company more competitive with US pipe producers, IPSCO acquired pipe mills in Camanche, IA, and in Geneva, NE.

Other companies also have found it expedient to export first. "I used to work for a company called Mexx, a Netherlands-based fashion supplier," Koopman said. "We entered Australia, South Africa, and the Eastern bloc countries via an export

strategy, and when that worked, we set up local warehousing and distribution subsidiaries."

Buying an overseas plant, as opposed to starting one de novo, is a high-stakes proposition for many companies. "The culture within the walls is critical with respect to the ongoing operation of the firm," Setrakian stated. He advises a joint venture with a prospective acquisition "as a way of feeling it out before buying it."

Some companies may follow two routes in this regard: acquiring a going venture in one country but starting one from scratch in another. Mercer Management, for example, built its overseas consulting business via both strategies. "In Europe, we concluded that there were sound opportunities to build by acquisition, while in Asia we felt the best way to proceed was by opening our own offices de novo," Setrakian said.

Mercer bought consulting firms in Germany, France, and Spain, but opened its own offices in Hong Kong and Singapore. "We felt Europe was a reasonably mature market with strong and well-grounded acquisition opportunities, but that similar opportunities did not exist in Asia," Setrakian added.

Companies seeking an international presence often must choose between its own dedicated sales force versus third-party agents doing the work for them. Others, such as University Games, follow an international sales strategy using third-party distributors.

"We identify the foreign markets we want to penetrate, and then form a business venture with a local distributor that will give us a large degree of control," Moog said. "In Australia, we expect to run a print of 5,000 board games. These we will manufacture in the US. If we reach a run of 25,000 games, however, we would then establish a sub-contracting venture with a local manufacturer in Australia or New Zealand to print the games." Smack dab between exporting and overseas manufacturing is another alternative: foreign product assembly. "Sometimes this is a better option because the duties in a particular country may be low on components but high on finished goods," Ehrsam said. "In a market in which a company has a fairly weak presence to begin with, it may actually be able to enjoy fairly good production and manufacturing costs by getting a local vendor to do the work for you."

CPC International favors full-scale overseas manufacturing to either foreign product assembly or exporting. "We rely on exporting chiefly as a means of entering a new marketplace," said Gale Griffin, vice president at the Englewood Cliffs, NJ-based food company. "We then like to move from an exporting environment into local manufacturing."

CPC manufactures such well-known food brands as Hellmann's Mayonnaise and the Knorr's line of soups. Altogether, the company manufactures in 62 of the 110 countries in which it markets its products.

CPC uses local personnel and managers almost exclusively when operating overseas. "We look for people who understand the markets and can compete very effectively within them," Griffin said. "They help you understand local government regulations, which can be tricky. We also let our local managers do their own marketing, figuring they know their own markets and how to compete there better than Englewood Cliffs does."

Mexx also sought out qualified locals to be its eyes and ears in a foreign market. "Such an individual can help develop the link between your business and the local marketplace," Koopman said. "Without this understanding of the local market, the risk of failure is tremendous."

Local relationships give local distributors and buyers peace of mind that they're dealing with a local company, he added. "You want to make the local buyer in France think he is dealing with a French company," Koopman said. "They want to feel they're dealing with the decision-making, not some emissary from New York in another time zone."

Finding someone qualified to fill these shoes is as easy as calling an executive search firm or accessing the Internet. "There are many qualified people looking to represent all kinds of companies on the Net," Powers noted.

Power's company, Insight, offers a computer software model that can help companies find the right overseas representatives. Called the Global Supply Chain Model, the software guides companies through the maze of decisions required to develop an international sales strategy, from how many plants needed to satisfy global markets to the best means to source products. The software costs $30,000, excluding consulting services. The task of finding a local rep should not be taken lightly, especially when it concerns finding someone to manage an overseas plant. "Having a plant manager who can create a culture from the ground up with the right discipline and values to develop a solid team of people is crucial to the success of the endeavor," Ehrsam said. "I've seen the best prepared and executed strategies succeed or fall to pieces on the basis of that one individual."

On the Ground

The litany of missteps by companies overeager to enter a foreign market makes entertaining reading. General Motors, for example, still winces at its decision to sell its Chevy Nova in Spain without pausing to consider that "nova" in Spanish translates into "doesn't go."

Other hastily made international sales strategies include K-Mart's decision to open a store in Singapore. The company's traditional and successful formula in the United States is to purchase land—usually on the perimeter of a town—at inexpensive prices. "In Singapore, such a large tract was unavailable at a cheap price, and the company ended up with an expensive location," Koopman said. "The strategy was not successful."

"If you're thinking of setting up shop overseas, assume that no matter how many things you thought of, there will be five you missed," Koopman advised. "At Mexx, for example, we learned that Frenchmen like their pants unfinished—so they can put cuffs on them. In Germany, however, 95 percent of pants are sold finished. There's a real danger exporting too far away from a market without someone on the ground to guide you."

While some elements making up an international sales strategy can be predicted with a degree of certainty, others—like currency exchange values—are capricious at best. "At Mexx, we planned twice to enter the Italian market," Koopman recalled. "In both cases, one week before we were set to launch our clothing line there, the Italian lira was devalued 20 percent—meaning our prices would increase by 20 percent. Both times we were forced to cancel our plans." Another unpredictable element is regulation. "A company may decide to set up shop in, say, Malaysia, because it considers the tariffs to be too high to export there successfully," Ehrsam said. "Next thing you know, the government of Malaysia decides to lower its tariffs significantly. Suddenly, you realize it may have been cheaper to export there rather than incur the huge capital costs of a plant."

Technology obsolescence and improvements in logistics play similar, unpredictable roles. A company may spend hundreds of thousands of dollars building a foreign facility weeks before a new automated manufacturing system renders its technology a buggy in an age of automobiles.

Moreover, a new way of moving goods faster, more efficiently and less expensively may materialize, reversing the status quo and making exporting a more cost-effective means of reaching a marketplace.

Ultimately, no matter which way a company chooses to enter a foreign market, it needs a pair of fleet feet. "It's very important, especially with newer economies, to get in as early as possible," Griffin counseled. "You want to establish market leadership for your brand, and the fact is, the first one there often has the best chance."

CPC should know: The company entered Eastern Europe within days of the fall of the Berlin Wall. It is now the market leader in much of the region.

"In Poland, we're number one in potato products, soups, and sauces; and number two in bouillons and mayonnaise," Griffin boasted.

Certainly, that's something to chew on.

**Smaller than Guatemala,
meaner than Serbia.**

THE MYTH OF THE CHINA MARKET

By John Maggs

e've got to be there," said Ron Brown as he led a delegation of American business leaders to China weeks after Bill Clinton's May 1994 about-face on Most Favored Nation status. "Hundreds of thousands of American workers are already depending on these jobs. China will be the engine for growth. It is the pot at the end of the rainbow."

No, it isn't. China is not a major export market for the United States, nor is it likely to be one any time soon. There's more U.S. investment in the Philippines, and almost as much in the Dominican Republic. And the factors keeping U.S. money out of China show no signs of disappearing; many won't be affected by China's eventual submission to the rules of the World Trade Organization, either.

Call it the great China market myth—the idea that everything from human rights violations to weapons sales is worth enduring because glorious riches await us in the People's Republic. But this expectation is a chimera. U.S. exports to China were $11.9 billion in 1996. In Asia alone, China ranks behind Japan, South Korea, Taiwan and Singapore. Boosters insist that exports to China are growing so quickly that these comparisons are irrelevant. But in fact, since 1980, exports to China have

risen about 10 percent annually, compared to an overall rise in U.S. exports of about 8 percent per year. Over the past decade and a half, U.S. exports to Brazil, Poland and dozens of other countries have grown faster than exports to China.

In 1996, China's economy grew at a torrid 9.7 percent, but, to the surprise of economists, American exports to China stayed virtually the same. The best explanation for this centers on another factor that mythologists of the China market don't like to mention. To advance internal economic and social goals, China's leaders continue to pull the levers of what remains a command economy. As in 1988, when inflation spun out of control, there's evidence that a 1996 inflation drive was built around the throttling of imports. Because of the large appreciation of the dollar last year, imports from the United States were the most expensive, and logically the best target.

hina's intervention in trade markets goes far beyond the inflation crackdown. American companies say the greatest obstacle to imports is a vast and shifting network of administrative barriers that are manipulated by Chinese bureaucrats. "Trading rights" must be granted to importing companies; and U.S. companies are sometimes told their goods have been barred by secret laws known as "nebu" that they are not allowed to inspect.

U.S. businessmen concede that trade with China depends foremost on what its government decides is best. Joseph Gorman, chairman of auto-parts giant TRW, says

---

JOHN MAGGS writes about international business and economics for *The Journal of Commerce.*

he has been trying to sell power-steering equipment in China for years. TRW is the world leader in power steering—Volkswagen, in fact, uses TRW equipment in the cars it assembles in China. Still, "we haven't been able to sell or market there directly," said Gorman. "China has a very detailed plan for the auto sector and that's pretty much the way it is going to develop."

Since most economists expect China's growth rate to slow, there's every reason to believe that U.S. exports will continue to hover at their 10-percent-a-year growth. This means that exports to China, now only 1.8 percent of total U.S. exports, will remain insignificant for at least a decade. More surprisingly, it also means that, over this decade, a number of Asian countries are likely to outpace China as markets for U.S. exports. In addition to South Korea, Taiwan and Singapore, Malaysia, too, will overtake China in the next two or three years. Thailand, where U.S. exports have been growing 20 percent a year, now imports half as much from the United States as China, but will overtake it early in the new century.

Many true believers in the China market argue that the United States will eventually get its share of imports because, unlike Japan, China has been running a net trade deficit with the world and will continue to do so. "The good news is that China can't keep growing without imports," said Richard Brecher of the U.S.-China Business Council. "They are going to have to run a trade deficit."

Not anymore. On January 10, China announced that its 1996 trade surplus with the world was $12.24 billion.

U.S. exports are the most important index of how the United States is benefiting from its economic relations with China. When Clinton talks about China meaning jobs for Americans, those jobs can only be measured in exports. But what about investment? China marketeers argue that, in that arena, there *has* been explosive growth for U.S. business. American companies, they say, are bringing home mega-profits from newly built factories in China.

Again, not nearly. The cumulative amount of U.S. direct investment in China edged up to $1.9 billion at the end of 1995, the last year on record, from $1.7 billion in the end of 1994. That's about 0.5 percent of the total, which is $170 billion. Colombia receives three times as much U.S. investment, despite a guerrilla insurgency, the threat of imminent U.S. sanctions for noncooperation on drug interdiction and an economy roughly one-tenth the size of China's. In defending free trade, Bill Clinton got laughs when he said that if low wages were the only factor, then U.S. investment would be flooding into the Dominican Republic. But U.S. direct investment in the tiny Dominican Republic was in fact $1.4 billion at last measure, not too far off from China's total. Some China boosters choose simply to disbelieve these statistics, which are compiled by the Commerce Department. "That's ridiculous," huffed Brecher, who faxed back a page of Chinese government data that was heavy on feel-good stats like "number of contracts signed." But even Beijing says the total U.S. investment is only $3 billion, a relative drop in the bucket.

While it's true that China is attracting more foreign investment than any other developing country, the overwhelming majority of that money continues to come from the three traditional sources for China's capital—Japan, Taiwan and Hong Kong. Beyond commonalities of language and culture, proximity is the most powerful factor driving investment patterns, and East Asia's geography will not change. Neither will the giant foreign reserves in these countries shrink very much, especially if they maintain their huge trade surpluses with the West.

Investment banker John Whitehead understands why U.S. investment in China remains so low. "There's a lot of activity lining up partners, but not a lot of money going in," he said. "China remains a relatively untried market and place to do business" for U.S. companies. Whitehead, a former chairman of Goldman, Sachs and deputy Secretary of State, borrowed Alan Greenspan's comment on the Wall Street bubble to describe an "irrational exuberance" among U.S. businessmen over China. Though Whitehead says he allies himself with Henry Kissinger, Alexander Haig and other "friends of China," he has no illusions about its business environment. "There is inherent instability in any dictatorial regime," he said. "In China, central authority is breaking down. Regional leaders have a great deal of authority. There is no legal structure for protecting private property, and the financial structure is uncertain."

With few exceptions, the China deals that fill the newspapers are agreements in principle, years away from actual investment. Many never come off. That's what happened with the Lippo Group's investment, brokered by Clinton fund-raisers, to build a $1 billion power plant in China with Entergy Corp. Other deals seem to remain perpetually just around the corner. General Motors announced recently that it was in "final negotiations" for a $2 billion deal to build passenger cars with a Chinese partner in Shanghai. GM officials also announced this deal in October of 1995, and have been talking about it since 1993. A GM spokesman said there was no estimate of when ground would be broken on the plant.

Businessmen say that, in China, "the negotiation begins when the contract is signed." Chinese industrialists never stop demanding concessions, which often include the giveaway of valuable technology. For Chrysler Corporation, the price was too high. China demanded that the company turn over all its manufacturing technology and design secrets in exchange for being allowed to invest $1 billion in a minivan joint venture. "They want us to set them up as a world-class competitor to Chrysler, and pay for it, too," said Chairman Robert Eaton.

McDonnell Douglas paid the price, then went out of business waiting for the China market to materialize. After agreeing to build twenty airliners in China, it couldn't sell one. The company was willing to play by China's rules, but then those rules changed: China's newly capitalistic airlines decided that Chinese-built planes would be of poorer quality than those made in Europe. McDonnell Douglas's inability to establish itself as an aircraft manufacturer in Asia was one of the major forces that drove it into its proposed merger with Boeing.

If the GM deal goes through, and GM officials are willing to part with the technology they bring with them to China, other restrictions will still limit the deal's value. In most developing countries, GM starts assembling cars almost entirely with parts manufactured elsewhere, mostly in the United States. Under China's auto development plan, Chinese-made parts will have to comprise 40 percent of the first cars that roll off the line in Shanghai. Within five years, the minimum "local content" will rise to 80 percent, ensuring that the engines, transmissions and other high-value components in these cars will not be exported from the United States. As for the fast-growing China market, auto analysts say that production capacity there will outstrip demand within three years. This suggests that GM and other U.S. companies will need to find other markets for these cars, further displacing exports from the United States.

Above all else, believers in the China market believe in the future. They believe the problems of today will surely disappear tomorrow. They believe that China is opening up to more imports when it is not. They believe that development will inevitably lead to greater fairness in the market when it has not.

Westerners have always seen what they want to see in China, beginning with Marco Polo. You don't have to be a protectionist or a Red-baiter to ask whether U.S. priorities in China have been skewed by this false image. If the United States recognizes that it has less to lose economically, perhaps balancing all its goals in China will be a little easier.

North Korea's economy and ruling cadre are self-destructing. An East Asian security nightmare will soon follow, predicts this veteran observer of the Korean peninsula.

"Compromise increases the risk of war"

An interview with Katsumi Sato by Neil Weinberg

IN THE LATE 1950s and early 1960s Katsumi Sato worked for a Japanese organization helping ethnic Koreans return to communist North Korea. As word filtered back about how life really was in the Workers' Paradise, Sato became one of North Korea's best informed and fiercest critics. Now 68 and the author of four books on North Korea's Stalinist state, Sato is President of Japan's Modern Korea Institute and publishes its magazine, Gendai Korea (Modern Korea), ten times a year.

On Feb. 26 Sato sat down with FORBES to discuss the impending disaster he sees unfolding on the Korean peninsula.

Modern Korea Institute's Katsumi Sato
"I give North Korea a few months or less."

FORBES: **Is North Korea now close to collapse?**
Sato: It is not close to collapse. It is collapsing. I give it a few months, or less.

North Korea has been more erratic than ever since President Kim Il Sung's death in 1994. In one week last fall, for example, it held a seminar for foreign investors—and sent a submarine full of commandos into South Korea.
It is not erratic policy. It's an internal power struggle. Since the death of his father, Kim Jong Il has been unable to take full control. Instead, he has effectively created his own party, with followers who think an open-door economic policy would destroy socialism. But technocrats centered around (recently purged) Prime Minister Kang Song San believe the economy will be destroyed unless the door is opened.

In the midst of this, [Workers' Party of Korea Secretary] Hwang Jang Yop defected Feb. 12 in Beijing and stated clearly that North Korea will be destroyed unless Kim Jong Il is removed. Since it would be a great defeat for Kim Jong Il and his followers not to do anything in response, they have started to remove the reformers by force. After Defense

Minister Choe Kwang died suddenly [on Feb. 21], the list of leaders for his funeral included almost no open-door reformers. It means Kim Jong Il is trying to grab power by force with support from within the military.

But Defense Minister Choe also had a very big group of anti-Kim Jong Il military supporters. It is possible that these people will take action that leads to civil war. Is China, which supports the reformers, going to stand by and do nothing? I don't think so.

What is China's long-term objective on the Korean peninsula?
China wants to keep a cushion between itself and South Korea. That means opposing war, since China knows North Korea would lose and the armed border would move north to the Yalu River.

China already has a sense of crisis due to the 1994 KEDO [Korean Peninsula Energy Development Organization] agreement, which gave the

U.S. a foothold in supplying North Korea with fuel oil and light-water nuclear reactors. It symbolizes the U.S. moving into what China thought of as its own turf. What's developing is a race between the U.S. and China for hegemony on the Korean peninsula in the post-Kim Jong Il era.

Since China's main objective is to retain its cushion, it opposes the current purge of reformists by military people who know nothing but war. China will try to check it.

How?

By stopping aid. Or blocking the border. China doesn't have to announce anything. Just close the border and nothing will get into North Korea.

The U.S., like China, still hopes to engineer a soft landing by exchanging aid for less belligerent behavior. Nuclear reactors in exchange for North Korea's promise to stop its nuclear program. What are the chances of success?

Zero. Zero from the beginning. That was the mistake of the U.S. government. The light-water reactors are made in South Korea. Building them would require 500 to 1,000 South Korean technicians to enter North Korea. The North would never allow such a large exchange of infor-

mation and so it will find excuses to stop the project.

The U.S. position has been exactly the same as China's. The U.S. thought it could create a soft landing in North Korea with goods and money, but didn't understand the culture and politics. North Koreans don't listen to other people's opinions and don't compromise. What controls people in North Korea is power, period.

How should the U.S. deal with North Korea?

It should have used power from the beginning. When the U.S. started negotiations with North Korea in June 1993, soon after the Clinton Admini-

stration came to power, it compromised by saying it would never use nuclear weapons and promising to help supply two light-water reactors. If instead the U.S. responded to a breakdown in negotiations by sending the Seventh Fleet into the Sea of Japan, the North would have had to propose further discussions.

Your State Department thinks if it forces North Korea into a corner North Korea will explode. It is the opposite. Compromise increases the risk of war. We gave them rice and it went to the military or high officials. None got to the people's mouths.

How would North Korea's political collapse affect South Korea?

Economic refugees will naturally flow across the military border into South Korea. Once it begins, it will put a tremendous burden on the South Korean economy. If refugees come to Japan as well, all of East Asia will become unstable.

Another thing to watch: The most important statements released by Hwang Jang Yop since his defection are that there are North Korean spies [in the South Korean government]. If names are disclosed, Kim Young Sam's regime could be destroyed.

The Heat Is On

Asia faces renewed WTO pressure to open markets

By Shada Islam in Brussels

Asian trade ministers had better be prepared. They will be attending 50th anniversary celebrations of the multilateral trading system at the World Trade Organization's headquarters in Geneva on May 18–20. But the party looks set to turn into a fierce debate on the future of world trade.

European Trade Commissioner Leon Brittan has said he intends to use the meeting to campaign for a new "millennium round" of global-trade negotiations. WTO Director-General Renato Ruggiero says it's time the agency's 132 members stopped focusing on pacts that boost regional trade in favour of a more ambitious plan to create "one global free-trade area." (The U.S. is being less ambitious, seeking sector-by-sector negotiations.)

This push for further trade liberalization, however, is making many Asians uneasy. Most governments in the region argue that given the troubled state of Asia's economies, this is hardly the time to start tinkering with the world trading system. Asians fear increased economic turmoil if they open their domestic markets further to foreign competition. As a result, many are unenthusiastic about a new round of inter-linked trade negotiations.

"We see the idea as being premature," says an Asian trade official in Geneva. No country in the region wants to backtrack on current market-opening pledges, he says. "But this isn't the time for new commitments."

There are other problems, too. Translating the WTO's current liberalization pledges into domestic legislation is proving difficult for Asian governments, says Jacques Pelkmans, senior research fellow at the University of Maastricht. "Many are only just realizing the complexity of the exercise." The priority, agrees a Malaysian trade official, must be to implement the commitments made under the Uruguay Round, the last comprehensive multilateral negotiations, which ended in 1994. "We can't be pressed into jumping ahead," the official warns.

But others are equally adamant that such measures must continue. Singapore and Hong Kong are in favour of the new round, believing that it's the best way of keeping world trade on a forward, protection-free track. "We think new negotiations will inject strong impetus" toward freer trade, argues Mary Chow, deputy head of the Hong Kong Economic and Trade Office in Brussels.

In fact, even without Brittan's plans for a millennium round, Asians will be under pressure to liberalize some more: WTO members are committed to start talks before 2000 on intellectual-property rights and the further opening of markets in areas such as agriculture and services. In addition, the WTO must review progress made by working groups, set up in late 1996, on trade and investments, competition policy and eliminating corruption in government procurement. And both the EU and the U.S. have called on the WTO to start discussions on electronic commerce, which they insist must be kept free of tariffs.

Since new trade talks appear inevitable, Victor Ognivetscz, a trade expert at the Geneva-based United Nations Conference on Trade and Development, says that Asian countries must drop their traditional "defensive" stance in favour of a more assertive approach. Instead of reacting to EU and U.S. agendas, they should prepare their own proposals, he says.

One key benefit of global talks is that participating nations can try to exchange concessions made in one area for trade advantages in another. Take agriculture. The so-called Cairns Group of countries, including Australia, New Zealand, Indonesia, Thailand and Malaysia, want better access to EU markets and the elimination of all market-distorting subsidies. But securing these concessions will probably be easier if negotiators can link farm trade to, say, discussions on services.

Removing industrial tariffs is also important. Asian exporters of textiles, electronics and chemicals still face duties of more than 12% for about 10%–15% of their goods, says Unctad's Ognivetscz.

Securing changes in the EU's controversial anti-dumping legislation which punishes countries accused of selling their goods in Europe at below-cost prices—is another priority. "We're talking about an instrument which is plainly protectionist, and political," says Patrick Messerlin of the Paris-based Institute of Political Studies. Since the EU wants negotiations on global competition rules—so that anti-competitive cartels, price-fixing and market-sharing arrangements are banned worldwide—Messerlin suggests that Asians should link this to a revision of anti-dumping rules.

And Ake Weyler, head of the Swedish Importers' Association, offers this advice: Asian countries unhappy with the slow pace of liberalization in textiles and clothing should offer to undertake a fast-track removal of their own textile tariffs in exchange for speedier quota-free access to EU markets.

HOT TOPICS

Asian countries face a host of tough issues in upcoming WTO negotiations

Issues scheduled for further action

- Agriculture
- Services
- Intellectual-property rights

Issues under discussions now

- Anti-bribery measures
- Trade and competition policy
- Trade and the environment

New issues to be addressed

- Electronic commerce
- Liberalization of investment flows
- Elimination of textile quotas
- Anti-dumping policy
- Labour standards
- Reduction of industrial tariffs

Source: REVIEW Data

REVIEW GRAPHIC/RENE CHOW

Building Successful Partnerships in Russia and Belarus: The Impact of Culture on Strategy

Linda M. Randall and Lori A. Coakley

From the former Soviet industrial-military complex come insights into the difficulties of merging the disparate mindsets of Eastern and Western business strategists.

Since Mikhail Gorbachev's economic reform efforts (*perestroika*) and Boris Yeltsin's aggressive policies toward encouraging privatization and foreign investments, large numbers of investors have been considering collaborative ventures with enterprises in the Former Soviet Union (FSU). One of the potentially attractive sectors in which to pursue business partnerships is the defense industry, in which massive industrial restructuring and conversion efforts are under way. More important, this sector of the economy is historically known for employing only the most highly skilled workers and warehousing the FSU's most critical and cutting-edge technological advances.

The attractiveness of this market is premised on the assumption that the swift and dramatic ideological, political, and economic changes of Yeltsin's "New Russia" and the former Soviet republics demonstrate a clear and inevitable, though difficult, transition to a market economy. Many prominent figures in Moscow have consistently reinforced this idea, and noted Western economists personally involved in macroeconomic reforms in the FSU have not doubted the reality of this transition in the least.

However, during the course of our own fieldwork in the FSU over the past year, we have had the opportunity to be involved in both formal and informal interviews with managers in Russia and Belarus (formerly Belorussia). This has led us to question seriously any assumption of a transition to a strictly market economy in either country. By looking at change through the critically important lens of former defense companies that are developing strategic plans for product commercialization, we argue that we are witnessing a very disjointed type of transition—a switch from a centralized, command economy to a more diffuse and decentralized one with a cadre of managers whose cultural values still adhere to a socialist (command) economic ideology. In other words, despite such structural changes as privatization, establishment of a banking system, and development of a market-based legal system, behavioral changes and attitudes of business managers as reflected in their strategic choices have yet to follow suit. Thus, as U.S. businesses consider entering into partnerships with for-

From *Business Horizons*, March/April 1998, pp. 15-22. © 1998 by the Foundation for the School of Business at Indiana University. Reprinted by permission.

mer defense companies, it is imperative they recognize that although Russia is a "market in transition," actions taken by Russian and Belarussian managers are still heavily influenced by the deeply embedded cultural values germane to the Soviet era.

Today, much of the research published in the United States about the Russian business environment is concerned with issues of joint venture management and worker differences, as well as general business and economic environment. Yet the need to understand the cultural context in which particular managerial, organizational, and strategic decisions are made is paramount to any successful business endeavor.

We provide results from in-depth, face-to-face interviews with Russian and Belarussian managers, regional government officials, and Russian defense industry scholars exemplifying how strategic choices concerning former defense enterprises are heavily influenced by cultural constraints and conditions endemic to socialist ideologies. The results of this study may be applicable not only to defense-oriented firms, but to many companies in Russia and Belarus trying to transform from a socialist to a market-based system. What may become apparent is that strategies implemented by managers of FSU enterprises are often contrary to what would occur in the United States and may frustrate collaborative efforts with American businesses.

Defense Sector

With the decline in military orders ranging from 65 percent to 90 percent since 1992, successful defense conversion in the FSU is of great importance. One primary reason is the tremendous concentration of national resources–both capital and labor–in the defense sectors. According to Lipsits (1995), a noted Russian expert on defense conversion, 20 to 25 percent of the gross national product and one-third of income generated for the country in the 1980s came from the Soviet Union's military-industrial complex. Nine to ten regions were economically dependent on the manufacturing of defense-related products. And approximately 8 million people, plus another 1.8 million scientists and engineers, were employed in defense-related activities in the FSU. In St. Petersburg, Russia's second largest city, one in four employees still works in a defense firm.

Because of Russia's dependence on its military-industrial complex, the need to convert its defense companies successfully has become urgent for the general viability and health of its economy. These firms contain some of the region's best resources. Moreover, they have the potential to become a globally competitive economic force, with particular attractiveness for foreign businesses.

The strategic choices of these defense companies are limited in comparison to their American counterparts. In the United States, strategic options vary from shrinking or eliminating their defense operations (conversion) to, in many instances, maintaining or expanding their defense-related products through acquisition. Such options are not always available to Russian and Belarussian defense companies largely because of insufficient capital–resulting from the lack of money or potential investors to fund conversion projects–coupled with commercial bank interest rates as high as 200 percent.

Complicating the requisite structural changes demanded by the move toward a more market-like system are the still prevalent socialist ideologies and values governing the behavior of critical change agents found in those defense enterprises. These individuals should be facilitating, not impeding, change. Thus, the strategic choices made by FSU defense managers not only reflect the need for greater capital and resources but are underscored by the cultural norms and expectations that have influenced managerial behavior and actions for most of the past 80 years.

UNDERSTANDING FSU MANAGERIAL CULTURE

Scholars have come to appreciate the role culture plays in influencing the economic behavior and strategic decisions made by managers. Culture frames the reasons why certain goals and objectives are developed and are in turn used to create strategic responses for companies. Such scholars as Max Weber have noted the role of history and culture in the development of capitalism in the United States. Combining the Anglo-Saxon values of private ownership of property, preference for individual over community gain, and the general acceptance of economic inequality (as opposed to Americans' theoretical approval of political equality–"one man, one vote") with the philosophy of Adam Smith, the American free market system was created. Values of profit maximization and individual gain became entrenched in managerial thinking and are integral components of many American strategic management models today.

Strategic management theory is replete with a number of frameworks, such as Porter's (1985) industrial organization-based theory, Miles and Snow's (1978) concept of distinctive competence, and Pfeffer and Salancik's (1978) resource-dependence theory. All of these are embedded with the underlying American values described above. Specifically, they illustrate ways in which companies can achieve competitive advantage in their business environments by generating wealth for their owners, maximizing profit, and increasing entry barriers for other potential competi-

The Former Soviet Union (FSU)

tors. Moreover, all these models emphasize aligning a firm's core competencies with opportunities in the environment.

Sacrificing competitiveness, FSU defense managers implement strategies that often run contrary to what would occur in the United States. They too are bound by cultural conditions and constraints that influence the "appropriate" courses of action. These cultural conditions and constraints are grounded in the ideology of socialism, under which the first and foremost endeavor of managers is to act out of the need to improve "collectivity." This means maintaining technological "superiority," preserving full employment, making decisions that are in the best interests of the workers (in contrast to the "shareholders"), and attaining production goals over profit maximization. Below we provide a more detailed description of three of the most prominent cultural ideologies evidenced in the companies in this study.

Role of Technology

During the Soviet era and before, Russia's desire was to be at least a technological equal with the West, if not to surpass it. Historically, technology holds a critical position in Russia partly because of its national security needs. Russia believed that the acquisition and development of technology abetted protection from its enemies. During the reign of Peter the First (1682–1725), Germans and other Western Europeans were brought to the country for their technical expertise. In the Soviet era, not only did the USSR have the

greatest number of engineers in the world, but the way to achieve top management positions was to be an engineer—and, of course, a member of the Communist Party. It is interesting to note that in 1980, roughly 80 percent of the Politburo members were engineers.

Based on this convergence of technology and national security needs, defense enterprises held a preeminent position in the Soviet economic system. Even with the reduction of the military threat from the West, present-day Russia needs to continue to protect its borders, an imperative that is still linked with its desire to maintain its best technology.

Such an emphasis on technology has deeply affected actions of FSU defense company managers. The attitude is most evident in the approach taken by the firms in this study to retain their technological expertise and make decisions in contrast to what would be expected in a more market-oriented strategic plan. This will be illustrated in the case examples discussed later.

Management's Perspective on Labor

FSU managers' views regarding labor differ from their American counterparts. Under a market system, American managers view labor as a cost item needing to be managed in order to maximize a company's profitability. During the late 1980s and 1990s in America, the phrase "lean and mean" came to describe many corporate strategies to maintain competitiveness by reducing work forces. As U.S. defense companies grapple with conversion and enter commercial markets, one of their primary concerns is that their cost structure (that is, the cost of manufacturing a product) is too high to price their commercial products competitively. One major move is to lay off their work force to put their cost structure in line with their commercial counterparts.

In contrast, because most FSU managers attitudes and goals are still so greatly influenced by the former command or socialist system, many of their views diverge widely from the American attitude of "lean and mean." In our study, several Russian managers commented that the employment of workers was a very important goal. As one manager remarked,

> I have heard that the goal of the American manager is to get rid of as many workers as possible. Isn't it the job of a manager to seek ways to provide employment for his workers? How can people buy all of the goods produced in America if no one has jobs and therefore cannot afford to buy them?

In the FSU, layoffs *are* occurring but not quite in the same manner as in the United States. For example, even though several companies in this study reduced labor by 30 to 40 percent, they are still over-employing people by American standards. Moreover, managers have a social obligation to these families to provide employment and services. Unfortunately, the enterprises are facing tremendous cash deficits and do not pay well. In many instances, workers had not been paid for several months. Again, although structural transformations in the economic system dictate change, the strategic options open to these Russian and Belarussian managers are governed by cultural values and obligations—despite the realities and potentially grave consequences of a lack of capital.

Production versus Market Orientation

The FSU managers in this study considered the achievement of production goals paramount, often retaining excessive capital and equipment no longer required to manufacture the newly (converted) commercialized product. This production mentality overshadowed the demands of the emerging market economy, minimizing the strategic options considered by the managers. Some of the companies were willing to manufacture any product, but the decision to do so was based on idle production capacity and not on costs, consumer needs, or competitive advantage.

Such behavior also stems from the edicts of a command system. Managers were trained and compensated for achieving production quotas determined by the central government administrators in the minis-

tries and the State Committee for Planning (Gosplan). These production goals reflected the Soviet Union's drive for military superiority and technological preeminence during the Cold War. Today, despite the end of the Cold War and the transition toward a more market-like system, production goals remain a dominant influence in the overall managerial decisions made by the directors of the enterprises studied.

INTEGRATION OF STRATEGY AND CULTURE

Six case studies are provided here that more clearly illustrate the impact of culture on the strategic choices made by managers. The field research for this study was conducted from early 1995 through the winter of 1996. The Russian and Belarussian managers were operating state-run or newly privatized defense enterprises. Based on previous studies of Russian management issues, a method of qualitative research was considered the most appropriate for exploring culturally specific issues affecting the strategic choices made by the managers. Top-level managers–directors and vice directors–were asked a series of semi-structured questions. Interviews were also conducted with workers and Russian scholars involved in the defense industry.

In total, six defense companies were studied in three cities: Nizhny Novgorod and Samara in Russia (located in regions once closed to foreigners because of their heavy concentration of sensitive defense technologies) and Minsk, the capital of Belarus (which, despite a large number of defense firms, was never closed to foreigners). In Nizhny Novgorod, managers were observed and interviewed in three companies, referred to as Nizhny A, Nizhny B, and Nizhny C. Nizhny A develops and manufactures products that use microwave technology for MiG aircraft. Nizhny B is a radio electronics manufacturer. Nizhny C manufactures radar equipment, videocassette recorders (VCRs), and televisions. In Samara, interviews were conducted at Samara A, a company that manufactures launching equipment for missiles and rockets. In the capital of Belarus, Minsk A manufactures equipment that makes super-thin fibers for insulation in defense-related products, whereas Minsk B manufactures integrated circuits and wafer-grinding machines.

A summary of the companies' characteristics are provided in the **Figure**. Based on the results of this study, the six firms are categorized depending on which cultural ideology dominated their strategic choices: technology, labor, or production.

Technology-based Strategies

Minsk B. Minsk B, the large integrated-circuit manufacturer, developed a strategy to convert its perceived

Figure

Summary of the Six FSU Defense Companies in the Study

Name	Location	Ownership	Core Competency	# Employees	Commercial Products
Minsk A	Belarus	100% Private	Super-thin fiber for insulation	45	Insulation for commercial equipment
Minsk B	Belarus	40% Belarus govt. 30% Russian govt. 15% Collective workers 15% Foreigners	Computer electronics	3,500	Wafer-grinding equipment used for semi-conductors
Nizhny A	Russia	50% Government	Microwave technology and radio electronics	1,800	Microwave ovens and transmitters for civilian radio stations
Nizhny B	Russia	38% Government 62% Private	Radio electronics	N/A	Audio recorders, medical equipment, and ultrasound
Nizhny C	Russia	100% Private	Radio electronics	N/A	Black & white televisions and VCRs
Samara A	Russia	100% Government	Space technology	N/A	Low-cost space launches and distribution of medical equipment

(N/A–Information not available)

technological advantage into a commercial business. Its focus was to concentrate on core technological competencies that would result in products it hoped would surpass those available in the United States and Germany. Management also stressed the importance of receiving a patent in several key countries, including Germany, Japan, and the United States. Despite realizing the importance of knowing competitors' technological strengths and weaknesses, and despite a recognition of the need to find a Western partner who could contribute capital and equipment to fund the technology, there was a pervasive belief among the top managers that by simply building a more technologically superior product, the company would succeed in the global marketplace. This differs from the general American approach for entering a foreign marketplace, whereby information concerning customers' needs, government regulations, and both domestic and global competitors is equally, if not more, important for gaining a competitive edge.

Samara A. Samara A, a 100 percent government-owned manufacturer of missiles and rockets, considers itself crucial to the advancement of scientific knowledge in Russia. Specifically, Samara A believes its knowledge of rocketry and space technology, particu-

larly heat-sensitive material, is its most marketable commodity. However, unlike Minsk B, the company is reluctant to take its knowledge of heat-sensitive materials and apply it toward commercial products because of uncertainty in how to use the technology without revealing proprietary information to competitors. Managers often reiterated that their main goal was to warehouse their proprietary technology and covet their core competencies. So the strategies for product development strayed from their technological capabilities in lieu of "safer," commodity-like alternatives with little market potential. One example was to consider producing wooden rulers and distributing "low-tech" medical equipment as a means of enhancing its financial viability.

For both Minsk B and Samara A, technology—whether preserved for reasons of national security or exploited for economic gain—was the primary driving force behind their managerial decision making. Their technology-oriented courses of action, which ignored the needs of customers or the presence of competitors, speaks to many of the old socialist values and general cultural assumptions that often conflict with expectations from potential foreign partners and American market-oriented models of strategic management.

Labor

Minsk A. Minsk A was founded by scientists from a larger defense company that produced fibers for insulation. After their split from the parent company, these scientists developed a super-thin fiber more effective and less expensive than their competitors'. The director talked about the extensive market research conducted to determine the uniqueness of the company's product. Sufficient funds were raised to develop and manufacture a prototype, and the scientists strongly believed that the improved technology exemplified would make their product sufficiently attractive to the world markets. As part of their strategic thinking, they considered the Russian market an integral part of their strategic plan, realizing that the Belarus market would be too small. Further, they believed the West offered the next area of export potential, but only after the Russian market had been penetrated. Presently, the company wants to patent its technology throughout the key industrial areas of the world and is searching for Western partners to provide capital and, in essence, to purchase the newly advanced fibers. One interesting caveat in the search emerged when the managers of Minsk A asked several Western business people to recommend the best strategic move for their enterprise. The Westerners strongly suggested licensing the technology to a Western company as the best way for Minsk A to enter the world market. A practice common in the United States, this serves to minimize risks and assess potential competitors, industry demand for the product, and so on. The managers discussed it among themselves and concluded that if they licensed their technology, they would not be able to employ as many people. They decided they would rather have a co-production agreement with a Western firm.

The tenets of socialist ideology are evident in the decisions made by the managers of Minsk A. Maintaining full employment is paramount to successfully achieving what Minsk A considers its "bottom line." "The first and foremost endeavor of socialism is to provide jobs," writes Kornai (1992). "Everyone who is able to work has the constitutional right to work." In the hierarchical tiers of society, it is the responsibility of those in positions of power to serve as the vanguard in preserving the people's interest and as the repository of a permanent public good. So for management to remain "legitimate" in the eyes of the workers, its first criterion for partnership must be full employment. Only from this position is a "successful" partnership feasible.

Nizhny C. Like Minsk A, Nizhny C's management is greatly concerned with maximizing core competencies while somehow maintaining the company's role as the provider of health care, education, social goods and services, and basic full-time employment for all its employees. A fully privatized company that makes televisions and VCRs, Nizhny C has been in a dire financial situation since 1994. No money has been received to develop conversion projects, and the company has survived only by exporting 40 percent of the stockpiled defense goods left over from a canceled 70 billion ruble order for the Ministry of Defense. Moreover, because production has dropped 40 percent from 1994 levels, the firm is now confronted with the difficult prospect of having to reduce its labor force and sell a number of the social services it has always been expected to provide. These include a kindergarten, a sports complex, housing for workers, a canteen, and a health clinic.

Whereas American managers would likely see the difficulty in making such decisions, they may not appreciate the overwhelming cultural dilemma in which this places a Russian manager. On the whole, both Minsk A and Nizhny C were disciplined in targeting their resources toward the technology each claimed as its respective core competency. The director of an enterprise is expected to make decisions that effectively benefit the collective good of the people. This implies that any actions he takes should preserve the number of workers employed by the company, as well as maintain certain social benefits. However, the burden of operating within the constraints of a socialist culture that promotes maintaining full employment of all workers while attempting to participate in more "market-like" environments may frustrate those trying to negotiate a potential partnership.

> "The managers discussed it among themselves and concluded that if they licensed their technology, they would not be able to employ as many people."

Production

Nizhny A. Nizhny A is a manufacturer of radio transmitters for MiGs and microwave ovens for Russian and Ukrainian consumers. Since 1993 it has lost 90 percent of its government defense orders, which had contributed 80 percent of its total revenues. Despite this 72 percent drop in total sales, however, the company continues to operate at 40 percent capacity, instead of the expected 25 to 30 percent figured by American standards. As a result, Nizhny A is stockpiling its production and will continue to manufacture as long as it has the requisite materials and supplies on hand—even though it has not received a new order since the loss of its defense contracts. This strategy may not appear much different from U.S. managers' desire to increase production. But Americans' efforts are the direct result of market demand, with primary emphasis being the minimization of production costs. On the other hand, Russian managers' goals are focused specifically on the quantity of goods produced, with little regard for the costs incurred by maintaining idle plants and labor and making products for the sake of production.

Nizhny B. For Nizhny B, a radio-electronics manufacturer, production was also a main focus point. In the process of developing its strategy, management hired a Russian consultant who recommended that the company produce audio recorders for the general communications industry—anything from "walkmans" to professional recorders for music. Initially, this strategy could be considered comparable to what Western managers would possibly implement, as it was nicely aligned with Nizhny B's core competencies and required little to convert production lines successfully. The primary difference, however, is in the underlying motives for producing such equipment. For the Russians, it was imperative to maintain production capacity at any cost, with little regard for market demand or competition—a key consideration for most U.S. manufacturers. Unfortunately, by the mid-1990s the Russian consumer market was flooded with Japanese, Korean, and German-made products that were reputed to be of better quality than that of Nizhny B.

Both these firms' management responses are consistent with cultural expectations concerning capacity use and full employment needs as paramount over any consideration of costs. This is in direct contrast with an American company's view of production as a balance between the minimization of cost and the maximization of quantity of goods manufactured, resulting in overall profits for the company.

The complexity and difficulty of the unprecedented market transformation that is currently under way in the FSU is largely due to the fact that there is no collective or individual historical memory of a free and open society or a market economy. More than 70 years of communist rule have left an indelible mark on the FSU. Ironically, countries such as Russia and Belarus are expected to make an economic transition in less than a decade that is similar to what has gradually evolved in the United States over the past 220 years.

For an economic system to make such a transition successfully, both structural *and* behavioral shifts are required by those involved in making change happen. In essence, the structural changes currently under way in the FSU's defense sector remain the focal point of much that has been written concerning transformation. Discussions have centered on changes

made to the economic, political, and legal infrastructures necessary to support a market economy. And the promise of such change continues to attract foreign investors by the bucketful to the FSU, particularly to Russia.

But what unfolded in the course of interviews conducted for this study was an awareness that the behaviors of Russian and Belarussian defense managers do not adhere to what would be expected by American managers faced with similar business conditions. Instead, as Russian managers attempt to mesh their cultural norms, past training, and work experiences with the new demands of the market-in-transition, they confront mounting obstacles that reflect the inconsistency between economic structure and expected managerial behavior. As we have illustrated, managerial behavior remains steeped in the achievement of production goals in lieu of marketplace edicts, the maintenance of labor in spite of cost and profit implications for the company, and the adherence to a perspective that technological superiority is paramount in the attainment of social welfare and national security.

As behavioral change continues to lag behind structural change, it becomes imperative to understand that this inconsistency between what economics demands and cultural norms require manifests problems and complexities far beyond mere structural change. In short, the implications of the different perspectives on technology, labor, and production shown in these six case studies for potential partnerships between U.S. and FSU companies need to be fully grasped by all parties entering into any form of relationship. Although this study has focused on the defense sector, all industrial sectors of Russia and Belarus were once part of the socialist economy and thus the conclusions drawn likely pertain to them as well. Perhaps through an awareness of these cultural differences and beliefs of others, productive, creative, and profitable collaborations can be achieved.

References

Anders Aslund, *How Russia Became a Market Economy* (Washington, DC: 1995).

H. Balzer, "Engineers: The Rise and Decline of the Social Myth," in Loren Graham (ed.), *Science and Soviet Social Order* (Cambridge, MA: Harvard University Press, 1990): 141–167.

Christopher A. Bartlett and Sumantra Ghoshal, "Global Strategic Management: Impact on the New Frontiers of Strategy Research," *Strategic Management Journal,* Summer 1991, pp. 5–16.

Joseph Berliner, *Soviet Industry from Stalin to Gorbachev* (New York: Cornell University Press, 1988).

Peter Buckley, "The Role of Management in International Business Theory: A Meta-Analysis and Integration of the Literature on International Business and International Management," *Management International Review, 36,* 1, (1996): 7-54.

Marshall Goldman, *What Went Wrong with Perestroika?* (New York: Norton, 1992).

D. Hecht, *Rubles and Dollars* (New York: Harper Business, 1991).

Interview transcripts of managers from enterprises located in Minsk, Nizhny Novgorod, and Samara, conducted in January and February 1995.

S. V. Kazantsev, "Oboronnyi Kompleks Rossii: Navti Svovu Nishu Na Rynke" (The Russian Military Complex: Finding Itself a Niche in the Market), *Zh. Ehko,* No. 8 (1995): 117-127.

János Kornai, *The Socialist System: The Political Economy of Communism* (Princeton, NJ: Princeton University Press, 1992).

D. Kotz, "The Direction of Soviet Economic Reform: From Socialist Reform to Capitalist Transition," *New York Monthly Review,* September 1992, pp. 14-33.

Paul Lawrence and C. A. Vlachoutsicos, *Beyond Factory Walls* (Cambridge, MA: Harvard Business School Press, 1990).

Moshe Lewin, *The Gorbachev Phenomenon: A Historical Interpretation* (Berkeley, CA: University of California Press, 1991).

I. Lipsits "Problemy Rossiyskoi Konversii" (Problems of Russian Conversion), *Zh. Ehkonomist,* No. 1(1995): 14-21.

Robert Massie, *Peter the Great: His Life and World* (New York: Ballantine Books. 1980).

D. McCardiy and Sheila Puffer. "Perestroika at the Plant Level: Managers' Job Attitudes and Views of Decision Making in the Former Soviet Union," *Columbia Journal of World Business,* Spring 1992, pp. 86-99.

R. Miles and C. Snow, *Organizational Strategy, Structure, and Process* (New York: McGraw-Hill, 1978).

J. Pfeffer and G. Salancik, *The External Control of Organizations: A Resource-Dependence Perspective* (New York: Harper & Row, 1978).

Michael Porter, *Competitive Advantage: Creating and Sustaining Superior Performance* (New York: Free Press, 1985).

A. Shama, "Management Under Fire: The Transformation of Managers in the Soviet Union and Eastern Europe," *Academy of Management Executive, 7,* 1 (1993): pp. 22-35.

Adam Smith, *Wealth of Nations* (Buffalo, NY: Prometheus Books, 1991).

Alan Smith, *Russia and the World Economy: Problems of Integration* (New York: Routledge, 1993).

Max Weber, *The Protestant Ethic and the Spirit of Capitalism,* trans. Talcott Parsons (New York: Scribner's, 1930).

D. H. B. Welsh, F. Luthans, and S. M. Sommer, "Managing Russian Factory Workers: The Impact of U.S.-based Behavioral and Participative Techniques," *Academy of Management Journal, 36,* 1 (1993): 58-79.

Boris Yeltsin, *The Struggle for Russia* (New York: Random House, Inc., 1994).

Linda M. Randall is an assistant professor of management at the University of Rhode Island, Kingston. **Lori A. Coakley** is an assistant professor of management at Bryant College, Smithfield, Rhode Island.

Strengthening the Architecture Of The International Financial System

THE FINANCIAL CRISIS IN ASIA AND THE IMF

Address by ROBERT E. RUBIN, *United States Secretary of the Treasury*
Delivered to the Brookings Institution, Washington, D.C., April 14, 1998

Today I would like to discuss the international financial system in the wake of the financial crisis in Asia; what we can learn from these events about the opportunities and risks of a global financial market; and how we can strengthen the architecture of the international financial system to realize the potential of a 21st century global economy.

These issues of architecture will be at the top of the agenda this week when the world financial community gathers here in Washington for the spring meetings of the Group of Seven industrialized nations and the policy making bodies of the International Monetary Fund and the World Bank. In addition, Chairman Greenspan and I will host a special meet-

ing of a group of ministers and governors from advanced, emerging and transition economies to discuss architecture. In a moment I will discuss the U.S. approach to changes in the international financial architecture, which we will bring to these meetings, just as the other nations of the world will bring their ideas and suggestions. But first, I think it is im-

From *Vital Speeches of the Day*, May 1, 1998, pp. 421-425. © 1998 by City News Publishing Company, Inc. Reprinted by permission.

portant to place these discussions in broader historical context.

Over the last ten to fifteen years, we have seen the rapid evolution of a new era of the global economy and global financial markets, an era that presents enormous opportunities for workers, farmers and businesses around the globe. And the changes have been dramatic. Greatly increased flows of trade, capital, information and technology have helped promote global output. Most large businesses, both here in the United States and elsewhere have become global. Developing countries have become important participants in the global economy; for example, they now absorb more than 40 percent of our country's exports. Financial liberalization and technological innovation have produced an ever broader range of new services and products.

A decade ago, official capital flows to developing countries were much greater than private capital flows. Today, annual private flows of capital to developing countries around the world are more than seven times larger than official flows. In 1996, more than $250 billion in private capital flowed to emerging markets—compared to roughly $20 billion ten years ago. All of this explains why fluctuations in the Thai baht, or the fortunes of the Korean stock market can now affect workers, farmers and businesses in the United States and all over the world and appear daily on the front page of our newspapers. A decade ago practically no one outside the affected countries would have noticed.

Global economic and financial integration with respect to trade and capital flows have brought tremendous benefits here in the United States through increased exports, more high-paying jobs, higher standards of living and lower inflation. The huge increase in private capital flows to developing countries have, among other things, helped finance a great increase in imports from industrialized countries, including our own. Developing countries from Latin America to Asia have also benefited greatly, as increased capital flows financed greater investment and contributed substantially to the high rates of growth in many such countries, promoting higher standards of living and lifting millions out of poverty. The recent economic turmoil in Asia should not, for example, detract from what Asia has achieved over the last 25 years. Even under the more pessimistic forecasts, living standards in Korea, Thailand and Indonesia would still be three times higher at the end of this year than they were 20 years ago, and the poverty rates much lower. Even with the current crisis, per capita income would be higher than in 1995.

As we have seen in recent years, however, this new era brings not only great opportunities and benefits, but also new challenges and risks. How effectively the international community meets these challenges and manages the risks, will have an enormous impact in the years ahead on our economic well-being, and the economic well-being of all countries.

One great challenge is to greatly broaden participation in the benefits of the global economy. Despite vast global economic growth over the past decade, over half the people of the world still live in poverty and that is a problem not only for the countries with high poverty rates but for all of us. The developing countries are our markets for the future, and their economic well-being promotes our economic well-being. Here at home, global financial integration benefits the great majority of Americans, but one of the concerns often expressed—and it is a concern that I share—is that, throughout the industrialized countries, including the United States, those who are well-equipped to compete in the global economy are doing better and better, and those who are not so well-equipped risk falling further and further behind.

But the answer to these challenges is not to turn inward, or to dismantle the global economy that has benefited so many. The answer is for all nations, including the United States, to make it easier for those who are dislocated to reenter the economy successfully; to focus on education and training to equip citizens with the tools to prosper in the global economy; to build social safety nets to protect the people who would otherwise be left behind; to work for broad implementation of core labor standards throughout the globe; and to promote democracy and human rights. The benefits of the global economy will only be realized if we and all other nations build broad-based support at home for forward-looking international economic policies. That support will only occur if these benefits are broadly shared.

A half century ago, when the world was emerging from a very different period of history, Franklin D. Roosevelt urged Americans to support him in working with other nations to create international institutions that would spell the difference "between a world caught again in the maelstrom of panic and economic warfare . . . and a world in which the members strive for a better life through mutual trust, cooperation and assistance." The result was the Bretton Woods institutions—the International Monetary Fund and the World Bank—followed later by a range of other collaborative arrangements, such as the World Trade Organization, central bank networks, and the regional development banks. This international architecture has worked to support growth and financial stability and open markets around the globe, greatly benefiting generations of Americans.

Throughout their history, the international financial institutions have had to adapt to a changing global economic landscape, and they have, by and large, done so successfully. But over recent years, the pace of change in the global economy has accelerated. The Asian crisis has demonstrated how badly flawed financial sectors in a few developing countries, and inadequate risk assessment by international creditors and investors, can have significant impact in countries around the globe. Once, unsound macroeconomic, financial and other policies in emerging economies would have had little impact on other nations. Now, unsound policies in these countries can harm economies throughout the global economy—such as our large budget deficits did in the 1980s—and the problems of each country are the problems of all of us.

That is why, even before the turmoil in Asia, the United States and the international community have been working to strengthen the international financial architecture. Our goals are clear: to promote broadly shared growth in both the developed and developing world, to be better able to prevent future crises, and to deal with them when they occur, and by making the architecture as modern as the markets. The United States began this effort four years ago at a G-7 leaders' meeting in Naples and, working with other nations, the first concrete steps were launched at the G-7 summit the following year in Halifax. Going forward will not require the kind of far-reaching institutional change that we saw in 1945, but the international architecture does need to adapt substantially for the very different circumstances that have developed over the past decade, and to fully prepare for the challenges of tomorrow. This adaptation involves great intellectual complexities and great international political complexities and will occur not at one time, but in pieces over an extended period of time.

There are a whole range of issues that are profoundly important to the strength of individual economies and the global economy—sound macroeconomic policies, education, health care, and the environment number among them. There is also

a detailed agenda for reform of the IMF concerning, among other things, its lending programs. But today I would like to focus on three challenges that have been brought home by the financial crisis in Asia and that are most directly related to financial stability and building a stronger global financial market. These are: providing better information through improved disclosure and transparency; building strong national financial sectors; and creating mechanisms so that the private sector more fully bears the consequences of its credit and investment decisions, including in times of crisis.

The first critical area is better information. When investors are well-informed, use that information wisely, and expect to bear their consequences of their actions, they will make better decisions. That is good for them and can be a powerful force in promoting good policies among nations. National policy makers also need better information, to guide their actions, and anticipate potential problems.

However, there are obstacles to getting good information about economic and financial matters. One is the temptation—in the private sector and in government—to avoid disclosing problems. But sooner or later, as we have seen in Asia, the problems will make themselves known—and in the meantime they only become more severe. In the Asian economies that suffered crises, very effective strategies for achieving many years of rapid growth had masked the growth of problems. In many cases, lack of data meant that no one had a true understanding of this build up or of these economies' vulnerabilities.

Another obstacle is the difficulty of collecting relevant information on a timely basis. In the modern, very complex global financial markets investors and policy makers need more types of information then ever before. For example, public and private institutions have to better identify and disclose the effects of

derivatives and other off-balance sheet items on financial risks and vulnerabilities.

Just as important as having good information is using that information well. Risk and credit evaluation have often not kept pace with the development of new products and markets. Indeed, in the Asian crisis we were struck by how few of the international creditors and investors in these economies had the appropriate expertise and knowledge on weighting of risk.

While to some measure this may simply reflect the seemingly inevitable tendency for investors and creditors to at times get overly optimistic or pessimistic—and at those times to forgo adequate analysis—the incentives to be rigorous should be maximized, which at the least involves questions of moral hazard and regulatory regimes. When creditors and investors come closer to functioning with full analytic rigor, markets will more effectively perform their critical disciplining function in favor of good policy, disclosure, strong financial sectors and the like.

Even before the Asian crisis we had been involved in an intensive effort to improve the quality and quantity of international economic and financial information, including greater IMF transparency. Many countries are now publishing more and better data as a result of these efforts and the IMF is more open about its analysis. But events in Asia have shown we need to strengthen these initiatives. We propose four steps to do so.

First, there needs to be a substantial expansion in the types of economic and financial data made available. In particular, it is essential to get good information on the external liabilities of both the public and private sectors. The IMF's Special Data Dissemination Standards should require countries to provide a complete picture of usable central bank reserves, including any forward liabilities, foreign currency liabilities of the commercial banks, as well as indicators on the health of the financial sector. The Bank for International Settlements should expand its reporting on cross border bank flows to get better, broader, and more timely data on external lending to a country.

Governments and international financial institutions also need to make this data more easily accessible to investors, particularly through the internet.

Second, we need to explore how to obtain and publicize a broader range of qualitative descriptive information on financial sector matters that affect the risk of investing in emerging markets, including detail on banking supervision, bankruptcy procedures, perhaps judicial systems, credit cultures and skills in the banking sector. We must now resolve the many difficult issues with regard to these qualitative matters, for example, how best to describe them and who should perform this function.

To support these efforts on disclosure, private sector groups should provide their own ideas about the data and information they would find most helpful, and ways to encourage wider use of available information and appropriate focus on risk.

Third, the IMF needs to make its analyses and lending conditions more transparent. This will involve more frequent and regular publication of a number of IMF documents, analyses, and letters of intent. However, while greater transparency to help investors reach an informed judgment about potential problems is essential, giving the IMF the responsibility to publicly predict formal warnings of crisis is not. While it is possible to identify problems that may develop into difficulties and occasionally into crisis, it is not possible in our view to reliably predict combustion into crisis.

Fourth, we need to increase incentives for countries to improve transparency. The discipline of the market is always the best and most powerful incentive, and can work here to induce better disclosure. Analysts and rating agencies also need to pay close attention to the availability and quality of data and information when determining credit worthiness and asset allocations. In addition, the IMF and other international financial institutions should publicize their concerns about important gaps in countries' disclosure and consider conditioning access to loans on countries' willingness to improve their transparency.

The second critical area we are focused on is strengthening national financial systems. A common element amongst the countries involved in the crisis in Asia—and, for that matter, in virtually all countries experiencing financial crises—is a badly flawed domestic financial sector.

Developing a strong financial system that is a match for the challenges of a global financial market is a long and difficult process. The institutions and laws we have in the United States to supervise our domestic financial system were developed over a period of a hundred years and must constantly be updated. We ourselves had an enormous financial sector problem with our Savings and Loan crisis in the 1980s. That crisis stemmed in part from a failure to supervise those institutions adequately as they moved into new services, and to a delay in taking decisive corrective action. Building strong financial sectors will unquestionably be key to financial stability and growth in emerging economies.

Given the effects that weak financial systems can have internationally, the time has come for a more systematic approach to strengthening national financial systems that would involve a more intensive assessment of the vulnerabilities in national financial systems and steps to promote reforms. To do this, we need action in the following areas.

First, we need to develop a more complete range of global standards to guide individual governments' efforts. As a result of the Halifax initiatives, the Basle Committee has now developed the "Core Principles for Effective Banking Supervision." IOSCO, the organization that brings together securities regulators from around the globe, is already well on the way to developing an analogous set of principles for the supervision of securities firms. But we believe core principles should be developed and adopted in additional areas that affect the underlying strength of a financial system, including bankruptcy regimes, accounting and disclosure, loan classification, and overall corporate governance. Other practices which need to be adopted include promoting credit risk management, helping address the problems of connected and directed lending, maturity and currency mismatches, and encouraging a strong credit culture and the requisite skills in a nation's banking system. Different countries have and will continue to have different ways of doing these things, but we must agree to certain high quality internationally acceptable standards.

Second, we need to fill a gap in today's international architecture to provide for international surveillance of countries' financial regulatory and supervisory systems, just as the IMF now carries out surveillance of macroeconomic policies. There are a number of different ways that this could be done—perhaps through a joint initiative with the IMF and the World Bank, with the use of existing expertise of regulators. But it is critically important to find an appropriate way to fill this gap.

Enhanced surveillance will help induce national authorities to bring their practices up to internationally-acceptable levels, as I set forth in the standards I just discussed, and reduce financial risk. These assessments can lay the groundwork for policy discussions and appropriate assistance, where needed, from the IMF and the multilateral development banks for programs to strengthen financial systems. In addition, analysis of this kind should feed into the range of key documents we believe the IMF should be releasing more systematically. This would then bring into play the most powerful incentive, the markets.

Third, we should consider examining other incentives that could be brought to bear for strengthening financial systems. For example, authorities in major financial centers could consider conditioning access to their markets by banks from other countries on a strong home country supervisory regime, as demonstrated by adherence to the Basle Core Principles, plus whatever relevant additional standards are developed.

Let me also make two additional points relating to financial sectors and capital markets. Experience shows that when countries allow foreign financial service providers into their markets—with all the competition, capital and expertise they bring with them—the strength of financial systems is greatly enhanced. The recent WTO agreement in financial services is a major step forward here.

In addition, while attempts to limit inflows of capital, such as Chile's short-term capital controls, have been advocated by some, it is key—independent of the merits or drawbacks of such measures—that this sort of approach not distract policy makers from implementing the underlying sound policies that are the real foundation for stability and growth. Having said that, it may be worth exploring narrower, prudential limits on banks to prevent an excessive buildup of short-term foreign currency liabilities.

The third and final critical area that I want to discuss today is building effective mechanisms for creditors and investors to more fully bear the consequences of their actions. We cannot prevent crises from happening entirely. When crises do occur, as most recently in Asia, the provision of temporary financial

support by the IMF, conditioned on countries pursuing sound policies, is essential in providing countries the breathing room they need to stabilize their currencies, restore market confidence and resume growth. It limits the risk that the crisis will worsen or spread. But, and the balance here will always be difficult, the private sector must fully bear the consequences of its decisions in the context of restoring financial stability.

There are two reasons to focus on the private sector bearing the consequences of its actions. In a world in which trillions of dollars flow through international markets every day there is simply not going to be enough official financing for the crises that could take place. There is also a risk with international assistance of what economists call "moral hazard": that providing official financial assistance shields creditors and investors from the consequences of bad decisions and sows the seeds of future crises. Some protection of creditors may be an inevitable by-product of the overarching objective of restoring financial stability, but this protection should be kept to the minimum possible.

When investors bear more responsibility for their actions, they have a better incentive to analyze and weigh risks appropriately. This, in turn, will promote good policy in all countries, including our own, and help prevent instability and crisis. Markets are a powerful force and our goal must be to make markets work better, while still providing the essential international support to help countries in crisis and guard against contagion risks.

There are a number of ways that the private sector can be involved when the IMF is providing emergency support at a time of country crisis, as the recent cases in Asia have shown. In Korea, international banks stretched out and renegotiated a substantial proportion of outstanding loans while the IMF has provided emergency financing to Korea, drawing upon its new, short term, high interest lending facility,

conditioned on strong policies. In Indonesia, foreign banks are now negotiating with a committee representing private sector corporate debtors, while the Indonesia program with the IMF is aimed at putting in place a more stable macroeconomic environment.

While the whole question of private sector involvement is extremely complicated—and there are many areas that may not have yet been fully explored—let me just mention a few thoughts as to possible mechanisms.

In general, the promotion of new, more flexible forms of debt agreements and indentures would provide a framework for direct negotiations between creditors and investors. In addition, the IMF should explore lending into arrears—in other words, the IMF continuing to provide financing to countries even when those countries may be behind on the debt payments to some private creditors to create a situation in which debtors and creditors work things out themselves. A broader, international bankruptcy regime of some sort may have great appeal, but, at least with current knowledge, the political obstacles may be insurmountable. However, strong bankruptcy laws and institutions covering debtor-creditor relations can mean business failures have a better chance of being resolved quickly and with less impact on the broader economy. Governments could then reduce the scope of formal guarantees to create a more healthy environment with the presumption that corporate debt will not be protected, and that where appropriate banks will be allowed to fail. Various insurance plans for creditors have also been suggested, but none so far proposed seem likely to be effective and some may create additional moral hazard problems.

Before I conclude, I want to comment on a critical immediate issue. The IMF has been central to the effort to restore financial stability in Asia and the IMF will be central to restoring financial stability in response to crises in the years ahead—matters that are critically important to the economic well-being of the American people. All of this underscores the importance of Congress approving full funding for the IMF, as requested by the President. As a result of the recent situation in Asia, the IMF's normal financial resources are approaching historically low levels. The IMF might not have the capacity to respond effectively if the Asian crisis were to deepen, spread to other developing countries throughout the globe, or if a new crisis were to develop in the near term. Every day that this continues is an-

other day of vulnerability for American workers, farmers, and businesses. Congress should act and act now. And our capacity to influence the IMF to deal with these new challenges turns upon our capacity to support the IMF with the funding it needs.

As I said earlier, there are many steps we need to take to build a strong global economy that benefits everyone. But the objectives I have described today—better information; stronger national financial systems; and mechanisms so that the private sector more fully bears the consequences of its investment decisions—are critical elements in

strengthening the architecture of the international financial system, especially with regards to preventing and dealing with financial instability and crisis.

Progress will take time and immense amounts of energy on the part of the international community, and in our country, close cooperation between Congress and the Administration. But our success in meeting the challenge of strengthening the international financial architecture will be critical to global prosperity—and our own country's economic well-being—for years and decades to come. Thank you very much.

MANUFACTURING

The world as a single machine

Rich countries worry that manufacturing is passing into the hands of poor countries. It is, but it's not a worry, says Iain Carson

CHANGE always frightens people. And today the world's economy is going through two great changes, both bigger than an Asian financial crisis here or a European monetary union there.

The first change is that a lot of industrial production is moving from the United States, Western Europe and Japan to developing countries in Latin America, South-East Asia and Eastern Europe; the classic example is the exodus of textiles from the rich world over the past two decades (see chart 1, next page). In 1950, the United States alone accounted for more than half of the world's economic output. In 1990, its share was down to a quarter. Even then, North America, Europe and Japan were between them still producing three-quarters of the world's output. But, as DeAnne Julius and Richard Brown, two economists working in Britain, pointed out in a famous essay in 1993, times are a-changing. Quite soon now, many big western companies will have more employees (and customers) in poor countries than in rich ones.

The second great change is that, in the rich countries of the OECD, the balance of economic activity is swinging from manufacturing to services (see chart 2, next page). In the United States and Britain, the proportion of workers in manufacturing has shrunk since 1900 from around 40% to barely half that. Even in Germany and Japan, which rebuilt so many factories after 1945, manufacturing's share of jobs is now below 30%. The effect of the shift is increased as manufacturing moves from rich countries to the developing ones, whose cheap labour gives them a sharp advantage in many of the repetitive tasks required by mass production.

These trends have caused an agonised debate about the "deindustrialisation of the West". When the oil-price rises of the 1970s brought inflation to Europe and America, many people feared a rapid decline in manufacturing as output shifted to developing countries with cheaper labour. By the mid-1980s, a lot of Americans had come to believe that their country's industry was being "hollowed out" as its basic activities moved to low-wage areas in Mexico and Asia. A sudden cancer, it seemed, had gripped the entrails of American industry.

It was not like that. A change was happening, but it was not simply a destructive change, and it had already been happening for quite a long time. For years before the mid-1980s, the structure of American industry had been altering. The familiar picture of solid old companies like IBM, General Motors and Ford pulling together for the greater good of corporate America had long since turned

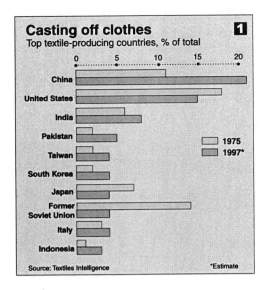

Casting off clothes
Top textile-producing countries, % of total

1975
1997*

China
United States
India
Pakistan
Taiwan
South Korea
Japan
Former Soviet Union
Italy
Indonesia

Source: Textiles Intelligence   *Estimate

There is something curious about this. Why did French and Belgian politicians get themselves into a lather when Renault, France's leading car maker, decided to close a factory near Brussels last spring? Why do fears of similar protests lead General Motors and Ford to keep surplus capacity across Europe, when a closer look at how many cars they can actually sell should lead them to axe their least efficient factories?

The broad answer, especially in Europe, is that many people still vaguely believe that manufacturing somehow matters more than any other economic activity; that making things you can drop on your foot is in some way superior to fingering a computer or cutting somebody's hair. Never mind that more than two-thirds of output in the OECD countries, and up to four-fifths of employment, is now in the service sector. Making things in factories is still what real men do (as, 150 years ago, growing things in fields was what real men did). Quietly strip 3,000 jobs out of a national network of retail banks, and no one will raise an eyebrow. Open a telephone sales centre in the north-east of England, creating 3,000 new jobs, and it might get a mention on the local news. Close a steel mill, and the gasps of dismay go on for weeks. Open a semiconductor plant, and the hosannas echo for months.

For most of today's rich countries, there was indeed a period when economic success was synonymous with manufacturing. Plenty

brown at the edges. International competition had arrived ages ago.

Much of what an innocent American consumer might have thought of as "Made in America" was by 1985 the product of factories in many different parts of the world. By 1990, 40% of IBM's employees were non-Americans; Whirlpool, America's leading supplier of domestic appliances, made most of its products in Mexico and Europe, having cut its American labour force by 10%; and General Electric was the biggest private-sector employer in Singapore, where American-owned factories employed over 100,000 Singaporeans to make electronic components to be shipped to the United States. By the early 1990s about a fifth of the total output of American firms was being produced by non-Americans outside America. As chart 3 on the next page shows, foreign investment in the past three decades has risen faster than trade and world output.

American industry had for years been changing, as the low-cost production of things like textiles, clothing, shoes, handbags, car seats and electrical wiring migrated to Mexico. Much that wore a Detroit car maker's badge or a computer company's brand was really the product of an elaborate international web of suppliers and assemblers. But it took a couple of decades for the politicians to realise what was going on. When they eventually did—as the car makers of Detroit and the computer companies of California imported more and more of their components, from axles to microchips—there arose desperate cries about "Japanese dominance" of high-tech industries and the "collapse" of much American production. And it was not only in America that people were falling into despair.

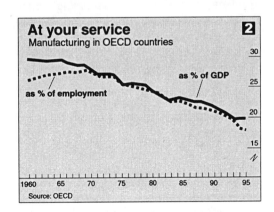

At your service
Manufacturing in OECD countries

as % of GDP

as % of employment

1960   65   70   75   80   85   90   95
Source: OECD

of Britons who have no memory of the real thing still feel a pang of artificial nostalgia about Birmingham as "the workshop of the world" and Clyde-built ships that ruled the waves. Moreover, success in manufacturing was linked to geopolitical power. The democracies were able to defeat Germany in two world wars because America's industrial machine poured out such a flood of tanks and warships and bombers. Best of all, in some ways, manufacturing was for long a source of reasonably reliable and well-paid jobs for young men with plenty of muscle and little else. It still is, to some extent. "We employ the guys who are never going to be Microsoft programmers," says one manufacturing boss at Chrysler.

It isn't special

So should the rich world worry that its manufacturing sector now seems to be migrating to low-wage competitors? Without big factories that ship steel, cars, machine tools and television sets to foreign customers, how can rich countries earn their keep in the world, finding the wherewithal to buy their food and oil and other raw materials? Ms Julius and Mr Brown, in that 1993 essay, called this the "Manufacturing is Something Special" argument. Manufacturing, in this way of looking at things, brings more growth, better-paid jobs, fatter export earnings and greater technological progress than any other economic activity.

Not so, the Julius-Brown essay explained. A household can use only so many cars and refrigerators and dishwashers in its members' lifetime. As countries get richer, a rising share of income goes on holidays, health and education. Busy people want to hire other people to clean their homes, launder their clothes and so on. Anyway, many jobs traditionally thought of as part of "manufacturing", such as the design and marketing of products, are really service jobs. As demand for them increases, these service jobs become better paid and more interesting compared with the drudgery of factory work—much of which is in any case moving overseas. Services are growing fast as a component of international trade, encouraged by widespread deregulation. The chunky, capital-intensive making of cars, chemicals and computers is starting to look middle-aged. If you want the vitality of youth, turn to things like telecommunications, aviation, biotechnology or the health-care industry.

In all rich countries, manufacturing's share of total output is shrinking, and its payroll is shrinking even faster. The same thing happened with agriculture. At the beginning of

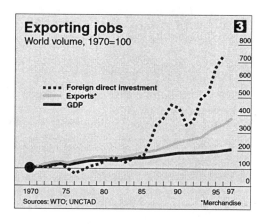

Exporting jobs **3**
World volume, 1970=100

- ······· Foreign direct investment
- Exports*
- GDP

1970　75　80　85　90　95 97
Sources: WTO; UNCTAD　　　　　*Merchandise

this century, 68% of Japan's labour force worked on the land, 44% of America's and about 20% of Britain's. Today, agriculture accounts for only 7% of workers in Japan, 3% in America and 2% in Britain. Yet the fading of agriculture did not bring impoverishment to these countries. Nor will the fading of factories. There will be other things for their people to do, which will bring comfortable incomes and may anyway be more interesting than hoeing fields or pulling levers on production lines.

This survey will look at the ways in which manufacturing is changing in both rich countries and poorer ones. Its various stages are becoming separate and dispersed, rather than being under one roof, or inside one company. The distinction between manufacturing and services is getting blurred. And, not least, new computer software is helping companies to organise themselves better around the task of serving their individual customers; this is rewriting the rules of mass production.

All this feeds back into the structure of manufacturing. Whole industries no longer migrate, as shipbuilding did from Europe to Asia in the 1970s. Drawing on examples from the industrial heartland of America, from the *maquiladora* factories in Mexico and from the Hong Kong-based manufacturing network, the survey will argue that today manufacturing is becoming a genuinely international affair. The fancy work gets done in rich countries by skilled workers, the simpler parts elsewhere in the global supply chain. More and more of the process is handled by multinational companies, quick to see what is best done where. There is nothing to fear in this. Any country that is willing to use the skills it possesses will gain from joining in.

Erasing Boundaries

GLOBALIZATION

Address by PETER HELLMAN, *President and CEO, TRW, Inc.*
Delivered to the University of Michigan Management Briefing Seminars, Traverse City, Michigan, August 6, 1997

One of the wisest decisions taken by those who create this king-sized management briefing each year is the setting. Traverse City sits in one of America's most pleasant areas.

Of course, there is no idea so good that someone will not try to improve on it. I'd like to begin my remarks by doing just that. If you will be kind enough to ride along with me, I'd like to transport this entire group to an even more tranquil setting—just right for an after-lunch session—and for a good purpose.

Let's make some changes. First, a boost from a mood setter named Beethoven.

That helps. Now, let's change the scenery.

We'll go somewhere first by crossing a big body of water. Not Lake Michigan, but an ocean. It doesn't matter which ocean or which direction.

Just to be completely away from anyplace we can identify, we'll soar high up into a great mountain range. Maybe it's the Himalayas or the Andes or the Alps. Far away and way up. Where the air is clear and we can see a hundred kilometers into the future. And we'll come to rest in a broad and beautiful meadow on a high plateau. A green pasture. We are now nowhere, and everywhere. We have taken ourselves to the center of the world, which is, of course—as always—wherever we want it to be. This is a great place to think new thoughts. That's why we're here.

Now, with clear heads and creative minds, let's deconstruct this industry and then reconstruct it for tomorrow.

Our subject will be . . . globalization.

Globalization is an opportunity for prosperity that is equal to any in our history. It can be a force for positive change, if we manage it skillfully as an industry.

Why does globalization beckon this industry? The most common answer to date is that auto companies want to grow at a faster rate.

Existing auto markets in the world's major economies are growing today at a moderate pace—one to two percent a year.

Significantly, nations and regions all around the world that are moving toward fully industrialized status provide this industry a market that will grow far faster for many decades to come.

That demand will double the industry's total global potential for growth. Auto companies sensibly want to grow where the world is growing. Growth is the industry's stated goal. Growth defined as expanding markets, a higher volume of sales—and in due time, profitability.

It's that assumption about delayed profitability that has caught my interest. I would like to pose a major question at this point.

Is growth with the assumption of eventual earnings the right primary objective? Is it well defined enough, or fundamental enough, to shape the industry's strategies?

I think not. I share the view that we need far greater impatience on the subject of efficiency—as a means both to enlarge earnings and accelerate them.

The very process of globalization should be aimed. . . from Day One . . . at efficiency.

Specifically, our goal can be—should be—to target efficiency as an immediate way of reducing operating costs. This is the true advantage of globalization.

If we accept efficiency as the industry's primary globalization goal, we immediately see that thinking only about assembled cars can limit our perspective.

Sometimes, the right way to think about cars is not to think about them at all. Let's try a small experiment, and think first about supply.

Sixty percent of total costs come from the supply chain.

When you ship a car, you ship a lot of expensive air. But you can nest hundreds of valves in a single crate.

From *Vital Speeches of the Day*, November 1, 1997, pp. 57-60. © 1997 by City News Publishing Company, Inc. Reprinted by permission.

Parts are movable, and the movement is affordable and easy.

Today's tariffs present few problems.

Transportation costs are low.

Nations are cooperating regionally. Supply . . . as well as assembly . . . opens the door wide to cost cutting as we globalize.

As usual, there are obstacles.

Some of them are the brightest new ideas of recent years—ideas that no one dares to question.

One such untouchable idea is the current accepted thinking on just-in-time delivery by the supply chain.

JIT is essential, but no idea—however successful—should be exempt from re-thinking as we change our world.

Take what is already a typical situation.

An automotive company from anywhere in the industrialized world builds an assembly plant close to an emerging or growing market.

That plant becomes a magnet—for parts, components, systems and modules.

The supply industry has the challenge of feeding that assembly line.

Immediately, capacity is expanded or created within just-in-time range—geographically nearby.

That pattern looks good, doesn't it? It's comfortable and familiar.

It is also an inefficient use of resources—with costs built into the supply chain that must inevitably end up in the ultimate price of the vehicle.

This is globalization for growth. From the viewpoint of supply, it is not globalization targeted specifically and immediately at cost-effectiveness.

This traditional model ignores the real opportunity of globalization.

That's because each source of supply must be capable of meeting peak demand by the assembly plant. And that's a treacherous concept in a cyclical industry.

Floor space, machines, people and supporting systems must be built to 100% peak capacity, even though we know from hard experience that demand will fall, and the whole system will operate frequently at 80% or less of its total capability.

This is especially true in emerging markets with volatile economies.

We estimate that the full capacity of such supply plants is used only seven percent of the time.

Ninety-three percent of the time, some capacity sits idle, adding costs that must be covered.

There is a great management inconsistency in this pattern.

One interesting example makes the point . . .

In every automobile plant, there are today specialists who are applying the newest computerized control systems in order to reduce the peak electrical demand of the facility.

Their primary focus is not how much electricity the plant consumes.

The efficiency focus is peak demand, because the electric utility charges a much higher cost for high peak demand.

The electricity supplier makes that charge to cover the cost of having turbines and generators standing by to meet short periods of high demand.

It's a legitimate charge. No one disputes the concept.

The management inconsistency stares us in the face.

OEM's are applying every new idea in electrical system control to anticipate and avoid peak demand costs for electricity, just as they are applying the newest concepts in lean manufacturing.

At the same time, today's sanctified concepts in just-in-time delivery are used to insist on right-next-door peak supply.

Why are the costs of energy demand and parts demand handled differently—the one fought with sophisticated technology, and the other apparently unchangeable?

That is a stark and costly contradiction in an age of continuous improvement to cut costs.

Again, the real value of globalization is the green field opportunity it presents to root out such accepted ideas.

Let me suggest a new pattern in supply management—one that targets cost effectiveness in a globalizing automotive industry.

OEM's can insist, as a basic strategy in globalization, that suppliers invest in local facilities that operate at what electric utilities call base load.

Assuming, for the sake of argument, that the plant's base load is **80%** of its peak production requirement, only that **80%** should be built.

Overcapacity should be cut out of the expansion right from the start.

When the assembly plant defines its supply chain in base load terms, it must then address its peak load needs in new, aggressive ways.

When peak loading is handled creatively, the OEM immediately has a powerful, flexible solution to the high cost problems created by the traditional cyclicality of this industry.

We know that the greatest effect of cyclicality is regional.

I believe that regional swings will become more significant as we globalize.

We should anticipate the impact of such cyclicality from the outset by refusing to build in overcapacity.

Moreover, the effect of regional demand savings can be integrated by cross-regional sourcing.

The high cost of peak demand capacity can be alleviated by backing up base load supply plants with modern techniques in global sourcing.

Base loaded factories can be backed up in days or even hours by regional warehouses . . . or by other plants anywhere in the region or the world by means of airborne delivery.

Modern electronic systems can contribute enormously to the sensitivity and therefore reliability of such global supply systems.

Today's information technology can evaluate inventory and order parts within minutes—and do so many times a day.

Their new sensitivity reduces time as a problem.

They are a far more modern solution to just-in-time performance than mere physical proximity.

And they are needed under any scenario we can conceive for cost-effective globalization.

Base loaded supply facilities supported by sensitive, fast backup capacity and all but instantaneous communications can dampen the cost of down cycles and serve the needs of up cycles in any dimension.

We have already demonstrated that when demand exceeds a given supply plant's base load capacity, additional supply can be drawn from plants in other nations not facing the same demand.

Experience tells us that globalized patterns of supply management can reduce unit costs dramatically—we estimate as much as twenty percent.

And the savings will show up soon—not at some distant date when growth alone will work its magic.

An overall strategy on this scale is important to the supply industry because of the sheer scale of globalization.

The capacity for expansion of supply companies is not endless.

To support a full globalization effort, they will have to husband those resources and apply them to greatest effect.

Building green field plants with 20% excess capacity is not the best way to do this.

There is a second opportunity for cost effectiveness in global supply that is a pre-requisite to the base load concept.

Its essence, too, is to avoid the costs of doing more than is necessary.

It is standardization.

Not total standardization.

Not standardization as the enemy of innovation.

But standardization where it makes sense . . . just as standardization in the design of assembly plants makes sense.

Let me offer a typical example—the kind of small component that attracts little notice.

Today, there are far too many designs for seat belt buckles in this industry.

We estimate that there are over a thousand designs worldwide.

Seat belt buckles are not sales determiners.

So why do we have so many designs?

We have them because our industry prefers to start with a clean piece of paper when designing a new platform.

Somehow, high volume industrialized markets hide the inefficiencies of such activities.

But take the same proliferation of buckles to an emerging market, and their costs become as visible as fireworks.

Tooling, machines, people, inventories—all the basics of the expanding business—multiply.

Standardization is clearly a sensible solution to such waste and cost.

It is a valuable concept under any circumstance.

The simple truth is that all of our auto markets—established and emerging—need no more than a few good designs in many parts.

That's just one example.

We could say the same of wheel covers, door handles, cigarette lighters and many other parts.

OE's have made progress in standardizing across their platforms, but more can be done, especially in terms of standard industry-wide design.

Cost-effective globalization of supply attained through both standardization and base load capacity is a simple, attainable, immediate vision.

The technology and management systems to make it work already exist. Its attainment will benefit everyone.

The assembly plant itself benefits from this coordinated baseload/ standardization approach in supply.

The plant will have fewer part numbers with standardization, as well as reduced in-plant inventories, faster and easier training of assembly workers, quality that becomes more attainable through repetition, fewer changes on the line for a wider range of models, reduced need for supervision and management intervention.

All of these advantages impact cost control from the day the assembly plant goes into operation.

The benefits of base loading with high speed backup extend also to the host country.

Emerging nations want stable employment.

Unstable employment can have political as well as economic consequences.

A base load factory should rarely if ever lay anyone off.

When political leaders insist on local content, they are not thinking about the inevitable cycles of this industry.

Base load supply can and should be local content.

But to require peak supply as local content benefits no one.

No vision, however simple and elegant, can automatically become reality.

That truth brings us to the most profound conflict in any industry—the endless wrestling match between past success and future success.

The methods which brought past success always form a wonderfully effective pattern for future failure.

Cultural barriers within organizations are formidable.

Breaking the mold is not easy—especially when the mold has enjoyed success on the scale of today's effective supply chain methods.

To persuade an entire industry that workable, modern systems can be cost improved by a major strategic change will be a hard sell.

But I believe it is a sale that can and must be made.

What I have been advancing is a theory—in my case, a pet theory.

But it is a theory of such promise that I think it deserves its day in court.

More critically, it is a threshold theory that can bring major cost effectiveness to the process of globalization.

Unless we learn quickly whether such new patterns in supply and design are ideas with real promise for every vehicle manufacturer—we could watch the globalization process move forward dragging too much of our past unchanged into our future.

What we need is an independent examination of the true potential of the 80–20 supply pattern and its essential ingredient—selective standardization.

I think I know who that independent voice might be.

I have a proposal to make—one that I hope will catch the practical, serious interest of a few movers and shakers in this group.

This will require us to return to the here-and-now, to Traverse City . . . right back to this room, and to the longstanding relationship between this industry and the University of Michigan.

I have already spoken to key people at the University's Office for the Study of Automotive Transportation, whose sponsorship of this annual gathering says everything about their commitment to innovation.

I have asked them whether they would be willing to examine the feasibility of this whole supply concept.

They are prepared to begin such a study almost immediately.

They suggest an early definition of the nature of the study—supported by seed money from a supply company.

TRW has already committed the necessary seed money. OSAT stresses that such a study is a major undertaking. Nothing like it has been ventured by anyone to date.

Even though it is global, and though it requires input from the senior analysts of our industry, it will be affordable—costing about $200,000.

OSAT says that the study can be completed to the stage of a preliminary report in about a year—perhaps soon enough for a verbal presentation at this meeting next year.

The final report can be issued in print a few months later.

Let me stress that, despite the initial support of my company, this will be an industry oriented study.

We and the University will soon be calling on key global suppliers to take part—and to support the study financially.

My company has already assured OSAT that we will play that role as well.

The University has also suggested an OEM Advisory Council as part of the study process.

It will ideally have members from all major automotive centers worldwide.

These OEM's, however, will not be asked to supply financial support.

This is a supply industry initiative all the way.

OSAT's research team will examine the status of other industries which already have such flexible, efficient global sourcing patterns in place.

They'll examine specific supply management patterns, and quantify cost savings.

Reliability will get plenty of attention.

The most promising candidates for standardization will be identified.

Most of all, they will define the new form of partnership that will clearly be necessary between automotive manufacturers and their suppliers as this industry accelerates its globalization activities.

My thanks to the professionals of the University of Michigan's Office for the Study of Automotive Transportation.

They are, as always, great friends to this industry.

It is time to get some specifics on the table for ideas of this kind.

Globalization is already well underway, but it offers no guarantees. Our emerging new markets are fragile.

We must go all out to keep break-even costs low, and suppliers appear to be missing some important opportunities.

We are behind the curve as a fully coordinated industry in working to link globalization and optimization—to target efficiency first and growth second.

We can catch up—if we start now.

I am confident that we will all embrace the creative changes that OSAT will identify. Imagination . . . boldness . . . and enterprise are the qualities that drive our world.

This is an industry that has from its first days placed great importance on innovation. Now, as we address one of the greatest opportunities in our history—true, cost-effective globalization.

I know we'll do the job that has to be done. Thank you.

■ **Global Language Training**

Are Expats Getting Lost in the Translation?

Expatriates can't just get by with English-only anymore. They need to speak their customers' languages—if their business relationships are going to flourish. Here's why all expat programs should include language training, and what can happen if they don't.

By Stephen Dolainski

We all know the image of the ugly American expatriate. It's the business professional who bulldozes his or her way through another country—speaking only English and making everyone around him or her pull out their English phrase books just to keep up.

Although the ugly American image is yet another stereotype that's shattered each and every time a U.S. businessperson goes abroad with a good knowledge of the customer's native language, it's still an image that's perpetuated in the expatriate community and in other business circles. But it shouldn't be. Not knowing the language of the land is a persistent business problem that's holding many professionals back from reaching optimum performance during their trips abroad.

Although English is widely spoken in the global business world, the language of business, as the adage goes, is the language of the customer. Increasingly, that language may not be English. And as U.S. companies—both big and small—look for new markets outside the major foreign financial centers such as Hong Kong, Paris and Geneva, they're beginning to realize they can't get by with just speaking English anymore. International human resources managers, already facing many challenges associated with relocating employees out of the United States, have the added responsibility of providing some form of language training for outbound expats, a task that may not be high on everyone's priority list.

But it should be—because companies are sending more expats to other countries than ever before, and because a better understanding of a customer's language can translate directly into profit.

Language training for expats is critical to global business success. The globalization process has been responsible for large numbers of Americans sent out of the country to expatriate assignments all over the world. An estimate by the New York City-based National Foreign Trade Council (NFTC) puts the figure at more than 250,000 on overseas assignments currently. According to the survey "Global Relocation Trends, 1995," conducted by the global relocation consulting firm Windham International based in New York City and the NFTC, the number of U.S. expats is expected to grow in the future.

Although these U.S.-based expatriates may bring expertise of their particular business or industry with them on assignment, they often only can communicate it in the English language. And as American companies start turning their attention to China, Mexico, Russia, Malaysia and markets outside the big foreign financial centers, something's surely going to get lost in the translation.

"If Americans spoke other languages the way Norwegians, for example, speak English, we'd take over the world." So says Jack Keogh, the director of client services for Mayflower International Inc.'s relocation division in Carmel, Indiana. In the global business world, U.S. business professionals—monolingual by and large—are at a disadvantage, relying on bilingual secretaries and interpreters to translate for them.

For example, using interpreters many help U.S. expats understand basic conversations with clients, but it won't necessarily help them with the nuances of what their customers are trying to discuss. While interpreters are an important business tool, they also can be another barrier to client relationships. "Your interpreter can have a 20-minute conversation with [your client] and you'll get a four-word answer," says Carrie Shearer, manager of compensation for Caltex Petroleum, a Dallas-based oil company that recently tutored 300 employees in the Thai language before sending them to Thailand.

More than just words are lost, says Robin Elkins, senior manager of Bennett and Associates Inc., a relocation and cross-cultural consultation firm in Chicago that works with *Fortune 500* clients and others. "English may be spoken in the office, in the workplace and in the expatriate community, but it's not always spoken outside those environments," says Elkins.

Employees who are about to go on an expatriate assignment must realize when they accept that assignment in another country where English isn't the norm, that learning the basics of the country's language should be viewed as a direct part of the assignment—not as a nice add-on skill.

And there's often more than just business at stake. There's also the not-so-small matter of the person simply getting around in the location they're visiting. "If expats can't interact with the locals in the markets and in the streets, they're missing a lot about the thinking and character of the local people," says Elkins. These experiences also influence expats' ability to assess situations back at work, and they'll often make wrong assumptions about people they're managing.

Kevin Murphy, director of international HR for Community Energy Alternatives, Inc., a small Ridgewood, New Jersey-based power producer with 18 expat employees on assignment, says, "Language training is incredibly important. It just makes everything easier.

"In China or Latin America, English isn't the major language, and you're at a tremendous disadvantage if you don't speak the language. So it makes sense to get whoever is going [there] up to speed with the language as soon as possible." Easier said—in any language—than done. But it's vitally important to the success of expatriate assignments.

Language training helps global business relationships thrive. The NFTC estimates that the average one-time cost of an expatriate relocation is $60,000. Corporate language

Need Help in Setting Up a Language Training Program?

HR managers who've never set up a language-training program can get some help establishing criteria to evaluate the features and benefits of language-training programs in the "Standard Guide for Use-Oriented Foreign Language Instruction." This seven-page guide is issued by the American Society for Testing and Materials (ASTM) and includes criteria for assessing needs and selecting instructors, descriptions of listening and speaking proficiencies, guides for evaluating instructors' performance and students' progress.

To order the guide, which costs $18, call ASTM customer service at 610/832-9585 or write ASTM, Customer Service, 100 Barr Harbor Drive, West Conshohocken, Penn. 19428.   —SD

training programs need to contribute to the success of international assignments.

Says Beth Gegner, regional manager in Europe for Blanchard Training & Development Inc., which is based in San Diego, California: "If someone in a foreign country has two vendors, and one speaks the language and the other doesn't, it's almost guaranteed that the one who has the language skill has more of a chance to get the account than the one who doesn't."

Language skills, says Murphy of Community Energy Alternatives, help build the kind of teamwork needed to succeed overseas. "Once you get into a country, and you don't have your act together as a team, you'll find out very quickly that the people in that country will not only steal your lunch, they'll eat it too. So you've got to glue [yourselves] together as a team. Part of that is picking up the language skills."

Cementing business-related communication may be the primary objective, but it's not necessarily the only objective. Knowing the language of the land can also help an expat feel less isolated. Shearer felt that language training was especially important when Caltex sent approximately 300 employees to a rural location in Thailand during the initial stages of building a refinery there. Because of the refinery's remote location, not as many people would speak English as in the capital city, Bangkok.

"You could get by at work without speaking Thai," says Shearer, "but how are you going to converse with the maid or [with a vendor] when you go to the open-air market? There's no way to even look at a coin and know what it is, because Thai is based on Sanskrit and doesn't look [anything] like English."

The good news for Shearer was that she knew about the project in 1994, 18 months in advance. Caltex, which employs approximately 10,000 people worldwide, only has 250 employees in the United States. Many employees who worked on the Thailand project were Caltex workers from South Africa, Australia and other countries.

"A lot of front-end work was being done in Dallas, so we had eight or nine [people of different] nationalities working in Dallas on this project, which made it easier to organize language training for everybody," Shearer explains.

In 1994, she contracted Berlitz to give Thai-language classes to the English-speaking employees and their spouses. A refinery can be a dangerous place, so Caltex employees also were taught to understand Thai vocabulary like "danger," "fire," "watch out," words that might be shouted out in an emergency. "When people are under stress, they're going to speak in their native language [unless trained otherwise]," says Shearer.

Caltex also brought 75 Thai workers to Dallas for technical training before the project commenced. They first were given a six-week, live-in immersion course in English. All together, Caltex ran 30 weeks of training.

Caltex has since decided to set up English-language training in Thailand for workers before they're brought to Dallas for technical training. Knowing what the need is ahead of time helps employees, their managers and HR to plan on which language training program method is best for a given situation.

Typically, before any language training takes place, the expat's personal and professional readiness for the assignment is assessed. But expats aren't the only ones who can benefit from language training. Gegner thinks there's also value in a company training all its employees "on a minimal level" in the language of the foreign companies it does business with. "If delegates visit the United States, they're going to feel much more at home if [workers] here could just say, 'Hello, how are you?' to them."

Helping inbound foreign national employees improve their English skills is another objective of companies like St. Paul, Minnesota-based 3M Co. and Caltex. Most of 3M's tutors are assigned to work with inbound workers already familiar with English but who want "to improve their English skills so they can be more produc-

> Learning a language in the in-between moments can be better for many soon-to-be expats than scheduled classes.

tive on the job in St. Paul," says Margaret Beaubien, 3M's language services administrator.

Tutors are usually employees' spouses, an advantage for inbound workers, says Beaubien, because "our tutors have a knowledge of how 3M works and can field questions from the foreign-service workers . . . and we're providing a lot more than language instruction."

The immersion approach usually works best.
Although tutors, classes and other methods are available sources of language training, perhaps the best place to learn a language is in its homeland, called "total immersion." Because this may not always be a practical option, the next best thing is a simulated immersion program—an environment in which only the target language is spoken and the student is exposed to different accents, three-way conversations, telephone role-playing, and other clearly defined social and business situations. An intensive program like this, which can cost several thousand dollars, might comprise a predeparture three-day crash course emphasizing business and courtesy communication. For the expat who has time, the immersion approach could be the way to go.

Berlitz, based in Princeton, New Jersey, is well-known for its immersion programs. International relocation and cross-cultural consulting firms like Bennett and Associates also offer highly personalized immersion preparation that's tailored to the expat's international assignment.

Ideally, training can continue once the expat is at his or her destination. Bennett and Associates uses its worldwide network of resources to locate qualified tutors. Berlitz operates more than 320 language centers worldwide. According to Michael Palm, Berlitz's North American marketing manager, curriculum, texts and instructional methods are universal (the centers aren't franchised), offering what might be called a seamless advantage: An expat can begin studying Japanese, for example, at a

Berlitz center in America and then once the expat is in the assigned country, he or she can pick it up again on the same page.

Intensive predeparture training, like immersion instruction, however, may not meet a company's needs. Kathy Hoffman, director of international human resources of the Norwalk, Connecticut-based ABB, recalls, "About five years ago, we tried some intensive courses, but reports back from the individuals said they found it better to get trained when they were actually overseas." She agrees that it may be more motivating when you're in the environment and can practice daily, than if you're sitting in a classroom trying to pick up a language. ABB, the U.S. arm of a global engineering group, sends approximately 200 people all over the world each year, most of whom are project workers who don't generally receive language training. Approximately 70 ABB employees, mostly management-level employees, receive foreign-language training once they're in the country, says Hoffman.

But who has time?
Many expatriates who are preparing for an international assignment, however, have little or no time for lengthy, intensive language training. That's when HR managers have to intervene with other tactics.

John Freivalds, managing director of JFA, an international public relations firm in Minneapolis, thinks he has a solution: *guerrilla linguistics*—learning several carefully chosen words and phrases, targeted to a country's business culture, that an expat can speak at the appropriate moment to impress locals that he or she knows more about a language and culture than he or she really does.

Although guerrilla linguistics may bring momentary success, the tactic is only temporary and probably works best for someone who has much global experience and speaks several languages.

Self-instructional materials such as audio tapes provide a practical alternative to tutors, classroom study and guerrilla linguistics, according to Jeffrey Norton, president of Guilford, Connecticut-based Jeffrey Norton Publishers Inc., one of the country's largest producers of self-instructional language courses. Learning a language in the in-between moments (between meetings or at lunch) or during off-hours can be better for many busy soon-to-be expatriates than scheduled classes.

Typically, an HR person is the primary impetus behind employees using self-instructional tapes, Norton notes, and adds that inquiries about such tapes have increased in the last three years. It figures that even if soon-to-be expats can't schedule large blocks of time to learn a new language, they probably can find snippets of time here and there to learn a language.

What Language Can Cost

If language training is an investment in the success of the expatriate on international assignment, then how much does a good investment cost? That, of course, depends on what kind of training is used, who provides it, where it takes place, how long it goes on and how many employees are participating. Here are a few examples of costs for language training, self-instruction, translation and interpretation:

■ Ten-day immersion program for one individual, including all materials (any language): $4,500.

■ *Guerrilla linguistics*—a written phonetic list of 30 to 40 key terms and phrases: $500–$1,000.

■ Two-part, self-instructional, beginning Japanese course of 24 cassette tapes (30 hours) and two texts: $430.

■ One hour of interpreting time (any language): $325.

■ Twelve-week (48 hours), university extension, intermediate Spanish conversation class: $280.

■ Three-part "executive" Japanese self-instructional course of six cassette tapes ($5-1/2$ hours) and three texts: $225.

■ "Russian for business" self-instructional program of three cassette tapes (three hours) and phrase book: $65.

■ Document translation: About $.25 per word for translations to or from French, Italian, German or Spanish (FIGS); more for other languages.

—SD

But beyond these language training methods, there's another longer-term approach and philosophy that companies can adopt for language acquisition.

Make language acquisition a company goal.
International human resources professionals might consider making language acquisition more of a global company objective, rather than just a situational tactic.

At 3M's headquarters, what began 30 years ago as informal, lunch-time get-togethers to practice German, has become a well-loved employee tradition and a unique company asset. It's called the "Language Society." In the beginning stages of the society, volunteer teachers were recruited

Language Training Improves Global Business at ARCO

Johnna Capitano isn't planning to go to China, but this spring she took a 12-week class in Mandarin Chinese. Now she can exchange greetings in the dialect, and she knows enough to be careful when she uses the Chinese word *ma*, which, depending on the intonation, has different meanings, including horse, mummy and mother.

"It was very challenging, because the tones are difficult to master," says Capitano, a Los Angeles (LA)-based human resources development consultant for ARCO Products Co., the downstream refinery and marketing arm of ARCO. "At times it was very frustrating, not being able to pronounce a word the way the instructor kept repeating it."

But Capitano stuck with it and was one of 10 employees who completed a pilot class in conversational Mandarin Chinese that the company conducted this spring. Twice-weekly classes, which met for 1-½ hours at a time, were held at ARCO Products Co.'s two sites in Los Angeles and in Anaheim, California. The company is exploring potential business opportunities in China and has already hosted Chinese delegations on tours of its LA refinery. Capitano will probably be involved in hosting future delegations.

Paula Johnston, ARCO Products' human resources consultant for international projects, set up the pilot language training in response to employees' requests. "Members of our technical team who had been to China to analyze business opportunities found it was difficult to communicate because everything was done through interpreters. We've also had several Chinese delegations visit ARCO, and did everything via interpreters. We thought since we're just looking at opportunities now, why not use the time appropriately and offer Mandarin classes before things heat up?"

Johnston requested bids from three vendors: a university, a consulting firm on the East Coast and Berlitz. Berlitz was selected, Johnston says, "not only on the basis of economics, but [also because] it offers a great deal of flexibility. It's a firm we could utilize not only at the beginning level, but also later for a total immersion program if somebody was actually selected for an assignment, and even in China for follow-up training. [The company offered] continuity and consistency."

Johnston set up classes during work hours at the company's LA refinery site, where Capitano took the class. She also set up a class at the firm's engineering and technology facility in Anaheim so employees wouldn't have to travel. About 28 employees began the classes, but enrollment ultimately dwindled to about 10.

"It was very tough, because some people's schedules were just too busy or they were placed on special projects," explains Johnston. "Some people probably couldn't keep up or just lost interest."

Capitano agrees. "People would get tied up in other projects, and it was difficult to pull away and say, 'Oh, I've got to go to my Mandarin class now.' Employees—and the company—all have to make language acquisition a priority.

"A language isn't easy to learn, especially when it's so different, like Mandarin. It really has to become a work priority that everyone understands," says Capitano.

Johnston is in the process of seeking feedback. Although her impressions, so far, are good, she doesn't want to overplay it. Why? "Because we did lose people for a variety of reasons," she says. Of the people who completed the program, the response, she reports, is "pretty enthusiastic." Although the reports are mixed, learning their customers' language can never be a futile endeavor. Because language training at ARCO hasn't been an afterthought, the wheels of global business are spinning with greater efficiency.   —SD

---

from employee ranks by other employees and classes were formed. Today, at the company's St. Paul location, the Language Society has about 1,000 members who are current or retired 3M employees or immediate family members. Classes in 17 languages, which are taught by a cadre of 70 volunteer teachers, meet once a week for 45 minutes during lunch. There's a nominal fee ($5) to join the society, and 3M supplies texts at cost to members.

Participation in Language Society classes has no official connection with employees' jobs, says Beaubien. Participation is voluntary, and employees are motivated by a variety of personal and professional reasons to study a foreign language.

"We have people who may be working in customer service and who are studying Spanish and they may receive calls from Latin America. They're better able to field those calls," says Beaubien. "3M has also opened a homepage on the Internet, and we're receiving inquiries from all over the world, and, of course, they're coming in different languages. The society is being contacted to translate those messages."

Language training at 3M isn't limited, however, to Language Society classes. Beaubien also manages a tutoring program for outbound and inbound employees, using more than 20 tutors who are either former teachers or hold ESL certification. The decision to receive language tutoring is left up to the individual employee and his other department manager, says Beaubien.

But not all employees are eager to learn a new language—even if it will benefit them in their jobs.

Motivate expats to know their customers' languages. "It's difficult," says Brian Connelly about the Spanish classes he's currently taking twice weekly after work. Connelly is manager of Pan-American operations for Blanchard Training & Development, a position that will require him to travel several times a year to Latin America. "I work 10 to 12 hours a day, and then go to class two times a week, and try to study in between."

Learning a new language requires time, effort and motivation. With all the responsibilities of an international assignment, it's difficult to take the extra time necessary to learn a new language. It's especially hard if language learning must be reserved for unpaid, after-work hours, even if companies reimburse instructional costs (and generally, they do). More than 60 percent of the companies surveyed by Windham International and the NFTC for the "Global Relocation Trends" survey offer cross-cultural orientation to expats (which generally includes a language training component).

And, according to Elkins, about 80 percent of Bennett and Associates' *Fortune 500* clients offer language training. "But," she says, "not many corporations encourage language fluency. They think they only need enough language to get by, because they'll have a [bilingual] assistant or secretary or have an interpreter."

Shearer of Caltex says that motivation is an "individual thing. You can force people to do something, but you can't force them to learn something." Caltex didn't require its outbound employees to learn Thai before going to the remote refinery project, and classes were offered after work. Still, about 85 percent of the employees took the training, with 75 percent completing it. A few people did so well, Shearer arranged private tutoring lessons for them, and Caltex paid for it.

Financial incentive is a tried-and-true motivator, and one that Murphy of Community Energy Alternatives employs. "If you hire a secretary [who knows] stenography, you'll pay that person a little more for [that] skill. So when a person picks up language skills, I want to be able to give [him or her a reward]." Murphy uses a performance appraisal submitted by the expat's manager that includes a language-skills evaluation. No matter what language a person speaks, everyone speaks the language of money.

Murphy tries to make it as easy as possible for expats at his firm to pick up language skills. He negotiates to purchase a block of time for the year with an outside vendor to provide onsite language training at his company's Ridgewood, New Jersey, headquarters. He schedules classes for employees during work hours. Murphy believes in continuing language training in-country, and negotiates that into his contract as well.

This is the type of long-term approach to language training that companies must adopt for future success in global business.

When all is said and done... As cel phones and the Internet link the Earth's remotest locations, the world grows a little bit smaller. Ironically, American businesses are realizing just how vast and culturally diverse this planet is—and that most of its inhabitants don't speak English.

Says 3M's Beaubien: "It's becoming critical that companies have employees who not only have studied other languages, but also who have received some cultural training and who understand how we can do business with people who are different, how we can work together as productively as possible. That only happens when you understand another culture and the best way to do that, of course, is through language."

As for HR professionals' part: Language training must be an integral part of a company's expatriate program. It can no longer be viewed as just another accent or add on. Because when your client in Mexico says, "Quiero comprar un contrato de un millón," (I want to buy a million dollar contract), the last thing you want your expat employee to say is, "Huh?"

Stephen Dolainski is a Studio City, California-based free-lance writer. E-mail laabsj@ workforcemag.com to forward comments to the editor.

GLOBAL EXECUTIVE

Getting What You Pay For

Most agree that it's best to hire local people, even at executive level, when setting up shop overseas.

By John Davies

The script is about greed, power, lust and the trouble you can get into if you don't know much about hiring foreign nationals overseas: A promising young computer executive suddenly learns from a factory in Malaysia that his breakthrough product has stopped working. The mystery deepens when a former girlfriend is named his boss, and she moves to eliminate him. In the high-tech battle that follows, the executive breaks into the world of virtual reality to discover how people she hired overseas are leading the firm to disaster.

That's the outline of *Disclosure,* a novel and film that author Michael Crichton says is based on events that occurred at a Seattle computer company.

On the screen, Michael Douglas portrays the bewildered executive, who discovers how quickly years of international effort can go bad. There are no rampaging dinosaurs as in *Jurassic Park.* Incompetent handling of foreign workers proves to be an equally effective monster.

For global executives, it's a cautionary tale.

With the worldwide growth in business, more US executives find themselves assigned to establish or expand overseas operations with foreign nationals, from top executive to assembly line workers, who are best-suited to carry out corporate strategy.

They must decide whether to hire an overseas agent, find a qualified expatriate, bring in a consultant, form a joint venture or employ an executive search firm. They may have to choose from several potential countries to select a base.

What do you want?

A company planning to set up overseas can't do any effective hiring until it has formulated goals and established strategies to meet them. International business advisers at management schools, consulting firms and executive search firms all say that while it may seem elementary, too many companies plunge into overseas hiring without knowing what they want to accomplish.

> "People sometimes think they'll save by sending an expatriate instead of paying the premium to hire a foreign national. It doesn't always work out that way."

"You have to know your objectives and strategy before you start," states A. Paul Flask, managing director in the Chicago office of Korn/Ferry International, the world's largest executive search firm. "Either your own people can figure out the goals, or you can use a consultant, or hire somebody to help you figure out those goals, but you don't want to get an expert at implementation and ask him to figure them out."

Once goals are set, a company has to decide whether its operation will be small enough to deal with a foreign-based representative, who may or may not have other interests to look after, he says. Sometimes, a company is lucky enough to find a joint-venture partner that fits in with US corporate culture and uses the American business to increase its clout or take up slack from otherwise unused capacity.

But a mismatch between agent and company, or between firms, can cause problems as the business grows, Mr. Flask points out. At that point, many companies search their own ranks and may try to establish a foreign office with an expatriate. Others advertise, only to be inundated with hundreds of resumes, mostly from unsuitable people.

Larger companies, however, may turn to executive search firms, sometimes called "headhunters," to find qualified candidates. For a fee of 15 percent to 30 percent of the candidate's first-year salary, a search firm takes a careful look at what a company wants. Researchers then comb through databases of qualified people known to be looking for jobs and then confidentially approach those working for competitors to see if they would be interested. They screen the candidates, verifying their claims, and narrow down the list of candidates.

Mr. Flask, who specializes in emerging markets, contends that when the person sought is to be in charge of an overseas unit, the search may focus on foreign nationals who know the territory they will work. "A fee of $20,000 to $80,000 to hire a foreign national may sound expensive, but when you consider that in Beijing, you're going to pay $13,000 a month in rent to get quarters for an expatriate, having someone who can live in Chinese housing may be a plus," he contends.

Such foreign nationals also don't suffer from the American style in negotiations. "In Asia, things are often done very obliquely," Mr. Flask says. "Americans have to understand they just can't stand up and ask 'Am I going to get screwed here?' when they're dealing with Asians. You have to build relationships." An effective top executive for an Asian operation must be bi-cultural.

Rapid growth in Asia also means that there is a shortage of effective and trustworthy, bi-cultural top executives, and American companies will pay a premium to retain them.

In other parts of the world, it may be easier to find a successful foreign manager who is just as much at home within the culture of the US corporation as at home, he suggests. More expensive labor benefits and tougher layoff rules may apply to personnel hired in Europe, but the differences in business culture are not as severe as between the United States and Asia.

"There's still a lot of chauvinism in Europe. For instance, you still have to be careful if you want someone who's calling on Poland not to hire a former enemy. But the problem in Europe is not so likely to be cultural background," Mr. Flask continues.

At the same time, the number of international companies hiring European workers is relatively small compared with the number of foreign companies in Asia hiring Asians. One study estimated that the number of Asians working for foreign companies grew by almost 30 percent per year during the early 1990s.

"There's no doubt that Asia is going to see the largest percentage of growth in the hiring of foreign nationals for at least the next few years," Mr. Flask adds.

Cross-cultural know-how

Others also cited understanding two cultures as the trickiest part of hiring executives and staff in a foreign country. "That's the single biggest problem we have when we try to help US companies set up offices and hire people in Japan," says Hiroyuki Euguchi, industrial cooperation specialist at the Japan External Trade Representative Office in New York.

American companies usually understand that they must tailor their products for the Japanese market, he explains, but still don't understand Japanese traditional ways of doing business. Without some immersion in Japanese language and culture, they cannot follow standardized formats for carrying on negotiations, such as the junior man-senior man relationship, in which each partner in

a negotiating team is expected to fulfill certain roles.

"An American company doing business in Japan has to be able to negotiate with the Japanese. And because negotiations in Japan are not like negotiations in America, foreign hiring is one of the more difficult problems," he claims.

Allen Christian, an international trade specialist in the Japan office at the US Commerce Department, adds that cultural differences, lifetime employment at Japanese firms and the slowdown in Japan's economy have all made it difficult for US firms to hire Japanese workers there.

But he adds that the Commerce Department is also advising would-be exporters that it may be time to reconsider setting up an operation in Japan. A sharp drop in office prices (See *IB*, April 1996) and the growing success of American-made goods in Japan's software, furniture, apparel and sporting goods markets are creating new opportunities.

At the same time, a growing number of Japanese women are looking for jobs and advancement in a society where very few rise to the rank of manager. American firms can take advantage of that combination.

The problem that most US companies encounter when they try to do business in Japan, and elsewhere in Asia, is that potential obstacles are rarely spelled out in law or regulations the way they might be in the United States, the trade specialist indicates.

Instead, Japan relies on a huge bureaucracy that may conceal countless obstacles to product distribution. "They're working on changing that, but the progress is slow," he says.

Hiring Japanese workers away from companies that have traditionally offered lifetime employment isn't difficult for larger US companies with a reputation for treating employees well, but may be hard for smaller ventures without that reputation. Smaller firms often find either a representative or a joint-venture partner.

Mr. Euguchi says he sometimes describes himself as "a gateway to Japan" for companies seeking information on how to find a Japanese representative or a suitable partner there. The US International Trade Administration also has desk officers who can get smaller companies started.

Hong Kong Ease

If Japan remains a somewhat enigmatic place to do business, the same isn't true in Hong Kong, notes Benjamin Chu of the Hong Kong government's Industrial Promotion Office.

Hong Kong is such a good place for foreign companies to set up business that between a quarter and a third of its workforce of nearly 3 million people are employed by foreign firms. "No one knows the exact num-

ber because we treat foreign offices the same way we do domestic offices," he observes.

There is no minimum wage, business taxes are low and employers can hire and fire at will, although some employees may be entitled to severance. Prime sites in downtown Hong Kong can be among the most expensive in the world, but a range of lower-cost property is also available. Foreign companies can hire directly from the market, in contrast to the situation across the border in China, where they must either form joint ventures or accept workers assigned by the government.

With its long history as a British colony, Hong Kong residents typically speak English and represent a part of the Chinese culture most interested in commerce and trade. A large percentage of residents have two or more jobs, creating an affluent consumer group interested in buying western products.

Chinese puzzle

Conditions for hiring workers are a lot more complex across the border in China, claims Jenny Pei, marketing manager at China Business Consultants Group in Chicago. There, companies setting up either representative offices or wholly owned subsidiaries must hire only from government agencies, not from the work force. Only approved joint ventures can hire on their own behalf.

Sometimes, Chinese government officials will search out joint venture partners in the United States, but US companies normally have to search for themselves to find a joint venture. "We do a lot of case studies about prospective joint ventures," she asserts. "Some companies can do it on their own, but a lot of them find having a consultant very helpful." (See *IB* December 1996/January 1997)

Lower inflation and a convertible currency makes China more attractive to US business, but extreme government regulation makes such business development difficult.

"You just cannot imagine the extent to which things are regulated," she says. "China is a planned economy and the government plays a much heavier role than even in Japan—government is in your face anywhere you go. It's not just a different cultural system for negotiating, it's an entirely different economic and political system."

But China shares one thing in common with Japan. Companies that think they've figured out the regulations often discover that they apply to foreigners in a special way. "There's usually some hidden agenda that will make it more difficult for foreign people to do business in China," she comments.

About 75 percent of American businesses in China hire their local employees through joint ventures. As long as they abide by any employment contract they might have signed, those companies can hire and fire freely. For instance, a large US corporation like General Motors, which has 30 operations in China, might face pressure from officials near that plant, but couldn't be forced to keep it running.

"It's no problem to find a place to rent, as long as you're prepared to pay," she adds. A recent survey of the world's 10 most expensive cities to rent office space included Beijing, Shanghai and Guangzhou.

Screening Clout

Once a firm has defined its goals, selected a top executive, chosen a site and established the best form of government, it still must hire lower-level employees. Often, that's left up to the top executive in each country, particularly if he is a foreign national with a superior understanding of the region's labor market. But if an operation is large or will involve employees from a variety of sites, screening tests may still be required.

Mobil Corp. of Fairfax, VA, for example, reports that its personnel managers have developed tests for foreign job applicants. One such test, used for applicants at a job site in Indonesia, helped them evaluate mechanical skills and the ability to learn, things Mobil couldn't always gauge clearly from educational records. The oil company

worked with the American Psychological Institute and the UK's Cambridge University to design the test. Its executives said the result was a valid test that accurately measured the skills Mobil sought.

But many companies don't have the time or resources to design their own tests. Medium-sized firms sometimes rely on educational consultants to evaluate job applications. Companies such as World Education Services Inc. in New York City and Evaluation Service Inc. in Albany, NY, screen thousands of applications each year to ensure job candidates are truthful and to give an employer some idea of how a foreign education might compare with a domestic one.

Much of their screening is done for foreign students who want to work in the United States, but such firms can also screen would-be foreign employees. Evaluations may be required to identify foreign-trained job applicants who meet specific standards needed for medical, teaching, scientific or engineering posts.

Employers hiring a foreign staff may also use outside services to verify work experience records, test language fluency for those who will be translating as part of their job, and look into the possibility of criminal violations.

Inquiries about criminal activity are the most difficult to carry out, because some countries either don't permit countries to ask, or are not obligated to say.

Under US immigration law, any foreign employee convicted of even a minor crime

might be denied entry into the United States for training or consultation purposes if the possible sentence for the offense exceeded a year. What's more, even foreign employees who have never broken the law in their own country can run into trouble if they made payments that would constitute bribes in the United States.

Legal payments to an adviser involved in a contract award might be a "finder's fee" or a "consulting cost" in some nations, but in the United States these payments constitute violation of the American Foreign Corrupt Practices Act, which may prevent a foreigner from entry to the United States.

In the movie, *Disclosure,* an inexperienced manager faces government pressure to hire more workers in Malaysia. She decides that she can avert a politically motivated labor problem by simply cutting equipment costs and hiring more workers.

To cut costs, she eliminates the air filters that keep dust out of computer drives during assembly, and cuts back on the number of precision mounting machines that ease computer chips into place. Instead, the extra workers push ultra-delicate computer chips into circuitboard sockets with their thumbs. Within days, computer drives are malfunctioning erratically.

"People sometimes think they'll save by sending an expatriate instead of paying the premium to hire a foreign national," observes Mr. Flask at Korn/Ferry. "It doesn't always work out that way."

HUMAN RIGHTS

A COMPANY WITHOUT A COUNTRY?

Unocal says it won't leave Burma, but it may de-Americanize

The U.S. is becoming a distinctly inhospitable place for Unocal Corp. to hang its hat. In March, a federal district court judge in California ruled that the oil and natural-gas company could face trial in the U.S. for human-rights violations in Burma, where it has a $340 million stake in a natural gas project. Then, on Apr. 22, the Clinton Administration imposed sanctions against the rogue state that prohibit further investment by U.S. companies.

Faced with this political pressure at home and drawn by the lure of growth opportunities abroad, the $5.3 billion company is taking a radical step: It is de-Americanizing.

Legally, the company is headquartered in El Segundo, Calif. But in company literature, Unocal says it "no longer considers itself as a U.S. company" but a "global energy company." In practice, it is slowly moving assets, research spending, and management to Asia.

On Apr. 21, Unocal opened what it calls a "twin corporate headquarters" in Malaysia. President John F. Imle Jr. and several senior executives will be posted there while CEO Roger C. Beach remains in California. This after it sold off its U.S. refining operations and gas stations to Tosco Corp. in March for $2 billion. Analysts say Unocal may decide to

LIGHTNING ROD Democracy groups say this gas pipeline—a Unocal joint venture—will fund the brutal military regime

spin off its Asia headquarters into an entirely separate company—and in so doing, may be able to bypass U.S. sanctions. "They have structured their operations now so it would be easy for them to pull out of the U.S. if that's what they needed to do," says Jennifer Weinstein, research associate at NatWest Securities Corp.

Unocal says it has no immediate plans to relocate or spin off the international division. Its Burmese operations, the company says, are grandfathered under the sanctions, and 62% of Unocal's revenue is still generated in the U.S., mostly from production in the Gulf of Mexico and Alaska. But two-thirds of its $1.34 billion in capital spending currently goes to Asia—Central Asia, Bangladesh, China, and elsewhere in Southeast Asia—as well as Burma. "Our major focus area for future investment is Asia," Beach wrote in a recent letter to shareholders. In Burma, Unocal owns 28% of a joint venture with France's Total, the Petroleum Authority of Thailand, and Myanma Oil & Gas Enterprise, a state-owned company. The four are investing $1.2 billion to develop a natural-gas field in the Andaman Sea south of Rangoon and a 254-mile pipeline to Thailand set to open in mid-1998. A proposed second pipeline, to Rangoon, could be halted by U.S. sanctions.

Unocal isn't the only U.S. company operating in Burma. Texaco Inc. and Arco Corp. have invested in smaller natural-gas projects. But pressure is mounting against multinationals that deal with the State Law & Order Restoration Council

(SLORC), the military junta that has run the country since forcibly taking power in 1988. PepsiCo, Philips Electronics, and Motorola, among other U.S. and European companies, have pulled out of Burma in the last year. That leaves Unocal the biggest U.S. player in the country by far—and, so, a magnet for activists.

RUNAWAYS. The anti-SLORC campaign may only drive Unocal closer to divorcing itself from the U.S. Overnight, it could join a growing community that includes Hongkong & Shanghai Banking Corp., which moved to Britain in 1993 ahead of China's takeover of Hong Kong, and ABB Asea Brown Boveri Ltd., which now calls itself a "multidomestic corporation."

Other multinationals will be watching. The human-rights case appears tenuous: Total is building and running the Burma operation, while Unocal is just an investor. But if the trial is heard in the U.S., it could have broad implications for other U.S. companies operating abroad. "It should be a warning that companies should be aware of what

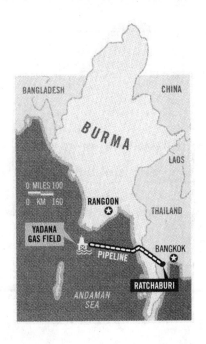

any of their government partners are doing," says Robert W. Benson, professor of international human-rights law at Loyola Law School in Los Angeles. Or they should start thinking about a new home.

By Sheri Prasso in New York, with Larry Armstrong in Los Angeles

Opportunity Knocks

Few companies have escaped the region's economic hammering unscathed;
fewer still have taken advantage of it. Here, we showcase three nimble
groundbreakers who are honing their competitive edge
in the midst of the crisis.

**By Simon Elegant in Hong Kong,
Kuala Lumpur and Singapore**

Lunchtime at Singapore's venerable Cricket Club and stately, plump Hugh Peyman is in full flow, discoursing learnedly on everything from Malaysian politics to the intricacies of Singapore banks' balance sheets. But one question brings a moment of uncharacteristic silence from Dresdner Kleinwort Benson's chief Asian strategist: Can he name an Asian company that has responded aggressively—even creatively—to the turmoil of the last seven months?

Peyman's silence is eloquent, but not nearly as pointed as the laughter with which some analysts greet the same query. Elizabeth Tran, a fund manager in Hong Kong for American Express, though, isn't laughing when she complains that many Asian companies have been acting "like hedgehogs in headlights."

For his part, Alex Liu of management consultants A.T. Kearney compares what companies in Asia are going through to the experience of terminally ill patients although these firms aren't doomed, just glacially slow in facing up to reality. "There are five stages, shock, denial, anger, sorrow and acceptance," Liu explains. "It's still way too early for most of them to get all the way through the process, but the sooner any individual enterprise can do it, the better. Eighty percent of companies are still in denial."

There are a few exceptions, of course—corporations that have risen to seek opportunity in the mayhem of recent months rather than just sitting on their hands. "It's like wartime," says Liu. "A few heads are beginning to emerge from the rubble." Such companies, whose very scarcity makes their actions all the more notable, are responding to the crisis by taking over weakened competitors and other companies on the cheap, and expanding away from dependence on their ailing domestic markets. The scramble for firesale Asian assets, they prove, need not be restricted to Western buyers.

It will be many months—even years in some cases—before observers can pass full judgment on such decisions. But how these companies chose to act offers a vivid illustration of the dangers and opportunities thrown up by the region's financial crisis. Perhaps more importantly, these groundbreakers are taking steps that the mass of less adventurous companies will follow when markets stabilize and corporate chieftains start to look anew for investment opportunities.

The following pages offer detailed glimpses of three such pioneers. It is a mixed group, ranging from Hong Kong-based First Pacific, one of Asia's most diversified companies, to Malaysian canner and packager Kian Joo and the Development Bank of Singapore, the largest Southeast Asian bank. But all share two characteristics: the willingness to move quickly and decisively once they have spotted an opportunity, and a shared corporate strategy whose advantages are so obvious that it hardly seems worth mentioning: nurturing a sound balance sheet.

His own balance sheet was very much on the mind of First Pacific's managing director Manuel Pangilinan late last year. Asian markets were in apparent free fall and some $3 billion in debt weighed heavily on First Pacific. It also suffered from a limited cash flow from its principal businesses.

Several months and a massive restructuring later, Pangilinan can allow himself a small smile as he acknowledges that First Pacific will soon have shrunk that debt to around $300 million. Resplendent in a purple tie and matching braces the soft-spoken Filipino adds that the company should have more than $900 million in cash by the end of March. And it is most definitely looking to be among the first Asian companies to take advantage of the crisis to make some major acquisitions.

Pangilinan has always been known as ready—even eager—to cut a deal a quality that proved useful when he was contemplating a way to extract First Pacific from its predicament last year. To his unsentimental eye, the group's main businesses were a distinctly mixed bag, some of which were expendable.

Most important was the Dutch trading group Hagemeyer, which had returned a whopping 24% on investment for 15 years and accounted for a third of First Pacific's income. But there were negatives. Despite the spectacular figures, the investment "didn't deliver enough cash," according to First Pacific spokesman Robert Sherbin.

From *Far Eastern Economic Review*, March 12, 1998, pp. 10-12, 14. © 1998 by Review Publishing Company Limited. Reprinted by permission.

Roving Eye

First Pacific

Base: Hong Kong

Business: Property, banking, consumer goods; diversified conglomerate

1997 net profit (estimate):
HK$1.4 billion
1998 net profit (estimate):
HK$1.1 billion

Action taken: sold two prime businesses, realizing some $2 billion, part of which was used to pay down its considerable debt burden.
Attempted but failed to buy 20% stake in San Miguel; now looking to make another acquisition.

Source: Lehman Brothers

On the March

Development Bank of Singapore

Base: Singapore

Business: Banking and financial services

1997 net profit (estimate):
S$412 million
1998 net profit (estimate):
S$490 million

Action taken: Bought controlling stakes in Thai-Danu Bank in Thailand and Bank of Southeast Asia in the Philippines

Source: UBS Research

Only one-third of First Pacific's $67 million accounting profit from Hagemeyer in 1996 was paid as a cash dividend. Furthermore, a series of purchases by Hagemeyer partly funded through new share issues was forcing First Pacific to pay out more and more to keep its controlling stake from being diluted.

What to do? To deal-maker Pangilinan, the answer was straightforward: sell. In mid-January, the company announced that it would sell not only Hagemeyer but its Hong Kong mobile-phone business, Pacific Link, as well. The sales realized some $2 billion. About half of that, the company said, would be used to reduce debt and recapitalize its Asian operations, most notably Metro Pacific, its troubled Philippine property and telecommunications arm. It was a move described by Lehman Brothers at the time as "necessary, effective and constructive."

Even in pre-crisis times, there was debate among the group's senior executives about Hagemeyer's role in the company, Pangilinan says. "We'd go for a road show in Europe and the States and invariably the question was asked, 'You're an Asian group, what are you doing with a fairly significant European and American asset?' " Then, there was no real reason to sell, Pangilinan says, because "First Pacific could raise the funds on its own ... Now, clearly the situation has changed with the Asian crisis."

Although growing competition was the driving force behind the decision to sell Pacific Link, Pangilinan adds that in light of what has happened to the region, and to Hong Kong in particular, "the timing couldn't have been better. We got under the bar just in time before the door closed."

The decision to undertake a major restructuring and its nimble execution in the midst of a chaotic market has drawn broadly positive reviews from analysts. Shareholders also seem to approve: First Pacific's share price has almost doubled since the restructuring plan was announced in mid-January, far outpacing the Hang Seng index, which it had lagged by some 43% in the previous six months.

If the company has an Achilles' heel, analysts agree, it is Metro Pacific, the company's Philippine arm. Metro holds two apparent aces: the development rights to Fort Bonifacio, a huge chunk of prime real estate in Manila; and Smart Phone, a mobile-phone provider that added 623,000 new subscribers in 1997. But Fort Bonifacio is unlikely to start showing a profit for a number of years, while Smart Phone is still vacuuming up development costs and equally unlikely to provide any cash flow for some time.

Thanks to the restructuring, however, First Pacific will pump up to $300 million into Metro, which should go a long way to seeing it through all but a complete meltdown of Asian economies.

First Pacific's restructuring will leave it with almost $1 billion in its pocket and a hungry eye. The eye has already focused on San Miguel Brewery in the Philippines, which fits the company's desire to buy into a market-leading concern with a recognizable brand name. That deal fell foul of politics in the Philippines, however, and Pangilinan says the company will move carefully, biding its time until another similarly sound prospect appears.

Another example of corporate nimbleness comes from the most unlikely of sources, the headquarters of the Development Bank of Singapore. The largest bank in Asean, DBS long had a reputation for conservatism that less kind observers described as over-cautiousness. But like a dowager stepping into sneakers and performing a pirouette, DBS waded into the turmoil of the Asian financial crisis in December and January to take control of banks in Thailand and the Philippines that were available at firesale prices.

The moves weren't completely unprecedented. For several years now, both the Monetary Authority of Singapore—the country's de facto central bank—and government officials have pointed out the limitations of the domestic banking market and underlined the need to regionalize. Heeding that call, DBS has led the way in expanding out of Singapore, both in its lending and in setting up branches and joint ventures in the region. "Basically," says the bank's president and chief operating officer, Ng Kee Choe, "we have this vision: to become a regional bank with global reach."

But that vision became entangled in the regional financial panic. John Doyle, who tracks the Singapore banking scene for brokers UBS, notes that with some 30% of its loans outside Singapore, DBS has the largest exposure to the region of any of the country's big four banks. He projects that the bank will see a net profit plunge of about 35% in fiscal 1997 because of that exposure, with only a slight improvement in its prospects over the next few years. Considering that DBS is already paying a heavy price for its earlier adventurousness, its two recent acquisitions are tangible proof of a gritty determination to fulfill its vision.

The purchase of Thai-Danu Bank—DBS injected 6 billion baht ($137.5 million) into the Thai institution, upping its original 3.4% stake to 50.27%—was particularly noteworthy: Despite acquiring a controlling stake, and seven of the bank's 15 board seats, DBS agreed to leave management control in the hands of existing Thai executives. That deal—the first major sale of a financial institution to a non-Thai buyer since the finan-

Can Do

Kian Joo Can Factory Berhad

Base: Kuala Lumpur, Malaysia

Business: Canning and packaging

1997 net profit (estimate):
56.8 million ringgit
1998 net profit (estimate):
59.4 million ringgit

Action taken: aggressive debt collection early in 1997; expanded overseas sales; bought competitor Carnaud Metal Box

Source: Dresdner Kleinwort Benson

cial crisis hit—was seen in Bangkok as a face-saving compromise that could prove a precedent for further buyouts in a country skittish about placing Thai companies in foreign hands.

While few would question the timing or cost of DBS's recent acquisitions, some analysts do have questions about what exactly the bank wants from its new purchases. "You have to have a sense of what you want to accomplish," says Doyle of UBS, "whether you want to be competing in the retail market" in Thailand or the Philippines. "In the long term five or 10 years down the road—consumer banking will be quite attractive in those countries. But right now, you have to question whether they are tying up capital they could use more profitably elsewhere."

"We do not want to be a mass retail bank per se," Ng responds. "We want to be in a selective market niche in individual banking in these countries . . . individual banking at the higher levels, which would combine investment-banking products, private-banking products. It's a different market niche, a different focus." The takeovers of Thai-Danu and the Bank of Southeast Asia in the Philippines, Ng is at pains to stress, are long-term strategic investments. "We are prepared to sit it out and wait for the region to recover, as it will."

Thinking about the long term and taking action accordingly is a lesson that Anthony See, who runs canner and packager Kian Joo

in Malaysia, learned the hard way. "Ten years ago, during the recession of 1987, our gearing was very high," he says, sitting in his factory office outside Kuala Lumpur and shaking his head at the memory. "We learned our lesson. Now, we do have a cash surplus of about 100 million ringgit [$27 million] in the bank."

It's just as well that Kian Joo had that cash hoard. The collapse of the Malaysian ringgit, which saw the currency shed half its value before recovering some ground earlier this year, was grim news indeed to a company whose raw materials—chiefly aluminium and tin plate—are imported and priced in U.S. dollars but whose income was chiefly in ringgit. "When I saw him then, he was very down about the company," one analyst confides of a meeting with See last October.

But despite his apparent gloom, See had already begun taking measures to stave off the effects of the market turmoil. As early as the first months of 1997, he says, changes in his customers' purchasing patterns and other signs had warned him of a possible economic slowdown. He instructed his sales staff to stop offering credit and push hard on collecting outstanding bills. As a result, he says, the company now has almost no bad debts to worry about.

'We have this vision: to become a regional bank with global reach'

—DBS President Ng Kee Choe

Such moves were prudent but paled next to the huge increases in overheads the weakened ringgit triggered. Hence the decision to focus more on overseas markets. Kian Joo immediately called distributors in Japan, for example, where the weaker ringgit allowed the company to offer much more competitive prices. See also began contacting distributors in nontraditional markets such as Cambodia, Laos, Burma and Saudi Arabia. Previously, the small numbers involved in such markets

hadn't been worth pursuing aggressively. But the need for foreign exchange—all such sales are conducted in U.S. dollars—changed all that. See says the push should raise the percentage of Kian Joo's overseas business from 11% of total sales to 15% this year, a figure some analysts say could hit 20%.

Michael Greenall, head of research at the brokerage Caspian in Kuala Lumpur, points out that Kian Joo wasn't only taking defensive measures. The company also set out to consolidate its hold on the Malaysian domestic market, snapping up ailing competitor Carnaud Metal Box for the bargain price of 17.5 million ringgit. The market turmoil had hammered Carnaud, one of Kian Joo's two major competitors in the canning market. Declining domestic revenues and ballooning expatriate costs prompted Carnaud's owners, giant U.S. packager Crown Cork & Seal, to sell. With the purchase, Kian Joo will boost its share of the Malaysian can market from around 42% to 55%.

Greenall also says that Kian Joo was in final negotiations late last year to acquire another competitor—Guo Lene Packaging—for 50 million ringgit from the Hong Leong group. The deal—which would have left Kian Joo with more than 75% of the domestic market—fell through because of what analysts describe as differences over price. Woo Mun Thye, an analyst at Kleinwort Benson in Kuala Lumpur, says that Hong Leong may well come back to Kian Joo, "after Guo Lene has bled a bit more."

See won't comment on the failed Guo Lene deal. Instead, he drives a visitor to a dark, barn-like structure the length of two football fields that houses two production lines for aluminium cans. Inside, the noise is physically palpable: the liquid thrashing of well-oiled machines and the rumble of conveyor belts combining to form a constant, thrumming roar, above that an irregular cacophony of crashing, banging and thumping as the cans are pressed, punched and moulded.

When the tour ends, See steps into the sunlight outside, closing a heavy door and abruptly cutting off the inferno of sound. He is in a reflective mood. "By rights, it should never happen, that something like that," he points back at the factory, "that takes so long to build up could be destroyed overnight." But his natural pragmatism soon asserts itself and See dismisses the vagaries of far-off markets with a wave of his hand. "We've got nothing to complain about. We learned our lesson: keep your gearing low and cash in the bank."

■ **Global Workforce**

Global Culture

Who's the Gatekeeper?

International business and trade are growing at breakneck speeds. Two book authors describe why HR is pivotal in guarding and communicating a global corporate culture in the 21st century.

By Michael S. Schell and Charlene Marmer Solomon

The growth of international business is phenomenal. According to the U.S. Department of Commerce, in the last 25 years U.S. investment overseas catapulted from more than $75 billion to in excess of $717 billion in 1996. Foreign investment in the United States went from $13 billion to $630 billion during the same period, and about one-third of all of this growth occurred since 1990. And the estimate of the number of U.S. expatriates is 350,000 by the National Foreign Trade Council. Activity—both in dollars and in human resources—continues to heat up and will only get more complex and demanding as the new century approaches.

This adapted excerpt from "Capitalizing on the Global Workforce: A Strategic Guide for Expatriate Management" by Michael S. Schell and Charlene Marmer Solomon (McGraw-Hill 1997), offers global HR managers a preview of what to expect. Based on interviews with dozens of senior human resources managers from Europe, Asia and the United States, it enumerates the primary challenge facing human resources in the next decade: creating a global corporate culture.

Driven by global competition and accelerated by technological achievements, organizations and their workforces are in an unparalleled transformation process. In 1987, Indianapolis-based Hudson Institute's landmark study, "Workforce 2000: Work and Workers for the 21st Century" (by William B. Johnston and Arnold H. Packer) predicted the increasingly diverse composition of the American workforce by the turn of the century and also examined several of the economic factors shaping this trend. Yet, changing demographics of the workforce are only part of the picture. What about the revolutionary changes in organizations that these people would staff? Moreover, despite its accuracy, the report forecast demographic trends based on predictable events. And while those predictions stunned American business leaders at the time, they pale in significance when compared to the impact of globalization on business in the 21st century.

In 1991, hard on the heels of that study, Armonk, New York-based International Business Machines (IBM) and New York City-based consulting firm Towers Perrin undertook an extensive survey that examined the role of human resources professionals in helping organizations gain a competitive advantage. Building on the findings of "Workforce 2000," this study melded the workforce issues with business challenges to explore the implications of both the changing organization and workforce on the human resources management function. Entitled, "Priorities for Competitive Advantage," it predicts the following vision for the Year 2000.

Human resources will be:

- Responsive to a highly competitive marketplace and global business structures
- Closely linked to business strategic plans
- Jointly conceived and implemented by line and HR managers
- Focused on quality, customer service, productivity, employee involvement, teamwork and workforce flexibility.

Even though those predictions still are currently accurate, they didn't anticipate the importance of the following factors:

- The impact of the global workforce and the proactive role that the HR function must assume in order to capitalize on it
- The need to create a corporate culture with global application
- The need to build HR competencies into the line manager function—in streamlined, reengineered organizations
- The urgency to reengineer the HR function to make it consistent with the strategic business mission and structure of the organization

It's certainly not surprising that many forward-thinking organizations have already embarked on the arduous task of reinventing the human resource function—and the organization as a whole—with this paradigm shift in mind. But through thoughtful analysis and ongoing efforts, it's possible to avoid many obstacles and pitfalls while evolving toward a global mindset.

What organizations will look like in the future. The trend toward smaller, independent operating units and smaller companies staffed by employees recruited from a worldwide talent pool will continue as we cross into the next millennium. These firms will focus on, and strive for, an empowered workforce. They will become increasingly flatter and faster than their predecessors, and they will move toward a strong corporate culture that binds employees into a unified organization. Managers in these organizations will require global skills and cultural fluency. Driven by the demands of a global workforce and the central role these individuals will play in the viability of the business, the human resources function will be part of the core business activity.

As the influence of technology expands and the business world relies on instant access to information to make quick decisions, global managers must be prepared. Those changes come at an ever-increasing rate accelerated by technology and the simultaneous momentum it picks up. Worldwide telecommunications, particularly computer networks, have made the transfer of information—and knowledge— a task achieved in seconds. That makes it possible for companies—and even individual workers in Malaysia or India—to play a key role in developing new products and making key discoveries. In the 21st century, new products and discoveries will as likely be generated in Malaysia and will need to be available in the United States.

Develop a cohesive culture.
As access to markets, raw materials, capital and an educated workforce standardizes around the world, American companies lose some of the unique advantages enjoyed in the past. They compete with companies around the world that use the same technology, have equal access to materials and people, and might even have lower labor and other operating costs.

What will distinguish companies from one another? The vision of the organization and how clearly its values are integrated into the business function. In other words, how effectively those values can be translated and implemented into a powerful corporate culture. The global HR manager plays a pivotal role in developing, protecting and communicating the corporate culture. It occurs through every step of the process, from developing policies that can be embraced by all members of the organization to communicating corporate values at the recruiting and hiring stages, as well as to training and performance management that maintains consistent corporate messages.

Since organizations no longer will be ethnically uniform, corporate culture will take on far more important meaning. It will be the blending of the various values of the worldwide workforce into a single value system that embodies the organization's vision. That corporate culture, together with

---

Action Steps for Global HR

Based on interviews with dozens of senior human resources managers from Europe, Asia and the United States, authors Michael S. Schell and Charlene Marmer Solomon recommend ways in which HR can be most proactive and effective. This information is based on their book, "Capitalizing on the Global Workforce: A Strategic Guide for Expatriate Management" (McGraw-Hill 1997). The steps below enumerate components of the primary challenge facing human resources in the next decade: creating a global corporate culture.

1. Take every piece of the HR function and see how it can be impacted beneficially by technology.
2. HR must be a partner to line managers. Don't abdicate your responsibilities to line management.
3. Educate self and others about business issues.
4. Facilitate change management. Help people prepare and adapt to change and complexity through education.
5. Understand customers, products/services and so on. HR must be able to educate others about how the company does business and how HR is helping in that process.
6. HR must be considered on the same level as business development, finance and marketing. It must be seen as being either as important as these functions, or the most important function, in the organization. If HR isn't reporting to the top, there's something wrong.
7. Be willing to transfer responsibility to employees. By empowering employees, HR can do away with tunnel vision of one's function and focus on broader issues.
8. Identify skills for new HR professionals. These will include financial/business skills as well as sales skills by which HR can sell their partnership to the business manager's world.
9. HR professionals must force themselves to speak the language of business managers. They must be aggressive about being included and respected.
10. The HR function must constantly prove it's relevant to the project.

Source: "Capitalizing on the Global Workforce: A Strategic Guide for Expatriate Management" (McGraw-Hill 1997) by Michael S. Schell and Charlene Marmer Solomon

---

its norms, will unify an organization's workforce, enhance communications and enable global teams to work together to achieve a single common purpose.

Corporate culture is the glue that binds this organization together, but the greater the number of elements and the more diverse they are, the tougher it is to hold everything—and everyone—together.

HR managers are the guardians of the corporate culture.
Melding a common vision is no easy task; communicating it consistently across cultures is even more difficult. Yet, coalescing various nationalities and cultures into a streamlined organization capable of speed, teamwork and flexibility will become essential to ratcheting up profits and productivity. The challenge: to recruit and hire the most gifted, talented and qualified employees from all over the world and enable this diverse group of people to join in a common cause.

In other words, the thinking required for today's (and tomorrow's) global leaders will enable them to make decisions and take actions for which there's no clear precedent and no predetermined corporate position. They will need to factor in and value intuitive judgment and ambiguous data to create competitive products and services. Somehow, the culture of an organization will have to allow these global leaders the freedom to use their global intuitiveness and sensibilities with the same credibility as it accepts data from spreadsheets. This leadership will take courage and wisdom, which is, in reality, nothing new for winning organizations. Therefore, as the modern corporation is redesigned and the traditions and practices of the past are discarded, HR can choose to be at the forefront—reexamining, redefining and facilitating the change.

Michael S. Schell is president of The Windham Group in New York City.

Charlene Marmer Solomon is a contributing editor for WORKFORCE and the keynote speaker for the first installment of the GLOBAL WORKFORCE SEMINAR SERIES. E-mail charsol@aol.com to comment.

Don't Get Burned By Hot New Markets

Be ready to do your part in evaluating proposed new locations.

By Charlene Marmer Solomon

The numbers practically sizzle off the page. Just look at this: U.S. direct investment abroad skyrocketed from $467.8 billion in 1991 to more than $796 billion in 1996, according to the U.S. Department of Commerce. U.S. corporations have invested more than $10 billion in China alone, another $23.6 billion in Brazil, $16 billion in Thailand and $12.5 billion in Indonesia. Many of these hot markets are growing at a robust GDP (gross domestic product) of 7 percent, or 8 percent a year.

One after another, American companies seek—and seize—new opportunities in rapidly growing yet unfamiliar markets. China, India, Brazil, Russia and many others offer untold opportunities with their megamillion populations and growing consumer classes. And U.S. firms are right there, offering everything from light bulbs to power plants and selling their expertise about manufacturing, marketing and managing global operations.

The ventures into these new territories can be profitable. But they also can be risky. New entrants must navigate gingerly over a hotbed of coals that will singe those who are unprepared for myriad laws and regulations, unfamiliar political and social structures, and unpredictable infrastructures, all of which manifest themselves in workforce issues. That's why HR's role is central to strategizing, planning and ultimately helping to choose new business destinations.

It's clear that the critical issues to success in new markets often revolve around typical HR concerns: hiring, training, compensating and managing people—but in a multiplicity of environments and a maze of legal and political circumstances. These are complex and multilayered

business issues, to be sure, but they are, nonetheless, issues that require understanding and thorough business, labor, legal and social analysis through an HR perspective.

HR must participate in a business analysis of proposed locations. "We increasingly see whole new industries going out—information technology, telecommunications, specialized pharmaceuticals, agriculture, insurance—and we're also seeing companies that have been established internationally for many years going into new markets," says Bill Sheridan, director of international compensation services at the New York City-based National Foreign Trade Council.

Sure, there's money to be made. But what makes global executives choose certain destinations as most receptive or at least worthy of the difficulties firms must surmount? The decision must always begin with the business objectives.

"Before we venture into new markets, we now start with a detailed strategic market analysis. We look at our markets over the next five to 10 years and try to determine where we need to be in four or five years' time," says Patrick Morgan, human resources manager, Latin America Region for San Francisco-based Bechtel Corp., the construction giant. "It's important to actually think through what it is you're going to do, where your market is, what your relative chances are of being successful, and then begin to prioritize where you want to go after that."

Morgan is always a key member of the management team that assesses the big picture. The cost-benefit analysis factors in: the position of competitors, infrastructure as it relates to personnel (such as telecommunications), regulatory and trade barriers, and the tax situation (both cor-

Tips To Get You Started

Planning and becoming educated about new destinations is fundamental to the success of your endeavor. Follow these easy but crucial tips as you begin your exploration of new marketplaces.
- Network with colleagues who are already doing business successfully in the country.
- Ask about cross-cultural differences.
- Conduct a review of the local environment in the context of your specific kind of business.
- Evaluate two or three destinations.
- Examine existing educational and training opportunities—either at local universities or available through other businesses. —*CMS*

porate and individual). Ideally, the new market would be a country where there's an untapped need for your products or services; a quality, skilled labor pool capable of manufacturing the products; and a welcoming environment (governmental and physical).

Are there such countries? Indeed, each has its pluses and minuses (see "15 Top Emerging Markets"). While Singapore has an educated, English-speaking labor force, basks in political stability and encourages foreign investment, it has a small population. While Mexico shines as an excellent example of a country that has aggressively lowered its income tax rates (from 60 percent in 1988 to 35 percent today) and attempts to alleviate other governmental hurdles in an effort to attract foreign investment, it has severe pollution. Many countries in Eastern Europe possess an eager, hungry-to-learn labor pool, but their infrastructures create difficulties. And, while India holds enormous promise, conducting business there is complex and difficult.

India's promise lays in its attributes. According to "Venturing in India: Opportunities and Challenges," a 1996 Conference Board report, India's impressive economic reforms have made it quite attractive for corporate investors. Because of its British roots, it has a strong legal system, developed technology and a growing financial sector. Known for its well-educated workforce, world-class scientific, engineering and management talent, and business schools that churn out excellent job candidates, India offers a labor pool that values education.

These positive attributes can be outweighed by potentially negative ones, however. India has an inadequate infrastructure, for example, with problems such as frequent power outages and crowded, unpaved roadways. And most daunting is India's political environment and highly bureaucratic and protectionist government that stir the flames of anxiety among multinational business leaders. For HR, the Indian business environment requires adroit management of people amid mountains of regulations.

For instance, the government wrought havoc with Houston-based Enron Development Corp. for five years.

Enron (along with Bechtel and General Electric Co., both of which had been successful in India with other projects) was in the midst of building a $2.8 billion power plant. It was the first foreign-owned power plant in India and one of the largest foreign investments ever. When a new regional government was elected, officials shut down construction of the plant and entangled the company in a judicial quagmire of 24 law-suits for 16 months. Knowing situations such as these are probable, HR must determine which issues (staffing vs. regulations) are more compelling.

Consider the quality and availability of the local labor force. The greatest challenge in entering a new market is often the work-force, specifically senior management. "After you determine that you have a marketplace that's going to utilize what you're producing, you need to see if there is the capability and talent in the local workforce to support the endeavor," says Richard Bahner, human resources head at New York City-based Citicorp. "You really need to do a total balanced evaluation. Some of these places offer less-expensive labor, but if they don't have the capabilities you're looking for, it may not be a savings because you'll have to supplement it with a large amount of computer support, training or expatriates."

The extent of the staffing challenges depends on your industry. "If you're distributing Pepsi™, you can manufacture it locally and teach people how to sell it easily enough, but if you're in global banking, you've got a lot more restrictions," Bahner explains.

Citibank has experienced this in the Asia-Pacific region. With relationships in China and Hong Kong for almost a century, it had an advantage when it looked to expand into Indonesia and Thailand. But it was hampered by the need for an educated workforce. Citibank developed the market in Indonesia and taught the people about electronic banking—eventually generating millions of Citibank Visa cardholders. But the HR issues were daunting.

"The biggest problem is the dearth of qualified locals," says Bill Fontana, formerly of Citibank in Indonesia and now vice president of international HR for the National Foreign Trade Council. It's a big, big problem. There are so few qualified people who can take senior positions (among 200 million Indonesians), that other U.S. companies will bid for this unique individual. "It jacks up the cost of your senior local person, and then you begin to pirate people away from other companies because they speak English, they've worked at another multinational organization, and therefore, you would pay almost anything to get them onto your payroll. It leads to spiraling inflation in the workforce."

As an example, Fontana was recruiting for a treasury head at Citibank in Indonesia. The position was staffed with an expat, and he wanted to fill it with a local. It took more than one year to identify a qualified person. Citibank offered the man $150,000 and a guaranteed base of $100,000. "He turned me down," says Fontana. "He told me that the Bank of Bali was offering him more

15 Top Emerging Markets

The "Global Relocation Trends 1996 Survey Report," containing research collected by the National Foreign Trade Council and Windham International (both in New York City), identifies the 15 countries presented in the next four pages as emerging destinations for international assignments. These countries were chosen most often by the 192 respondents (representing

Country or Region [1]	Type of Government [2]	GDP Per Capita (US$) [2]	Inflation Rate [2]	Native Languages [2]	Travel Per Diem (US$) [3]	Entry Requirements [4]	Standard Workweek [4]	Labor Law Snapshot [4]
People's Republic of China (PRC) (Zhonghua Renmin Gongheguo)	Communist state	$2,900	10.1%	Standard Chinese or Mandarin, Yue (Cantonese), Wu, Minbei, Minnan, Xiang, Gan, Hakka dialects, minority languages.	Range: $119 – 226	U.S. citizens must have a passport and visa. Most business visitors on initial visits enter on tourist visas, which don't require a letter of invitation.	Mon. through Fri., 08:00 – noon and 13:00 (or 14:00) – 17:00.	Rules for hiring Chinese nationals depend on the type of establishment: wholly-owned, joint venture or representative office.
Republic of India	Federal republic	$1,500	9%	English is important for national, political and commercial communication. Hindi is the primary tongue of 30% of the people.	Range: $186 – 306	A passport and visa are required. Also: evidence of yellow fever immunization if the traveler is arriving from an infected area.	Most offices: Mon. through Fri. Some offices: Mon. through Sat.	Less than 2% of the total workforce is unionized. Worker days lost to strikes and lockouts have declined since 1991.
Federative Republic of Brazil (Republica Federativa do Brasil)	Federal republic	$6,100	23%	Official language: Portuguese. Also Spanish, English and French.	Range: $56 – 252	Travelers must have a temporary business visa (valid for 90 days) if they plan to transact business.	Mon. through Fri., 08:30 or 09:00 – 17:30 or 18:00 with a one- to two-hour lunch. Some factories: half-days on Sat.	Labor unions, especially in the most skilled sectors, tend to be well-organized and aggressive in defending wages and conditions.
Russian Federation (Rossiyskaya Federatsiya)	Federation	$5,300	7%	Primary language: Russian.	Range: $191 – 319	U.S. citizens must have a passport and visa. Visas are issued based on support from a sponsor: a Russian individual or organization.	40 hours per week.	Local labor mobility within Russia is limited by housing shortages and difficulties in obtaining government-required residence permits.
United Mexican States (Estados Unidos Mexicanos)	Federal republic operating under a centralized government	$7,700	52%	Spanish and various Mayan dialects.	Range: $61 – 255	U.S. citizens can apply for a business visa for up to 30 days on arrival in Mexico. Longer stays require a FM-3 visa.	48 hours, including one paid day of rest.	For overtime, workers must be paid twice their normal rate – and three times their hourly rate when more than nine hours per week of overtime.
Republic of Singapore	Republic within a commonwealth	$22,900	1.7%	National language: Malay. Other official languages: Chinese, Tamil and English.	$211	Passports are required. Visas aren't necessary for U.S.-based travelers.	44 hours: Mon. through Fri., 08:30 – 17:30 and Sat., 08:30 – 13:00.	The government places a ceiling on the % of foreign workers various industries may employ and a monthly levy for each foreign worker.
Hong Kong	Territory of China as of July 1997	$27,500	8.4%	Chinese (Cantonese) and English.	$344	Visas allowing residence and local employment for expats are granted on the basis of simple procedures.	Mon. through Fri., 09:00 – 17:00. Sat. was traditionally a half-day, but many companies now advertise 5-day workweeks.	Minimal labor relations difficulties. The average number of days lost due to industrial conflicts is one of the lowest in the world.

46,900 expats) as among the three countries they see emerging as assignment locations for their organizations. The countries are listed in rank order beginning with China, chosen by 27 percent of companies—down through Australia, chosen by 4 percent. The corresponding data fields included in this table were compiled from a variety of sources to delineate some of the HR-related concerns companies should have as they evaluate international assignment locations.

[1] - [8]Please refer to "Heading Notes" on the next 2 pages for additional details about each of the categories below

Labor Force [2]	Unemployment Rate [2]	Literacy Rate [2]	Telephone System [2]	Health & Medical Care [4]	International Schools [5]	Corruption Rating [6]	Hardship Premium [7]	Direct Investment (US$) [4]	U.S. Companies [4]	Embassy Information [8]
583.6 million (1991)	5.2% (1995)	81.5% (1995)	Domestic and international services are increasingly available for private use. Unevenly distributed system.	Co. insurance should cover emergency evacuations. Serious cases are often handled in Hong Kong.	9 schools in 6 cities	2	15 – 25%	Foreign investment (including U.S.): $38 billion in 1995.	Information not available.	**Embassy of the PRC** 2300 Connecticut Ave. NW Washington, D.C. 20008 Tel: 202 / 328-2500 E-mail: webmaster@china-embassy.org URL: www.china-embassy.org/
314.751 million (1990)	Info not available.	52% (1995)	Probably the least adequate system of the industrializing countries. Slows industrial and commercial growth.	Adequate care is available in population centers. Doctors and hospitals often expect payment in cash.	6 schools in 6 cities	2	10 – 20%	U.S. investment: $192 million in 1995.	CMS Generation Coca-Cola General Motors Guardian J. Makowski Williams Corp.	**Embassy of India** 2107 Massachusetts Ave. NW Washington, D.C. 20008 Tel: 202 / 939-7000 URL: www.indiaserver.com/embusa/
57 million (1989)	5% (1995)	83.3% (1995)	Good working system.	Information not available.	12 schools in 10 cities	3	0 – 10%	U.S. investment: $23.6 billion by end of 1995.	Alcoa Caterpillar Dow Chemical Ford IBM Xerox	**Embassy of Brazil** 3006 Massachusetts Ave. NW Washington, D.C. 20008 Tel: 202 / 745-2700 E-mail: scitech@brasil.emb.nw.dc.us URL: www.brasil.emb.nw.dc.us/
85 million (1993)	8.2% (1995)	98% (1989)	Enlisting foreign help to speed up modernization. A severe handicap to the economy.	Far below Western standards with severe shortages of basic supplies.	3 schools in 3 cities	2	10 – 25%	Foreign investment (including U.S.): $2.1 billion in 1996.	Information not available.	**Embassy of the Russian Federation** 2650 Wisconsin Ave. NW Washington, D.C. 20007 Tel: 202 / 298-5700 URL: www.russianembassy.org
33.6 million (1994)	10% (1995)	89.6% (1995)	Adequate domestic service for business and gov't, but the public is poorly served.	Dependable in the principal cities. Most private doctors have U.S. training.	15 schools in 10 cities	2	0 – 5%	Information not available.	Information not available.	**Embassy of Mexico** 1911 Pennsylvania Ave. NW Washington, D.C. 20006 Tel: 202 / 728-1600
1.649 million (1994)	2.6% (1995)	91.1% (1995)	Good domestic facilities and international service.	Information not available.	7 schools in a small country (3X the size of Wash., D.C.)	8	0%	Foreign investment (including U.S.) in manufacturing: $4.1 billion in 1996.	Approximately 1,300 U.S.-based firms.	**Embassy of the Republic of Singapore** 1824 R St. NW Washington, D.C. 20009 Tel: 202 / 537-3100
2.915 million (1994)	3.5% (1995)	92.2% (Age 15+ had some school; 1995)	Modern facilities provide excellent domestic and international service.	Information not available.	11 schools in a small region (6X the size of Wash., D.C.)	7	0%	U.S. investment: $13.8 billion by the end of 1995.	More than 1,100 U.S.-based businesses.	**Embassy of the PRC** 2300 Connecticut Ave. NW Washington, D.C. 20008 Tel: 202 / 328-2500 E-mail: webmaster@china-embassy.org URL: www.china-embassy.org/

Country or Region [1]	Type of Government [2]	GDP Per Capita (US$) [2]	Inflation Rate [2]	Native Languages [2]	Travel Per Diem (US$) [3]	Entry Requirements [4]	Standard Workweek [4]	Labor Law Snapshot [4]
Republic of Idonesia (Republik Indonesia)	Republic	$3,500	8.6%	Official language: Bahasa Indonesia (modified form of Malay). Also English, Dutch and local dialects.	Range: $110 – 305	Business visitors from the U.S. may obtain a 60-day short visit pass on arrival. Temporary residence visas may be obtained from the embassy.	Mon. through Fri., 08:00 – 16:00 and Sat. 08:00 – 13:00. Moslems are released for prayers every Fri. 11:00 – 12:00.	The government sets minimum wages by region. The minimum wage in Jakarta and West Java as of April 1997 is approx. US$ 2.40/day.
United Kingdom of Great Britain and Northern Ireland (U.K.)	Constitutional monarchy	$19,500	3.1%	English, Welsh, Scottish form of Gaelic.	Range: $150 – 294	Employees of British subsidiaries of U.S. firms encounter little difficulty in obtaining permission to enter and remain in the U.K.	Mon. through Fri. 09:00 – 17:30.	Information not available.
Argentine Republic (Republica Argentina)	Republic	$8,100	1.7%	Official language: Spanish. Also English, Italian, German and French.	Range: $120 – 223	Visas are no longer required for U.S. citizens traveling to Argentina. Passport holders are granted a 90-day visa on entry.	Mon. through Fri.	The labor code traditionally has been a disincentive in hiring. New regulations that allow greater flexibility in personnel mgmt. will help job growth.
Kingdom of Thailand	Constitutional monarchy	$6,900	5.8%	Primary language: Thai. English is the secondary language. Also, regional dialects.	Range: $80 – 167	Passports and onward/return tickets are required. Visas aren't needed for stays of up to one month.	Mon. through Fri., 54 hours for commercial workers and 48 for industrial workers.	All employers must determine the terms of employment for their staff. Those with 10 or more employees must specify working regulations.
Malaysia	Constitutional monarchy	$9,800	5.3%	Official language: Malay. Also English, Chinese dialects, Tamil and numerous tribal dialects.	Range: $121 – 165	U.S. business visitors don't need visas unless coming for employment purposes. Instead, they'll be given passes at the point of entry.	Mon. through Thurs. 08:00 – 12:45 and 14:00 – 16:45. Fri. 08:00 – 12:15 and 14:45 – 16:15. Sat. 08:00 – 12:45.	There are a number of national unions, but the government prohibits the formation of a national union in the electronics industry.
Republic of Venezuela (Republica de Venezuela)	Republic	$9,300	57%	Official language: Spanish. Also native dialects spoken by 200,000 Amerindians in the interior.	$184	To obtain a business visa, contact the nearest consulate.	40 hours per week maximum (non-manual labor). Offices: 08:30 – 12:30 and 14:30 – 18:00.	Law places restrictions on the employment decisions made by foreign investors; e.g., foreigners may not exceed 10% of employees.
Socialist Republic of Vietnam (Cong Hoa Chu Nghia Viet Nam)	Communist state	$1,300	14%	Official language: Vietnamese. Also French, Chinese, English, Khmer and tribal languages.	$244	Passports and visas are required. Any Vietnamese embassy can process visas.	Mon. through Fri., 08:00 – 17:00 and Sat. 08:00 – 11:30.	Labor is becoming more regulated. Foreign employers must pay income taxes for their employees, including steep rates for middle managers.
Commonwealth of Australia	Federal parliamentary state	$22,100	4.75%	Official language: English. Also native languages.	Range: $107 – 283	A passport and either a visa or an electronic travel authority are required for Americans traveling for business.	Mon. through Fri., 38 hours.	The negotiation of contracts covering wages and working conditions is gradually shifting away from the centralized system.

Heading Notes 1 – 4:

1: Source: Countries or regions were selected for this table because they were identified as emerging destinations for international assignments in "Global Relocation Trends 1996 Survey Report" put together by the National Foreign Trade Council and Windham International, both in New York City.

2: Source: The CIA World Factbook (www.odci.gov/cia/publications/nsolo/factbook). *GDP Per Capita* and *Inflation Rates* are 1995 estimates. *Literacy Rates* pertain to the percentage of the population aged 15 and over that can read and write, unless otherwise stated.

3: Source: The U.S. Department of State (www.state.gov/www/perdiems/9709/perdiems.html). Numbers are recommended per diem allowances for foreign travel.

4: Source: STAT-USA, U.S. Department of Commerce (www.stat-usa.gov). *Entry Requirements* and *Labor Law Snapshot* are short excerpts from the source and shouldn't be perceived as complete information. Some *Direct Investment* figures are "cumulative to date" and others are "annual." Some are "U.S." and others are "foreign."

Labor Force [2]	Unemployment Rate [2]	Literacy Rate [2]	Telephone System [2]	Health & Medical Care [4]	International Schools [5]	Corruption Rating [6]	Hardship Premium [7]	Direct Investment (US$) [4]	U.S. Companies [4]	Embassy Information [8]
67 million (1985)	3% (1994) (under-employ-ment: 40%)	83.8% (1995)	Domestic service is fair; international service is good	There are a few modern clinics in Jakarta, but expats generally fly to Singapore for treatment of serious illnesses.	23 schools in 20 cities	2	10 – 15%	Approved U.S. investment since 1967: $12.5 billion.	Arco Freeport McMoRan General Electric General Motors Mobil NYNEX	**Embassy of the Republic of Indonesia** 2020 Massachusetts Ave. NW Washington, D.C. 20036 Tel: 202 / 775-5200
28.048 million (1992)	8% (1995)	99% (age 15+ finished 5 years of school; 1978)	Technologically advanced domestic and international systems.	Information not available.	12 schools in 9 cities	8	0%	U.S. investment: $4.314 billion 1994 – 1995.	Information not available.	**Embassy of the United Kingdom of Great Britain and Northern Ireland** 3100 Massachusetts Ave. NW Washington, D.C. 20008 Tel: 202 / 588-6500
10.9 million (1985)	16% (1995)	96.2% (1995)	Modern system, but few private phones. System often goes out in rainstorms.	There are many competent doctors, dentists and specialists available in Buenos Aires.	6 schools in 1 city	2	0%	U.S. investment: totals $10 billion by mid-1996.	Information not available.	**Embassy of the Argentine Republic** 1600 New Hampshire Ave. NW Washington, D.C. 20009 Tel: 202 / 939-6400 URL: athea.ar/cwash/homepage/
32.153 million (1993)	2.7% (1995)	93.8% (1995)	Service to the general public is inadequate.	Medical care, especially in Bangkok, is adequate. Doctors often expect immediate cash payment.	10 schools in 4 cities	3	10 - 15%	U.S. investment exceeded $16 billion in 1997.	Ford General Motors IBM Kellogg	**Royal Thai Embassy** 1024 Wisconsin Ave. NW, Suite 401 Washington, D.C. 20007 Tel: 202 / 944-3600 E-mail: thai.wsn@thaiembdc.org URL: www.thaiembdc.org/
7.627 million (1993)	2.8% (1995)	83.5% (1995)	Adequate or good domestic service, depending on location. Good international service.	Information not available.	4 schools in 2 cities	5	0%	Based on approvals, U.S. projects valued at $1.2 billion in 1996.	Baxter International Exxon Intel Mattel Mobil Motorola	**Embassy of Malaysia** 2401 Massachusetts Ave. NW Washington, D.C. 20008 Tel: 202 / 328-2700
7.6 million (1993)	11.7% (1995)	91.1% (1995)	Modern and expanding.	Information not available.	6 schools in 5 cities	2	5%	Information not available.	Avon BellSouth Black & Decker Citibank Colgate-Palmolive Ralston Purina	**Embassy of the Republic of Venezuela** 1099 30th St. NW Washington, D.C. 20007 Tel: 202 / 342-2214
32.7 million (1990)	25% (1995)	93.7% (1995)	Considerable progress in some areas, far behind in others.	Most medical facilities don't meet interna-tional hygiene standards and lack qualified doctors and supplies.	3 schools in 2 cities	2	25%	Licensed capital for U.S. projects: $773 million in 1996.	Information not available.	**Embassy of the Socialist Republic of Vietnam** 1233 20th St. NW, Suite 400 Washington, D.C. 20037 Tel: 202 / 861-0737 E-mail: vietnamembassy@msn.com URL: www.vietnamembassy-usa.org/
8.63 million (1991)	8.1% (1995)	100% (1980)	Good domestic and interna-tional service.	Medical and dental services and all types of health facilities are comparable to those in the United States.	2 schools in 2 cities	8	0%	Information not available.	American Express Campbell Soup Coca-Cola Microsoft Philip Morris Toys 'R' Us	**Embassy of Australia** 1601 Massachusetts Ave. NW Washington, D.C. 20036 Tel: 202 / 797-3255 URL: www.aust.emb.nw.dc.us/

Heading Notes 5 – 8:

5: Source: "The ISS Directory of Overseas Schools 1997 – 1998" compiled by International Schools Services Inc. in Princeton, NJ (www.iss.edu).

6: Source: The 1997 TI-Corruption Ranking is a joint initiative of Göttingen University in Germany and Transparency International. The index uses seven survey sources and measures the perception of corruption by business professionals, risk analysts and the general public. Scores range from 0 (highly corrupt) to 10 (totally clean). (www.gwdg.de/~uwvw/rank-97.htm)

7: Source: Rochester, Wisconsin-based Runzheimer offers these U.S. State Department percentages as a general indicator of the appropriate salary increase that should be offered to an expatriate for accepting an assignment in these locations. Runzheimer cautions that it's best to seek customized data relating to your specific company.

8: Source: Contact information for all embassies was provided by The Electronic Embassy Site (www.embassy.org).

Research was conducted by Valerie Frazee, special projects editor for WORKFORCE and GLOBAL WORKFORCE. E-mail frazeev@globalworkforce.com to comment.

money! And the expatriate was only making about $115,000."

The situation is similar in other parts of the region. Experienced, multilingual Thais and Taiwanese can look to their talented colleagues in Hong Kong and China for ways to bid-up their going wages. As these countries develop, the competition for talent is becoming ferocious. Local companies are vying with foreign firms for the same employees.

One obvious solution is education. In addition to the traditional training that internationally experienced firms such as Motorola, Coca-Cola and McDonald's have conducted for years, there are now joint ventures between universities and businesses. For instance, Baltimore-based Johns Hopkins University has paired with Nanjing University in China. Based in the city of Nanjing, 100 students each year participate in a bicultural business program and living experience (a Chinese and an American student are roommates) that prepares them for senior-level management positions.

The receptivity to education varies by location. Eastern Europe is different from Asia-Pacific. "The work ethic is very strong, and equally important, there's a strong interest in learning," says Fontana. "When we went into Eastern Europe, the question [from employees] was, 'When do I get my next training course?' The thirst for training and knowledge is staggering." Training can rarely keep pace with need.

Evaluate laws and regulations. The next thing you need to think about is whether the government has created an environment receptive to foreign businesses. The question is: Do the laws enhance or inhibit the chance of success?

No matter where in the world your company ventures, as economies develop and competition increases, local companies become stronger, and they often exert pressure on local governments to tighten regulations regarding foreign firms. For example, work permits for expats aren't as easy to obtain in many parts of the world as they once were. Mandated workforce practices can either aid or decrease your company's opportunities. Labor law and its effect on compensation and benefits requires research and comprehensive understanding.

One of the first questions must be: How restrictive is the labor law? "As an example, generally, in countries where the British flag has flown, the labor code is simple, straightforward and employer-friendly. Where the Napoleanic code has predominated, you find labor legislation that's complete, complex, confusing and expensive," says John de Leon, regional director of international HR consulting services for Deloitte & Touche LLP, based in Wilton, Connecticut. "In Asia-Pacific, generally speaking, labor law (although very different from the U.S.) isn't as restrictive and permits companies greater freedom to make decisions."

These restrictions refer to the presence of work councils that get involved in activities Americans would consider purely management decisions. They may restrict part-time and temporary employees. They will have provisions that affect termination. For example, in the United Kingdom, although there's a cost associated with terminating employment, it's far less expensive and less complicated to calculate than in most parts of Latin America.

You can't assume you're operating with a U.S. frame of reference. In many countries, the labor code includes a concept called *acquired rights*. The code says you can't take away anything from an individual. So, for example, job content, responsibilities, pay and benefits must remain constant. Another concern is strong labor unions. And, still another difficulty is that many rapidly growing countries spur growth by being less restrictive when a company enters the country to set up business. "It's at the back end where you get a lot of intervention," says Fontana. "I let go of nine people in Indonesia at a cost of $1.2 million in severance pay.

And then there's compensation and benefits. Social costs, medical-care costs, pension and social security costs differ greatly from one country to another. And often, the ways in which salaries are quoted and designed are significantly different. "Until recently, India capped the base salary for executives at a pretty low level in hard currency because of the socialist mindset," says Sheridan. "So, firms offered myriad allowances—cars, drivers, servants, clothing. American companies saunter in and want to roll it all into one basic salary, and they aren't seeing the other factors involved."

In other words, if you aren't discerning, country-specific labor laws and regulations can begin to eat severely into profits. Or, if you re not careful, you may get burned because you've unwittingly trespassed legal boundaries.

Ask yourself, "How hospitable is this country to the business?" Beyond the more narrowly defined and obvious HR issues, receptivity and overall friendliness to foreign business are major factors in selecting a destination country. How protectionist is the environment? What types of bureaucratic, regulatory and economic constraints exist? Is there political tension or security risk? Corruption? A workable legal system? Economic stability?

All of these issues complicate the ability to staff your operations. For instance, if your company faces political security risks, how will that affect the expatriation of employees? If it's a highly bureaucratic and regulated country, what will that do to your ability to hire and fire employees? If there's gross corruption in the local business environment, how will you train your staff to handle the situation?

How do all these elements interact? Latin America, for example has always ranked prominently in international operations for Farmington, Connecticut-based Otis Elevator Co. Worldwide. The company had maintained escalator factories throughout Latin America at one time, and then it consolidated most of the operations in Brazil (as well as small operations in Argentina and Uruguay). "Even though the business climate was kind of 'iffy' because of the hyperinflation (at the time), we chose Brazil because we were still making money. We had invested in a factory: we had a good relationship with the government so we could repatriate funds, and the labor market was good," says Jim Defau, director of compensation and benefits for the firm. "Overall, it's a conducive environment for doing business."

Defau explains that a receptive government provides a foundation from which to start the assessment of the business climate. The intangible quality of hospitality is a mixture of distinct factors. Is the legal and ethical environment one that your company can handle? Is the location a place that will attract or repel managers and workers from other countries? Will the government help or hinder your day-to-day concerns? Overall, is the country a place where all the factors combine so you'll be able to help your employees do the best job for the company and where your company can thrive?

Success depends on so many elements. It requires more skillful management of every aspect of the organization when you edge into new markets. There are so many hot spots and fumaroles, and the unprepared will surely get burned. HR is part of the holistic picture. "The functional silos that once existed are no longer in place. We're all business partners—HR, legal, finance, engineering, and, every aspect of the business affects every other aspect," says Defau.

If ever HR was core to business success, it has never been more obvious than in the pursuit of these active, hot markets.

Charlene Marmer Solomon is a contributing editor for Workforce *and* Global Workforce. *E-mail char-sol@aol.com to comment.*

BY CARLA JOINSON

Why HR Managers Need To Think

G L O B A L L Y

Don't have any international operations?
Better learn about them before you do.

American businesses are sending their employees to foreign locations in record numbers, largely because of international mergers, start-ups, acquisitions and joint ventures. The way human resource executives handle international issues can make or break an expatriate assignment, as well as affect a company's success in foreign markets. For many in HR, though, international responsibilities can come with little or no warning. Acquiring a global outlook now can help domestic HR staff more easily assume international duties later.

Global marketplace drives international assignments

The National Foreign Trade Council (NFTC) estimates that 300,000 U.S. expatriates are on assignment at any given time. *The Global Relocation Trends 1996 Survey Report*, sponsored by Windham International and the NFTC, shows a solid trend toward more international assignments by responding companies, with 64 percent expecting expatriate growth. Additionally, 81 percent of participants in Arthur Andersen's 1997 *Global Best in Class* study of international human resource programs ex-

pected expansion into new regions in the world.

Even when businesses try to reduce their expatriate population by transferring their responsibilities to local nationals, expatriate growth continues. According to the *Global Relocation Trends* survey, a growing dependence on global sales has actually stepped up the demand for expatriates. Companies responding to the survey generate 43 percent of their revenues outside their headquarters country. Consequently, they need expatriates who can support their expansion through both technical expertise and cultural understanding.

Telecommunications, aerospace, engineering and information technologies, as well as banking and financial services, are prime fields for continued global expansion. Even small companies trying to expand their markets may need to send two or three people overseas.

Heidi O'Gorman, a manager of international HR consulting services at Arthur Andersen, says that all business these days is global. "A mid-sized business may get components from one company and sell to another company—either of which may be outside the U.S.," she explains. "Or that same company may suddenly find itself with a labor force in another country if it's part of a merger."

Surprises for HR

Many HR managers with international responsibilities enjoy their jobs but admit that there can be surprises along the way. HR software based on U.S. needs might be inadequate in another country. Recruiting may involve caste systems and nepotism, while productivity during holidays such as the month-long Ramadan may lag because employees are fasting. No one can know everything about another country, but "business as usual" may be difficult if you're not prepared for an international spin.

"Try to remove the assumption you have that 'this will happen because I asked them to do it,'" says Olivier Maudiere, international HR manager at Walt Disney World. "Remove the assumption that once you put something in place, it will work. Follow-up, follow-up, follow-up."

"It's a totally different job from domestic HR," he continues. "And because you generally have more than one country you're responsible for, you can't rely on just one system or way of doing things. You have to be open to all the different problems."

It's important for HR staff to upgrade any weak areas such as negotiation skills, then quickly acquire country- or regional-specific knowledge and skills about laws and the political system. "Otherwise, you'll be perceived as woefully incompetent," says Scott Russell, senior vice president for human resources at Cendant Mobility in Danbury, Conn.

Experts say other surprises most often occur in the following areas:

Communications. Jerry Torma, director of international human resources and compensation at Nordson Corp. in Amherst, Ohio, says it's easy to take communication—in terms of time, distance, language and culture—for granted. That is, until geography makes it difficult.

"It's so much easier to communicate across four time zones in the United States than across 24 time zones around the world," he explains. "You can't decide to talk to people only when you're in the office.

"If you're communicating with someone in the Middle East, for example, you have four days of the week in which it will be hard to catch people in the office: Thursday and Friday for them, and Saturday and Sunday for you. This can be extremely frustrating, though e-mail can help."

Physical demands. "You need physical stamina for this job," says Russell. "Someone calling on his lunch hour with a gripe may be waking you up at midnight, or you may get a call about a business issue at 3 a.m."

Travel also can be demanding. "HR people need to travel to the countries they support, or they'll miss out on a lot of issues," says Maudiere. "It's like trying to use the Internet in place of face-to-face relationships; you must know what your subsidiaries need, or you'll fail to be their ambassador when you get back."

Involvement with employees. "One thing that surprised me," says Jeanne Dennison, director of HR for International Telecommunications Group at Bell Atlantic in White Plains, N.Y., "is how involved you get with an employee's family and personal life.

"Employees will often look to HR to know all about things that affect their families," Dennison explains, "and you can get involved at a level unheard of with domestic generalists."

Cross-cultural gaps. The differences between cultures can surprise both HR and the expatriates on assignment. Without cross-cultural training, anyone involved in the assignment can have trouble. "HR spends untold hours teaching people how to manage here in the U.S.," says Russell. "But they'll send someone to China without any training on how to manage the local workforce." He tells of an American company in Japan that charged its Japanese HR manager with reducing the workforce. "He studied the issue but couldn't find a solution within cultural Japanese parameters," says Russell. "So when he came back to the Americans, he reduced the workforce by resigning—which was not what they wanted."

Texas A&M International University professor Paul Herbig, author of the *Handbook of Cross-Cultural Marketing* (Hayworth, 1997), notes that these kinds of management mistakes happen all the time. "A sales manager in Brazil recruited 30 college graduates and gave them a week's training," he says. "Then he told them they would be selling door to door, and they all quit right in front of him. In Brazil, college graduates don't do that kind of work."

A manager in England saw workers making their own hot tea during breaks and thought he'd introduce some break-room efficiencies. "He took away their teapots and replaced them with an American vending machine selling iced tea," says Herbig, "and then he had a revolt on his hands."

Bill Sheridan, director of international compensation services at the NFTC, believes Americans often encourage behavior that is not appropriate to another culture. "In many countries, people are risk averse or don't want to stand out in a crowd. We tell them, 'be the best you can be' or try to motivate them within an American framework, and we just make them very uncomfortable."

O'Gorman notes that HR managers suddenly thrust into an international situation can be frustrated by the amount of time it takes to get things done. "Our fast-paced way of life isn't shared by other cultures," she says, "and you have physical and time boundaries you have to work around. For example, trying to collect compensation data for expats can be difficult," she continues. "Form W-2s need to come to you by the end of January, but that's an American institution. April 15th doesn't mean much in other cultures."

Torma warns HR people that their positions may not always generate respect. "Outside the United States, countries have 'personnel' or 'industrial relations,' which are several layers below HR," he says. "You need to be a businessperson first, then a practitioner. Interface with line people as much as possible, and learn as much as you can about your customers' products."

He, too, advises international HR staff to travel to the areas they support. "E-mail is not enough. With the possible exception of third-world countries, your customers will want you to go to them." He stresses that HR people should "try to get invited up-front to all the possible strategic planning sessions, so you can be proactive instead of reactive."

The HR learning curve

"Things are hard enough to do in your own culture," says Rita Bennett, managing partner of Bennett Associates. "Companies underestimate the competency and skills, and the unbelievable demands, required of HR when they're given international responsibilities."

One of the most crucial skills a newcomer to international HR has to acquire is cultural

---

RESOURCES

Where in the world to get help

Though a single clearinghouse for international HR information isn't available, newcomers can still find plenty of help. Advice from experts includes the following:

1. Network within your own company or contact a counterpart in the host country.

2. Contact professional associations, such as the Society for Human Resource Management's Institute for International Human Resources (800-283-7476), the American Compensation Association (602-922-2020) or the International Personnel Association (203-358-9799).

3. Turn to domestic advisers such as tax or employment attorneys, if they have international expertise.

4. Hire international HR consultants, especially to help you lay the groundwork when you first start your program.

5. The two Arthur Andersen stud[ie]s mentioned in this article are available free of charge from Arthur Andersen LLP, Mailstop 05-40, 33 W. Monroe, Chicago, IL 60603.

6. National Foreign Trade Council Inc. (1270 Avenue of the Americas, New York, NY 10020-1700; (212) 399-7128) will send you its *1998 Directory of International Service and Information Providers*.

---

sensitivity. "Even if a compensation specialist never leaves New Jersey, she'll still interact cross-culturally and will need to know how to communicate and deal with the other culture," says Bennett. She, and others, can rattle off a list of practical matters that need handling: visas, work permits and currency; housing, schools and medical care; language and cross-cultural training; avenues of communication; evacuation insurance, taxes and compensation. These factors, along with things such as host country recruiting and management, have to be juggled across cultural, economic and political systems that may be very different from one other.

The first thing HR must do, however, is to provide policy and guidance for these issues. "You don't want to be writing your international HR policy when the first guy's already on the plane," says Jo-Anne Vaughn, a consultant with Global Human Resource Services Ltd. of Bethesda, Md. Realistically, however, she finds that most companies won't put a plan together unless they do think they're getting ready to send someone overseas.

A study by Arthur Andersen, *Exploring International Assignees' Viewpoints*, shows clearly that few employees will accept an assignment if their families object or are unable to accompany them. The backbone of your international HR policy should be expatriate support, tempered by your company's corporate culture, needs and growth. Flexibility is key, since an assignment in the United Kingdom differs from one in Saudi Arabia or Zimbabwe. "If someone is living in a difficult area, you need to help them," says Vaughn. "An employee in Jakarta might be given a week of R&R in Singapore, where the family can also take care of medical needs."

Bell Atlantic's Dennison believes compensation is one of the key areas in which HR needs to come up to speed very quickly. "Some of the issues are quite varied and unique, such as the impact of hyperinflation or deflation. Many of the elements of compensation are far removed from base pay: COLA, housing, mobility premiums and the like."

Money matters also are close to the expatriate's heart. Retirement benefits, tax equalization and host country tax law, spousal lost-income compensation, and social security issues can have many ramifications for the expatriate. HR must develop policies to ensure that the expatriate isn't hurt financially by accepting an assignment, and then make certain that he or she understands all the options and responsibilities.

Legal issues and host country laws can also be areas of difficulty. "There's an idea of life-long employment in many countries," says Herbig. "In Japan, for instance, it can be hard to fire someone. Then it can be hard to hire other Japanese when they see this implied agreement broken." Sheridan echoes this concern. "Many countries have very pro-employee laws," he says. "Termination may

COMMON CONCERNS

What **expatriates** are worried about

The most important concerns of expatriates have been identified as follows:

FAMILY NEEDS

The first consideration is for the trailing spouse's job, and the second is for their children's education.

SAFETY

Arthur Andersen's *Exploring International Assignees' Viewpoints* study indicates that employees are less concerned about cultural or religious differences than they are about political stability and threats to their safety. Assignments in the Mid/Near East and Africa are least likely to be accepted.

NEED FOR CROSS-CULTURAL TRAINING

In Arthur Andersen's *Global Best in Class* study, respondents rated this training as very important for success, yet it was only the third most frequently offered support program. Many experts cite a wish for more cross-cultural training as the No. 1 comment made by expatriates after their return.

CAREER PLANNING

Only 46 percent of responding companies in the *Global Relocation Trends* survey, conducted by Windham International and the National Foreign Trade Council, formally address long-term career planning with their expatriates. Among the companies that do, 42 percent limit it to pre-assignment planning.

DISENGAGEMENT FROM THE COMPANY

Many expats report a sense of alienation or a feeling of being forgotten by the home office. Giving expats a contact and keeping them up-to-date on changes and news within the company can counteract these feelings.

REPATRIATION

Almost 60 percent of respondents to Arthur Andersen's *Exploring International Assignees' Viewpoints* study said they were not guaranteed a job upon completion of their assignments. Combined with a general lack of career counseling and few formal repatriation programs, companies often have significant attrition rates for returning employees.

EXPATRIATE PACKAGES

Creating **international** HR policies

The following elements should be considered when formulating international HR policy:

EMPLOYEE ASSESSMENT

How will you identify candidates for expatriate assignments? Will you interview/assess families?

What qualities does management view as most important for a successful assignment?

COMPENSATION

Will the payroll function be established at the domestic or host-country location?

Will you offer a home, host or international retirement plan?

Will you offer any of the following: mobility premium? tax equalization? housing allowance? tuition for children? home sales/storage assistance? home/emergency/bereavement leave? rest and relaxation leave? cost of living adjustments?

EXPATRIATE/FAMILY SUPPORT

How many of the following services will you offer: job hunting assistance for a spouse? cross-cultural and/or language training? counseling services? paperwork assistance with visas, work permits, powers of attorney, banking and taxes? "look-see" trips prior to relocation?

MANAGEMENT TRAINING

Have you provided guidance concerning unfamiliar business practices such as gift-giving situations or facilitator payments?

Do managers understand what will motivate host-country nationals?

Do managers understand host country labor laws?

CONTINGENCY PLANNING

Where will expatriates go for medical emergencies?

Who monitors host countries' political situations or decides when to evacuate?

Have you provided expatriates with a domestic point of contact?

Have you provided safety information for areas with anti-American sentiment?

REPATRIATION

Will you provide career counseling during the expatriate assignment?

Will you provide for employee development overseas?

What support does HR provide to help expatriates reassimilate into the company?

How does HR help returning expatriates find a new job?

Will you provide a repatriation buyout if an expatriate's job no longer exists?

---

mean very high monetary compensation, and some of these laws apply to expats, too."

Vaughn says HR should be aware that U.S. law doesn't necessarily follow the expat overseas. "Sexual harassment issues may be ignored or poorly enforced," she says. "Your U.S. employees can also evade things like child support or other domestic litigation," she continues. "This can be very hard on HR—they may know nothing about the problem until they get a court order demanding information."

Trends in global HR

"Companies of all sizes are continuing to expand internationally," says Sheridan. "Sud-denly, U.S. companies have a lot of expertise and capital that are needed in other countries. Enough barriers are coming down so that even businesses that traditionally didn't go overseas, such as insurance, are now able to expand. It's a push from U.S. business to find new markets, and a pull by host countries for our expertise."

Additionally, many companies are recruiting overseas for technical workers, and inpatriate HR responsibilities require the same cultural sensitivity and HR skills as expat management. "We send out 15 expats but bring in 80 to 100 inpatriates," says Monica Crone, an international HR generalist with British Aerospace N.A. Inc. in Chantilly, Va. "A lot of things we take for granted, our inpats know nothing about, such as how to open a bank account or get a driver's license in the United States."

Crone expects more intercompany transfers within the aerospace industry, and more joint ventures and global collaboration in general. Other experts see trends toward shorter, unaccompanied assignments where that's feasible, or where the location is less desirable. The Windham International/NFTC study shows that China and India are the top "emerging" destinations, but are perceived as the most challenging destinations and may require greater support from HR.

Disney's Maudiere believes today's expats have a new mindset. "It used to be only for the money," he says. "Now people are viewing expat assignments as something to put on their resumes." One last trend is within HR itself. Nordson's Torma sees more bilingual and bicultural people coming into HR, and even non-HR employees taking on these international responsibilities.

Experts agree that the effort HR gives to formulating policy and acting as advocates for expatriates is key to any international assignment's success. HR support of an expatriate's personal and family needs, training requirements, career development and repatriation may be the crucial factor in earning a return from the company's three-year, $1 million investment.

Carla Joinson is a San Antonio freelance writer who specializes in business and management issues.

by Richard T. Hise

Globe Trotting

Uncle Sam is spending $3 billion a year to help smaller businesses get into the export game.

Getting small- and medium-sized enterprises (SMEs) more involved in exporting would achieve a number of major benefits. At the national level, it has been estimated that if exports of these firms could be increased by as little as 5%, our level of trade would double in 10 years, virtually eliminating the trade deficit. In addition, more jobs would be created; the U.S. Department of Commerce believes that for every $4.5 billion increase in export sales, 10,000 jobs are added, and these export-related jobs would pay approximately 17% more than comparable jobs in the domestic sector.

At the company-level, individual SMEs that begin exporting (or expand their level of exports) would find a more lucrative market than the domestic one: 95% of the world's population and 80% of its purchasing power are found outside the United States, potentially resulting in additional customers, sales, and profits. Overseas market opportunities can be exploited as competition intensifies in the home market. Exporting diversifies risk, and life cycles of products nearing the end of their usefulness can be extended overseas. For seasonal businesses, exporting can smooth production and sales imbalances. Most impor-

tant, it has been found that companies that export are less likely to experience financial trouble than nonexporters. And, on a personal note, exporting provides abundant opportunities to see new places and make new friends.

The problem is that SMEs have demonstrated much reluctance to engage in exporting, currently accounting for only 10% of U.S. exports. At least 250,000 SMEs are currently not exporting. In Texas, with a 2,000-mile border with Mexico, only 20% of SMEs with excellent export potential have elected to do so.

Getting SMEs to initiate export operations appears to be the key. They tend to employ a number of reasons to justify their failure to export, such as not knowing how to get started, lacking the financial backing, shortage of qualified personnel, success in the domestic market negating the need to go overseas, not knowing the best marketing strategies to employ in international markets, and paucity of information about nondomestic opportunities. However, such barriers to exporting are not as formidable as perceived by SMEs because the U.S. government now has a large number of free or low-cost export assistance programs available.

EXECUTIVE *BRIEFING*

By *exporting their products and services, small- and medium-sized companies could improve their financial performance, significantly reduce the U.S. trade deficit, and create more jobs with higher pay. Unfortunately, many have been reluctant to do so, for several reasons. To overcome this, the U.S. government has many free or low-cost assistance programs to improve the marketing skills of first-time exporters or those seeking to expand current overseas activity.*

Stimulating Exports

Through the Export Enhancement Act of 1992, the United States began a strategic, coordinated effort to stimulate exports. The overarching objective was to create jobs by:

- Solidifying our competitive position in the Big Emerging Markets–the China Economic Area (China, Taiwan, and Hong Kong), South Korea, ASEAN, India, South Africa, Poland, Turkey, Argentina, Brazil, and Mexico–which are expected to

Marketing Assistance From U.S. Government Programs

- Introducing products or services to interested buyers located in foreign countries.
- Obtaining economic, trade and demographic information about overseas markets.
- Understanding the negotiation styles and cultural practices of overseas buyers, agents and distributors.
- Getting help in developing customized international marketing strategies.
- Being informed about upcoming seminars and conferences on exporting.
- Finding out what trade barriers exist—and where—and what can be done about them.
- Finding out how "export ready" your company is—and what you need to do to get ready.
- Having products test marketed in other countries.

- Obtaining data about key competitors in foreign markets.
- Receiving updates about political and social unrest and terrorism in other countries.
- Finding out about foreign product standards, labeling, and certification programs.
- Lining up joint venture partners.
- Getting trade potential estimates for products or services.
- Learning the most appropriate entry and expansion strategies in overseas markets for products or services.
- Participating in overseas trade missions. Receiving marketing information, advanced planning and publicity, logistical support, and prearranged meetings with potential buyers and governmental officials.
- Participating in overseas trade shows. Getting access to pre- and post-event logistical support, de-

sign and management assistance, and on-site assistance.
- Identifying prospective overseas representatives and distributors.
- Obtaining briefing on the economic and business climate existing in overseas countries.
- Having products promoted in videos that are distributed to potential agents, distributors and buyers in foreign markets.
- Getting the names of overseas distributors and agents that have indicated an interest in handling the specific type of product or service your company has to offer.
- Getting the names of foreign companies that are interested in purchasing the specific type of product or service your company has to offer.
- Determining the reputation, reliability and financial status of prospective overseas distributors, agents and purchasers.

account for more of our exports by 2000 than the EC or Japan.
- Developing a strategy to support U.S. companies competing for large foreign contracts (chiefly infrastructure).
- Developing the means to enable SMEs to fulfill their export potential. Slightly more than $3 billion is spent annually in support of the legislation.

Implementation of the Export Enhancement Act rests with the Trade Promotion Coordinating Committee (TPCC), a coalition of 19 agencies and departments, that provides a means for all federal agencies to coordinate their trade promotion activities, eliminate duplication and obtain a more focused government approach to trade promotion. Committees and working groups meet on a weekly or biweekly basis to develop positions on issues ranging from export finance to marketing assistance.

Approximately 125 federal programs exist to help companies get started in exporting or expand current export operations. Much of what they do for their clients involves helping them to develop or improve their international marketing practices. The box on this page indicates the types of marketing assistance available. They can be grouped into four major areas:

marketing counseling; market information; obtaining sales leads, agents, and distributors; and promoting export products and services.

The federal export assistance programs that follow are only a sample, but the initiatives are the most helpful and have the widest appeal. There are, however, opportunities for specialized companies to benefit from export assistance initiatives tailored to their particular needs. Programs available to assist agricultural, energy, environmental, minority-owned, and travel and tourism companies improve their marketing strategies for overseas markets are listed [in box Marketing Assistance for Specific Types of Companies].

Before companies approach any of these export assistance offices, they are advised to work through the Trade Information Center, (800) USA-TRADE. The TIC is a comprehensive resource about all federal government assistance programs. It is operated by the U.S. Department of Commerce for the 19 federal agencies comprising the TPCC. Their international trade specialists will advise companies on methods for locating and using government programs and guide callers through the exporting process. Through trade specialists, callers can learn how to access reports from the National Trade Data Bank, which contains 200,000 government documents related to export promotion and international markets. Staff also can direct businesses to state and local organizations that provide additional export assistance.

Marketing Counseling

U.S. Export Assistance Centers. USEACs are customer-focused, federal export assistance offices that offer one-on-one counseling to help clients identify target markets and develop marketing strategies. USEACs streamline export marketing assistance by integrating in a single location the counselors and services of the U.S. and Foreign Commercial Service of the Department of Commerce, the Small Business Administration and, in Long Beach, Calif., the U.S. Agency for International Development.

Through co-location and cooperation with local public and private export service partners, USEACs will increase the depth and range of export services available to clients and promote a more rational and integrated delivery network. USEACs will target primarily export-ready businesses, particularly small- and medium-sized firms. A total of 12 USEACs were open by the end of 1996 in Atlanta, Baltimore, Chicago, Cleveland, Dallas, Denver, Long Beach, Miami, New York, Philadelphia, St. Louis, and Seattle.

> # Commercial officers in the overseas posts collect information about trends and barriers to trade in their areas and seek out trade and investment opportunities to benefit U.S. firms.

International Trade Administration. The International Trade Administration offers assistance and information to help exporters. ITA units include: (1) domestic and overseas commercial officers, (2) country experts, and (3) industry experts.

The U.S. and Foreign Commercial Service (U.S.F.C.S.) has a network of trade specialists located in the United States and overseas who provide information on foreign markets, agents and distributors, trade leads, and counseling on business opportunities, trade barriers, and prospects abroad.

There are 96 ITA/U.S.F.C.S. district offices and branch offices in cities throughout the United States and Puerto Rico. Most maintain business libraries containing the Commerce Department's latest reports. District office trade specialists can provide the business

community with local export counseling, and a variety of export programs and services, including the Export Qualifier Program in which specialists help firms determine their readiness to export through a computerized program. Specific recommendations are proposed to help strengthen and enhance a company's exporting ability. Commercial officers in the overseas posts collect information about trends and barriers to trade in their areas and seek out trade and investment opportunities to benefit U.S. firms.

IEP (International Economic Policy) is a source for information on trade potential for U.S. products in specific countries. Individual IEP country desk officers, representing 194 countries, plus several regional business information centers, highlight new opportunities for trade and investment. These specialists can look at the needs of an individual firm wishing to sell in a particular country in the full context of that country's economy, trade policies, and political situation. Desk officers collect information on their assigned country's regulations, tariffs, business practices, economic and political developments, trade data, and market size and growth, keeping a current pulse on the potential markets for U.S. products, services, and investments.

Trade Development Industry Officers (TDs) work with manufacturing and service industry associations and firms to identify trade opportunities and obstacles by product or service category. They also help clients develop export marketing plans and programs. In addition to counseling they conduct executive trade missions, trade fairs, and marketing seminars. TD officers specialize in approximately 500 different product[s] or services from A to Z (abrasive products to zinc).

District Export Councils. DECs are organizations of community leaders whose knowledge of international business provides a source of professional advice to firms seeking to begin or expand international sales. DECs, closely affiliated with the U.S. Department of Commerce, provide specialized expertise to the department and its clients.

DECs respond to exporters' needs by working with the U.S. and Foreign Commercial Service's domestic offices and promote greater international trade activity at the local level. DECs counsel exporters, sponsor trade events, and help build local export assistance partnerships with other organizations.

The 51 DECs nationwide combine the expertise of over 1,500 volunteers, representing business, universities, and government. DEC members, appointed by the U.S. Secretary of Commerce, are recognized for their extensive knowledge of international business and access to specialized trade resources. Members provide an important source of professional advice that complements the assistance provided by U.S.F.C.S. international trade specialists.

Marketing Assistance for Specific Types of Companies

Agriculture

- Foreign Agricultural Service. Sixty overseas offices carry out market promotion and collect information for the agricultural sector.
- Agricultural Trade and Marketing Information Center. Locates relevant material from their large collection of trade and marketing information.
- Computerized Information Delivery Service. CIDS provides instant access to Department of Agriculture reports and news releases.
- Country Market Profiles. Describes 40 overseas markets for high value agricultural products.
- Market Promotion Programs. Administered by the USDA's Foreign Agricultural Service, the MPP promotes a wide variety of U.S. commodities in every region of the world.
- Trade Shows. About 15 major overseas shows are held annually by the Foreign Agricultural Ser-

vice. They include international food shows and sales missions that target emerging markets for consumer-ready foods.

Energy

- Committee on Renewable Energy Commerce and Trade. CORECT is an interagency working group of 14 federal agencies of the U.S. Department of Energy that coordinates federal programs to assist export efforts of renewable energy and energy-efficiency industries.
- Export Assistance Initiatives. The U.S. Department of Energy helps energy exporters to identify overseas opportunities.

Environmental

- International Technology Transfer Activities. The Environmental Protection Agency promotes the sale abroad of environmental technologies and services.

Minority-Owned Businesses

- Minority Business Development Agency. The Department of Commerce promotes one-on-one assistance via Minority Business Development Centers, Native American Business Development Centers, regional Minority Enterprise Growth Assistance Centers, Business Resource Centers, and the Minority Business Opportunity Committees.
- Office of Minority Small Business and Capital Ownership Development. The Small Business Administration provides marketing management and technical assistance by contracting for the services of professional management firms.

Travel and Tourism

- Travel and Tourism Administration. This agency stimulates international demand for travel to the United States.

Each DEC has a membership mix that includes exporters (manufacturing and service industry), export service providers, and public sector trade promotion organizations. DECs help develop local networks to provide a complete spectrum of international trade services to the exporter. The result is a local export facilitation infrastructure that matches available resources with business needs.

Office of International Trade. This arm of the Small Business Administration (SBA) works in cooperation with other federal agencies and public- and private-sector groups to encourage small business exports and to assist small businesses seeking to export. The office's outreach efforts include sponsoring and developing "how-to" and market-specific publications for exporters.

Small Business Development Centers. Another SBA operation, SBDCs provide counseling service at no cost to small business exporters, but fees are charged for export training seminars and other SBDC-sponsored export events.

SCORE Program. One-on-one counseling and training seminars are provided by members of the SBA's Service Corps of Retired Executives, many of whom have

years of practical experience in international trade. Specialists assist small firms in evaluating export potential by identifying technical, managerial and marketing problems.

Market Information

National Trade Data Bank. Operated by the U.S. Department of Commerce, the NTDB is a "one-stop" source for international trade data collected by 17 U.S. government agencies. Updated each month and released on two CD-ROMS, the NTDB enables anyone with a CD-ROM-equipped IBM-compatible PC access to 200,000 trade-related documents. The NTDB contains:

- The latest census data on U.S. imports and exports by commodity and country.
- The complete *CIA World Factbook*.
- Current market research reports compiled by the U.S. and Foreign Commercial Service.
- The complete *Commercial Service International Contacts* directory, which contains more than 46,000 names and addresses of individuals and firms abroad interested in importing U.S. products.

- U.S. State Department country reports on economic policy and trade practices.
- The publications, *Export Yellow Pages, A Basic Guide to Exporting,* and *the National Trade Estimates Report on Foreign Trade Barriers.*
- The Export Promotion Calendar.

Eastern Europe Business Information Center. The Center, operated by the ITA, has a wide range of publications on doing business in Eastern Europe and the Baltic states, including lists of potential partners, trade and investment regulations, priority industry sectors, and notices of upcoming seminars, conferences, and trade promotion events. EEBIC publishes a monthly newsletter, "Eastern Europe Business Bulletin," as well as the bimonthly "Eastern Europe Looks for Partners," which highlights business partnership opportunities for U.S. firms with Eastern European companies.

International Data Base. The Center for International Research compiles and maintains up-to-date global demographic and social information for all countries in its International Data Base. It is run by the U.S. Bureau of the Census and available to U.S. companies seeking to identify potential markets overseas. Printed tables on selected subjects for specific countries can be purchased for a minimum charge of $75.

SBAtlas. SBAtlas (automated trade locator assistance system) provides free of charge two types of reports: product-specific and country-specific. The SBAtlas product report ranks the top 35 import and export markets for a particular good or service. The country report identifies the top 20 products most frequently traded in a target market.

Country Commercial Guides. These are now produced annually by U.S. embassies in 120 countries. They replace eight overlapping economic and commercial reports formerly generated by the Departments of State, Commerce, and Agriculture. The guides provide business users with a comprehensive look at the local market, including the political, economic and commercial environment, best export prospects, marketing approaches, key contacts, and trade regulations and standards.

Economic Bulletin Board. The EBB provides time-sensitive market information and the latest statistical releases from a variety of federal agencies.

Industry Sector Analyses. ISAs are market research reports produced on location in leading overseas markets. They cover market size and outlook, characteristics, and competitive and end-user analysis for a selected industry sector in a particular country.

Customized Market Analysis. CMAs are made-to-order market research studies for companies needing to develop or refine a marketing strategy for a specific product or service in a targeted country. A comprehensive analysis provides specific information on the sales potential of a product or service in the target market, on the competition, on the price of comparable products, and on distribution channels. It also lists potential buyers. Depending on the country, prices range from $1,000–$5,100.

Sales Leads, Agents, and Distributors

The Department of Commerce's ITA offers several services for exporters.

Agent/Distributor Service. A customized search helps identify agents, distributors, and foreign representatives for U.S. firms based on the foreign companies' examination of U.S. product literature. A fee of $250 per country is charged.

Export Contact List Service. This database retrieval service provides U.S. exporters with names, addresses, products, sizes, and other relevant information about foreign firms interested in importing U.S. goods and services. Similar information on U.S. exporters is also given to foreign firms seeking U.S. suppliers. Names are collected and maintained by Commerce Department district offices and commercial officers at foreign posts.

Matchmaker Trade Delegations. These Commerce Department-recruited and planned missions are designed to introduce new-to-export or new-to-market businesses to prospective representatives and distributors overseas. They involve intensive trips filled with meetings with prospective clients and in-depth briefings on the economic and business climate of the countries visited. Trade specialists from the Department of Commerce evaluate the potential of a firm's products in target markets, find and screen contacts, and handle logistics.

Customized Sales Survey. This custom-tailored research service provides firms with specific information on marketing and foreign representation for their individual products in selected countries. Interviews or surveys are conducted to determine overall marketability of the product, key competitors, price of comparable products, customary distribution and promotion practices, trade barriers, possible business partners, and applicable trade events. Fees for CSS surveys vary from $800–$3,500 per country.

Trade Opportunities Program. TOP provides companies with current sales leads from international firms seeking to buy or represent their products or services. TOP leads are printed daily in leading commercial newspapers and also are distributed electronically via the Department of Commerce Economic Bulletin Board. There is a nominal annual fee and connect-time charge.

International Company Profiles (ICPs). ICPs indicate the reliability of prospective trading partners. Information provided includes type of organization, year established, size, general reputation, territory covered, sales, product lines, principal owners, financial information, and trade references with recommendations from commercial officers as to suitability as a trading partner. The cost of one report is $100.

Promotion

The ITA also offers U.S. companies several opportunities to promote their products and services overseas.

Foreign Buyer Program. FBP supports major domestic trade shows featuring products and services of U.S. industries with high export potential. U.S. and foreign commercial service officers worldwide recruit qualified buyers to attend the shows. The exhibitions are extensively publicized through embassy and regional commercial newsletters, catalog-magazines, foreign trade associations, chambers of commerce, travel agents, government agencies, corporations, import agents, and equipment distributors in targeted markets. An International Business Center at each foreign buyer show provides interpreters, multilingual brochures, counseling, and private meeting rooms.

Commercial News USA. Published 10 times yearly by the U.S. and Foreign Commercial Service, this catalog-magazine promotes American products and services to overseas markets. *Commercial News USA* is disseminated in paper copy to 125,000 business readers via U.S. embassies and consultants in 155 countries, and to more than 134,000 active bulletin-board subscribers. Selected portions are also reprinted in newsletters that are tailored in content and language to the individual country and distributed to potential buyers, agents, American chambers of commerce abroad, and other multipliers. U.S. firms can have their products or services highlighted for a fee that varies by the size of the listing.

Trade Fairs and Exhibitions. About 80–100 worldwide trade fairs are selected annually by the Commerce Department for recruitment of a USA pavilion. Selection priority is given to events in viable markets that are suitable for new-to-export or new-to-market, export-ready firms. Fees range from $2,500–$12,000, depending upon the country. Exhibitors receive pre- and post-event logistical and transportation support, design and management of the USA pavilion, and extensive overseas promotional campaigns to attract appropriate business audiences.

Trade Missions. Focusing on one industry or service sector, trade missions provide participants with detailed marketing information, advanced planning and publicity, logistical support, and prearranged appointments with potential buyers, government officials, and others. Participants pay between $2,000–$5,000, depending on location and number of countries visited.

The missions usually consist of 5–12 U.S. business executives.

Product Literature Centers. Trade development industry specialists at ITA represent U.S. companies at various major international trade shows by distributing product or service literature. In addition, trade specialists at these centers identify potential customers for companies displaying their literature.

Success Stories

Companies that have used U.S. government export assistance programs have benefited significantly. The following stories pinpoint a variety of sources that either helped clients get started in exporting or increased their export sales:

- The Lemna Corp. of St. Paul, Minn., began selling duckweed in Poland, Slovakia, Russia, Belgium, Mexico, Sweden, and Italy seven years ago. Working with the U.S. Department of Commerce's National Trade Data Bank, the Export-Import Bank and the U.S. Foreign Commercial Service, by 1995, the company's exports accounted for 50% of its sales.
- Mobile Telesystems Inc. of Gaithersburg, Md., is a 58-employee company that evolved from COMSAT and sells portable telecommunication systems that allow users to communicate to and from any point in the world. Sales in 1989 were $7 million in seven countries. By 1992, they reached

> **Programs available are not "cookie cutter" in approach, but tailored to the level of clients' export readiness.**

$28 million in 40 countries. At first, export sales accounted for 10% of total revenues, then reached 70% in 1992. The company's export sales growth was sparked by working with the U.S. Department of Commerce, the Baltimore Export Assistance Center, and the Export-Import Bank.

- Working with the export services of the New Orleans district office of the ITA, Intralox Inc. of Harahan, La., experienced dramatic increases in export sales: 28% the first year, 44% the second year, 59% the third year, and 79% the fourth year. The company sells modular plastic conveyor belting for can manufacturing, bottling, and food processing to Latin America.

- Folio Corp. of Provo, Utah, expects to increase its percentage of export sales to 40% within five years, up from a current 8%. The 130-employee firm, founded in 1986, sells infobase software. The company has used the Salt Lake City district office of the ITA and the National Trade Data Bank, and made contact at the Comdex Trade show in Las Vegas with distributors recruited through the Foreign Buyer Program.

- Thermaflo is a 250-employee manufacturer of refrigerant recovery and recycling products and services that prevent the escape of CFCs into the atmosphere. The Springfield, Mass., firm used a variety of assistance programs to get export sales into the United Kingdom, Finland, Sweden, Norway, and Denmark, including the Boston district office of the ITA and a Matchmaker trade mission to Germany in conjunction with a trade fair in Nuremberg.

Opportunity Knocks

Small- and medium-sized businesses can call upon a large number of U.S. government export assistance programs to acquire the marketing expertise needed to be successful exporters. Programs available are not "cookie cutter" in approach, but tailored to the level of clients' export readiness—whether they are a first-time or experienced exporter, the types of products or services involved, and countries designated as export markets. The effectiveness of the assistance provided, the wide spectrum of marketing problems addressed, and their low- or no-cost feature, means that SMEs cannot, in good conscience, point to a lack of international marketing skills for deferring their export initiatives. And, because government programs also exist to provide export financing, insurance and legal assistance (including the time-consuming, onerous chore of documentation), there are essentially few, if any, valid objections that can be raised.

Certainly, the impetus exists for the 250,000 SMEs that are not currently exporting to consider doing so, while those already exporting should be motivated to identify additional international product/market opportunities. Using U.S. government export assistance programs means reduced risk for exporters and excellent potential for improved bottom lines.

Additional Reading

Edmunds, Stahr and Sarkis J. Khoury (1986), "Exports: A Necessary Ingredient in the Growth of Small Business Firms," *Journal of Small Business Management*, 24 (October), 54–65.

Hise, Richard T. (1997), "Barriers To Doing Business In Mexico," in "Trade Insights," a paper series published by the Center for the Study of Western Hemispheric Trade in Austin, Texas.

Holderman, Karen (1996), "Improved Market Research Programs Help U.S. Exporters Find Opportunities Abroad," *Business America*, 117 (October), 7–10.

Sharkey, Thomas, Jeen-Su Lim, and Ken Kim (1989), "Export Development and Perceived Barriers: An Empirical Analysis of Small Firms," *Management International Review*, 29 (2), 33–40.

"Successful Exporters Share Their Secrets," *Business America*, 118 (March, 1997), 4–10.

Yang, Yoo S., Robert P. Leone, and Dana L. Alden (1992), "A Market Expansion Ability Approach to Identify Potential Exporters," *Journal of Marketing*, 56 (January), 84–96.

About the Author

Richard T. Hise is Professor of Marketing and Holder of the Foley's Professorship in Retailing and Marketing at Texas A&M University, College Station, where he teaches and does research in international marketing and international logistics. A consultant to major companies for more than 20 years, Dick has offered a number of export marketing workshops for Texas-based firms. His articles have appeared in the *Journal of Marketing, Business Horizons, Journal of Global Marketing, Sloan Management Review, Journal of Product Innovation Management, Research-Technology Management,* and *Industrial Marketing Management.* He also has authored or coauthored five books on personal selling, product management, and marketing strategy.

nuclear reactors, North Korea and, 165–166

O

Office of International Trade, 221
"OLI" (ownership, location, and internationalization), 24, 25
opportunistic exporters, 137
Organization for Economic Cooperation and Development (OECD), 42, 44, 45, 129
Otis Elevator Co. Worldwide, 210–211

P

Pacific Basin Economic Council (PBEC), 50
Pacific Economic Cooperation Council (PECC), 50
Pacific Link, 200
Packer, Arnold H., 202
Pakistan, 124
Pangilinan, Manuel, 199, 200
Peninsula Group, 77
PepsiCo, 89, 149–150
Philippines, 49–50
piracy, 147
Policy Framework Papers (PFPs), 64
potatoes, NewLeaf, 10
Powers, Richard, 159, 160
Premier Siècle Après Beatrice, Le (Maalouf), 106
"Priorities for Competitive Advantage" (Towers Perrin), 202
private banking, technology and, in Asia, 71–72
privatization, 156; in Vietnam, 145
product literature centers, 223
protectionism, 112–118
pyramid schemes, 105

Q

Qiao Shi, 122

R

Ramos-Horta, Jose, 53
Rao, P. V. Narasimha, 155
real estate, in Japan, 39–40
Reciprocal Trade Agreements Act of 1934, 113
Reng Qing, 92–93
research and development (R&D), 30–38
Ricardo, David, 114
Roundup Herbicide, 11
Rousseau, Jean-Jacques, 70
Russia, building successful partnerships in, 168–175
Russian Federation, advertising in, 141

S

Saint-Simon, Henri, 70
Sanders-Frank amendment, 64, 65
Sato, Katsumi, 165–166
SBAtlas, 222
SCORE (Service Corps of Retired Executives) Program, 221
search firms, hiring foreign nationals and, 194–195
See, Anthony, 201
Setrakin, Scott, 159
Schapiro, Robert B., 8–17
Sharp, 34–35
Siemens, 33
Singapore, 61, 141–142, 199, 200
small- and medium-sized enterprises (SMEs), exporting and, 218–224
Small Business Administration (SBA), 221
Small Business Development Centers (SBDCs), 221
Smart Phone, 200
soil erosion, 11
South Africa, 155
South Korea, 61, 62, 155, 168
Special Data Dissemination Standards, of IMF, 178–179
"spectrum illusion," 104
stakeholders, business ethics principles and, 100–101
standardization, globalization and, 187
State Security Law of 1993, in China, 122–123
steel industry, in Germany, 127
Suharto, 154–155
Sun Microsystems, 27
sustainability teams, of Monsanto, 13, 14–16
sustainable development, technology and, 8–17

T

Tariff Act of 1828, 113
taxes, trusts and, in Hong Kong, 72
technology: advances in, and sustainable development, 8–17; private banking in Asia and, 71–72
Texas Instruments, 25
Thai-Danu Bank, 200–201
Thermoflo, 224
Third International Maths and Science Study (TIMSS), 41–43
3M Co., 190–192
Thyssen, 127
top-line opportunities, 136
topsoil erosion, 11
Toshiba, 33
"total immersion" approach, to language acquisition by expatriates, 191
toxic waste, 54
Toyota, 26–28
trade deficit, 116

Trade Development Industry Officers (TDs), 220
Trade Expansion Act, 113–114
Trade Information Center (TIC), 219
trade missions, 223
Trade Opportunities Program (TOP), 222
Trade Promotion Coordinating Committee (TPCC), 219
trade shows, 221, 223
transaction costs, 136
Travel and Tourism Administration, 221
trusts, in Hong Kong, 72
TRW, 162–163
Turkey, 156

U

unions, impact of globalization on Germany and, 127–128
University Games Corp., 159, 160
Unocal Corp., 197–198
U.S. and Foreign Commercial Service (U.S.F.C.S.), 220
U.S. Export Assistance Centers (USEACs), 220

V

Vo Van Kiet, 144
Vietnam, 140, 141, 143–152

W

Wal-Mart, 58
Wang, Dan, 122
water, 15
Whig Party, 113
Whirlpool, 183
"Whorf Hypothesis," 104
women, in Japan, 195
workers' rights, International Labor Organization and, 124
"Workforce 2000: Work and Workers for the 21st Century" (Johnson and Packer), 202
World Bank, 139
World Trade Organization (WTO), 52, 55, 107, 109–111

X

Xerox, 31, 34–35, 36

Z

Zarsky, Lyuba, 55, 56
Zedillo, Ernesto, 154
zero-sum games, Hungarians and, 105

AE Article Review Form

We encourage you to photocopy and use this page as a tool to assess how the articles in **Annual Editions** expand on the information in your textbook. By reflecting on the articles you will gain enhanced text information. You can also access this useful form on a product's book support Web site at **http://www.dushkin.com/ online/.**

NAME: _____   DATE: _____

TITLE AND NUMBER OF ARTICLE: _____

BRIEFLY STATE THE MAIN IDEA OF THIS ARTICLE: _____

LIST THREE IMPORTANT FACTS THAT THE AUTHOR USES TO SUPPORT THE MAIN IDEA:

WHAT INFORMATION OR IDEAS DISCUSSED IN THIS ARTICLE ARE ALSO DISCUSSED IN YOUR TEXTBOOK OR OTHER READINGS THAT YOU HAVE DONE? LIST THE TEXTBOOK CHAPTERS AND PAGE NUMBERS:

LIST ANY EXAMPLES OF BIAS OR FAULTY REASONING THAT YOU FOUND IN THE ARTICLE:

LIST ANY NEW TERMS/CONCEPTS THAT WERE DISCUSSED IN THE ARTICLE, AND WRITE A SHORT DEFINITION:

ANNUAL EDITIONS revisions depend on two major opinion sources: one is our Advisory Board, listed in the front of this volume, which works with us in scanning the thousands of articles published in the public press each year; the other is you—the person actually using the book. Please help us and the users of the next edition by completing the prepaid article rating form on this page and returning it to us. Thank you for your help!

ANNUAL EDITIONS: International Business 99/00

ARTICLE RATING FORM

Here is an opportunity for you to have direct input into the next revision of this volume. We would like you to rate each of the 46 articles listed below, using the following scale:

1. Excellent: should definitely be retained
2. Above average: should probably be retained
3. Below average: should probably be deleted
4. Poor: should definitely be deleted

Your ratings will play a vital part in the next revision.
So please mail this prepaid form to us just as soon as you complete it.
Thanks for your help!

We Want Your Advice

RATING

ARTICLE

1. Growth through Global Sustainability
2. America and the Global Economy
3. International Business: The New Bottom Line
4. Building Effective R&D Capabilities Abroad
5. Back to the Land
6. World Education League: Who's Top?
7. Balancing Act
8. Riding the Dragon
9. Multinational Corporations: Saviors or Villains?
10. The Great Escape
11. Reining in the IMF: The Case for Denying the IMF New Funding and Power
12. International Monetary Arrangements: Is There a Monetary Union in Asia's Future?
13. Asia Sets a New Challenge
14. Africa's New Dawn
15. Global Transfer of Critical Capabilities
16. Scaling the Great Wall: The *Yin* and *Yang* of Resolving Business Conflicts in China
17. Can Multinational Businesses Agree on How to Act Ethically?
18. Us and Them
19. Government and National Parliaments
20. Trade Free or Die
21. Antitrust Regulation across National Borders
22. Rule by Law
23. Wanted: Muscle

RATING

ARTICLE

24. Global Economy, Local Mayhem?
25. Global Deregulation: Deutsche Hegira
26. Controlling Economic Competition in the Pacific Rim
27. How to Succeed in the Global Marketplace
28. A World of Advertising
29. Asia's Next Tiger? Vietnam Is Fraught with Promise and Peril for Marketers
30. Troubles Ahead in Emerging Markets
31. Not-So-Clear Choices
32. The Myth of the China Market
33. "Compromise Increases the Risk of War"
34. The Heat Is On
35. Building Successful Partnerships in Russia and Belarus: The Impact of Culture on Strategy
36. Strengthening the Architecture of the International Financial System
37. The World as a Single Machine
38. Erasing Boundaries: Globalization
39. Are Expats Getting Lost in the Translation?
40. Getting What You Pay For
41. A Company without a Country?
42. Opportunity Knocks
43. Global Culture: Who's the Gatekeeper?
44. Don't Get Burned by Hot New Markets
45. Why HR Managers Need to Think Globally
46. Globe Trotting

(Continued on next page)

NO POSTAGE
NECESSARY
IF MAILED
IN THE
UNITED STATES

BUSINESS REPLY MAIL
FIRST-CLASS MAIL PERMIT NO. 84 GUILFORD CT

POSTAGE WILL BE PAID BY ADDRESSEE

Dushkin/McGraw-Hill
Sluice Dock
Guilford, CT 06437-9989

ABOUT YOU

Name _____ Date _____

Are you a teacher? ☐ A student? ☐
Your school's name _____

Department _____

Address _____ City _____ State ___ Zip ___

School telephone # _____

YOUR COMMENTS ARE IMPORTANT TO US !

Please fill in the following information:
For which course did you use this book?
_____

Did you use a text with this *ANNUAL EDITION*? ☐ yes ☐ no
What was the title of the text?
_____

What are your general reactions to the *Annual Editions* concept?
_____

Have you read any particular articles recently that you think should be included in the next edition?
_____

Are there any articles you feel should be replaced in the next edition? Why?
_____

Are there any World Wide Web sites you feel should be included in the next edition? Please annotate.
_____

May we contact you for editorial input? ☐ yes ☐ no
May we quote your comments? ☐ yes ☐ no